JUSTIFYING PRIVATE RIGHTS

Many of the most influential contributions to private law scholarship in the latter part of the twentieth century go beyond purely doctrinal accounts of private law. A distinctive feature of these analyses is that they straddle the divide between legal philosophy, on the one hand, and the sort of traditional doctrinal analysis applied by the courts, on the other. The essays contained in this collection continue in this tradition. The collection is divided into two parts. The essays contained in the first part consider the nature of, and justification for, private rights generally. The essays in the second part address the justification for particular private law rights and doctrines. Offering insightful and innovative analyses, this collection will appeal to scholars in all fields of private law and legal theory.

Volume 36 in the series Hart Studies in Private Law

Justifying Private Rights

Edited by
Simone Degeling
Michael Crawford
and
Nicholas Tiverios

•HART•
OXFORD • LONDON • NEW YORK • NEW DELHI • SYDNEY

HART PUBLISHING
Bloomsbury Publishing Plc
Kemp House, Chawley Park, Cumnor Hill, Oxford, OX2 9PH, UK
1385 Broadway, New York, NY 10018, USA
29 Earlsfort Terrace, Dublin 2, Ireland

HART PUBLISHING, the Hart/Stag logo, BLOOMSBURY and the Diana logo are trademarks of Bloomsbury Publishing Plc

First published in Great Britain 2020

A catalogue record for this book is available from the British Library.

Library of Congress Cataloging-in-Publication data

Names: Degeling, Simone, editor. | Crawford, Michael J.R. (John Rooke), editor. | Tiverios, Nicholas A., editor.

Title: Justifying private rights / edited by Simone Degeling, Michael JR Crawford and Nicholas A Tiverios.

Description: Oxford, UK ; New York, NY : Hart Publishing, an imprint of Bloomsbury Publishing, 2020. | Series: Hart studies in private law ; volume 36 | Includes bibliographical references and index.

Identifiers: LCCN 2020042231 (print) | LCCN 2020042232 (ebook) | ISBN 9781509931958 (hardback) | ISBN 9781509944620 (paperback) | ISBN 9781509931972 (pdf) | ISBN 9781509931965 (Epub)

Subjects: LCSH: Civil rights. | Possession (Law) | Right of property. | Torts. | Equity.

Classification: LCC K3240 .J8744 2020 (print) | LCC K3240 (ebook) | DDC 342.08/5—dc23

LC record available at https://lccn.loc.gov/2020042231

LC ebook record available at https://lccn.loc.gov/2020042232

ISBN: HB: 978-1-50993-195-8
ePDF: 978-1-50993-197-2
ePub: 978-1-50993-196-5

Typeset by Compuscript Ltd, Shannon

To find out more about our authors and books visit www.hartpublishing.co.uk. Here you will find extracts, author information, details of forthcoming events and the option to sign up for our newsletters.

CONTENTS

LIST OF CONTRIBUTORS

Andrew Botterell is a Professor in the Faculty of Law and Department of Philosophy, and Associate Dean (Research and Graduate Studies) in the Faculty of Law, Western University.

Peter Cane is a Senior Research Fellow at Christ's College University of Cambridge and Emeritus Distinguished Professor of Law at the Faculty of Law, Australian National University.

Michael JR Crawford is a Lecturer in the Faculty of Law, University of New South Wales.

Simone Degeling is a Professor in the Faculty of Law, University of New South Wales.

Nicholas J McBride is a Fellow at Pembroke College, University of Cambridge.

Ben McFarlane is Professor of English Law and a Fellow of St John's College, University of Oxford.

Paul B Miller is Professor of Law and Associate Dean for International and Graduate Programs, Notre Dame Law School.

James Penner is Kwa Geok Choo Professor of Property Law, National University of Singapore

Andrew Robertson is a Professor of Law at the University of Melbourne.

Lionel Smith is Sir William C Macdonald Professor of Law, Faculty of Law, McGill University and Visiting Professor, Faculty of Law, University of Oxford.

Stephen A Smith is James McGill Professor in the Faculty of Law, McGill University.

Nicholas A Tiverios is Senior Lecturer in the Faculty of Law, University of Western Australia.

1

Introduction

SIMONE DEGELING, MICHAEL JR CRAWFORD
AND NICHOLAS A TIVERIOS

This collection of new work in private law theory is the product of a two-day workshop held at the University of New South Wales Faculty of Law in July 2019. The contributors and participants were drawn from the legal academy across the common law world. Contributors were invited to submit essays on a diverse range of topics, including the juridical nature of rights and private law, the virtues of different methodological approaches to justification in private law, and the justifications, or lack thereof, for particular doctrines of private law.

The content of this collection reflects this diverse list of themes. The chapters are divided into two parts. Part I considers the nature of private rights generally. The chapters in this section discuss, among other things, the nature and sources of rights, the nature of juridical reasons, and the sorts of justifications that have been, and ought to be, given for the conferral of the rights that subjects of law have against each other. Part II focuses on the justification for particular rights and doctrines of private law. The chapters in Part II range from the nature of equity to the justification for doctrines such as deceit, equitable estoppel, possession, and relief against forfeiture. Although divided into two parts, many of the issues discussed in Part I inform and illuminate the discussion of the substantive doctrines discussed in Part II (and vice versa). Each contribution to this book provides detailed references should the reader wish to engage more thoroughly with the topic discussed.

Part I. The Nature of Private Rights

This Part commences with Peter Cane in chapter two who provides a 'naturalistic' account of the external assessment and justification of private legal rights, in which that assessment and justification depends neither on claims of superior authority nor on appeals to univocal human reason or moral intuition. He explains that naturalism is an assumption on which analysis is based, which is that 'any and every human activity can be explained, at a "deep" level, in terms of biological facts'.[1] Further, Cane points out that when we consider the position of *homo sapiens*, our lens must be expanded to take into account that changes in human behaviour may not have been the product of biological evolution but also social, cultural and behavioural evolution. Thus, social and normative 'facts' must also be considered. The social fact or imperative on which Cane's argument rests is the species' universal human need and want to cooperate.

Cane commences his analysis by providing an account of the emergence of law as a social phenomenon based on interpersonal cooperation. Highlighting the role of people, both legal officials and citizens, in making law and the legal system, Cane describes law as an 'evolutionary human achievement'[2] pointing out that '[s]uch cooperative compliance with and conformity to a legal regime is what enables law to be used to create powers, obligations, permissions, prohibitions and institutions merely by saying so'.[3] He then turns to private law as a separate legal category. Taking an historical approach, he briefly traces the twin development of notions of private and public law, and the growth of what in modern parlance we describe as 'private law theory' or reflections on law as practice. Continuing with this historical approach, and commencing with the Roman jurist Gaius, Cane traces the common law legal literature which has attempted to identify the principles or order which lies underneath the substantive law.

A particular feature of private law theory identified by Cane is that scholars have chosen private 'rights' as their organising category. Rights may be viewed as a device for reconciling positions. Viewed from a naturalistic perspective, Cane observes that a species' universal characteristic is the need to be separate and autonomous but, at the same time, to be able to cooperate with others. There are good reasons to cooperate in order to achieve benefits for all, but cooperation also carries costs. Thus, Cane observes: '[i]ndividuality and sociality are both species-universal human characteristics, but there is no species-universal balance between the two'.[4]

So then how may a naturalistic account justify private rights? Cane returns to his central theme which is the human need and desire that social norms of cooperation be 'justified'. In order for human beings to weigh the cost of cooperation for common purpose and bear those burdens, their internal system of values or 'red lines' must be engaged to determine their next step. Judges have institutional authority to make the law. Thus, the prescriptive or normative elements of their reasons are conferred by the legal system. However, legal scholars or private law theorists have no such remit. Scholars would be well advised, argues Cane, to make clear where their prescriptions, including about private rights, are coming from and how they are based. He points to the human felt need for justification, which may in some cases, such as judicial decision, be met by authority. However, claims by legal scholars have no such authority.

[1] P Cane, chapter 2 at 25.
[2] ibid, 28.
[3] ibid, 27.
[4] ibid, 38.

In 'Justifying Private Law: "Reasons Fundamentalist" Instrumentalism and the Kantian Account', James Penner compares John Gardner's 'reasons fundamentalist' instrumental account of private law[5] with Arthur Ripstein's Kantian account.[6] As Penner explains, 'reasons fundamentalist' accounts of the law make two basic claims about humans and our relationship with the law. The first is that humans, as rational creatures, respond to reasons. We owe the moral duties we owe because we can justifiably expect others, as rational beings, to respect those reasons when they relate to important interests. On Gardner's account, engagement with moral norms is an inescapable part of being rational and being rational is an essential part of being human. The second interlocking claim is that, unlike engagement with moral norms, engagement with legal norms is not an inescapable part of being human. In contrast to our obligation to obey moral norms, there is no inherent moral obligation to obey the law. The virtue of the law is simply that, as a tool for guiding behaviour, it can assist us to better comply with our duties to observe reasons that relate to important interests. Private law is thus of purely instrumental value and its norms are only desirable in so far as they assist the law's subjects to better comply with their conceptually antecedent, and inescapable, moral duties. On this understanding, law only becomes morally necessary when it is the sole way of enabling members of a community to comply with their moral duties.

By contrast, Arthur Ripstein offers a non-instrumentalist account of private law, invoking Kant's concept of private right, which is based on the foundational, and negative, claim of equal freedom, according to which no one is in charge of anyone else. As Penner explains, the best way of understanding the notion of Kantian 'private right' is that it creates a realm of 'agency'; a private realm in which, free from the interference of others, we can use our personal *means* to pursue the ends that we have set ourselves. The centrality of means explains why, on Ripstein's Kantian account, all private wrongs become reducible to either usurpations of one's means or uses of one's own means that have the effect of damaging the means of others. As Penner makes clear, this understanding of private law draws a very strong distinction between interferences with means, which amount to a 'misfeasance', and acts that merely alter the environment in which the right-holder operates, which amount to a 'nonfeasance'. Whilst conduct that falls within the latter category might be injurious to the right-holder, it is never wrongful. As Penner explains, Ripstein's explanation of private law is non-instrumentalist because, so Ripstein argues, the very structure of private right can, without more, explain the entirety of private law.

However, as Penner goes on to demonstrate, whilst these sorts of 'universalist' explanations do indeed account for much of the law, it is not clear that they entirely live up to their ambitious claims. The Kantian notion of private right clearly explains why two parties can enter a contract that gives one a right of way over the

[5] See, eg: J Gardner, 'The Negligence Standard: Political not Metaphysical' (2017) 80 *Modern Law Review* 1; J Gardner, 'Nearly Natural Law' (2007) 52 *American Journal of Jurisprudence* 1.

[6] A Ripstein, *Private Wrongs* (Cambridge MA, Harvard University Press, 2016).

land of the other. However, as Penner notes, what it cannot easily explain is why the law of easements also permits that same bilateral agreement to have *in rem* effect so as to bind those who were not party to it. Likewise, it is unclear how Ripstein's minimalist scheme based on interferences with *means* can explain the existence of 'deprivation-based' torts such as nuisance. Whilst Gardner's instrumentalist account of private law does not suffer from these particular shortcomings, it is, as Penner notes, often difficult to apply in practice. This is not least because of the inherent difficulty in identifying and settling on the antecedent moral norms which legal norms are to serve. Penner's thoughtful and carefully argued chapter serves both as a timely evaluation of two leading contemporary accounts of private law and as a fitting tribute to John Gardner's outstanding contribution to private law scholarship.

Ripstein's account of Kantian private right,[7] discussed by Penner, is an example of what Stephen Smith describes in his chapter 'Intermediate and Comprehensive Justifications for Legal Rules' as a 'comprehensive view' of the law. Unlike narrow justifications for legal rules that appeal to, for instance, precedent, coherence or jurisdiction, 'comprehensive views' are founded on fundamental conceptions of the right and the good. Another example of a comprehensive view, and the eternal competitor to the Kantian and corrective justice view,[8] is the law and economics movement that has dominated US legal scholarship since the second half of the twentieth century. Where the Kantian may explain and justify private law on the ground of equal freedom,[9] law and economics scholars, most prominently Richard Posner,[10] have argued that the law both is and should be an instrument that promotes economic efficiency.

The purpose of Stephen Smith's chapter is to explain the limits of comprehensive theories in legal argument and justification. He argues that 'comprehensive views', though of great philosophical interest and importance, are not the sort of justifications that judges and other legal officials should give when justifying legal rules. Instead, Smith argues that judges both should, and in fact do, offer what he calls 'intermediate justifications'. These are justifications for legal rules that are consistent with a broad range of comprehensive views, including those who hold the anti-theory view that rejects comprehensive views. So, for instance, one might justify liability for breach of contract on the basis that the promisor ought to 'keep his promise'. This is an intermediate justification because it is consistent both with the broadly utilitarian justification that the law should enforce efficient bargains,[11] and

[7] ibid.

[8] For the corrective justice view of purely instrumental accounts of the law see EJ Weinrib, *Corrective Justice* (Oxford, Oxford University Press, 2012) 297–333.

[9] For leading accounts see, for instance, Ripstein (n 6); EJ Weinrib, *The Idea of Private Law* (Oxford, Oxford University Press, 2012).

[10] RA Posner, *The Problems of Jurisprudence* (Cambridge MA, Harvard University Press, 1993) 360–62.

[11] Meaning that the benefit of performance to the promisee outweighs the detriment to the promisor. This would satisfy the Kaldor-Hicks conception of efficiency, but not Pareto's more onerous requirement. See further, SA Smith, *Contract Theory* (Oxford, Oxford University Press, 2004) 110–13.

with a deontological or religious view that regards promise-keeping as an inherently valuable moral practice, and not merely a means to some other end. Building on the seminal work of Cass Sunstein,[12] Smith offers two arguments in favour of what he calls the 'acceptability thesis' of legal justification and against the use of comprehensive justifications. The first is the 'practical objection' to comprehensive views. This objection is not, as one might expect, that (most) judges are not philosophers, or that it would be too difficult to sufficiently acquaint judges with all the rival comprehensive theories. It is instead concerned with the ability of the law to achieve its most basic objective of guiding human behaviour. As Smith argues, whilst people may be persuaded to comply with the law because of the presence of sanctions, 'legal rules are immeasurably more effective if their subjects are inclined to follow them, and they will be more inclined to follow them if they agree with the justifications offered to support them'.[13] Because comprehensive views are likely to be controversial, if not objectionable, to large sections of the community, justifications for rules that avoid foundational claims and employ more broadly accepted intermediate principles will make those rules more likely to guide the behaviour of those who are subject to them. The second, 'principled objection', to comprehensive views is concerned, not with the efficacy of the law, but instead with the legitimacy of state power. As Smith notes, in political theory it is often argued that, because law is obligatory and ultimately backed by the coercive power of the state, its constituent rules should be justified in terms that most, though perhaps not all, its subjects can accept and endorse. Once again, because intermediate justifications are consistent with many of the comprehensive views held by reasonable people, satisfaction of the legitimacy imperative favours justifications that are expressed in terms of intermediate, rather than comprehensive, principles.

Importantly, and thought-provokingly, Smith goes on to argue that the 'acceptability thesis' is not confined to judges and other legal officials who apply the law. On his account, it also applies with equal force to those in the academy. As he persuasively writes, '[a] justification succeeds or fails regardless of who offers it. The reasons underlying the acceptability thesis are not just reasons for judges; they are reasons for anyone trying to justify legal rules'.[14]

Nicholas McBride in chapter five seeks to break the logjam in current debates about the nature of rights, by observing that all parties to those debates assume that we can be wrong about rights. They assume that it is possible to make true and false statements about the nature of rights, and debates about the nature of rights are directed at ascertaining which statements are true and which false. McBride observes that this assumption is maintained in the face of the fact that it would be easy to see claims about the nature of rights as being designed not to uncover truths about the nature of rights, but as concerned simply to advance particular

[12] C Sunstein, 'Incompletely Theorized Agreements' (1994) 108 *Harvard Law Review* 1733.
[13] SA Smith, chapter 4 at 72.
[14] ibid, 81.

power-seeking agendas. It would be easy to see such claims in this more cynical way because of the significance of rights in the way they give us power over others, and also because no real progress has been made in resolving various debates about the nature of rights, when one would expect such progress to be made where there is a truth of the matter about the nature of rights. McBride focusses on the following debates:

(1) Are rights best described as protecting the right-holder's interests ('Interest Theory'), or as giving the right-holder the power to determine how someone else will behave ('Will Theory'), or as combining these two functions ('Hybrid Theory')?
(2) Are there such things as moral rights (as opposed to legal rights)?
(3) Are rights peremptory or not? Does the existence of a right dictate to someone what they should do in a given situation, or does the existence of a right only affect what considerations someone should take into account in determining what they should do in a given situation?
(4) Are rights purely private in nature, held by and against individuals, or are there distinctively public rights, held by or against the government?

McBride argues that if we can – as all parties to the above debates assume – be wrong about rights, a way of making progress in these debates would be to ask: what positions in these debates are *least likely* to advance a particular power-seeking agenda? Whichever position is least likely to advance a particular power-seeking agenda is, correspondingly, most likely to reflect some truth about the nature of rights as there seems to be no other reason why such a position might be adopted. As a result, we should presume that the position in relation to a particular debate about rights that is least likely to advance a particular power-seeking agenda is correct unless and until we are given a good reason for thinking that it is incorrect.

Turning first to debate (1), McBride distinguishes between the Interest Theory and Will Theory, further distinguishing between two versions of the Interest Theory, which he labels the Interest-Ground Theory ('IG Theory'), and the Interest-Effect Theory ('IE Theory').[15] According to the IG Theory, A has a right against B if B is subject to a duty to do x, and that duty exists because B's doing x will (other things being equal) serve A's interests.[16] According to the IE Theory, A has a right against B if B is subject to a duty to do x, and B's doing x will (other things being equal) have the effect of serving A's interests.[17] Referring to the Will Theory,[18] McBride

[15] NJ McBride, chapter 5 at 89.

[16] See J Raz, *The Morality of Freedom* (Oxford, Oxford University Press, 1986) 166.

[17] See, eg: MH Kramer, 'Rights Without Trimmings' in MH Kramer et al (eds), *A Debate Over Rights: Philosophical Enquiries* (Oxford, Oxford University Press, 1998); MH Kramer, 'Getting Rights Right' in MH Kramer (ed), *Rights, Wrongs and Responsibilities* (London, Palgrave, 2001); MH Kramer, 'Some Doubts About Alternatives to the Interest Theory of Rights' (2013) 123 *Ethics* 245; MH Kramer, 'In Defence of the Interest Theory of Right-Holding: Rejoinders to Leif Wenar on Rights' in N McBride (ed), *New Essays on the Nature of Rights* (Oxford, Hart Publishing, 2017).

[18] McBride relies on the formulation of the will theory given by Hart. See HLA Hart, 'Legal Rights' in his *Essays on Bentham* (Oxford, Oxford University Press, 1982) 184.

explains that A has a right against B if B is subject to a duty to do x, and A has (i) the power to waive or extinguish that duty; (ii) the power to enforce[19] that duty if B breaches, or threatens to breach her duty to do x; and (iii) the power to waive or extinguish any obligation that B might owe A to pay compensation to B in the event that B breaches her duty to do x. Observing that on the Will Theory there is no limit on what rights we can have against other people, such that 'I will have a right against you any time you are subject to a duty and I have the ability to control you through the means of your being subject to that duty',[20] McBride concludes that, as between the Interest Theory and the Will Theory, the Interest Theory is less likely to have been adopted for reasons of political advantage. Moreover, as between IG Theory and IE Theory, IG Theory is less likely to have been adopted to advance a particular power-seeking agenda.

In relation to debate (2), McBride observes that the resources in contemporary society available for evaluating the actions of ourselves and others are 'grotesquely impoverished',[21] and that the 'adoption of the language of moral rights will be motivated by a desire for power – either the power to protect oneself from others, or the power to dominate others'.[22] Applying his methodology leads the author to take the side of those who deny that moral rights exist.

Turning to debate (3), the author elsewhere reframes this question by asking whether rights are best characterised as '*rights that*' or '*rights to*'.[23] 'Rights that' are peremptory in nature whereas 'rights to' are non-peremptory in nature. Thus, '[i]f I have a right that you take care not to run me over, then you must have a duty to take care not to run me over: nothing else could be implied by my having a right that you take care not to run me over'.[24] My right is peremptory: 'once the right is demonstrated, the question at issue is conclusively resolved'.[25] By contrast, if I have a right to life, it is uncertain what that means for other people. The nature and extent of the legal protection against me being deprived of my life must be worked out. My right is non-peremptory. Returning to the issue of claim-rights, McBride again asks his central question. Pointing to the fact that 'rights to' are 'shapeshifters',[26] the author suggests that 'rights to' are likely to be attractive to those who seek power over others. Therefore, he argues that

[19] McBride explains that this requirement is rendered problematic if we are talking about a *moral* right (if there is such a thing as a moral right) and would need to be modified by a Will Theorist in order to apply to that kind of right.

[20] NJ McBride, chapter 5 at 91.

[21] ibid, 95.

[22] ibid 96. McBride notes that this was (unsurprisingly) also Nietzsche's view: see his *Daybreak* (1881) Book II, §112 ('On the natural history of rights and duties').

[23] NJ McBride, 'Rights and the Basis of Tort Law' in D Nolan and A Robertson (eds), *Rights and Private Law* (Oxford, Hart Publishing, 2012) 335–36, 343–46; and subsequently in NJ McBride, *The Humanity of Private Law, Part I: Explanation* (Oxford, Hart Publishing, 2019) 43–48.

[24] NJ McBride, chapter 5 at 97.

[25] NE Simmonds, 'Constitutional Rights, Civility and Artifice' (2019) 78 *Cambridge Law Journal* 175, 183.

[26] NJ McBride, chapter 5 at 97–98.

'rights that' are less likely to have been adopted for political purposes. In result, the author concludes we should adopt, as more likely to be true, the view that claim-rights are peremptory 'rights that …', in the absence of further arguments in favour of the view that at least some claim-rights must be described as taking the form of 'rights to …'.[27]

In considering debate (4), the discussion observes that the common law seems to recognise the existence of distinctively public claim-rights where a government body or employee (D) has misused its powers in a way that harmed a private individual (C). In such a case C can argue that he had a claim-right that D not do what it did if (i) D intended to harm C; or (ii) D knew that he was misusing his powers and he knew that his doing so was likely to result in harm to C.[28] Is there anything wrong with the common law recognising the existence of such a distinctively public claim-right?

McBride suggests that the answer may be 'yes'. Returning to the IG Theory (which won out in debate (1)), McBride considers the hypothetical example of a claim-right against the government that it set up a 'fully-functioning police station and hospital within five miles of where I live'.[29] Arguably such a claim-right could not be supported under the IG Theory, as my interest in being safe and healthy could not be sufficiently weighty to ground a duty on the government to establish a hospital and police station within five miles of my residence. Moreover, McBride observes that a broader version of the IG Theory, which accommodates not only my interests, but also the interest of others in my interests being protected, courts the danger of allowing claim-rights to be used to advance a particular power-seeking agenda. Therefore, he suggests, the IG Theory should not be taken as supporting an onerous public claim-right such as the one in his hypothetical example. Returning to the particular public claim-rights currently recognised via the tort of misfeasance in public office, McBride argues that while such claim-rights could be supported under the IG Theory as they are a lot less onerous to comply with, such claim-rights arguably have not been recognised in order to protect individual interests, but as a way of bringing abusive government officials to heel. Overall, therefore, whilst conceding the possibility of there being distinctively public claim-rights, claim-rights are most secure when found between private individuals.

[27] A variety of such further arguments are canvassed in McBride, *The Humanity of Private Law* (n 23) 48–54, but none compel us to think of claim-rights in terms of being 'rights to …'. In particular, Razian rights, that ground duties, can be assimilated to Dworkinian principles, so that a Razian 'right to life' can be redescribed as a 'legal principle that life should be protected' (for the same suggestion, see C Webb, 'Three Concepts of Rights, Two of Property' (2018) 38 *Oxford Journal of Legal Studies* 246, 253–54). And while Kantians will not be able to give up the language of 'rights to …' as they need such language to denote the necessary connection between C and X that has to exist for C to be able to complain that D has violated C's Kantian right to independence by damaging or using X, that kind of 'right to …' is not a claim-right at all, but an *interest* in X.

[28] *Three Rivers DC v Governor and Company of the Bank of England (No 3)* [2001] UKHL 16, [2003] 2 AC 1.

[29] NJ McBride, chapter 5 at 100.

In 'Juridical Justification of Private rights', Paul Miller considers the issue of justification in the context of private law methodology. In particular, Miller is concerned with the status and significance of *juridical* justifications for private rights. Juridical reasons are the reasons the law itself posits to justify obedience to its rules. An analysis of juridical justifications is a form of interpretive analysis because it prioritises the 'internal' perspective and very obviously attempts to understand the law on its own terms.[30] As Miller writes:

> [t]he task of *interpretive legal theory* is one of offering a simplified but faithful rendering of posited law that aims to make it more amenable to understanding. The rendering involves descriptive and normative elements, but the latter are supplied not by the theories, but by law.[31]

Importantly in a chapter concerned with methodology, Miller makes clear that not all interpretive theories of law are concerned with *juridical* reasons. Theorists, such as the Kantians, who offer 'foundationalist' explanations for private rights that are reducible to a single value are certainly engaged in interpretive theory. However, unlike a theorist concerned with juridical justifications, they are not primarily concerned to explain the legal structures they see by appealing to the reasons that the law itself provides.

Miller's analysis of juridical reasons takes it as axiomatic that the law is a public practice of practical reason, the aim of which is to provide normative guidance to its addressees. The law supplies this guidance by both issuing rules and, crucially, articulating the reasons for those rules to people capable of appreciating their persuasive force. As Miller observes:

> [r]easons are given juridically for rights and other legal rules in order to more effectively guide the behaviour of beings endowed with practical reason. Private rights are legally binding to the extent that they are validly posited, but juridical reasons are only practically persuasive to the extent that they are practically reasonable.[32]

This leads to a fascinating puzzle. If law guides behaviour by both positing rules and the *reasons* for those rules, why is it that, as Miller notes, juridical reasons so often appear superficial and, in some cases, unconvincing? Surely, if the law offered more persuasive reasons for its rules, it would better fulfil its behaviour guiding function. Importantly, Miller provides an explanation for what he describes as the characteristic 'thinness' of juridical reasons. On his account, the relative simplicity of juridical reasons is explained by the fact that they must function as a sort of normative shorthand, capable of being understood and applied by lawyers and laymen alike. Whilst 'thicker', more elaborate, reasons might seem desirable in the abstract, the characteristic 'thinness' of juridical reasons enables people with no expertise in ethics, economics, or whatever, to easily determine what the law

[30] This is, of course, not to say that interpretive legal analysts do not see the value in critical analysis. It is simply to say that it is a different enterprise.

[31] P Miller, chapter 6 at 111.

[32] ibid, 120.

requires of them. As Miller notes, the need to provide effective guidance results in 'a delicate real-world economy of practical reasoning that favours law and legal reasons that are clear and comprehensible'.[33]

Miller concludes by noting the limits both of juridical justifications and of interpretive theory more generally. Whilst it is unlikely that the law, as a system of practical reason, is pervasively irrational or unreasonable, the interpretive theorist must still be wary of 'reading into the law a level and extent of practical reasonableness that simply is not there'.[34] Likewise, whilst the thinness of juridical reasons aids normative guidance, it is possible that, in some cases, those reasons are simply too thin. Consistently with the distinction Miller draws between interpretive and critical theory, theorists need not always adopt the internal perspective. They can also step outside the law and argue that, on occasion, the reasons offered by the law for its own rules are inadequate.

In chapter seven Lionel Smith builds on recent scholarship in Quebec civil law, notably the work of Justice Benoît Moore,[35] to argue that the idea of the source of a private right is deeply ambiguous, and that the failure to see this has bedevilled attempts to classify the sources of rights. Much has been written in both the common law and the civil law about the 'sources' of rights or of obligations. Jurists have attempted to classify and organise these sources as a way of shedding analytical light on the different kinds of rights that exist in private law. Just as every effect has multiple causes, every right has multiple sources. Smith argues that Moore's work allows us to observe the following ambiguities in the idea of a 'source' of a right or obligation. The first is 'justificatory principle'. A justificatory principle is not a legal rule, but is itself a principle that is capable of justifying legal rules. The example Smith gives is 'seriously made promises should be kept' which may lie behind rules of offer and acceptance and adequacy of consideration. Smith thus describes a justificatory principle as a 'non-legal ideal or aspiration or value'.[36] The second sense of source is 'formal source', which is that which permits us to conclude that the rule is a legal rule, rather than, say, a moral or religious precept. It is that which 'qualifies a rule as a rule of law'.[37] For example, a statute, a constitution or binding case law. The third is 'normative source', which is a 'legal rule that is capable of creating or modifying particular rights, liabilities and other legal relationships between citizens'.[38] Thus, the legal rule is itself the thing which can create or modify obligations and rights between parties. Smith gives

[33] ibid, 126.

[34] ibid, 127.

[35] B Moore, 'De l'acte et du fait juridique ou d'un critère de distinction incertain' (1997) 31 *Rev Juridique Thémis* 277; B Moore, 'La classification des sources des obligations: courte histoire d'une valse-hésitation' (2002) 36 *Rev Juridique Thémis* 275; B Moore, 'La théorie des sources des obligations: éclatement d'une classification' (2002) 36 *Rev Juridique Thémis* 689.

[36] L Smith, chapter 7 at 151.

[37] ibid.

[38] ibid.

as an example the 'general rule that "every natural person has a right to bodily integrity"'[39] which is arguably the normative source of my right to claim damages in battery from the particular person who punches me. Finally, the notion of 'material source' describes that legal rules are only engaged when the relevant facts are proved to have occurred. These facts are the material source of the right or obligation etc. The material source 'is one of the factual events that activate[s] a normative source'.[40] Importantly, Smith emphasises that these classifications will often overlap. For example, a principle that people should honour their serious commitments (a justificatory principle) may be shared by a number of legal rules, all of which give effect to this principle: variously in the law of contract, the law of covenants, the law of express trusts and the law of estoppel. Each of these discrete instantiations of legal liability will have its own normative source and formal source.

Lionel Smith argues that a similar ambiguity inhabits the common law's idea of a 'cause of action', and that in the common law cause of action is sometimes used to mean a material source, sometimes a normative source, sometimes a justificatory principle and sometimes to mean the obligation that arises when the material source has activated a normative source. Distinguishing between the different senses of the ideas of 'source' and 'cause of action' helps to clarify a number of debates in private law theory.

The specific example Lionel Smith takes us to is the well-known system of classification proposed by Peter Birks according to which private law is classified according to one of four generic 'causative events' (or, as Smith describes, the classification of the *legal characterisation* of events that take place in the world): consent, unjust enrichment, wrongs and 'other'.[41] Returning to the idea of 'sources', Smith asks about the extent to which these Birksian categories of event are unified sources and whether they are categories organised by any of Moore's understandings of source.

Smith observes that whilst consent has material unity, in that a manifestation of intention underpins all legal relations and responses in this category, the category of wrongs is not so unified. Returning to the Birksian notion of a wrong, which is that it is an unexcused infringement of a right, Smith points out that there is no unity in this category by normative source nor by material source. Rather, as shown by the diversity of members of the category, for example, breaches of trust, breach of contract, breaches of rights granted by the law to all and also those granted by the law to only some (eg, proprietary rights in a particular asset), Smith argues that there is plurality. Further, 'there is no unity as to justifying principle, as these many rights have many justifying principles'.[42]

[39] ibid, 138.

[40] ibid, 151.

[41] P Birks, 'Definition and Division: A Meditation on *Institutes* 3.13' in P Birks (ed), *The Classification of Obligations* (Oxford, Clarendon Press, 1997) 1; P Birks, 'Introduction' in P Birks (ed), *English Private Law*, 2 vols, vol 1 (Oxford, OUP, 2000) xli–xlii.

[42] L Smith, chapter 7 at 147.

However, it is in relation to the event labelled unjust enrichment that the chapter takes on its greatest significance. Even if we excise from that category the phenomenon of restitution for wrongs, so that it contains only subtractive unjust enrichment, Lionel Smith observes that the category is unified by a justificatory principle against unjust enrichment. However, at the level of normative sources, he argues that unjust enrichment contains multiple and diverse normative sources.[43] Therefore, argues Smith, a classification based only on justificatory principle does not provide a category sufficient to 'insist on uniformity across the whole category'.[44] Returning to the Birksian taxonomy, this observation is important because, as the author points out, 'a classification based on justifying principle could never be made to do the work that Birks wanted it to do'.[45] This is because classification according to justifying principle risks ignoring the differences of detail at the level of normative source. Birks sought to unify various claims or causes of action as the causative event labelled unjust enrichment. Drawing on the Moorean scheme, Smith points out that in doing so, Birks ultimately purported to achieve this unity according to a single normative source. However, the wide range of situations in which defendants 'may become responsible to plaintiffs without having consented or having done anything wrong'[46] suggests not only a category organised by a single justificatory principle against unjust enrichment, but a variety and diversity of normative source.

Part II. Particular Private Rights

Part II of this collection considers the more specific justifications appliable to directly applicable legal rules. In doing so, many of the tensions between fundamentalist accounts in Part I are 'played out' in concrete case examples. Part II begins with a contribution by Michael Crawford. Many analyses of property theory focus on whether private property is justified.[47] In 'Justifying Possession (or How We Get from Here to There)', Crawford considers a different question. Assuming that private property is desirable, he asks how such a system gets up and running in the first place. To become operational, all systems of private property need, at a minimum, agreed-upon rules that determine how unowned things can be removed from the commons and become objects of private ownership. The question is,

[43] See too Robert Stevens, 'The Unjust Enrichment Disaster' (2018) 134 *Law Quarterly Review* 574.

[44] L Smith, chapter 7 at 149.

[45] ibid.

[46] ibid, 152.

[47] As Lisa Austin has noted, this is even true of many of the analyses that purport to focus on the rules that determine initial acquisition. See LM Austin, 'Possession and the Distractions of Philosophy' in JE Penner and HE Smith (eds), *Philosophical Foundations of Property Law* (Oxford, Oxford University Press, 2013) 182.

what mechanism should the law employ to do this and why? Under the influence of law and economics scholarship, these questions have received surprisingly little attention. One might speculate that this is because, under the hypothetical conditions of the Coase theorem,[48] questions of initial allocation become uninteresting if one's only goal is efficiency.

Perhaps the most influential discussion of this issue is contained in Richard Epstein's seminal essay, 'Possession as the Root of Title',[49] in which he argues that, in systems that recognise private property, the most basic questions of mine and thine are resolved by application of the possession rule. According to this rule, the first person to take possession of an unowned thing becomes its owner. In that essay, Epstein provides a modest defence of the possession rule on the grounds of conceptual necessity. In getting started, systems of private property are stuck between a rock and a hard place. On the one hand, the philosophical objection from 'unilateralism' seems to prevent the legitimate creation of any non-consensual right-duty relationships. On the other hand, insurmountable transaction costs and unavoidable strategic behaviour mean that no system of private property could be based on consent. So how to break this impasse? What rule should we use? Given the necessity for an allocative rule but the extreme difficulty of selecting one, Epstein's answer is: the best rule you can have is the rule that you have got. The mere status of the possession rule as the accepted means of answering the most fundamental questions of mine and thine is justification enough.

In his chapter, Crawford aims to go beyond Epstein's minimal defence of the possession rule. Following David Hume's famous account of property,[50] he argues that the possession rule is an emergent phenomenon. It was never consciously designed, nor was it selected as the basic mechanism for creating property rights because it was seen to be fair or morally justified. Rather, as with all emergent phenomena, the possession rule is strictly amoral and it triumphed at the expense of other potential means of creating property rights because it more effectively resolved the recurrent coordination problem created by the problem of scarcity. However, that the possession rule is strictly amoral does not mean that it is also immoral or otherwise unfair.

Drawing on insights from evolutionary game theory, Crawford dissents from the commonly expressed view that possession is a morally questionable way of creating original property rights. After discussing the inevitable moral constraints placed on any basic allocative rule, he argues that the possession rule satisfies a minimal conception of fairness because it ensures that, at the very least, no one is systematically excluded from acquiring rights to scarce resources. Put differently, the possession rule ensures that no one must forfeit a resource to anyone else

[48] RH Coase, 'The Problem of Social Cost' (1960) 3 *Journal of Law & Economics* 1.

[49] RA Epstein, 'Possession as the Root of Title' (1979) 13 *Georgia Law Review* 1221.

[50] D Hume, A Treatise of Human Nature (first published 1739–40, Oxford, Oxford University Press, 2000) pt 2 § 2–3.

because of who they are. Thus, the virtue of possession is not merely its incumbency. It also satisfies a basic standard of fairness.

In chapter nine Andrew Botterell seeks a better understanding of the underlying normative contours of the tort of deceit. At the heart of the puzzle he seeks to solve is the doctrinal emphasis placed in the tort of deceit on the requirement of economic loss, such as that stated in *McGregor on Damages*: *viz* that the 'principal, and generally the only, recovery in deceit is for pecuniary loss'.[51] But is this requirement of loss constitutive of the tort, so that until loss has been suffered the 'tort is inchoate'?[52] Alternatively, does the requirement of loss go rather to actionability? On this view, as Botterell explains, following *Briess v Woolley*,[53] the tort becomes complete only when the fraudulent misrepresentation is acted upon. In order to answer this question about the proper role of loss, the author sketches an account of private law and demonstrates how the tort of deceit accords with this general picture.

Botterell argues that the tort of deceit is not a normative or conceptual outlier in the private law universe. In his view, deceit is wrongful because it interferes with people's normative entitlements to things that are theirs. The tort of deceit does not protect a right not to be lied to, nor does it protect a right to decisional autonomy. Rather, it protects everything that is rightfully ours – anything to which we have a normative entitlement to – from dispossession due to fraud. This view rests on what the author describes as 'The Toronto Plan',[54] an approach to private law that views it as a unified system of norms governing the reciprocal conduct of individuals that protects me and what is mine from the constraining actions and choices of others. Following Arthur Ripstein, Botterell suggest that a private wrong 'consists in pursuing purposes in a way that is inconsistent with some other person's entitlement to do so'.[55]

So how does this apply to the tort of deceit? Botterell takes us to the Kantian notion of a *juristic lie*, which is an untruth that bears upon rights or directly infringes upon rights.[56] On this view, a deception wrongs another person when it is done with the intention of infringing or interfering with another's right, and when that right is in fact interfered with. Thus, the author argues that the tort protects 'everything to which you have a normative entitlement'[57] by preventing the non-consensual dispossession of these things by the fraud of another. He argues that the basis of the tort of deceit is not the right to make decisions free from deception but rather the right not to be deceptively dispossessed of what is rightfully yours.

[51] J Edelman (ed), *McGregor on Damages*, 20th edn (London, Sweet & Maxwell, 2018) 1653.
[52] A Botterell, chapter 9 at 182.
[53] *Briess v Woolley* [1954] AC 333 (HL), 353 (Lord Tucker).
[54] A Botterell, chapter 9 at 189, 191–196.
[55] Ripstein (n 6) 30.
[56] A Botterell, chapter 9 at 197.
[57] ibid.

Returning to the puzzle Botterell identifies at the start of his chapter, the author takes the view that damage, but not loss, is essential to the tort of deceit. This conclusion rests on a particular definition of loss and damage. Consistent with the general approach of the Toronto Plan, the damage at issue in the tort of deceit is the damage that inheres in the dispossession of rights. However, Botterell defines loss to be a comparative concept, so that whether a person has suffered a loss at time *t* depends on what happens at the later time *t+1*. Therefore, loss is not essential to proving deceit, even though in many cases plaintiffs will also suffer losses as a result of being dispossessed of their normative entitlements.

In chapter ten, 'Justifying Liabilities and Duties', Andrew Robertson raises what may be thought to be an objection to a premise underlying this collection. Namely, while this collection is focused on the justification of private law *rights*, Robertson argues that any complete justification of the private law requires a detailed analysis of both power/liability and right/duty relationships. These terms are used in the sense of being Hohfeldian correlatives: with the right/duty[58] relationship characterised by B coming under an immediate duty to do or not to do a particular activity[59] with the correlative claim-right to compel such behaviour being held by A. Whereas the power/liability relationship is characterised by A being able to effect a 'particular change of legal relations' with B.[60] Robertson makes an important analytical point that can bring normative debates concerning private law theory and doctrine into sharper focus. In this connection, it is hard to improve on Arthur L Corbin's observation that:

> Hohfeld's analysis of concepts and his arrangement of terms does indeed give great aid to the analysis of legal problems in breaking down our complex and variable terms. It solves no problem of social or juristic policy, but it does much to define and clarify the issue that is in dispute and thus enables the mind to concentrate on the interests and policies that are involved, and increases the probability of an informed and sound conclusion.[61]

What then can be said about the importance of power/liability relationships to justifying private law? Robertson argues such relationships provide 'an important frame of reference for any justificatory exercise'[62] in private law for two key reasons. The first reason Robertson provides is that both 'historically and as a matter of practice'[63] the private law begins with antecedent questions focusing principally on the imposition of liability rather than the imposition of rights and duties.

[58] WN Hohfeld, 'Fundamental Legal Conceptions as Applied to Judicial Reasoning' (1913) 23 *Yale Law Journal* 16, 30.

[59] See, eg: J Finnis, 'Some Professorial Fallacies About Rights' (1971–72) 4 *Adelaide Law Review* 377, 379.

[60] Hohfeld (n 58) 44.

[61] AL Corbin, 'Foreword' in WW Cook (ed), *Fundamental Legal Conceptions as Applied in Judicial Reasoning* (Clark NJ, Lawbook Exchange Ltd, 2010) xi.

[62] A Robertson, chapter 10 at 201.

[63] ibid, 201.

The salient point made is that private law judgments are generally concerned with justifying either the imposition of liability or the denial of liability.

A second reason to consider liability as a frame of reference in private law is that unique questions of justification may arise in relation to justifying a primary liability in contrast to justifying the imposition of a primary duty. Those questions of justification will be missed or, worse still, fundamentally misunderstood in an analysis of private law doctrine that focuses exclusively on rights and duties. Robertson's chapter uses the example of equitable estoppel (explained on the basis of a power/liability relationship) and the right to performance of a contractual promise (explained on the basis of a right/duty relationship) to demonstrate the difficulty of distinguishing between right/duty relationships and power/liability relationships and also the importance of appreciating the diversity of jural relationships in any discussion of justification. The analytical distinctions between equitable estoppel, contract, equity and the common law drawn out by Robertson is a theme returned to in chapter eleven by Ben McFarlane. After laying this groundwork as to the importance of the power/liability relationship as a frame of reference, Robertson then considers a second example of vicarious liability. Concluding that if the puzzle of justifying vicarious liability is to be solved then the attribution of legal culpability to a third party is likely to be justified '*as* a liability, based on a broader sense of responsibility not involving notions of fault or wrongdoing'.[64]

The final part of Robertson's chapter 'discusses the need to take account of duties in the analysis of justification in private law'.[65] This includes a response to the work of John Goldberg and Ben Zipursky[66] and the idea that viewing the private law through the rubric of duty illustrates that the private law is about behaviour guidance (ie by placing B under an immediate duty to do or not to do a particular activity the private law is concerned about guiding B's behaviour by use of a coercive duty). Although, as Robertson correctly observes, other jural relations, and not just right-duty relationships, can also be perfectly adequate in guiding behaviour. In doing so he provides the example of the detailed steps required of a bank 'to avoid having constructive notice of the [surety's] rights' as enunciated by Lord Nicholls in in *Royal Bank of Scotland v Etridge (No 2)*, which are not imposed as a legal duty.[67] There is much force to this point. Consider the so called 'duty to mitigate' loss.[68] A contracting party does not breach a duty by failing to mitigate her loss, it is just that particular legal consequences arise if she fails to do so. Naturally, the rule of mitigation will guide the innocent party's

[64] ibid, 210.

[65] ibid, 202.

[66] As argued in JCP Goldberg and BC Zipursky, 'Seeing Law from the Internal Point of View: Holmes and Hart on Legal Duties' (2006) 75 *Fordham Law Review* 1563, 1577.

[67] *Royal Bank of Scotland v Etridge (No 2)* [2002] 2 AC 773, [70].

[68] *British Westinghouse Electric and Manufacturing Co Ltd v Underground Electric Railways Co of London Ltd* [1912] AC 673.

behaviour without the imposition of a duty in that context. The fact that legal consequences arise if B does x/fails to do x, and those consequences might be bad for B, does not mean that B has a duty to do x/not to do x but those set legal consequences may nonetheless still provide a forceful guide for B's behaviour. Robertson then concludes by arguing that a full understanding of a justification in private law can only be gained by taking account of liabilities, powers, duties and rights.

The importance of taking into account the diversity of jural relations is a theme continued in Ben McFarlane's chapter 'Equity and the Justification of Private Rights'. In particular, McFarlane observes that the dualism created by the common law and equity multiplies the number of specific legal rules requiring justification. Debates concerning fusion and the proper relationship between common law and equity are long running but remain relevant.[69] For instance, Lord Toulson's opening paragraph in *AIB Group (UK) plc v Mark Redler & Co Solicitors*[70] showed some willingness to reignite the fusionist debate: '140 years after the Judicature Act 1873, the stitching together of equity and the common law continues to cause problems at the seams'.[71] McFarlane's chapter illustrates why the metaphor of 'equity' and the 'common law' as being 'stitched' together is unhelpful. Developing a thesis that is consistent with the historical works of FW Maitland[72] and Sir Victor Windeyer,[73] McFarlane argues that equity and common law mostly avoid substantive conflict[74] as a result of analytical form and normative function. Illustrating why it is of the first importance for lawyers to appreciate the diversity in jural relations,[75] he argues that it is mistaken to consider equitable doctrines as mere facsimiles of common law rules. For example, Patrick Atiyah viewed equitable estoppel and contract as operating in the same substantive space. On this view, both doctrines enforce a contract albeit with detrimental reliance standing in for the consideration requirement whenever estoppel is invoked.[76] McFarlane observes that salient analytical differences between the jural relations involved in contract and estoppel show why this cannot be the case: the law of contract imposes an immediate right-duty relationship at the point of formation[77] which obliges the promisor to perform

[69] See, eg: J Austin, *Lectures on Jurisprudence*, 1st edn (Lomd, J Murray, 1863) i, 38–39; L Smith, 'Fusion and Tradition' in S Degeling and J Edelman (eds), *Equity in Commercial Law* (Sydney, Lawbook Co, 2005) 38.

[70] *AIB Group (UK) plc v Mark Redler & Co Solicitors* [2014] UKSC 58, [2015] AC 1503.

[71] ibid [1].

[72] FW Maitland, *Equity: A Course of Lectures*, revised edn (Cambridge, Cambridge University Press, 1936) 1–19.

[73] WJV Windeyer, *Lectures on Legal History*, 2nd edn revised (Sydney, Lawbook Co, 1957) 259.

[74] But for the opposite view see WN Hohfeld, 'The Relations between Equity and Law' (1913) 6 *Michigan Law Review* 537.

[75] Building on Hohfeld (n 58).

[76] PS Atiyah, 'When is an Enforceable Agreement Not A Contract? Answer: When it is an Equity' (1976) 92 *Law Quarterly Review* 174.

[77] See further, Smith (n 11) Ch 3.

the promise, whereas estoppel only imposes a primary *liability* on the promisor at some later point in time and only if there is a prospect of the promisee suffering a detriment as a result of his or her reasonable reliance on the promise. Likewise, lawyers also habitually speak of 'equitable' and 'legal' property rights as if these were merely alternative forms of title under the general law.[78] However, using the examples of equitable assignment[79] and equitable property,[80] McFarlane demonstrates how such concepts reflect the 'second order' or 'supplementary' nature of equity whereby equity engrafts onto, and controls the exercise of, a common law right or power. Given this analytical form of many equitable principles, what is said about their normative function? McFarlane makes two important points that ought to be borne in mind by those considering the interplay between common law and equity. First, noting the importance of equity in mitigating the risk of one party 'taking advantage of, or otherwise abusing, the existence of certain primary legal rules' and thus arguing that the existence of those equitable principles may be crucial to justifying the operation of those primary legal rules.[81] Secondly, noting how the bifurcated structure of 'equitable property' enhances the autonomy of a primary right holder by increasing the means by which that party can deal with his or her primary rights.[82]

The final issue addressed in this collection concerns what justification(s) are there, if any, for equity's jurisdiction to provide relief against forfeiture which is considered by Nicholas Tiverios. As Tiverios explains in his chapter 'Property, Therefore', pursuant to Anglo-Australian law, there are two conceptually distinct grounds on which equity may provide relief against forfeiture by *disabling* one party's strict insistence on his legal rights. Tiverios terms the first ground the 'security rights' basis. That is, where A's right to the forfeiture of B's right is inserted into the contract as a matter of substance to secure either B's payment of money or B's performance of some other transactional event, equity will relieve B from the forfeiture of her right on the condition that she compensates (including interest and costs) A for the failure of the secured event.[83] He terms the second ground of relief the unconscionability basis. This ground of forfeiture applies beyond the context of security rights and involves circumstances where A has engaged in

[78] See, eg: *R (Von Goetz) v London Borough of Tower Hamlets* [1998] EWCA Civ 1507, [1999] QB 1019, 1024 (Mummery LJ).

[79] See further, CH Tham, *Understanding the Law of Assignment* (Cambridge, Cambridge University Press, 2019).

[80] See further, FW Sanders, *Laws of Uses and Trusts* (London, E. and R. Brooke 1791) 108–11; W Hart, 'What is a Trust?' (1899) 15 *Law Quarterly Review* 294; K Jacobs, *The Law of Trusts in New South Wales* (Sydney, LexisNexis, 1958) 7.

[81] B McFarlane, chapter 11 at 240.

[82] ibid, 243. See also NA Tiverios and MJR Crawford, 'Equitable Property and the Law of the Horse: Assignment, Intermediated Securities and Data Trusts' (forthcoming) 14(3) Journal of Equity.

[83] *Waddington in Kreglinger (G&C) v New Patagonia and Cold Storage Co Ltd* [1914] AC 25 (HL), 49–50 (Lord Parker); *Cukurova Finance International Ltd v Alfa Telecom Turkey Ltd* [2013] UKPC 25; [2016] AC 923 (PC), [90] (Lord Neuberger).

an unconscientious exercise of a legal right or a legal power.[84] More specifically, B may be entitled to retain her right that would otherwise be lost on an event of default in circumstances where A's exercise of a legal right or power is affected by fraud, accident, mistake or surprise, provided that A has sufficient notice of the impugned circumstances such that the loss of B's right is unconscionable. One puzzle the chapter addresses is the potential additional requirement that the 'forfeiture' involves B losing a proprietary or possessory right on default in order to seek relief. In *Manchester Ship Canal Company Ltd v Vauxhall Motors Ltd (formerly General Motors UK Ltd)*,[85] a majority of the Supreme Court of the United Kingdom decided that under English law B must forfeit a proprietary or possessory right on default in order to seek relief against forfeiture. The majority was reluctant to interfere with what it saw as the 'careful development' of a 'principled limitation' on the doctrine of relief against forfeiture which had been 'worked out over many years in a succession of broadly coherent authorities'.[86] Australian courts have, however, adopted an approach that clearly differs from their English counterparts. This is because, in Australia, the equitable doctrine to grant relief against forfeiture can seemingly apply in the context of the forfeiture of non-proprietary rights (eg where B loses a contractual right on an event of default). In this connection, Edelman J in *Mineralogy Pty Ltd v Sino Iron Pty Ltd (No 6)*[87] raised the question for those who insist on the imposition of the proprietary or possessory right requirement:

> One difficulty with the insistence that relief against forfeiture operates only to relieve from forfeiture of proprietary rights is the issue of the principle. *Why* should the doctrine be confined to property rights? None of the cases addresses this point.[88]

Tiverios provides three arguments in support of the Australian approach over that adopted in England. The first argument is that the proprietary or possessory right requirement was not essential as a matter of Anglo-Australian legal history. The second argument is that the proprietary or possessory right requirement is not essential analytically or as a matter of moral philosophy as the security rights basis for relief against forfeiture gives effect to a principle of corrective justice[89] and the unconscionability basis for relief against forfeiture appears to fit the view that

[84] *Shiloh Spinners Ltd v Harding* [1973] AC 691 (HL), 722–23 (Lord Wilberforce); *Legione v Hateley* (1983) 152 CLR 406 (HCA), 424–25 (Gibbs CJ & Murphy J); *Australian Competition and Consumer Commission v CG Berbatis Holdings Pty Ltd* [2003] HCA 18; (2003) 214 CLR 51 (HCA), [42] (Gummow & Hayne JJ).

[85] *Manchester Ship Canal Company Ltd v Vauxhall Motors Ltd (formerly General Motors UK Ltd)* [2019] UKSC 46; [2019] 3 WLR 852.

[86] ibid [50].

[87] *Mineralogy Pty Ltd v Sino Iron Pty Ltd (No 6)* [2015] FCA 825; (2015) 329 ALR 1, [981]–[983] (Edelman J). See too the authorities listed in NA Tiverios, chapter 12 at 248.

[88] ibid [983] (Edelman J).

[89] See further, Weinrib (n 8) 96–98; 169–84.

equity is concerned about curtailing opportunism.[90] The final argument is that the proprietary or possessory right requirement risks strained reasoning as to what constitutes a proprietary or possessory right. He suggests that a careful reading of the decision in *Manchester Ship Canal* demonstrates that the Court nonetheless substantively granted B relief against the forfeiture of its contract rights with A notwithstanding judicial statements to the contrary. The arguments raised by Tiverios appear to remain contested in Australia due to conflicting authorities. This is because since the chapter was written Brereton JA in *Kay v Playup Australia Pty Ltd*[91] favoured the English approach and took a more restrictive reading of Australian law to conclude in *obiter* that 'the doctrine [of relief against forfeiture] is confined to proprietary or possessory rights, and does not extend to mere contractual rights'.[92]

Acknowledgements

As noted above, the majority of the chapters contained in this collection were presented at the 'Justifying Private Rights' workshop, held at UNSW Sydney in July 2019. The editors acknowledge and thank both those who presented papers at the workshop and those who attended as commentators, many of whom travelled to Sydney from both interstate and overseas, for their stimulating questions and commentary. The success of the workshop also owed much to those who worked tirelessly behind the scenes. In particular, the editors thank Maya Conradi and Joshua Gibson for their outstanding efforts. We are also indebted to Ruby O'Kane and Robert Rourke for their excellent research assistance and Sinead Moloney and Helen Kitto at Hart Publishing. Last, but certainly not least, the editors thank the Automic Group for its generous and ongoing financial support for private law research at UNSW, the Faculty of Law for financial support for the workshop and Jessica Hudson, who was instrumental in both conceiving of, and organising, the workshop that ultimately resulted in this collection.

[90] See further, WJ Jones, *The Elizabethan Court of Chancery* (Oxford, Oxford University Press, 1967) 447; HE Smith, 'Equity and Administrative Behaviour' in PG Turner (ed), *Equity and Administration* (Cambridge, Cambridge University Press, 2016) 326, 330–35.

[91] *Kay v Playup Australia Pty Ltd* [2020] NSWCA 33, [100]–[123] (Brereton JA with Macfarlan JA and Simpson AJA not deciding this point).

[92] ibid.

PART I

The Nature of Private Rights

2

Justifying Private Rights

PETER CANE

> For instance, Catholicism, the legal system, and space rockets are all products of an evolutionary process, and possess an evolutionary history that encompasses the repeated, typically gradual refinement and recombination of earlier variants.[1]

I. Introduction

In the call for papers for the workshop from which this volume arose, the organisers suggested the following question for discussion: what are the means and methodologies by which private rights are justified? Amongst modern private law theorists, one (quite common) methodology is what we might call 'moral intuitionism'.[2] This approach is 'external' to private law in the sense that it is not used to provide an 'interpretive' account of the rights that private law actually recognises (or fails to recognise), but to assess or justify the law's recognition of (or failure to recognise) those rights against some 'objective' benchmark, often loosely referred to as 'morality'. Under the name of 'Natural Law', John Bowker describes moral intuitionism in the following way:

> the basic claim … is that people endowed with reason can work out rationally what they should and should not do as they live with each other … Since rationality is a universal human competence, its exercise should result in objective ethical judgements on which all rational people can agree.[3]

In terms of 'morality', Bowker identifies this approach with 'morality independent of the agent's community and history' as opposed to 'morality as the consequence of context'.[4]

[1] KN Laland and GR Brown, 'The Social Construction of Human Nature' in E Hannon and T Lewens (eds), *Why We Disagree About Human Nature* (Oxford, Oxford University Press, 2018) 137.

[2] I would understand the methodologies of, for instance, E Weinrib (in *The Idea of Private Law*, 2nd edn (Oxford, Oxford University Press, 2012)) and R Stevens (in *Tort Law and Rights* (Oxford, Oxford University Press, 2007)) in this way: see P Cane, 'Rights in Private Law' in D Nolan and A Robertson (eds), *Rights and Private Law* (Oxford, Hart Publishing, 2011) 35–62.

[3] J Bowker, *Why Religions Matter* (Cambridge, Cambridge University Press, 2015) 197–98.

[4] ibid 197.

In the face of the reality of reasonable, persistent and intractable disagreements about values (including rights), I find such an approach to the justification of private law rights unsatisfying, depending – as it does – on the possibility of consensus about values. One way of managing such disagreement is by appeals to authority. What we might call the 'religious' method of external assessment of the law's authoritative claims (about rights, for instance) would be to appeal to (divine) authority superior to that of the law. I find such an approach no more satisfying than moral intuitionism. So, the challenge I take up in this chapter is to provide an account of external assessment and justification of private legal rights that depends on neither claims of superior authority nor appeals to univocal human reason or moral intuition. How might we understand claims that private legal rights are, or are not, justified without having recourse to authority superior to the law's, or to acontextual, 'rational' moral judgment?

The approach adopted in this chapter can be dubbed 'naturalistic'.[5] It rests on an assumption that everything that happens in the world, whether or not involving human agents, is traceable, *at some level*, to material facts and processes that can be accounted for by the laws of physics and chemistry, without recourse to the supernatural or metaphysical. This assumption implies, in turn, a particular 'method' or 'strategy' for 'justifying' private rights and other legal phenomena (legal 'facts'). We may describe this method as being 'diachronic' (temporally dynamic) as opposed to 'synchronic' (temporally static), 'historical' (in a broad sense that encompasses what may be called 'pre-history' or 'deep history'),[6] and 'evolutionary' in a loose post-Darwinian sense.[7] The precise terminology is not important even though, of course, these various terms are not synonyms. Each carries distinctive connotations that I am happy to accept. It may be that the methodology HLA Hart called 'descriptive sociology' (as opposed to 'analytical jurisprudence') could be similarly described.[8] Indeed, the story Hart tells about the transition from a pre-legal to a legal world[9] can be read in this way.[10]

The aim of this chapter is briefly to outline such a 'naturalist' account of the activity of justifying private rights. That said, the purpose is not to provide an explanation, in terms of laws of physics and chemistry, of the activity of justifying

[5] The term 'naturalism' may also be used to refer to what I have called 'moral intuitionism' and what John Bowker calls 'natural law'. Because of the risk of confusion, I toyed with the alternative term 'physicalistic' but decided against it because the core phenomena I am discussing – law and legal theory – are not physical.

[6] C Gamble, J Gowlett and R Dunbar, *Thinking Big: How the Evolution of Social Life Shaped the Human Mind* (London, Thames & Hudson, 2014).

[7] For helpful discussions see, eg, A Mesoudi, 'The Study of Culture and Evolution across Disciplines' and G Hanlon, 'Historians and the Evolutionary Approach to Human Behaviour' in L Workman, W Reader and JH Barkow (eds), *The Cambridge Handbook of Evolutionary Perspectives on Human Behavior* (Cambridge, Cambridge University Press, 2020).

[8] HLA Hart, *The Concept of Law*, 3rd edn (Oxford, Oxford University Press, 2012) vi.

[9] ibid ch V.

[10] P Pettit, 'Social Norms and the Internal Point of View: An Elaboration of Hart's Genealogy of Law' (2019) 39 *Oxford Journal of Legal Studies* 229.

private rights or even to gesture towards one. Rather, naturalism constitutes an assumption on which the analysis is based, namely that any and every human activity can be explained, at a 'deep' level, in terms of biological facts. At the same time, there are various 'shallower' levels of useful explanation of human activities, such as those of human psychology and social life, that presuppose the deeper level of biological explanation. Explanation of human activity (such as justifying private rights) at shallower levels will be cast not, for instance, in terms such as the firing of neurons or the human genomic map, but in terms of human actions, decisions, desires and intentions. This chapter explores in the shallows without attempting to provide any account of the nature of the relationship between the various levels of explanation beyond the idea that shallower-level explanations 'presuppose' deeper-level explanations. In particular, I have nothing to say about whether or not shallower phenomena are, in any way or to any extent, 'determined' by deeper phenomena.[11] A useful term commonly used in this context is 'emergence' – to say that one state of affairs emerges from another is to say something like: the latter state is 'more (or, perhaps, "other") than the sum of the parts' of the former state. In such terms, one might say that legal facts 'emerge' from physical facts.

The 'evolutionary' element of the approach is crucial for explaining change. In this view, change is a function of interaction between physical phenomena. The phenomena in question may be respectively dubbed an 'organism' and its 'environment', the latter referring to everything in the world apart from the organism, including other organisms. An evolutionary approach assumes the existence of entities capable of mutual interaction, deeply at the physical and chemical level, but also at shallower levels, such as that of social life. Such interaction may change the organism, the environment, or both.

On the naturalist approach, the activity of justifying private rights and, therefore, justifications of private rights, are products or aspects of human behaviour, as are legal systems, morality, football, and so on. 'Human' refers to the species *homo sapiens*. Intrinsic to the concept of a species is the idea that each and every member of a species shares certain 'species-universal characteristics' (as I shall call them). At the same time, however, the concept also accommodates great variation of characteristics amongst members of the same species. We may think of many species-universal characteristics (especially characteristic behaviours) relatively rather than absolutely – as being 'tendencies', 'aptitudes' or 'inclinations' that all human beings display to a greater or lesser extent within socially defined parameters of 'normality'.

Basic to the approach taken here – as to evolutionary accounts of human social behaviour more generally – is an assumption that in whatever ways *homo sapiens* has evolved in the 200 millennia since the species first appeared, it has

[11] So, I say nothing explicitly about the idea of gene-culture co-evolution: see eg PJ Richerson, 'The Use and Non-Use of the Human Nature Concept by Evolutionary Biologists' in E Hannon and T Lewens (eds), *Why We Disagree About Human Nature* (Oxford, Oxford University Press, 2018).

not yet changed in ways that have caused further speciation. Put differently, the assumption is that the species-universal characteristics of *homo sapiens* today are essentially similar to what they were in the 'pre-historical' period when the species emerged. It follows that whatever changes have occurred in human behaviour since then have not been the result of significant biological evolution sufficient to justify the recognition of a new hominid species.[12] They have been the product of 'social', 'cultural' or, more broadly, 'behavioural' evolution rather than biological evolution.

There are a great many landmarks in human biological and behavioural evolution. These include: the development of physical and mental capacities and skills (including consciousness), physical and mental strengths and weaknesses, 'dominances' and vulnerabilities; the emergence of cooperation and sociability; the invention of language and writing; and so on. The emergence of cooperation and sociability is crucial to our story because law and legal phenomena are social activities.

Whereas the engine of biological evolution is spontaneous variation and selection, behavioural, social and cultural change are largely products of learning and the transmission of knowledge and skills from one generation to the next. As human history shows, learning can bring about much more change in human behaviour much more rapidly than biological evolution can. However, learning is a precarious engine of change partly because of the inherent difficulties of teaching and learning, and partly because learning appears not to be inherited readily, if at all. The development of language and the invention, in turn, of writing, printing and information technology have facilitated exponential and ever more rapid increases in learning and its effective transmission. The continuity, stability and increasing social complexity and technological sophistication made possible by such technologies are central to an understanding of law and of how law changes.

The following discussion will begin by providing an account of the emergence of law as a social phenomenon based on interpersonal cooperation. It will then proceed to an historical account of the development, first, of the concept of 'private law' as we understand it today; and, second, of 'private law theory' in the contemporary sense. Next, it will turn to the emergence of the concept of 'rights' as a central feature of much modern private law theory. Finally, it will develop a behavioural account of justification based on the human propensity to seek, and the human need to find, good reasons for participation in cooperative practices such as private law. It goes without saying that each and every one of these elements of the story could be, and ideally needs to be, elaborated at much greater length than is possible here.

[12] For a very early and intriguing statement of this idea, see B Russell, *Authority and the Individual: The First Reith Lectures* (London, George Allen & Unwin, 1949) Lecture 1.

II. Law

Law is normative in the sense that it establishes standards and provides guides for behaviour. Standards of behaviour specify what we must do, what we must not do, and what we may choose to do or not. Each of these types of specifications provides 'reasons for action'. Law is one of various normative social phenomena. 'Morality' is another. All normative phenomena establish standards for, and in that way may guide, behaviour; and they can all provide reasons for action. Law has various distinctive characteristics by which it may be distinguished from other normative social phenomena. These include, most noticeably, a complex set of institutions for making, applying and enforcing norms.

Norms are a product of what I shall term 'normative behaviour'. Michael Tomasello speculates that while individual members of various animal species are able to coordinate their behaviour with that of other members of the species, each for their own personal, self-regarding best interest, only human beings are able to cooperate.[13] Coordination involves mutually self-interested conformity to agreed standards of behaviour. The benefits of coordination will accrue only so long as those benefits so satisfy the self-interest of all of the coordinators that each is motivated to comply with the agreed standards. To sustain the benefits of coordination in the face of countervailing self-interest, the participants must go further and cooperate with each other by complying with or, at least, conforming to the agreed standards of behaviour so long as this continues to be for the mutual benefit of the co-operators as a unit, regardless of whether it is individually beneficial for each of the co-operators alone. This move from coordination to cooperation transforms personal standards of behaviour adopted as a matter of self-interest into interpersonal standards of behaviour mutually applicable to self and other(s).

Just as cooperation can generate interpersonal norms, so active, committed compliance and passive, indifferent conformity lie at the basis of a legal system, which we may think of as a highly institutionalised system of inter-related, interpersonal norms. Such cooperative compliance with and conformity to a legal regime is what enables law to be used to create powers, obligations, permissions, prohibitions and institutions merely by saying so.[14] A statute provides that 'there shall be a Supreme Court' and there is (or, at least, can be) a Supreme Court. Declare in a legally prescribed form that 'I leave the balance of my estate to Oxfam' and Oxfam is the beneficiary of the balance of your estate. Enact 'possession of a prohibited drug is an offence' and it is an offence. Since the House of Lords decided

[13] M Tomasello, *A Natural History of Human Thinking* (Cambridge, MA, Harvard University Press, 2014). The terms 'coordination' and 'cooperation' are mine, not Tomasello's.

[14] M Köpcke, *Legal Validity* (Oxford, Hart Publishing, 2019); S Bertea, *A Theory of Legal Obligation* (Cambridge, Cambridge University Press, 2019); J Searle, *Making the Social World: The Structure of Human Civilization* (Oxford, Oxford University Press, 2010).

in 1932[15] that there is a tort of negligence, there has been a tort of negligence. When a criminal court pronounces a defendant 'guilty' the defendant is guilty. None of this happens by magic but by, and only by, the cooperative behaviour of a large number of people, both legal officials and citizens, who actively comply with or passively conform to legal norms. Law, we might say, is an evolutionary human achievement. It is an adaptation to the circumstances of human life made possible by certain species-universal human propensities and capacities.

III. Private Law

Because normative behaviour is a species-universal human characteristic, it seems reasonable to explain it in terms of other evolved human characteristics from which, we may say, it has 'emerged'. At the same time, of course, human normative behaviour is enormously various. At this point, it seems reasonable to change register from biological evolution to cultural and social evolution, especially since our concern is with specific features of modern legal systems. Cultural and social accounts of private law rights are much more likely to be available and persuasive than biological accounts.

How did the legal category of private law evolve? The Romans, the architects and builders of arguably the first recognisable legal system in a modern sense, thought of law primarily as a system of interpersonal norms. Inchoately, they distinguished between private law and public law; but the basic difference between them resided in the respective status of various subjects of the law rather than in any clear distinction between public and private areas of substantive law. The first major Roman legal theorist, Gaius, divided Roman law into three: the law of persons, the law of things and the law of actions. Some 1,600 years later, William Blackstone,[16] an early theorist of English law, divided the law into four categories concerned, respectively, with the rights of persons, the rights of things, private wrongs and public wrongs. By 'public wrongs' he meant crimes. His discussion of what we would now call 'public law' is contained in the volume dealing with the rights of persons.

On the continent, the Roman understanding survived until the eighteenth and nineteenth centuries. Important factors in its demise included the development of large and strong bureaucracies to regulate and manage increasingly complex societies and the replacement of Emperor Justinian's *Corpus Iuris Civilis* by legislative codes as the foundation of civilian legal systems. In France, the distinction between public law and private law was institutionalised as a result of the post-Revolutionary prohibition on 'ordinary' courts entertaining complaints or claims

[15] *Donoghue v Stevenson* [1932] AC 562.

[16] W Priest (ed), W Blackstone, *Commentaries on the Laws of England* (Oxford, Oxford University Press, 2016).

against state officials and the creation of the Conseil d'État. This development reached its logical, substantive conclusion in 1873 when the Conseil pronounced that the tort liability of public authorities was governed not by the 'ordinary' private law of tort but by a special, public tort law.[17]

In England, AV Dicey vigorously resisted such an arrangement partly because he opposed the growth of the State and the administration which, he feared, the recognition of a categorical and institutional distinction between public law and private law would facilitate.[18] In his account of the English constitution (harking back to Blackstone), government consisted of a collection of individual officials, each of whom was subject, like other citizens, to the 'ordinary law', including the law of tort. His opinion did not, of course, prevent or even slow the growth of the bureaucratic state or non-court, 'judicial' bodies, in the guise of 'tribunals', to entertain complaints against government. On the other hand, it did delay, until the latter half of the twentieth century, the introduction into English law of a substantive distinction between public law and private law which, when it came, was built on the back of an institutional public/private distinction, beginning with amendments to procedural rules in 1978 and culminating in the creation of the Administrative Division of the High Court in 2001. Ironically, at the beginning of the twenty-first century, 'administrative tribunals' were absorbed into the judicial system,[19] thus removing the element of institutionalisation of the public law/private law distinction introduced by the creation, in the twentieth century, of administrative tribunals separate and distinct from courts. Nevertheless, the substantive distinction survives.

Having traced the historical evolution of the concept of private law, we must now ask: what is private law? This question, too, can be answered historically. As noted earlier, the Romans distinguished between persons on the basis of their role and status. Nevertheless, even the relationship between the highest official and the lowliest citizen was understood interpersonally. This relationship was, of course, different from that of the relationship between (for instance) two ordinary citizens; but it was, for all that, a relationship between persons. The same is true of medieval English law. In a feudal system, all social relationships are between individual persons, regardless of their respective social, political or economic status. The monarch, for instance, obviously possessed unique powers and prerogatives; but for all that, the monarch was a person (even if, in Ernst Kantorowicz's famous words, the monarch – uniquely – had 'two bodies').[20]

[17] See, eg, D Fairgrieve, *State Liability in Tort: A Comparative Law Study* (Oxford, Oxford University Press, 2003) ch 2.

[18] JWF Allison (ed), AV Dicey, *The Law of the Constitution* (Oxford, Oxford University Press, 2013). This is the standard, modern edition of AV Dicey's *An Introduction to the Study of the Law of the Constitution*, first published in 1885.

[19] Tribunals, Courts and Enforcement Act 2007 (UK).

[20] EH Kantorowicz, *The King's Two Bodies: A Study in Mediaeval Political Theology* (Princeton, NJ, Princeton University Press, 1957).

Things started to change significantly in the eighteenth and nineteenth centuries. The change can easily be seen in places, notably France, where sovereign monarchies were abolished and replaced by an impersonal understanding of government, typically referred to as 'the State', built on the sovereignty of 'the People', understood as a singular entity. It did not follow that this relocation of sovereignty would lead to a substantive division of the law into public and private components. In France, as we have seen, the die was cast in 1873 when it was decided that the liability of the State for wrongs long recognised by law should be governed not by the pre-Revolutionary law of the *Corpus Iuris Civilis* and its successor *Code Civil*, by which such wrongs were first articulated, but by a separate law of public wrongs, applicable to the State but not to citizens. Such a solution was not readily available in England, where the monarchy continued to exist and where, to this day, central government continues to be conceptualised as one of the monarch's two bodies ('Her Majesty's Government') and many individual public officials are identified as part of 'the Crown'. As we have seen, English law did not begin to develop a distinct concept of public law until the late 1970s. However, because it is not based on an impersonal concept of the State, it is not as fully-fledged as its Continental counterparts.[21] The starting point and foundation of the English law of government liability continues to be 'the ordinary law' that binds all citizens alike, albeit now subject to significant modification and qualification to accommodate the distinctive rights and responsibilities of agents entitled to act, and acting, 'in the public interest'.

IV. Private Law Theory

Can a similar historical story be told about private law theory? Let us define theory simply as mental reflection on practice: thinking about doing. As far as we know, in the Western tradition it was the Romans who first started thinking seriously and systematically about law. As already noted, for them there was no categorical, substantive distinction within law between public law and private law. There was a single body of law. This body of law grew out of a practice in which citizens could secure from a public official a ticket entitling them to have a dispute resolved by third party. In modern terms, we may think of this practice as a form of public regulation of private dispute settlement: the judges were not public officials. Roman law, as we understand it today, originated in conditions attached to the issue of such tickets, and instructions, contained therein, from the issuing official to the dispute-settler. As the body of law grew larger and more complex, a professional group (called 'jurists') arose that specialised in advising

[21] JWF Allison, *A Continental Distinction in the Common Law: A Historical and Comparative Perspective on English Public Law* (Oxford, Clarendon Press, 1996).

litigants and officials on what the law was. In the second century CE, one of those jurists – Gaius – made a path-breaking attempt to state the law systematically and comprehensively. The *Institutes of Gaius* can plausibly be classified as the first extant work of legal theory conceived and written as a result of thinking about and reflecting upon the law as practised. Several centuries later, Roman law was again restated at the behest of Emperor Justinian in what became known as the *Corpus Iuris Civilis*. The first volume, the *Institutes*, followed the same conceptual scheme as Gaius had developed in his *Institutes* but drew, as well, on the work of a significant number of other leading jurists.

The English common law developed similarly to Roman law: out of a practice of issuing tickets ('writs') to litigants, giving them access to royal courts (as opposed to local and manorial courts). Originally, the trial process – which was, from an early stage, dominated by juries – dealt with all the issues in the case whether they were, in our terms, issues of law or issues of fact. The role of the common law judge was to manage access to and conduct trials, not to give judgment, which was the task of the jury. The judge was concerned primarily with what we would now call 'procedure', not substance: 'managerial judging' in modern terms. In thinking about these legal practices, the earliest theorists of English law – notably Glanville in the twelfth century and Bracton in the thirteenth[22] – were influenced by the Gaian scheme of arrangement which, at this time, formed the basis of legal education. However, by far the largest sections of Glanville's and Bracton's books concern procedure and writs – 'the law of actions', in Roman terms, as opposed to the substantive law of persons and things. Over the centuries, English judges became more and more involved in giving judgment on substantive issues of law (as opposed to issues of fact, which were for the jury); but this process took place within the formal framework of the procedurally-oriented writ system. In consequence, for a very long time most English 'theoretical' legal literature was similarly framed in terms of forms and causes of action, and of pre-trial, trial and post-trial procedure.

In the middle of the eighteenth century, Blackstone attempted to reflect the increasing 'substantivisation' of the law in his *Commentaries on the Laws of England*. He divided his exposition into two main sections: the law of rights and the law of wrongs. However, by Blackstone's day, substantivisation had advanced further in some areas of the law than in others, and tort law was one of the least affected. In fact, Blackstone's account of much of what we would now call tort law has a distinctly procedural cast.

The nineteenth century brought three developments of fundamental importance for understanding the role of theory and theorising in common-law systems. First, the writ system was abolished. Henceforth, instead of having to find a writ to fit the facts of one's case, litigants were to initiate court proceedings by stating

[22] See J Baker, *An Introduction to English Legal History*, 5th edn (Oxford, Oxford University Press, 2019) 185–87.

the facts ('fact pleading') and asking the court for an appropriate legal remedy. The effect was to shift the focus of both the practice and the theory of law away from procedure and on to substance. Second, jury trial was gradually abolished for almost all civil claims. One result was to throw onto the judge responsibility for giving judgment on all issues of both fact and law. Whereas juries had never been required to give reasons for their decisions, by this time it was common, if not obligatory, for judges to give reasons. This gradually generated a major new source of raw material for legal theory – judicial reasons for judicial decisions on law and fact.

Third, the nineteenth century was a period of enormous technological change. It soon became apparent that the courts did not have the resources to adapt the existing common law, and to invent new common law, quickly enough to keep up with the pace of social and economic change, and the social demands for government intervention in social and economic life. Parliament came into its own as the nation's prime law-maker; although it was not long before it, too, reached the limit of its resources and started delegating law-making power to government, where most of it now resides. Around the same time, utilitarianism was being formulated as a moral, social and political philosophy; and positivism as a legal philosophy (or 'theory'). Together, these forces had a fundamental effect on the way the common law was understood. In an older way of thinking (by which Blackstone was influenced), both statutory and judge-made law formed part of a much larger tapestry of the normative life of the community, albeit a distinct part with its own characteristic features and resources. In the new way of thinking, by contrast, both judge-made law and statutory law were conceived as being superimposed on the extra-legal normative life of the community – a frame for the tapestry, if you like, rather than integrated into its warp and woof.[23] Put differently, in the modern view, law and 'morality' were conceived as running in separate streams. From this perspective, the role of legal theory was not so much to understand the place of law in the normative life of the nation but rather to understand law as an external regulator of that life, with its own internal logic and, in a very significant sense, autonomous of the extra-legal tapestry that it frames.

In this institutional environment and intellectual atmosphere, the task presented to judges was to contribute, as needed, to the law-making project that was now dominated by Parliament and the Government. The task of private law theorists – such as Frederick Pollock,[24] John Salmond[25] and Percy Winfield[26] – was to discover or invent 'principles' that could plausibly be said to underlie the unruly mass of substantive law that had developed 'in the interstices of the forms

[23] These two ways of thinking about law are models or ideal-types, not descriptions.

[24] See R Stevens, 'Professor Sir Frederick Pollock (1845–1937): Jurist as Mayfly' in J Goudkamp and D Nolan (eds), *Scholars of Tort Law* (Oxford, Hart Publishing, 2019).

[25] See M Lunney, 'Professor Sir John Salmond (1862–1924): An Englishman Abroad' in Goudkamp and Nolan (n 24).

[26] See D Nolan, 'Professor Sir Percy Winfield (1878–1953)' in Goudkamp and Nolan (n 24).

of action', and which was now seen as a tool of public power more than an expression of community life.[27] This task proved to be more difficult in the case of tort law than of contract law. The problem (leaving aside the awkward case of what we now call 'unjust enrichment law') was partly that tort law was constructed out of the remainder of 'private law' after contract and property had been removed, leaving a miscellaneous group of causes of action with no immediately or obviously unifying principle or set of principles. One way of thinking about underlying principles was to classify torts according to whether liability was for intention or negligence, or regardless of either (strict): in Pollock's terminology, the various 'torts' were 'wilful', or 'the result of imprudence or omission', or 'apparently unconnected with moral blame'. Pollock also cut the tort pie into separate wedges called 'personal wrongs', 'wrongs to property' and 'wrongs to person, estate and property generally'.[28]

By contrast, Oliver Wendell Holmes took a quite different approach.[29] He proposed that tort law be understood as the law of 'accidents', concerned with striking a reasonable balance between the interests we all share in personal safety on the one hand, and freedom of action on the other. Holmes argued that an objective concept of 'negligence' was central to this understanding of tort law; but that, in certain circumstances, tort law imposes standards of conduct more or less demanding than negligence. This theory did not solve the classification problem; it simply ignored it by opting to treat tort law as a law of wrongs, having nothing to do with protection of rights. Pollock's explanation for the role of rights in tort law was that by the nineteenth century, older forms of action ('writs') designed for protection of rights had been superseded by trespass and trespass on the case, which were based on the concept of 'wrong', not 'right'. On this basis, Pollock felt able to conclude that moral wrongfulness was the basic principle underlying tort law and that tort liability, regardless of moral wrongfulness, was exceptional and explicable in terms of the procedural roots of the common law. Unfortunately (as Pollock realised), this explanation leaves vicarious liability and strict liability for infliction of harm (as opposed to interference with rights) unaccounted for;[30] but he was not prepared to banish them from the province of tort law.

Holmes's taxonomical approach (which was greatly influenced by utilitarian and positivist ideas) never took off, even in the United States. However, his utilitarian positivism triggered a process that would lead to another major change in the way law was understood, loosely called 'realism'. One of the ideas that realism came to stand for was that law (like other norms, perhaps) was best understood as an epiphenomenon of human social behaviour, not a distinct and autonomous

[27] For greater elaboration of some of the ideas in this chapter, see generally P Cane, 'Law, Fact and Process in Common Law Tort Scholarship' in Goudkamp and Nolan (n 24).

[28] ibid 374, n 51.

[29] See JCP Goldberg and BC Zipursky, 'Thomas McIntyre Cooley (1824–1898) and Oliver Wendell Holmes (1841–1935): The Arc of American Tort Theory' in Goudkamp and Nolan (n 24).

[30] P Cane, 'Law, Fact and Process in Common Law Tort Scholarship' in Goudkamp and Nolan (n 24) 380, n 81.

form of such behaviour. Let me explain. In my way of thinking, norms are social phenomena that can provide reasons for action. In a different way of thinking (commonly associated with the eighteenth-century Scottish philosopher, David Hume), norms cannot, as such, provide reasons for action in the way that beliefs, needs and desires can because beliefs, needs and desires are (we might say) 'natural', inbuilt aspects of human nature. In this view, norms provide reasons for action if and to the extent that they reflect needs, conform to beliefs and promote desires. It follows that in order to understand legal and other norms properly it is vital to understand the natural motivations that the norms (purport to) reflect. In one version of this approach, norms do not even provide *judges* with genuine reasons for reaching one decision rather than another. This approach encourages us to view law as, and as only, an instrument for meeting needs, vindicating beliefs and satisfying desires. In this view, social norms are not components of the life of the community but more like descriptions of certain aspects of social life and human behaviour.

Realist ideas deeply influenced such distinguished tort theorists as Leon Green,[31] Fleming James,[32] William Prosser[33] and John Fleming.[34] These jurists were not all extreme norm-sceptics; but they did share the conviction that law was primarily a tool that could be, was and should be used to promote what came to be called 'social policy'. Realism never took a firm grip on English tort scholars. Instead, 30 years or so later, figures such as Patrick Atiyah sailed under the flag of 'law in context'. The founders and leaders of this movement never doubted that law was worth studying in its own right and for its own sake. All they said was that law is only one part of life, and that it can always be better understood if it is not treated as being hermetically sealed off from its environment and its context. At this time, there was little interest in the late-nineteenth-century project of finding one or a few principles that could account for tort law or, indeed, other areas of private law. Principled coherence in the law was not prized for its own sake but only to the extent that it made the law better at what people wanted it to do.

It was into such an intellectual milieu that economic analysis of law burst in the 1960s and 1970s. Two schools may be identified: the Yale School, associated with Guido Calabresi; and the Chicago School, associated with Richard Posner. Their respective approaches were very different. From our perspective, Posner's has three distinctive characteristics. One is the assumption that what matters most for understanding the law is not what law-makers say they are doing but what they actually do: outcomes, not reasons. The second is a claim that there is a single unifying principle that can explain tort law, namely 'economic efficiency'. The third

[31] J Steele, 'Professor Leon Green (1888–1979): Word Magic and the Regenerative Power of Law' in Goudkamp and Nolan (n 24).

[32] G Calabressi, 'Professor Fleming James Jr (1904–1981)' in Goudkamp and Nolan (n 24).

[33] CJ Robinette, 'Professor William Lloyd Prosser (1898–1972)' in Goudkamp and Nolan (n 24).

[34] P Mitchell, 'Professor John G Fleming (1919–1997): "A Sense of Fluidity"' in Goudkamp and Nolan (n 24).

is the view that promoting economic efficiency is not only the principle that best *explains* tort law but also the principle that *justifies* it to the extent that it is justified. Calabresi, by contrast, argued that while economic values were amongst those the law could and should promote, there were non-economic (non-instrumentalist) values of which this could also be said. There was, for him, no single unifying principle that could either explain or justify tort law.

Economic analysis attracted many opponents with various methodological commitments. One such commitment is non-instrumentalism. There are two forms. In its first, more extreme form, non-instrumentalism claims that although law can be used to serve various purposes, it does not itself have purposes; it just is. In its second, and perhaps more common form, non-instrumentalism distinguishes between law's intrinsic or internal purposes on the one hand, and law's extrinsic or external purposes on the other, and claims that law is best understood as serving only internal purposes and not also external purposes. A second, related, commitment is formalism. For the strict formalist, the best understanding of law is dictated by law's form. For the moderate formalist, functions are also important for understanding law but, crucially, function follows form. A third commitment is implicit in the search for theoretical unity, namely 'coherence'. In order for the law to be coherent it must not only avoid self-contradiction and other logical errors. Additionally, every component of the law must be explicable in terms of one and the same principle, or one and the same, small set of principles. These various commitments force non-instrumentalist theorists, rather like their instrumentalist counterparts, to put much more weight on outcomes than reasons. Various makers of one and the same law (judges of the same court or members of the same legislature) may have different reasons for making it; and such variety militates against unified and highly parsimonious explanations and justifications. On the other hand, outcomes are things, not reasoning humans. There is no reason why those outcomes that do not fit the theory should not simply be rejected as mistakes. It is harder to argue that people should systematically be taken to have acted for reasons other than those they express or profess.

Another development in tort theory, relevant to our story, has taken place since the 1980s: an understanding that the tort theorist is engaged in a search for 'the philosophical foundations' of the law. The idea that law has *philosophical* foundations was, I suggest, partly a response to *economic* analysis of the common law, and partly designed to signal commitment to certain methodologies and strategies associated with moral philosophy and normative political theory. One of the consequences (or causes) of 'the Enlightenment' in the eighteenth century was a loss of faith in the Divine as an authoritative source of values, and its replacement by an ideal of human 'reason' or 'rationality' – human mental reflection undertaken in the right way, at the right time and under the right circumstances. In the new way of thinking, properly deployed human reasoning could provide a source of values which was uncontaminated by human frailty in the face of the harsh realities of the human condition. For many, 'true morality' was a product of the exercise of such rationality; in stark contrast, law (along with what Hart called 'positive morality')[35] was (potentially at least) a contaminated and less-than-perfectly rational social practice. Its rationality and, therefore, its 'truth' and 'legitimacy', were contingent.

This 'philosophical turn' is very different from the approach I am adopting in this chapter. The reason is not that it involves abandoning the evolutionary idea that change is a function of interaction between organism and environment. Rather, it is that the philosophical turn requires types of interaction between a sort of organism and a type of environment neither of which, as far as we know, has ever existed anywhere. Human beings are not ideal reasoners, and the ideal circumstances of human reasoning, as envisioned by the philosophers, have never existed, do not exist and are unlikely to be realised any time soon.

V. Private Rights

The previous section has told a developmental, historical story about private law theorising, particularly its philosophical, non-instrumental strand. However, it did not advert to a striking feature of much private law theory – namely, its focus on rights. In addition to the methodological commitments already identified, very common amongst non-instrumental theorists, particularly tort theorists, is another to the effect that the concept of a 'right' provides the foundation for non-instrumentalist theories of tort law. This commitment does not seem to follow from any of those previously discussed and is, for that reason at least, rather puzzling. Why 'rights' rather than 'duties', for instance? How might we explain the appearance of this common feature of theorising about private law?

The word 'right' is used in various different senses. The early twentieth-century American theorist, WN Hohfeld, identified four: 'claim', 'privilege', 'power' and 'immunity'.[36] Hohfeld thought that a 'a right in the strictest sense' was a claim. In Hohfeld's scheme, if a person has a 'claim-right', some other person (by definition) has a duty or obligation to satisfy the claim. For instance, if A owes B a duty of care in negligence, B has a right against A that A perform the duty, and a claim against A if A does not perform it. This is the sense the word normally bears in rights-based theories of tort law. Somewhat confusingly, however, many rights-theorists of tort law refer to breaching a duty not only as flouting or disregarding a right, but also as a 'wrong'. Neither in law nor in linguistic usage outside the law are all wrongs breaches of a duty owed to another; but rights-theorists tend to use 'breach of duty' and 'wrong' synonymously. They do not mean either that breaching duties is the only way of 'doing wrong' or that it is necessarily 'wrong' not to perform one's

[35] HLA Hart, *Law, Liberty and Morality* (Oxford, Oxford University Press, 1963) 20.

[36] WN Hohfeld, 'Some Fundamental Legal Conceptions as Applied in Judicial Reasoning' (1913) 23 *Yale Law Journal* 16.

duty. In fact, they arguably use the term 'wrong' precisely in order to bring within their conception of tort law torts that do *not* involve breaches of duty. For example, they want to be able to say that even if you trespass on another's land (ie, infringe their property right in the land) in complete ignorance and innocence, as far as tort law is concerned, you have committed a 'wrong' – something that you ought not to have done, for which you may be legally liable.

It is not clear to me why rights-theorists choose to include within their theories of tort law strict liability (for instance) for unauthorised entry onto another's land. In Pollock's view,[37] innocent entry came to be treated as a trespass as a result of judicial reactions to litigants' desire to avoid the procedural disadvantages of the medieval writs (such as the writ of right) that were specifically designed to protect the landowner's power of exclusion. It was early on in the history of the common law that courts started inventing 'fictions' to enable litigants to avoid procedural disadvantages of particular writs so that they could use other, less disadvantageous writs instead. Fictions were typically a response to changes in social conditions, coupled with the refusal of writ-issuing authorities to add to the list of available writs. Litigants and courts were faced with the need to adapt old technology and a limited toolbox of writs to meet new interests, needs and demands. The early modern theorists, such as Pollock, were perhaps still too much under the spell of the old writ system to be able to reimagine the substantive law in radical ways that simply ignored the history of the writs. One hundred and fifty years later, the star of tort appears to shine so brightly in the universe of legal theory and practice that it now blinds everyone to the possibility of radical new ways of thinking about the contents and structure of tort law. The philosophical turn in tort theory has not emboldened tort theorists to claim the freedom enjoyed by philosophers to ignore the past if that seems the 'rational' thing to do. They still feel more-or-less bound by the authority of law's past, embodied in the collection of causes of action for which the writs of trespass and trespass on the case happened to be available in the nineteenth century.

Why have so many seekers after unifying theories of tort law chosen 'rights' as their organising category? This is not an easy question to answer. A clue may lie in the magnetic influence of one of the pioneers of non-instrumentalism, Ernest Weinrib.[38] Weinrib observes that private law organises the world in terms of bilateral relations between individuals. Private law, in other words, is about how we interact, one-on-one, with other people. By itself, this observation is not very illuminating. After all, potentially there are as many bilateral relationships as there are human twosomes. How or according to what principle does private law construct such relationships? Weinrib looks to (moral) philosophy – Immanuel Kant in particular – for an answer. He finds it in what he calls 'Kantian right'.[39] This he

[37] See Stevens (n 24) 380, n 81.
[38] EJ Weinrib, *The Idea of Private Law*, rev edn (Oxford, Oxford University Press, 2012).
[39] ibid ch 4.

construes as the idea that private law recognises each and every human being as equal in the respect that each enjoys individual autonomy, the capacity (coupled, to a greater or lesser extent, with the propensity) to choose for oneself how to act. Put in more naturalistic terms, we may say that some sense of the separateness and autonomy of individual persons from one another is a species-universal human characteristic of *homo sapiens*. However, it is also a feature of the human condition that making and sustaining relationships with other human beings – compromising our separateness, if you like – is not only essential for survival but also productive of benefits that no individual could secure separately.

Because we are all 'born free' as it were, survival and flourishing through relationships requires us to construe our autonomy not in terms of doing what we choose, but in terms of freedom to act as we choose, consistently with the equal freedom of the other party to the relationship to act as they choose. It is the human capacity and propensity to limit our individual autonomy for the sake of cooperation that explains the invention of social norms. Human freedom is not unqualified freedom; it is *equal* freedom. That each party to a bilateral relationship should feel equally autonomous is a precondition of the sort of cooperation on which social life can be based. In this sense, we may say that everyone has an equal right to be free because such a right is a normative presupposition of cooperative, human, social life. This is not to say, of course, that cooperation between equals is the only basis on which social life may be founded. Coercion of inferiors by superiors may also provide a basis for life in groups.

However, even if some such concept of a right to equal freedom helps us to understand the role of interpersonal norms in generating productive human cooperation, it does not get us very far towards a theory of private law, let alone any particular area of private law such as tort law. This is because 'equality' is a comparative concept. It tells us that we all have the same rights but does not tell us what those rights are. The human condition is characterised by inherent, creative tension between autonomy on the one hand and cooperation on the other – between individuality and sociality. Observation tells us that there is great variety amongst human groups in how and where they strike the balance between the interests of the individual and the interests of the group. Individuality and sociality are both species-universal human characteristics, but there is no species-universal balance between the two.

This brings us to the climax of our story. Let us suppose, for the sake of the argument, that private law treats individuals as equals and that it does this by allocating an equal right of autonomy to each and every individual. A naturalistic approach can account for this characteristic of private law. However, so far, we have no naturalistic account of how much freedom we each have – in other words, what our rights are (in private law). In this regard, what we observe in human practice are variety and disagreement. If we are not willing to appeal to either higher authority or moral intuition to justify the rights we have or should have, how can we proceed? In the next section, I will attempt to extend the naturalistic approach to the justification of rights.

VI. Justifying Private Rights

Earlier, I argued that it is possible to explain human normative behaviour (making 'norms' that prescribe behaviour regardless of self-interest) in terms of cooperative compliance and conformity. The fact that human beings are willing and able to cooperate for common purposes can provide good reasons to behave, in particular ways and not in others, for the sake of realising benefits that could not otherwise be obtained. However (as I also suggested earlier), cooperation may also involve costs, and for any individual there may come a point where the personal costs of compliance with a socially agreed norm of cooperation become so great that the individual no longer has (all things considered) good reason to comply. In particular, human beings have evolved in such a way that they value not only the benefits of cooperation and sociality, but also of feeling that they are 'doing the right thing' in some 'ultimate' sense that may transcend and conflict with the facts and values of human sociality and cooperation.

People satisfy the experienced need for ultimate, transcendent justification in various ways. Some turn to religion and belief in a supernatural realm outside and above the natural that is not subject to the contingencies of life on earth. Others put their faith in some concept of ideal human reason that is, in a very different way, not subject to the contingencies of life on earth. For those of a naturalistic inclination, there is a different way of thinking about the human capacity and propensity to assess certain actions, and certain reasons for action, as wrong or bad, without qualification – 'really' wrong or bad. According to the naturalistic approach, norms are a product of interpersonal human cooperation. Cooperation involves sacrificing or compromising one's own self-interest, itself an aspect of the individual's innate awareness of separateness from other persons, for the sake of an interest shared with other self-interested persons. Cooperation is made possible by our innate capacity to see the world from another's point of view. Cooperation establishes a sort of equilibrium between self-interest and the interests of others in the form of shared interest.

However, cooperation is different from co-optation. Cooperation does not involve the individual giving up or losing the sense of their own separateness and autonomy. Relationships that involve such abandonment or loss are not cooperative but submissive and exploitative. The actual terms of interaction are critical to its maintenance and survival – not just any agreement will do. If those terms require a person to give up or abandon their sense of separateness and autonomy, cooperation is at an end and co-optation of self by other has taken over. Normally functioning human beings retain some sense of their own separateness and autonomy from each and every other person. Resisting co-optation involves rejecting proffered terms of interaction that threaten to destroy a person's sense of separateness and autonomy. In the very nature of things, only the individual can know whether or not the content and nature of proffered terms of proposed interaction would destroy their sense of separateness and autonomy. Only the individual can locate their own 'red lines'. The individual's red lines represent and express that person's ultimate values – 'ultimate' in the sense that they are proof against the demands of others even if and when such demands come from all relevant others. Personal, ultimate truths are those beliefs to which the individual will hold entirely regardless of whether (any) other people hold the same beliefs. Some will cling on to those beliefs even when doing so threatens not only ostracism from the society of other human beings, but also personal survival. Martyrs are prepared to die for their (personal) beliefs in an ultimate expression of individual autonomy and rejection of social cooperation. Our personal red lines are our values and beliefs, our reasons for behaviour, that outweigh all other reasons.

Justification is always undertaken within a framework of norms that provide criteria for justification. A person's ultimate values are those that they consider justified 'all things considered' (as the philosophers would say). Ultimate justifications provide reasons for action that outweigh *all others*. On the other hand, justification can be undertaken within a non-ultimate framework. Pertinently, norms may be justified, and may be justifiable, within a framework of legal norms that might not survive the rigours of all-things-considered, ultimate justification. Much justificatory private law theory is conducted 'internally', within the normative framework provided by the law itself. However, legal theorists sometimes aspire to go further and provide 'real', ultimate justifications, not just 'legal justifications'. Some may do this by reference to religion, others by reference to ideal human rationality, and so on. People who find the approach in this article attractive will understand themselves to be fixing their own, personal red lines.

In what sense can ultimate justifications be 'true'? Truth may be social. Good examples of socially true facts are those produced by the application of the best and most rigorous methods of the experimental natural sciences. These are good examples because most people accept scientific experimentation as a valid way of producing (scientific) 'truth'. Scientific method, like all methodologies, is well designed to answer certain sorts of questions, namely those that we believe can be answered by that method. As far as we know, there are many questions to which people want answers that cannot be answered by scientific methods. A pertinent example is 'what rights should tort law recognise and protect?' Crucially, too, no method is accepted nearly as widely for answering such questions as scientific method is accepted for answering the sorts of questions it is designed to answer. Some people might use '"religious" methodology', others '"philosophical" methodology'. Unfortunately, there is no practised religious or philosophical methodology that is anywhere near as universally accepted as scientific methodology. There are many questions to which we crave answers but which we do not know how to answer because we cannot agree on a methodology for answering them. Because of lack of social agreement about the appropriate methodology for answering such questions, any answers given are not 'social' truths. From the point of view of the person proposing the answer, it may be 'true' – personal truth; and it may be true for others who, although they adopt a different method of answering, agree with the answer, however reached.

For those who agree with the proposed answer however it was reached, who agree with its substance regardless of the methods by which its substance was generated, we might say that the answer is an 'ultimate' truth for that person, not just a social truth. Even in the case of propositions established by the most rigorous scientific methods, we might say that a 'leap of faith' is needed to turn the proposition into ultimate truth in this sense – true no matter what. After all, not everyone makes the leap of faith in science.

Legal theorists who set out to answer questions such as 'what rights ought tort law to protect?' are rarely explicit about their methodology for arriving at answers. I have suggested that the philosophical turn in legal theory may be understood as an attempt to find, in 'philosophical method', a way of answering such questions. The hope, in turning to philosophy, is – presumably – to find interpersonal, ultimately true answers. I have also proposed a different way of thinking about ultimate truth which makes it necessarily personal, not interpersonal, a shield to protect oneself from what one considers to be unreasonable demands from others. There may be many different ways to arrive at personal truth. In fact, personal truth may be purely personal or shared in common with (some) others. Indeed, for most humans, most of the time, their personal beliefs (necessarily) coincide with those of a significant number of others. It is an inherent human aspiration that one's personal truth should be accepted by others. Humans are social, cooperative creatures, and a measure of interpersonal agreement about reasons for action is a precondition of cooperation.

Legal theorists commonly equivocate between whether their justificatory theories are theories of law, constructed within the normative parameters of the legal project or, by contrast, all-things-considered justifications (often referred to as 'moral', as opposed to legal). A possible explanation for this is that much legal theory is concerned primarily with judicial law-making and its supporting reasoning. In common law systems, the first place that judges (must) look for the law is in the body of materials – cases and statutes – that have come down to the present from the past, however remote. This creates an imperative to 'describe' and 'explain' the existing law. Traditionally, such deference to the authority of 'the ancestors' was rooted in pre-modern understandings of law as a product of 'custom'. Now, by contrast, we tend to think of judge-made law, like legislation, as 'positive', created in the present to mould the future, not as a legacy from the past. One effect of democratisation has been to confer on popularly elected legislatures a legitimacy for making positive law that judges lack by virtue of their not being popularly elected. As a result, deference to past authority has come to be viewed not so much in terms of the customary nature of law but more as a condition of the legitimacy of judicial law-making, which (we think) should be 'interstitial' and 'incremental'. Projection of the legal past into the present and the future is no longer understood to be an aspect of the very essence of law. Rather, it is seen partly as a matter of maintaining a productive balance between stability and change in social life (too much of either can be dysfunctional), and partly as a way of justifying the non-democratic law-making powers of judges. It is acceptable for judges to modify and extend existing law but not, like legislatures, to make new law *ex nihilo*.

All this means that we want the past to be a magnetic source of instruction and inspiration but not a choking, binding authority. In the face of the need and desire for the law to adapt to social change, this judicial attitude to the existing legal materials (both common law and, to a lesser extent, statutory), in combination with the relative lack of legitimacy of judge-made law, encourages judges, as quietly and subtly as possible, to inject views about what the law ought to be into descriptions and explanations of what it is, in that way blurring the line between the descriptive and the prescriptive. This strategy enables the judge to avoid rejecting the past outright (by overruling previous decisions) in all but extreme cases and to paint the law as being in, or to bring the law to, the position they prefer without being too obvious about it. Ronald Dworkin called this process 'interpretation' and made it a virtue by maintaining that the aim of the process was to make the inherited law morally 'the best it could be'.[40]

The interpretive methodology obviously begs the question of the source of and justification for the normative judgments that are added to the legal materials either to make them the best they can be or, at least, fit for purpose in current circumstances. Judges often attempt to cover their tracks by appealing to 'community values', 'morality', 'justice' or 'consequences'. But they need not worry because judges have no obligation to justify their law-making activities even if it is institutionally prudent for them to do so. This is because, like the legislature, they have institutional *authority* to make law. Moreover, the reason-giving obligations of judges are primarily designed to guarantee that they respect the existing body of legal materials, not that they justify their forward-looking law-making. Apart from its legal authority, the legitimacy of judicial law-making depends on its acceptability to those who have to apply and enforce the common law and those to whom it applies.

VII. Conclusion

It is here that the theoretical rubber hits the hard road of legal practice. Interpretation is now understood by many to be the basic methodology of private law theory.[41] Like judges, many private law theorists quietly and subtly introduce into their accounts of the law external, extra-legal 'oughts' (often in the form of 'rights') that they use to paint law's portrait as they see it. However, scholars in common law systems lack the institutional authority of judges to extend and modify the law in this way. The prescriptive, normative elements of judges' interpretations are justified (or not) by

[40] R Dworkin, *Law's Empire* (Oxford, Hart Publishing, 1998) (first published by Harvard University Press in 1986).

[41] See, eg, S Smith, *Contract Theory* (Oxford, Oxford University Press, 1993) ch 1.

their systemically conferred authority to 'make law' by extension and modification of existing law. Theorists, by contrast, have no such authority. All they can do is attempt to persuade the rest of us (including the judges) that their normative views about modification and extension of the law are justified and true. In order to persuade, they would do well to distinguish clearly (in a way that judges are under no imperative to do) between the descriptive, explanatory elements of their interpretations and the prescriptive, normative elements. They would also be well-advised to make clear where their prescriptions (about rights, for instance) are coming from and how they are based: religion, perhaps; or some concept of interpersonal, ultimate morality; or human reasoning under ideal circumstances; or their own all-things-considered judgment; and also to explain how the foundations of their prescriptions support the prescriptions themselves. This is because it is a human characteristic to need and want good reasons to engage in the sort of cooperative behaviour on which the existence of law and legal systems depends. Under the naturalistic approach adopted in this chapter, human cooperative, normative behaviours (social, normative 'facts') are explicable in terms of (non-normative) psychological, motivational and, ultimately, biological facts about human nature and its interaction with its environment(s). The human need and desire that social norms of cooperation be 'justified', I have argued, is explicable in terms of a desire and need to preserve individuality in the face of demands for cooperation with others. Description and explanation of normative practices are centrally important functions of legal theory but alone cannot satisfy the felt need for justification. Up to a point, claims and exercises of authority may meet the need. However, the efficacy of such claims may be limited. Relevantly for present purposes, judicial claims of authority typically have less justificatory force than those of a legislature. Legal theorists can claim no authority for their justificatory proposals. Their important task is to state those proposals explicitly and persuade by argument that they are justified.

3

Justifying Private Law: 'Reasons Fundamentalist' Instrumentalism and the Kantian Account

JAMES PENNER*

I. Introduction

It seems to me that our current understanding of the question of how private law rights can be justified might be advanced by comparing and contrasting two leading theories which aim to provide an answer to this question: (1) the 'reasons fundamentalist' instrumentalist picture of private law, and (2) Ripstein's Kantian non-instrumentalist picture of the same. In doing so I shall reflect critically, and I hope fairly, on a few aspects of Gardner's instrumentalism and Ripstein's Kantianism whilst aiming at the same time to acknowledge their merits. With respect to Ripstein, I shall situate the discussion primarily within the law of torts, because Ripstein does so in his most recent book, *Private Wrongs*.[1] I have dealt elsewhere with both Gardner's and Ripstein's views on other aspects of private law.[2]

* Thanks to Elise Bant, Andrew Botterill, Alan Brudner, Peter Chau, Wayne Courtney, Michael Crawford, the late John Gardner, Josh Getzler, John Goldberg, Lusina Ho, Duncan Horne, Greg Keating, Jason Nyers, Henry Smith, Lionel Smith and Tan Zhong-Xing for helpful comments, and to many helpful discussions with Arthur Ripstein. I am also grateful to the National University of Singapore for funds provided to me as Kwa Geok Choo Professor of Property Law.

[1] A Ripstein, *Private Wrongs* (Cambridge MA, Harvard University Press, 2016). I shall also, in places, draw upon Ripstein's more general work on the Kantian structure of law: A Ripstein, *Force and Freedom: Kant's Legal and Political Philosophy* (Cambridge MA, Harvard University Press, 2009).

[2] For a critical review of J Gardner, *From Personal Life to Private Law* (Oxford, Oxford University Press, 2018), see JE Penner, 'Book Review: From Personal Life to Private Law, by John Gardner, Oxford, Oxford University Press, 2018' (2019) 10 *Jurisprudence* 300. For discussion of Ripstein's Kantian analysis of property, see JE Penner, *Property Rights: A Re-Examination* (Oxford, Oxford University Press, 2020) ch 8. On Gardner's and Ripstein's treatment of the 'continuity thesis' and issues in tort more generally, see JE Penner, 'Don't Crash into Mick Jagger When He is Driving His Rolls Royce: Liability in Damages for Economic Loss Consequent upon a Personal Injury' in PB Miller and J Oberdiek (eds), *Civil Wrongs and Justice in Private Law* (Oxford, Oxford University Press, 2020) 253–71.

II. Reasons Fundamentalist Instrumentalism about the Law

Reasons fundamentalist instrumentalism (RFI) about the law makes two basic claims, one moral, and one legal: (1) we have the moral duties we have because as the sorts of rational creatures we are, we can respond to reasons; and we have the moral rights we have because we can rightly hold others to respect those reasons when the reasons reflect important interests that we have; (2) there are circumstances where our compliance with our duties to observe reasons can be assisted by a public authority with the power rightfully to guide, and ultimately, to coerce our behaviour. The law is instrumental in the sense that it gives assistance to its subjects in making this compliance actual without doing too much collateral damage along the way.

As to (1), Gardner develops the idea in terms of 'basic responsibility' and the inescapability of morality. As to the former, Gardner writes:

> Basic responsibility is what it sounds like. It is an ability. More fully, it is the ability and propensity to have and to give self-explanations in the currency of reasons. The ability and the propensity are but two sides of the same coin. As beings who are able to respond to reasons we cannot avoid being disposed to respond to them. There is nowhere to hide from them. …
>
> Basic responsibility, I suggest, cannot be assigned or allocated by anyone. There is no normative power, by the exercise of which anyone can add to or subtract from it. That is not because it is impossible for any of us not to have it. Some of us lack it altogether. Well, actually, that depends on who counts as 'us'. But assuming we mean 'human beings', we might doubt the basic responsibility of very young children, those with advanced forms of dementia or severe mental illnesses, and those in comas. Surely basic responsibility is entirely lacking in at least some such cases? Yes, and that is already a matter of regret. Human beings ought to be answerable to reasons. That is part of their human ergon, to use the Aristotelian term, sometimes translated as 'function' but perhaps better as 'destiny'.[3]

The basic idea is that we are 'valuing' creatures. We respond to or react to or understand facts, including facts about events and human actions, as reasons. We see the world, in part, in terms of values (physical pleasure, social and aesthetic values, and so on) that we have reason to realise, and also in terms of disvalues

On Ripstein's Kantian rendering of fiduciary law, see JE Penner, *Justifying (or Not) the Office of Trusteeship with Particular Reference to Massively Discretionary Trusts* (on file with the author). For an instrumentalist account of criminal law and punishment and its relation to private law, see JE Penner, 'Punishment and Penalties in Private Law, with Particular Reference to the Law Governing Fiduciaries' in E Bant, J Goudkamp, J Paterson and W Courtney (eds), *Punishment and Private Law* (Oxford, Hart, forthcoming).

[3] J Gardner, 'The Negligence Standard: Political Not Metaphysical' (2017) 80 *Modern Law Review* 1, 7–8.

(pain, actions which we regard as cruel or debased or pointless) which we not only have reason to avoid but also have reason to prevent. Reasons underpin rights and duties in a straightforward way on this perspective: X has against Y a right to q if the value of q gives rise to a reason for action which is 'categorical' in the sense that it prevails over Y's otherwise innocuous plans to realise values. Y cannot push X out of the way, thus interfering with X's right to bodily security, in order to hasten himself on his way. Very roughly, X's interest in bodily security is of a strength and stringency such that it imposes a categorical (which is not to say absolute) duty on Y not to infringe it.

If this is right then morality is, as Gardner puts it, 'inescapable' for creatures like us.[4] Gardner frames this in terms of a thesis, IM (the *i*nescapability of *m*orality): '(IM) Engagement with moral norms is an inescapable part of rational, and hence human, nature'.[5] After having introduced this thesis, Gardner spends some time dealing with some objections which might be framed under the rubric of moral scepticism.[6] I shall not go into these in detail, except to say that I think his responses have the better of the argument. One of his points stands out. It is that immoral behaviour no more undermines the demands of morality in the practical realm than bad reasoning undermines the norms of logic and rationality in the 'epistemic' realm, the realm of belief fixation. It may be the case that many people, or most people, are poor at determining what morality requires of them, in the same way that we can observe that many people are poor thinkers in various ways in other realms of thought.[7] That this is so does nothing to impugn the validity of the norms that apply.

Unlike morality, the law is always escapable in the relevant sense. Hence Gardner's thesis (EL), the '*e*scapability of *l*aw': '(EL) Engagement with legal norms is not an inescapable part of rational, and hence human, nature'.[8] The basic idea is that, in contrast to the norms of rationality and morality, it is always possible to ask the question, 'yes, I see this is a valid law, but must I comply with it?'. Note, this is not the same as the similar-sounding question in relation to morality, 'why should I', (for example), 'keep my promises?'.[9] The latter question could be posed as a particular instantiation of the question, 'sure, keeping my promise is what I ought to do as a matter of morality (is a "valid" or sound moral norm), but why should I do what morality requires me to do?', or more generally, 'why should I act morally?'. That question is, as we have seen, illicit on Gardner's account,

[4] For elaboration and discussion see JE Penner, 'Rights, Distributed and Undistributed: On the Distributive Justice Implications of Lockean Property Rights, Especially in Land' in JE Penner and M Otsuka (eds), *Property Theory: Legal and Political Perspectives* (Cambridge, Cambridge University Press, 2018) 139–44.

[5] J Gardner, 'Nearly Natural Law' (2007) 52 *American Journal of Jurisprudence* 1, 2.

[6] ibid 2–5.

[7] The classic work here is that of Kahneman and Tversky: See D Kahneman, *Thinking, Fast and Slow* (New York, Farrar, Straus and Giroux, 2011).

[8] Gardner (n 5) 10.

[9] ibid 4.

no different in kind from the question, 'why should I reason rationally?'. But the question makes perfect sense nonetheless as a question about *what* morality requires of one – what the *content* of morality *is*. As Gardner says, all norms require justification, and this is particularly relevant for moral norms just *because* they are inescapable.[10]

Matters are different with the law. As Gardner explains:

> [Regarding the question] 'Why should I obey, or otherwise engage with, the law?' … that question is a good one precisely because law (unlike morality) is something that one needs (further) reasons to obey, or indeed to engage with. Legal norms answer to rationality. Unlike moral norms, they do not form an inescapable part of rationality. An unjustified moral norm is an oxymoron; an unjustified legal norm is always a live possibility. It follows that law is humanly escapable in the relevant sense (even if it is also humanly necessary).
>
> So in this respect – in respect of the property picked out in (EL) – legal norms are unlike moral norms and like the norms of a game or a recipe. Their existence as norms leaves open the question of whether they (or some of them) are worth using as guides to action.[11]

With this consideration in mind, we can now address (2), the main 'instrumentalist' side of RFI. In what circumstances does morality require us to follow the law – or to put it another way – in what circumstances does morality 'incorporate' legal norms, such that the legal norms are also inescapable moral norms? And the simple answer is whenever we would better comply with the moral norms that otherwise apply to us apart from the law when we follow the law rather than our own appraisal of the norms in question. This is nothing more than Raz's dependence thesis in relation to his service conception of practical authority.[12] Whilst I think this is right, there are many complications which go to show that this simple principle is often difficult to apply in practice.

One thing I want to dwell upon here is whether the law could, even in principle, attend to all or most areas of our interpersonal moral relations equally. For example, should the law pay attention to basic wrongs, murder, theft, etc, with more alacrity than it attends to, say, voluntarily undertaken obligations, such as contracts?

Consider, first, criminal law. Criminal law is conventionally regarded as reflecting and vindicating moral norms that would exist independently of the existence of any legal system. The injunctions not to murder, to respect the property of others, and so on, are (to the extent they are valid, of course) morally required of every individual regardless of the behaviour of others, or of the individual's expectations of the behaviour of others.

[10] ibid.
[11] ibid 11.
[12] J Raz, *The Morality of Freedom* (Oxford, Clarendon Press, 1986) 42–53.

But the criminal law does more than simply enforce pre-existing, independently valid moral norms of this kind. Its main function is to solve two kinds of 'coordination problem' where the idea of a coordination problem is broadly understood. The first kind concerns the problem of indeterminacy. The exact extent, scope and justification of these norms are controversial and uncertain. Whilst the law, to be legitimate, must by and large reflect the moral considerations which underpin these moral norms, the law can and does serve as an authority which solves the problem of indeterminacy by specifying, in more or less certain terms, legal norms which reflect these moral ones. Further, the criminal law specifies more or less certain responses to, in particular punishments for, breach of these legal norms.

The second sort of coordination problem is that of organising collective action. The 'coordination' problem the criminal justice system addresses here is the problem, or goal, of coordinating a community's response to crime so as to deal with it in the best way possible, enforcing compliance with these norms to deal with those subjects of the law who would otherwise disregard these moral norms, or have in fact disregarded them. By instituting a criminal justice system, the law creates a better, collective way of dealing with crime, ie dealing with criminals in a just, fair and certain manner, than would leaving it all to private action, self-help, revenge, feud, vendetta.

If it is, as I believe it is,[13] a moral obligation on any community to *take the side* of the victim over the criminal in some suitably expressive *public* way, a community cannot stand idly by when one of its members maliciously victimises another. By taking the side of the victim I do not mean that the community 'takes over' the victim's private personal interest in compensation or revenge. By taking the side I only mean that the community publicly vindicates the rights of the victim that were transgressed, and voices appropriate censure of the perpetrator, 'disowning' his act as the kind of act permissible in that community.[14] This is especially so in the case of serious violations, murder, assaults causing grievous bodily or psychological harm, plundering frauds, and so on. A community is less of a community in so far as it fails to do this. Victims, in the absence of this 'taking their side', are treated as equal to, or even less than, the perpetrator who victimised them. Taking the side of the perpetrator is the clearest signal possible that the victim is isolated. Such a victim justifiably feels even more aggrieved if, at the same time, the victim is regarded as still a 'citizen' – that only rubs salt in the wound. We can see this in the contemporary context, perhaps most vividly in the Black Lives Matter movement. It simply cannot be justified that police officers can wrongfully take the lives of citizens with no genuine repercussions, and this has nothing to do with feelings, say, of revenge.

[13] For a full defence of this view, and its relation to Gardner's similar thoughts, see Penner, 'Punishment and Penalties' (n 2).

[14] I thank Alan Brudner for helping me make this point clear.

Since feud, vendetta and so on, are *private* retaliatory responses, they cannot achieve this public, 'community', function. Because this obligation is necessarily collective or communal, it cannot be discharged by an individual, or any number of individuals. In order for this obligation to be discharged, some representation of the community must be instituted. This is not an empirical matter, but a conceptual one.[15]

As Gardner points out, the particular modern form through which most criminal justice systems 'take the side of the victim' is to require the wrongdoer to *answer* for their wrong. We make the criminal wrongdoer answer for the wrong, not the victim.[16] Of course, this is to put things too simply. The criminal process has multiple stages, and the accused has no obligation to put up a positive defence, or any defence at all. There is also opportunity to raise defences of excuse and justification. There is, finally, the idea of answering for the wrong by the imposition of punishment.[17]

Recognising the conceptual priority of the 'taking the victim's side' over the issue of punishment has an immediate pay-off. It explains why those interested in 'restorative' or 'reconciliatory' responses to crime, even though they may abjure punitive responses, are on the same page so far as this goes. In other words, this 'expressive' aspect of the criminal law is conceptually prior, as Gardner himself makes clear, to the issue of punishment. I shall not here delve into the justification of punishment when it is warranted as the right response to crime.

Is private law, in particular, the private law's determination and enforcement of a tort law duty of repair, necessarily implemented by a state in the same way that a state's obligation to institute a criminal justice system is? That, for example, is what a Kantian may feel bound to claim.[18] As far as I can tell, Gardner hasn't addressed the point in terms, but given his instrumentalism about all law, and private law in

[15] This, to my mind, is the one case where only the 'state' can act to preserve the 'civil condition'. To this limited extent, then, I am with the Kantians when they say that we have an obligation to enter into and maintain the civil condition when we cannot avoid coming into contact with each other. Unlike Kantians, I don't think the same obligation applies when it comes to private law generally, though I shall ask in a moment about a resemblance here with tort law.

[16] Or rather, we should. Just uttering this statement immediately and ineluctably, and rightly, brings to mind the lamentable historical (and regrettably, to some extent still, present) attitudes to and the prosecution of the crime of rape.

[17] Thanks again here to Alan Brudner for helpful discussion.

[18] See Ripstein, *Private Wrongs* (n 1) xii: 'Kant argues that a central part of interpersonal morality requires institutional instantiation in a body of positive law.' But cf ibid, 293–94, n 8, where Ripstein says that 'it is within the state's proper authority' to abolish tortious liability for personal injury and establish, in its stead, but not as a 'replacement', a public accident compensation scheme. For a reading of Kant that would deny this, see JR Otteson, 'Kantian Individualism and Political Libertarianism' (2009) 13 *The Independent Review* 389. For a discussion of the way private law fits, or fails to fit, within Rawls's 'basic structure' of institutions, see A Ripstein 'Private Order and Public Justice: Kant and Rawls' (2006) 92 *Virginia Law Review* 1391; Ripstein, *Private Wrongs* (n 1) 290–92; and S Scheffler, 'Distributive Justice, the Basic Structure and the Place of Private Law' (2015) 35 *Oxford Journal of Legal Studies* 213. For the claim that a tort law right to redress should be conceived as a constitutional right in the US, see JC Goldberg, 'The Constitutional Status of Tort Law: Due Process and the Right to a Law for the Redress of Wrongs' (2005) 115 *Yale Law Journal* 524.

particular as expressed in a number of recent writings,[19] he must surely believe the answer to be, as a matter of principle, no. For my own part I am not so sure.

An instrumentalist case may be made, I think, that certain duties of repair need to be instituted by the law just as much as some criminal law offences. Take for example the Bhopal disaster. I cannot see how a community could stand by and let the negligent plant operator just 'get away with it', ie get away with paying no compensation, and I am assuming this was a case of pure negligence, ie liability in tort without any criminal liability. Of course, this is perhaps an extreme case, and I am not arguing that all duties of repair have the same urgency; the same, as it were, 'public' urgency.[20] But I think some do.

The duty to repair following a breach of contract is a different kettle of fish again. As far as I can tell, the law could do without enforcing such duties entirely, in the same way that the law does not (outside the law of covenants) enforce gratuitous promises. Again, based on recent writings,[21] Gardner would seem to agree, and through various techniques such as binding arbitration clauses the law of contract seems to be heading in this direction anyway. Though Gardner deplores the recent efforts by corporate actors to make their side of an agreement enforceable whilst effectively denying the same to their consumer counterparties,[22] he, quite rightly I think,[23] doubts whether breaches of contract have anything like a 'public' element which would weigh in favour of state enforcement for that kind of reason. There are many obvious reasons against burdening the state in this way, the most obvious being that private parties may respond to contractual breaches in a number of ways (taking their business elsewhere in future, via reputational effects, and so on) which may be typically efficacious in resolving the issues, or at least to some extent preventing and reducing the ill effects of breach, and in any case, one can mostly avoid serious losses arising from breach of contract through the judicious selection of counterparties.[24]

For the instrumentalist, then, there may be cases where law is necessary in a very straightforward way – the law alone can allow us to act morally where doing so has an urgency for maintaining the basic interests we have in living together in a community. In such cases, complying with morality can only be achieved by complying with the law, and, in such cases, it is trivial to derive a moral obligation

[19] See, eg: J Gardner, 'What is Tort Law For? Part 1. The Place of Corrective Justice' (2011) 30 *Law and Philosophy* 1; J Gardner, 'What is Tort Law For? Part 2. The Place of Distributive Justice' in J Oberdiek (ed), *Philosophical Foundations of the Law of Torts* (Oxford, Oxford University Press, 2014) 335; J Gardner, 'Some Rule-of-Law Anxieties about Strict Liability in Private Law' in LM Austin and D Klimchuk (eds), *Private Law and the Rule of Law* (Oxford, Oxford University Press, 2014) 207; J Gardner, 'Dagan and Dorfman on the Value of Private Law' (2017) 117 *Columbia Law Review* 179.

[20] Indeed, I think some duties of repair under the current law of torts are preposterously unjust. See Penner, 'Don't Crash' (n 2).

[21] Gardner, 'Dagan and Dorfman' (n 19) 191–94; J Gardner, 'The Twilight of Legality' (2018) 43 *Australasian Journal of Legal Philosophy* 1, 8–9.

[22] Gardner (n 21) 6–7.

[23] ibid 8–9.

[24] Cases of monopolies and monopsonies aside.

to obey the law. As we know, Finnis can be read as saying essentially the same thing, as he also has what might be called a 'necessity' thesis about the law: in some respects law is a necessary institution if we are going to live in a minimally moral community at all.[25] But it is very apparent that this kind of case, one which is necessary for preserving a community with some minimally effective institution of moral norms, could not conceivably be treated as a general justification of all the law we see in modern societies. After that, for the instrumentalist, it is all a matter of the costs and benefits of the law's creating legal norms that reflect moral norms (or creating legal norms that have other functions, eg facilitating commerce). I hasten to add that this notion of costs and benefits is simply a way of pointing out that there will be reasons for and against any course of action, including legislation. It is not to restrict our reasoning to the cost/benefit analysis of economics, or utilitarianism, for example.[26]

III. Criticisms of Gardner's Account of Instrumentalism

I have elsewhere criticised Gardner's application of instrumentalist principles to particular areas of legal doctrine,[27] so here I want to concentrate on a particular criticism of Gardner's conception of morality which underpins his instrumentalism about the law. But to acknowledge a point only to pass over it, Green raises large issues about what might be called the philosophy of 'moral' psychology in respect of Gardner's 'moral rationalism', in particular the question of why a person would commit a wrong knowing it was wrong, and what this itself might tell us about the nature of morality.[28] And it is true that Gardner's account might be faulted for not addressing this sort of case clearly enough. For example, whilst he develops the point about how we regard a human in a vegetative state as a cause for regret, for such a person lacks the normal attributes of rationality (and perhaps more urgently, any form of agency at all), he does not, as far as I can see, address the similar worry about those whose moral faculties seem impaired, in particular the case of the psychopath or sociopath, at least if we understand that for such a person the interests of others 'have no meaning'. I do not think, at the end of the day, that this issue raises an insurmountable difficulty for Gardner's 'escapability' account, so I shall not pursue this here.

Green does, however, raise a more urgent issue, the issue of 'positive', or partly 'positive', morality, by which he means 'social morality', or the *mores* of our community.[29] How much of our moral understanding is rationally compliant,

[25] J Finnis, *Natural Law and Natural Rights* (Oxford, Clarendon Press, 1980) ch 10.

[26] See Gardner, 'What is Tort Law For? Part 1' (n 19) 16–27.

[27] Penner, 'Book Review' (n 2).

[28] L Green, 'Escapable Law: Gardner on Law and Morality' (2018) Oxford Legal Research Paper Series No. 15/2018, 2–3, 4–5, 24 <papers.ssrn.com/sol3/papers.cfm?abstract_id=3261903>.

[29] ibid 12, 14–15.

if our 'engagement' with it is shaped, for better or worse, by what we are told by others about what amounts to 'right' and 'wrong', and how much do social conditions giving rise to 'customary' morality determine not only our moral *culpability* when we err, but also what is right or wrong in the first place? This, for Green, is an especially salient question in the case of the 'inescapability' of morality, and he is right to point out that the law's edicts, even to the extent that they are incorporated by morality – in cases like the ones in which we have a moral obligation to obey the law – are still just what the law says. But in such cases, they are not inescapable *tout court* just because as laws they are norms that fall under EL.

I think all of these concerns are valid and insightful, but there is a Gardnerian reply, which is that morality, like any other realm of understanding, is replete with doubt, given the significant, but not to my mind actually disabling, frailties in human judgement. The difference between IM and EL does not lie in a difference in our epistemic certainty or uncertainty, but in the nature of the justifications we can offer for one or the other. If, despite uncertainty, we come to believe that φ-ing is morally wrong, without further ado we must refrain from φ-ing in the same way that if we examine the grounds for believing that p, and come to believe that p, there is nothing, at that point, more to be said. But there is another very important kind of case, the case of what philosophers call 'mediated' belief fixation. These are cases where we acquire belief indirectly, in particular by relying upon what others tell us, as for example in the case of experts, witnesses of events we did not witness ourselves, in cases where we follow the customs of our community, and so on. Here we have a second source of questions, such as, was the person a liar, was the expert competent, is the custom outdated (dressing for dinner) or sexist (requiring women in public to be chaperoned), and so on. This is, I think, built into the service conception of authority and testimony. The point is not that there can be no good reasons for submitting to different modes of epistemic access, or practical counsel – it is only that they are necessarily 'second-hand' or mediated. So, Gardner is right to think that when morality indeed incorporates law, the law is inescapable under IM. This is particularly so in the case of plausible 'determinacy' cases. For the kind of moralist Gardner is, there is a *moral* value in identifying a plausibly moral way forward even if we cannot know that that way forward is unique, or indeed know that there is no unique way forward because of the very indeterminacy of morality. That too is part of what is inescapable about morality. Its own indeterminacy, on this account, requires that we take up mechanisms, where the matter is sufficiently important, to decide one way or another. To round out the point, I can never escape my own rationality, my own moral judgements, even if part of those judgements involves relying upon the testimony or authority of others. But there is always a question to be asked about whether I am rational, including morally rational, in relying upon those second-order sources, including, of course, when that source is the law.

Though Gardner and I are both 'reasons fundamentalist' instrumentalists, we will naturally apply instrumentalist principles differently in different cases. To give a flavour of this, let me give just one example, which I have considered at length elsewhere.[30] Gardner suggests, I think, that the law of contract's instrumentalist aim is to support what might be called valuable commercial relationships, relationships which have value for their participants apart from the law. In a way this makes perfect sense. We can conceive of exchanges or sales as parts of morality apart from whatever the law says about them, and to the extent the law can contribute to their functioning properly, good for the law *ceterus paribus*. But Gardner seems to further suggest that some or all – it is not clear to me – such relationships have a kind of intrinsic value, rather than pure instrumental value, and here, if I have got Gardner right, we differ. As far as private law is concerned, it seems to me that the law situates parties to an action as strangers, for the most part, not as people situated in intrinsically valuable relationships.

IV. The Basic Kantian Position as Set Out by Ripstein

As is well known, Ripstein's version of private right turns on the idea that no one is in charge of anyone else. More specifically, Kant's private right ensures the independence of our choices from the interferences of others, choices concerning the 'means' that we have, our bodies and our property. Another way of putting this is that private right entitles us to a realm of agency: the ability to pursue purposes, the ends we set ourselves, in so far as we do that by using our means in various ways. For Kant, your private rights are relational and negative; they concern the actions of others, prohibiting their acting so as to interfere with your means by damaging or usurping them, and you do not have any 'positive' rights in your means: no one else is under a duty to assist you in the use of your means, or to provide a favourable environment for their use. Finally, the function of private rights is essentially allocative. In order to have a regime of right which makes necessary reference to the concept of a person's own means, we have to know which means are yours and which are mine. That problem needs no solution in the case of the right to our bodies, which right is for Kant 'innate', but it does require a solution as regards acquired rights, for example we need to have a power to create contractual rights and a power to appropriate unowned things.

According to Ripstein, a private wrong occurs in two ways, either when one person 'usurps' or uses the means belonging to someone else, say by taking someone else's property, or uses their own means in a way which has the side effect of damaging another's means. So, according to Ripstein, there are two basic forms of wrong, or tort: use-based wrongs and damage-based wrongs. Of course, both can be violated with respect to the same means: I can take your property and use it in a way that damages it. But the wrongs are, conceptually, distinct. Use-based wrongs, such as trespass or conversion, are wrongful whether or not any damage

[30] Penner, 'Book Review' (n 2) 303–10.

occurs. They are actionable per se. Damage-based wrongs, as the term indicates, are actionable only on proof of damage.

As I mentioned above, you do not have any 'positive' rights in your body or your property: no one else is under a duty to assist you in the use of your means, or to provide a favourable environment for their use. Much turns on this. For Ripstein, it explains the misfeasance/nonfeasance distinction in tort law. I am never liable for failing to help someone out, unless I have bound myself to do so by undertaking a voluntary obligation to do so, as under a contract. In particular, the distinction explains why there is no duty of easy rescue in tort law. Such a duty would require me to use my means in the service of yours, and no one is entitled to that service. More importantly, and this is a point we shall return to below when I offer some criticisms of Ripstein, the misfeasance/nonfeasance distinction is supposed to explain why the law does not give a remedy in what are sometimes called cases of 'pure economic loss'. The standard example we can call the 'bridge case'. X negligently damages a bridge owned by A. X will be liable to A both for (1) the cost of repairing the bridge, and (2) any consequential economic loss he suffers because the bridge is unusable until repaired, eg for the loss of custom A suffers because his customers no longer have access to his premises. Let us assume that B has a contractual licence from A to use the bridge, and to license his own customers to use it, so that they can access B's own business premises. As a result of X's damaging the bridge, B also suffers a loss of custom, but X is not liable to compensate him for that loss consequential on X's wrong. Why not? For Ripstein, as between X and B, this is a *nonfeasance* case. X has wronged A's means, not B's, so as between X and B X has not committed a wrong, so cannot be liable.

Thus the Kantian notion of right depends upon a clear conceptual distinction between acts which amount to the violation of a right, a misfeasance, and acts which merely change the context in which a right-holder operates, as in the 'bipolar' notion of nonfeasance as against B in the bridge case. The distinction may be empirically difficult to apply. A good example of the way this distinction arose and was dealt with in the common law concerned the development of the action of 'trespass on the case'. To use an old example, if I throw a log at you, that is a trespass.[31] But if I throw a log into the road which you later trip over, the law is faced with a question. Have I done something wrong, or have I merely changed the context or environment in which you operate? In my defence, why can I not say you should just be more careful when you are out walking?[32] So trespass on the case concerned making fine distinctions between acts which violate another's rights and those which merely change the context in which the right-holder operates and, as we know, the current law of negligence has roughly drawn the line by settling on

[31] *Reynolds v Clerk* (1725) 8 Mod 272, 276 cited by TW Merrill, 'Trespass, Nuisance, and the Costs of Determining Property Rights' (1985) 14 *Journal of Legal Studies* 13, 27–28.

[32] As late as 1880 Bramwell was reported as saying: 'If it was too dark for the man to see, he had no business to go there. If it was light enough for him to see, he had no business to stumble over the obstacle'. JH Baker, *An Introduction to English Legal History* (Oxford, Oxford University Press, 2002) 417.

the idea that I am liable for those indirect injuries which arise as the result of the materialisation of a risk I have 'unreasonably' created, or 'unreasonably' failed to take adequate precautions against. In cases where the risk of my activities is not unreasonable as regards others, there is no misfeasance; I have merely changed the context in which others operate, so as between them and me, this is a case of nonfeasance: I did nothing bearing on relations of right as between us.

This is a powerful and prima facie attractive account of private law. As Ripstein says:

> The idea of independence carries the justificatory burden of the entire argument, from the prohibition of personal injury, through the minutiae of property and contract law, on to the details of the constitutional separation of powers. Kant argues that these norms and institutions do more than enhance the prospects for independence: they provide the only possible way in which a plurality of persons can interact on terms of equal freedom. Kant's concern is not with how people should interact, as a matter of ethics, but with how they can be forced to interact, as a matter of right.[33]

In other words, right, as opposed to virtue or ethics, concerns how we stand in relation to others so that we can rightfully act at all, and have our own choices properly attributed to us, whether rightful or wrongful. In order even to act rationally and therefore, as we have seen, morally, I must be able to tell which means are rightly, or morally, available to me, and private right and private law establish just that.

V. Criticisms of Ripstein's Kantian Account

In the first place, a word about a possible 'instrumentalist' explanation of Kantian private law. As is well known, owing to Kant's 'assurance' argument, outside of a 'civil condition', roughly an established state with an executive, legislature and courts, private rights are only provisional or imperfect.[34] In order to 'perfect' these rights or make them real, the state must be established as it is the only means of doing so, owing to its legitimate right to legislate, adjudicate and coercively execute judgments. In this respect, the state is a necessary instrument for the realisation of our moral relations to each other as individual members of society. But just because it is a necessary instrument, does not mean that it is not an instrument (though it does raise the interesting question of what 'necessary' means here).[35]

[33] Ripstein, 'Force and Freedom' (n 1) 14. See also A Ganesh, 'Wirtbarkeit: Cosmopolitan Right and Innkeeping' (2018) 24 *Legal Theory* 159, 163.

[34] See Penner, *Property Rights* (n 2) 164–73, 186–93.

[35] For discussion, see Gardner, 'What is Tort Law For? Part 1' (n 19) 19–27.

Be that as it may, this has nothing to do with my treating Ripstein's Kantian account of tort as a non-instrumentalist account. Ripstein does not deny that the law has an instrumental function in the sense that the law implements right so as make right real, nor that the law makes determinate the duties and rights that obtain between individuals, and that this determination will require the judgement of judges, legislators, and so on.[36] In each of these ways Ripstein's account clearly acknowledges certain ideas of instrumentality.

What makes Ripstein's account non-instrumentalist is his claim that the structure of private right which he sets out determines all the substantive content of private law, or at least the core of private law. In particular where the structure of private right, reflecting its underlying idea that no person is in charge of another, explains legal doctrine satisfactorily, no further considerations are relevant for determining what private law should be. In this sense, private law is to be understood as the *implementation* of a morality of private interactions amongst individuals which determines, albeit through the judgement of judges, what the private law should be. So if, as suggested earlier, we had a private law which failed to give legal effect to voluntarily undertaken obligations, such as those undertaken in contracts, this would be a clear deficiency in our private law from this Kantian perspective, for in that case the law would fail to give effect to private right as elaborated on this Kantian conception of it.

There is one further feature of Ripstein's Kantian account of *tort law*, in particular, that needs to be noticed. Although Kant was clearly familiar with Roman law,[37] Kant did not so much as mention the word 'delict' in his discussion of private right. So, everything relevant to tort law has to be gleaned from Kant's general picture of private right and his idea of a wrong.

A. Rights and Interests

Let me begin with two critiques of Ripstein's tort theory both of which focus on interests as a ground of rights. Ripstein, by contrast, posits the opposite view – what he has called a 'rights theory of interests'[38] which, stated roughly, is that you can only identify something as an interest, at least as a matter of interpersonal morality, in so far as you have a right to it, that is, in so far as you can restrain the conduct of others in relation to it. So you have an interest in your body just in so

[36] See also M Stone, 'Legal Positivism as an Idea About Morality' (2011) 61 *University of Toronto Law Journal* 313; R Stevens, *Torts and Rights* (Oxford, Oxford University Press, 2007) 329–40. Stone argues that determinations of right can only be attained through the casuistic reasoning of impartial officials.

[37] He 'follows' Ulpian in setting out the general division of duties of right. Immanuel Kant, *The Metaphysics of Morals*, 2nd edn (first published 1797, Cambridge, Cambridge University Press, 1996) 29/[6:236], and his discussion of contract also clearly draws on Roman law: ibid 67/[6:284]–68/[6:287], 78/[6:297]–80/[6:300].

[38] Ripstein, *Private Wrongs* (n 1) 68–73.

far as others are prohibited from touching it, and so on. My own view, for what it is worth, is that interests are prior to rights, but I shan't defend it here.[39]

The first critique is Hershovitz's.[40] Hershovitz spends a lot of time objecting to Ripstein's claim that I am not entitled so much as to touch your body or your property under the Kantian theory of trespass to goods or the person. Citing a number of cases, Hershovitz points out that this is not, legally, literally true.[41] For example, non-offensive touchings of others, say lightly tapping you on the shoulder to get your attention, or bumping up against you on a crowded bus, are not batteries. I am not sure, however, whether Ripstein's account is much undermined by such examples. Despite these cases, it seems right to say that the underlying rule is that prima facie you are not allowed to touch other people's bodies without getting their consent first. Hershovitz is on stronger ground, however, when he considers the tort of invasion of privacy, citing a case where the tortfeasor drilled a hole in an adjoining door between hotel rooms so as to video a celebrity whilst she was naked and posting the video online.[42] Now the point of this example is not that Ripstein could not fit this tort within his scheme, arguing this is a use-based tort, an unlawful 'using' of the victim's body. The problem is that this doesn't seem to express what the wrong is. If we have an interest in privacy per se, then it is not clear how this fits into the 'means' account, for your privacy is not a means you have at all.

A similar point is raised by Sangiovanni.[43] He claims that Ripstein's account will eventually have to rely upon identifying interests as the ground for rights. He contrasts two cases, the 'harmless rape' and drawing someone's hands as they sit in a public place. The harmless rape case has been much discussed.[44] The situation is that of a person who is raped when unconscious and the rapist dies shortly thereafter having told no one about it so that the rape is never discovered. It is taken to be a paradigmatic example of a wrong without any harm. The drawing of the hands account is supposed to be a structural parallel, but the first, harmless rape, case is normally (and rightly) thought to be a wrong, whereas the latter, drawing hands, case is not. Sangiovanni proposes that the only way to show why is to claim that one has an interest in one's sexual integrity, but no similar interest in our not being drawn whilst in public. Thus to 'use' or 'usurp' the body of another is a *moralised* concept itself – it is not basic; rather, what shapes it is an underlying concept of uses or usurpations which violate our interests.

[39] For a discussion of the interest theory of rights in this volume, see McBride, chapter 5. For my own views, which differ in important respects from McBride's, see JE Penner, 'The Analysis of Rights' (1997) 10 *Ratio Juris* 300; JE Penner, 'Legal Powers and the Will and Interest Theories of Rights' in N McBride (ed), *New Essays on the Nature of Rights* (Oxford, Hart Publishing, 2017).

[40] S Hershovitz, 'Book Review: The Search For a Grand Unified Theory of Tort Law' (2017) 130 *Harvard Law Review* 942.

[41] ibid 949–52, 958–59, 961.

[42] ibid 953–55, 963–65.

[43] A Sangiovanni, 'Rights and Interests in Ripstein's Kant' in S Kisilevsky and MJ Stone (eds), *Freedom and Force: Essays on Kant's Legal Philosophy* (Oxford, Hart Publishing, 2017).

[44] J Gardner, *Offences and Defences: Selected Essays in the Philosophy of Criminal Law* (Oxford, Oxford University Press, 2007) 5; V Tadros, *Wrongs and Crimes* (Oxford, Oxford University Press, 2016) 102ff.

The gist of Ripstein's reply lies in the following passage, which is also relevant to Hershovitz's critique:

> Generally speaking, I can only use you by touching you or by getting you to participate in my plans without proper consent (eg by lying to you). If I stalk you or crowd you, these things can be assimilated to touching; perhaps the same thing can be said of spying on you, or other invasions of your privacy. But if I derive some benefit from you happening to be where you happen to be, that isn't even a candidate; it isn't a mild form of invasion of privacy.[45]

The last line seems correct, emphasising that a line must be drawn somewhere between a violation of right and merely changing, or taking advantage of, the context in which someone else operates. But it doesn't seem to answer the challenge posed by the stalking, crowding or invasion of privacy cases. The wrong in these cases seems to be primarily understandable *prior* to framing them as extended kinds of touching or use. The point, which I take to be Hershovitz's and Sangiovanni's point, is not that a Kantian cannot fit these torts within the use-or damage-based torts schema, but rather that there is not any neutral, non-moralised concept of use or damage under which they would be identified as torts, ie wrongs, in the first place.

This brings us to a much larger concern, liability for negligence. My critique here is almost wholly inspired by that of Brudner,[46] and I hope I do it no injustice here by setting out the motivating idea in my own way. As Ripstein makes clear,[47] Kant essentially, not merely metaphorically, regards our relations of right as akin to spatial relations. On this view, invasions of rights are conceived of as boundary crossings. In view of this, it is difficult if not impossible to appreciate the nature of negligent wrongdoing. This is not to say that some negligent wrongdoing may not involve a boundary crossing, as, for example, when due to my carelessness my factory explodes launching debris onto your land. But we can contribute to the creation of circumstances in which others' interests are endangered, and if this contribution is 'careless', we have breached a duty properly to take those interests into account, whether or not a boundary crossing results. There was no boundary crossing in *Donoghue v Stevenson*,[48] nor in the case of the log thrown into the road. In general, indeed, the victim of negligence is an author of her own downfall in the sense that it is her own 'moving into' those carelessly created circumstances which gives rise to her injury. This is, obviously, an 'interests', as opposed to a notional or indirect 'trespass', ie 'boundary crossing', conception of negligence, and it would take a paper of its own to substantiate it in detail. But the basic claim is that, unlike trespass torts, liability for negligence turns on a failure of the defendant, not to observe boundaries, but to govern his behaviour in light of the interests of others.

[45] A Ripstein, 'Embodied Free Beings under Public Law: A Reply' in S Kisilevsky and M Stone (eds), *Freedom and Force: Essay's on Kant's Legal Philosophy* (Oxford, Hart Publishing, 2017) 198.

[46] A Brudner with JM Nadler, *The Unity of the Common Law* (Oxford, Oxford University Press, 2013) ch 6.

[47] Ripstein, *Force and Freedom* (n 1) 12. For discussion see Penner, *Property Rights* (n 2) 161–62.

[48] *Donoghue v Stevenson* [1932] AC 562 (HL).

That is just what being careless in regard to others is. This is, I should say, not a criticism, or at least not a direct criticism, of Ripstein's own explanation of negligence. It is rather to point out that his idea of a 'damage-based' tort is not easily derived from, and therefore supported by, Kant's own conception of interpersonal rights and wrongdoing.

B. The Problem of 'Nonfeasance' with Respect to those Holding Merely Contractual Rights

Here we must address the bridge case: X negligently damages a bridge owned by A. X will be liable to A both for (1) the cost of repairing the bridge, and (2) any consequential economic loss A suffers. X will not be liable to B, A's licensee, for any consequential loss B suffers. What I am going to suggest is that it is not clear that Kant's framework of rights indicates that the law should address the bridge problem in the way that it does. The first has to do with the way the law characterises an interest in property. The easement of way, or a right of way, serves as a good example. An easement of way is not a possessory interest, but an 'incorporeal' hereditament. It is created by a voluntary undertaking, by a covenant, between the dominant and servient tenant holders. So, for Kantian theory, this is an acquired right akin to a contract. The origins of easements, and other members of the numerus clausus,[49] such as profits, mortgages, and so on, are historically murky, but the point to notice is that what makes them interests in land is the fact that they bind successors in title. This is not to deny that easements and profits, once created, also have in rem effects. Anyone who blocks another's right of way is liable to the easement holder in nuisance. But the point is that the law makes a choice in these matters, both in binding parties in rem, and binding successors in title. The law could have left this all 'in contract', and contractual licences granting rights of way only as between the parties (licences of way, one might call them) can perfectly well be created, as the bridge case itself shows. The question this discussion raises is why, as between X, the negligent bridge-damager, and B, the grantee of a right of way, B's right of way should be treated differently depending upon the fact that in one case, it binds successors in title, and in the other, it does not. For as between A and B, their relations are the same whether A covenants with B for an easement or A contracts with B for a licence of way. So, there is no difference here that would require a difference in treatment between B as easement-holder and B as licensee which should matter to the third-party tortfeasor, X. Neither is the fact that in the case of the licence, the licence does not bind successors in title though the easement does. Again, this feature of an easement does not seem to indicate any bearing on X's relationship with B. Obviously what does is the law's holding that the easement

[49] For extensive discussion, see Penner, *Property Rights* (n 2) 12–14.

binds third parties in rem. The question is, why? Why should a covenant have this magic effect where a contract does not? It seems to me that the only reason is one of policy, a facilitative policy. The law, in its wisdom, decided that A and B by voluntary arrangement could subject third parties to B's rights under the arrangement. But this is not dictated by the structure of private right, and certainly not by the very idea that A and B can agree to something. Kantian private right *can explain* why the relation between X and B has no legal significance, despite B's *in personam* licence, but it cannot explain the relation between X and B that the covenant is held to generate.

Consider another case, which we can call the 'Mick Jagger' case (MJ). I negligently injure MJ, breaking his leg, so he cannot appear on his upcoming South American tour with the Stones.[50] I will of course be liable for MJ's medical expenses and 'pain and suffering', but what will really ruin me is my liability for his lost earnings, say £2 million. Under the law as it stands, from a Kantian perspective, one might say what I also injure, besides MJ's body, is his 'acquired' rights under the contract with his counterparties, let's say his fans who bought tickets, leaving aside all the middlemen. As a matter of law, the contract is frustrated. But here's the problem – why do I also not have to compensate MJ's fans? On the Kantian story of acquired rights, contractual rights are modelled on property rights. Especially for 'transfer' theorists of contract,[51] what the fan acquires under the contract is a right to their counterparty's, MJ's, 'agency' in the philosophical sense of that term – they own a piece of MJ's agency by virtue of the contract or, to put it another way, they acquire an interest in his body. Why should I have to compensate MJ for *his* interest in his fans' plural agencies, their bodies, their obligations to pay to see him, but not compensate his fans for my interference with *his* body, rights which they have acquired under the Kantian theory of contract? If anything, my injury is more directly *against them*, since I make it the case that his ability to discharge his duty to perform, which they 'own', is damaged or destroyed.

The general point here is about framing the nature of 'consequential' loss. Any theory of private right has to deal with the bridge and MJ cases. It is not at all clear to me how the present state of the law, and these are pretty paradigmatic or central features of the law, is to be explained or justified by the application of Kantian principles, which is not to say that they cannot be justified at all.

C. Deprivation Torts

As we have seen, Ripstein claims that all torts are either use- or usurpation-based, or damage-based. I think this is wrong. A clear example occurs when I

[50] I have discussed a host of issues that arise in this sort of case in Penner, 'Don't Crash' (n 2).

[51] See, eg: P Benson, 'Contract as a Transfer of Ownership' (2007) 48 *William and Mary Law Review* 1673.

dump a load of bricks on the public highway preventing you from accessing your easement of way. This is an actionable private nuisance though I have neither damaged anything of yours, nor used anything of yours. I have merely deprived you of the subject matter your right. I think that nuisance, generally, is a deprivation tort, depriving you of the use or access to what is yours, not by physically removing you, but indirectly, say by smoking you out of your house or garden. Nolan aims to maintain that nuisance torts are damage-based torts by claiming that the damage is a reduction in 'usability'.[52] But this, I think, could just as easily be framed as a deprivation of usability – a deprivation of your liberty to use what is yours. The action of replevin also responds to a deprivation tort. No proof is required that the wrongful distrainor of goods used them (then he would also be liable for conversion) or that he damaged them. The gravamen of the wrong is that he unjustly deprived the plaintiff of his rightful possession. As with negligence liability, I can only flag this here. I have pursued it in depth elsewhere.[53]

Incidentally, it also strikes me that the tort of defamation sits uneasily on the use or usurpation tort/damage-based tort borderline. A defamatory statement could be conceived of along the lines of my 'using' your reputation without your consent, giving it the structure of a tort that is actionable per se without 'proof of damage' in the sense of consequential loss.[54] On the other hand, a defamatory statement must damage one's reputation, in the sense of its having to be shown that, if believed, it would lower one's reputation amongst right-thinking people.[55] Again, it is not clear to me that there are robust Kantian principles to resolve this.[56]

VI. Conclusion

As I have hoped to have shown, though I take a 'reasons fundamentalist' instrumentalist position on the law, my discussion of the work of Gardner shows that the application of instrumentalism to particular cases is not straightforward, and requires judgement, though that is not, I think, a flaw in the position. With regard to Kantian positions, whilst I hope I have fairly acknowledged the power of some basic Kantian insights, I have also tried to show that Kantian resources may be insufficient to illuminate some important aspects of tort law doctrine.

[52] D Nolan, 'The Essence of Private Nuisance' in B McFarlane and S Agnew (eds), *Modern Studies in Property Law*, Volume 10 (Oxford, Hart Publishing, 2019).

[53] Penner, *Property Rights* (n 2) ch 7.

[54] Ripstein, *Private Wrongs* (n 1) 195.

[55] At ibid 193, Ripstein says: 'Only you are entitled to *change* your reputation because others may not' (emphasis added). Since Ripstein correctly claims, ibid 207–08, that there is no tort of 'famation', 'change' here must mean something like 'injure' or 'damage'.

[56] For Ripstein's full account, see *Private Wrongs* (n 1) ch 7.

4

Intermediate and Comprehensive Justifications for Legal Rules

STEPHEN A SMITH*

This chapter explores two ways of justifying legal rules. The first, which is adopted by some (but only some) academics, justifies legal rules on the basis of comprehensive moral theories. As understood here, moral theories are comprehensive if they provide standards against which all or most legal rules may be evaluated, and if they ground those standards in a foundational principle, value or belief, or in a set of closely connected foundational principles, beliefs or values. In contemporary legal scholarship, the most widely adopted comprehensive moral theories are utilitarian and Kantian theories.

The second way, which is adopted by nearly all judges (though also by many academics), justifies legal rules on the basis of intermediate moral principles, values or beliefs ('principles'). As understood here, intermediate principles are broader than legal rules, but narrower than the foundational principles that define comprehensive theories. Examples of intermediate principles include fairness, honesty, dignity, reasonableness, keeping one's word, proportionality, clarity, stability and predictability.

My exploration of these ways of justifying legal rules focuses on two questions. First, why do judges restrict themselves to 'intermediate justifications' (as I will call them)? The most plausible explanation, I argue, is that, in the pluralist societies that are my focus, for legal rules to be practically effective and, more importantly, for legal rules to be legitimate, they must be acceptable to people who hold different (or no) comprehensive moral theories. And for justifications to be acceptable to such people, they must be limited to intermediate principles.[1] The second question is whether, assuming the 'acceptability thesis' (as I will call it) not only explains

* I would like to thank Felipe Jiménez and Michael Crawford for helpful comments. I also recommend that readers interested in this chapter's concerns read Paul Miller's contribution to this book. As Miller explains (see n 3 in his chapter, 'Juridical Justification of Private Rights'), there are significant overlaps (though also significant differences) in our arguments.

[1] My development of this argument is indebted to C Sunstein, 'Incompletely Theorized Agreements' (1994) 108 *Harvard Law Review* 1733. It was also inspired by – though disagreeing with – Ronald Dworkin's view of judicial reasoning. For Dworkin, judges should, and in practice regularly do (even

but also justifies the judicial approach, the thesis also applies to academics. Should academics also limit themselves to intermediate justifications for legal rules? My answer, with certain qualifications, is that they should. Although the 'practical objection' to comprehensive justifications has only a limited application to academics, the 'principled objection' (the objection from legitimacy) applies with full force. The argument that good justifications for legal rules should in principle be acceptable to people who hold different (or no) comprehensive theories applies regardless of who is offering the justification.

The idea that legal rules – rules that are backed up by the state's coercive powers – should be justified in a way that can be accepted by people who hold different (or no) comprehensive theories is intuitively appealing and is supported by well-established theories of state action. However, aside from explaining this appeal and support, I do not directly defend the idea here. My answer to the second question ('does the acceptability thesis apply to academics?') is therefore tentative. But – and this qualification brings me to this chapter's third major theme – it is tentative only insofar as we restrict our focus to scholarship whose sole concern is to justify legal rules. The qualification is important. Legal scholars who defend comprehensive justifications typically present them not as standalone justifications but rather as part of broader explanatory (or 'interpretive') legal theories. In such work, comprehensive justifications do not merely justify legal rules: they also explain them. For such theories, the judiciary's reluctance to invoke comprehensive moral theories raises a problem, regardless of its substantive merits. The subject matter of explanatory theories is, or at least should be, not just the law's rules, but also its understanding of those rules. That understanding, which the judiciary's justificatory practices reflect, is deeply at odds with comprehensive justifications. The significance of this inconsistency, I argue, is that explanatory theories that invoke comprehensive justifications run the risk of transforming the law into something unrecognisable.

The chapter is in three parts. In the first part, I describe the circumstances in which judges offer justifications for legal rules and defend my claim that those justifications are typically limited to intermediate principles. In the second part, I ask why judges limit themselves to intermediate justifications, and conclude that, while the practice is defensible on practical grounds, it is also defensible as a matter of principle. Specifically, it is defensible on the principle that justifications for legal rules should be acceptable to those to whom the rules apply. Finally, in the third part, I discuss the implications of this conclusion for academic justifications for legal rules, including justifications that form part of broader explanatory legal theories.

if implicitly and unconsciously), ground their determinations of even the most technical legal issues in a comprehensive moral theory: R Dworkin, *Law's Empire* (Cambridge, MA, Belknap Press, 1986) 240–50. Like Dworkin, I argue that judges and academics are engaged in the same task when they justify legal rules. However, my conclusion is essentially the reverse of Dworkin's. I not only argue that judges do not, and should not, adopt comprehensive moral theories, but also argue, albeit more tentatively, that legal philosophers should follow their lead.

This chapter makes a number of arguments in a relatively short space. It may be useful to mention in advance three arguments that it does not make. First, I do not argue that justifying legal rules is a preoccupation, let alone the exclusive task, of judges or legal academics. Most judges and academics spend little, if any, time trying to justify legal rules. Second, I do not argue that the rules of the Canadian legal system, or of any other legal system, are in fact justified, whether on the basis of intermediate principles, comprehensive theories, or on any other ground. My concern is for the form of judicial and academic justifications, not their truth. Third, I do not argue that most people, let alone all people, endorse comprehensive moral theories. Many people reject entirely the idea that morality could be the subject of a comprehensive theory, while others – probably the majority – never think about comprehensive moral theories at all.

My final preliminary comments are terminological. To avoid constant qualifications, I will refer to comprehensive 'views' when I want to refer to individuals' overall positions vis-à-vis comprehensive theories. Thus, while one possible comprehensive view is a belief in, for instance, utilitarianism, another possible view is to reject not just utilitarianism but all comprehensive moral theories. Individuals who hold the latter position, have a comprehensive view (the 'anti-theory' view), but they do not support a comprehensive theory.

I have framed this chapter as an exploration of justifications for 'legal rules', but its arguments apply equally to justifications for 'legal rights' (or 'duties', 'powers', etc). For convenience, I sometimes refer to 'the law' rather than 'legal rules', but I am not concerned with justifications for 'the law in general' (or for large parts of the law, for example, private law). Although academics often invoke comprehensive views when they offer justifications for the law in general – and most of what I say about comprehensive views applies to such work (with minor qualifications) – judges almost never try to justify the law in general. Finally, while some of my claims about judicial practice fit private law cases better than public law cases, for the most part my arguments apply equally to both private and public law. The only qualification is that I focus on judicial and academic justifications for legal rules in contemporary pluralist societies, such as Canada, England, or the United States. Further, certain of my claims about judgments and legal scholarship turn on their specific form and status in common law jurisdictions.

I. Judicial Justifications

Justifications for legal rules are moral justifications. Human activities, creations, institutions and so forth, are justified if they are good, valuable, appropriate, etc. In the case of legal rules – rules that stipulate rights, duties, powers and liabilities, and that are backed up by coercive sanctions – good means morally good. If legal rules are justified, they are justified on moral grounds. This proposition applies equally to rules that solve coordination problems. Moral considerations may not determine which side of the road we should drive upon, but there are obvious moral reasons for having a law that specifies that we should drive on one side or the other. Such a law helps to minimise accidents while facilitating movement. Insofar as laws solve, or help to solve, socially significant coordination problems, they can be justified on moral grounds.

From the law's perspective (and so from the perspective of judges when they act in their official capacity), legal rules are presumed to be justified. To say – as judges regularly say – that there is a 'duty to do X', is to say that, all things considered, X should be done.[2] In other words, it is to say that X is morally required. Of course, the existence of a legal duty to do X does not mean that, all things considered, X should actually be done. The law may be mistaken. This possibility explains why it is sometimes morally justified to ignore the law. But judges never adopt this view, or at least they never adopt it when they are acting in their official capacity. They never suggest that individuals should break the law. From the judicial perspective, to say there is a 'legal duty to do X' is the same as saying that there is a 'duty to do X'.

However, presuming that legal rules are justified is not the same as justifying them. For judges to justify a legal rule they must actually provide a justification, that is, they must explain the grounds on which the rule is justified. Judges rarely provide such justifications, at least explicitly. In most cases, the rules that judges apply are settled rules – rules that have been established by precedent or legislation – and judges generally assume that settled rules need no justification. In such cases, judges typically limit themselves to ascertaining the relevant facts, identifying the relevant rule and then applying that rule to the facts. Judges normally provide reasons at each stage in this process, but they do not offer them to justify the rules that they apply. They simply presume that these rules are justified.

Even when judges are developing the law – for example, by filling a gap, resolving an uncertainty or overturning or limiting a precedent – they rarely justify those developments, at least directly. In most cases, judges develop new rules by extending established rules. They present the new rule as, broadly, a logical extension of rules that already exist. Like the closely related practice of confirming established law, the practice of extending established law is not itself a justification for the rules that these practices apply or develop, at least if nothing more

[2] This is true even when, as occasionally happens, judges say that they wish the law did not contain a particular rule. In such cases, the judge is effectively saying that notwithstanding certain defects in the existing law, it is on balance preferable for reasons of roughly, predictability, coherence, consistency, democratic values, and the like, for the law to remain as it is. In other words, the judge is saying that, notwithstanding that the law is imperfect in certain respects, departing from the doctrine of stare decisis or ignoring a legislative enactment would make the law more imperfect or would be undesirable for broader systemic reasons. For example, reforming the law might require the court to ignore the decision of a democratically elected legislature, or it might require the kind of wholesale reform of a broad area of law that can generally only be brought about effectively by legislation. See generally J Gardner, 'How Law Claims, What Law Claims' in J Gardner, *Law as a Leap of Faith* (Oxford, Oxford University Press, 2012) 142; J Raz, 'The Inner Logic of the Law' in J Raz, *Ethics in the Public Domain* (Oxford, Oxford University Press, 1994) 240.

is said. These practices are techniques for identifying and developing the law. To be sure, there are well-known justifications for confirming and extending established law. Indeed, the justifications are basically the same for both practices, as I explain below. Most judges would no doubt refer to these justifications if they were asked to defend the practices. Still, assuming a justification is not the same as providing one.

In some cases, however, judges provide justifications for legal rules. These justifications are of two kinds. First, judges sometimes invoke what I will call 'everyday moral principles' – principles like fairness, dignity, honesty, autonomy, reasonableness, keeping one's word and proportionality – to justify or help justify rules that they are developing or confirming. In *Jacobi v Griffiths*, for example, Chief Justice McLachlin wrote, 'Our ultimate goal is a rule of vicarious liability that is fair to the plaintiff, the defendant, and society'.[3] It is true that in many (but not all) cases, judges offer such justifications as part of the practice of extending or interpreting established rules. In such cases, the judges first hold that the established rules give effect to a certain principle, and then they develop or (particularly in the case of legislation) interpret the law using this principle. Still, if the principle is a moral principle, then it is also, at the same time, a justification; indeed, it is justification not just for the new rule but also for the existing rule.

Second, judges sometimes invoke 'rule-of-law' principles, such as predictability, stability, coherence, clarity and non-retroactivity, when they are developing the law (or refusing to adopt a proposed development). Judges typically invoke such principles to explain why they are confirming or extending established rules, but they also invoke rule-of-law principles to justify correcting perceived inconsistencies in the existing law. For example, in justifying the introduction of a broader duty of good faith into Canadian law in *Bhasin v Hrynew*, Cromwell J wrote that 'it is time to take two incremental steps in order to make the common law less unsettled and piecemeal, more coherent and more just'.[4] It is true that the rule-of-law principles are principles specifically for developing and promulgating rules employed in legal and other rule-based normative systems. Still, rule-of-law principles provide

[3] *Jacobi v Griffiths* [1999] 2 SCR 570 [24]. Other examples include *Ira S Bushey v United States of America* 398 F2d 167 (2d Cir 1968), 172 (Friendly J) ('Consequently, we can no longer accept our past decisions that have refused to move beyond the *Nelson* rule … since they do not accord with modern understanding as to when it is fair for an enterprise to disclaim the actions of its employees'); *McFarlane v Tayside Health Board* [2002] 2 AC 59, 108 (Lord Millet) ('The court is engaged in a search for justice, and this demands that the dispute be resolved in a way which is fair and reasonable and accords with ordinary notions of what is fit and proper'); and *Campbell v MGN Ltd* [2004] 2 AC 457, 473 [51] (Hoffmann J), ('[T]he new approach takes a different view of the underlying value which the law protects. … it focuses upon the protection of human autonomy and dignity').

[4] *Bhasin v Hrynew* [2014] 3 SCR 494 [33]. See also *Bow Valley Husky (Bermuda) Ltd v Saint John Shipbuilding Ltd* [1997] 3 SCR 1210 [50] (McLachlin J) ('courts should not assiduously seek new categories; what is required is a clear rule predicting when recovery is available'); *Hedley Byrne & Co Ltd v Heller & Partners Ltd* [1964] AC 465, 525 (Lord Devlin) ('As always in English law the first step in such an inquiry is to see how far the authorities have gone, for new categories in the law do not spring into existence overnight').

justifications – moral justifications – for the rules that they explain. Exceptional cases aside, a retroactive law is, on its face, a bad law. More generally, rules that are stable, predictable, consistent and publicly available are preferable to rules that are unstable, unpredictable, inconsistent and unknowable. Aside from the practical benefit of not having to re-invent the wheel in every case, compliance with the rule-of-law principles makes it easier for citizens and legal officials to use the law as a guide. This benefit is particularly significant in the many cases where, if the courts were starting from a blank slate, there would be more than one acceptable direction in which they could develop the law. In such cases, the practice of extending the existing law can provide a predictable, non-arbitrary, solution. Even where the existing law might appear to offer little guidance, it nearly always offers some guidance, and so can limit the instances where judges might otherwise be at liberty to, in effect, toss a coin. More broadly, the rule-of-law principles help to ensure that like cases are decided alike. Of course, the existing law sometimes has little to commend it. In such cases, judges should, and often do, strike a new path (and when they do this, they typically invoke everyday moral concepts of the kind mentioned above to justify the new path). However, in a system where it is presumed that legal rules are generally justified – as our judges, in their official capacity, must necessarily presume – confirming and extending the established law is, in general, entirely appropriate.

Finally, while judges typically assume the validity of legislation without comment, they occasionally justify that assumption. They do this most often in cases where they are contemplating whether, and to what extent, legislation displaces the established, typically judge-made, law. The justification invariably offered (or at least alluded to) for affirming or extending legislation is the principle of parliamentary sovereignty and, more broadly, that of democratic rule. For example, in *Home Office v Dorset Yachet Co Ltd*, Lord Diplock wrote:

> So long as Parliament is content to leave the general risk of damage from criminal acts to lie where it falls without any remedy except against the criminal himself, the courts would be exceeding their limited function in developing the common law to meet changing conditions if they were to recognise a duty of care to prevent criminals escaping from penal custody owed to a wider category of members of the public …[5]

A. Judicial Justifications are Intermediate Justifications

The distinction that I have drawn between, on the one hand, identifying and applying legal rules and, on the other hand, justifying legal rules, is of course more complex than my brief comments suggest. One complication is that courts invoke everyday moral principles not just as justifications for rules, but also (and indeed

[5] *Home Office v Dorset Yachet Co Ltd* [1970] AC 1004, 1070.

far more frequently) as part of a rule's substance. For example, many legal rules require courts to consider whether a particular action was 'reasonable' or whether imposing liability would be 'fair'. Another complication is that the rule-of-law justifications for confirming and extending established law are so well known that it is arguable that they are implied – that they go without saying – in any judgment where legal rules are confirmed or extended. The same is true of the democratic justification for recognising legislation. However, for the purposes of my argument, it is not necessary to determine how often, or in what circumstances, judges provide justifications for legal rules. It is sufficient that they do this at least sometimes. My concern is the nature, or more strictly the form, of these justifications, whenever judges offer them.

The distinguishing feature of judicial justifications for legal rules, at least so far as their form is concerned, is that they are almost always expressed in terms of intermediate moral principles.[6] The examples that I mentioned above all fall into this category. The everyday moral principles of fairness, dignity, honesty, reasonableness, autonomy, keeping one's word and proportionality are intermediate principles. So too are the principles associated with the rule of law, such as predictability, stability, clarity and non-retroactivity.[7] The same is true of the democratic justification for recognising legislation. These principles are intermediate because, on the one hand, they are more general than the particular rules that they are employed to justify. Judges invoke fairness, dignity, non-retroactivity and so forth, in a variety of contexts. On the other hand, they are narrower than the foundational principle or principles that define comprehensive moral theories. The best-known foundational principles in the legal literature are the 'utilitarian' principle of maximising overall social utility (where 'utility' typically refers to something like the satisfaction of individual preferences) and the 'Kantian' principle of prioritising individual rights, in particular an individual's right to be independent from the choices of others. These principles provide standards for evaluating most, if not all, legal rules (which is why the theories are 'comprehensive').[8]

[6] Versions of this claim have been advanced by various writers, including Sunstein (n 1) and Gerald Postema. The common law's search for 'common reason', Postema writes, 'explains in part the willingness of a common law judge to seek only local coherence, rather than broad theoretical coherence of a single moral vision or systematic rationality … [the] law, common lawyers maintained, is not concerned with the moral vision of any individual, however soundly argued it may seem to be, but rather with the convergence of the views and judgments of the larger community, and forging and maintaining a common sense of reasonableness': G Postema, 'Philosophy of the Common Law' in JL Coleman, KE Himma and SJ Shapiro (eds), *The Oxford Handbook of Jurisprudence and Philosophy of Law* (Oxford, Oxford University Press, 2004) 7.

[7] This category of reasons supports highly complex and over-arching judicial accounts of the law's structure. For example, courts may rely on a general theory of the law's structure to determine if a particular claim should be assessed using contract law rather than tort law principles. Such theories are comprehensive, but they are not comprehensive moral theories.

[8] I describe foundational principles as providing standards to evaluate rules as opposed to standards to produce rules because some comprehensive theories, including Kantian theories, suppose that, in respect of certain legal issues, there is more than one acceptable legal solution. In such cases, the theory tells law-makers *how* to come up with a rule – roughly, choose from among the following options – but it does not tell them which rule to affirm.

Of course, principles can be more, or less, intermediate, while theories (and the foundational principles that define them) can be more, or less, comprehensive. Further, intermediate principles are often justified on the ground that they give effect to foundational principles, while foundational principles are often justified on the ground that they explain intermediate principles.[9] From the perspective of comprehensive theories, intermediate principles are intermediate because they mediate between foundational principles and particular rules. I discuss these links in more detail below. For the moment, it is sufficient if it is accepted that judges rarely justify legal rules on the basis of utilitarianism, Kantianism or any other similarly comprehensive moral theory. Nor do they justify legal rules on the basis of the anti-theory comprehensive view, that is, on the basis of the view that rejects comprehensive theories entirely.[10] Judges simply do not raise comprehensive views; instead, they rely on intermediate principles, such as fairness, reasonableness, consistency and predictability. There are exceptions, but they are rare, and they usually involve only passing mention of comprehensive views. The important question is not whether judges limit themselves to intermediate principles, but why they limit themselves and whether their reasons for doing so also apply to academics.

II. Why do Judges Limit Themselves to Intermediate Justifications?

The judiciary's practice of limiting itself to intermediate justifications for legal rules is explicable in terms of two objections – one 'practical' and one 'principled' – to comprehensive justifications.

A. The Practical Objection[11]

The practical objection to judges advancing comprehensive justifications is not, as might be assumed, that judges are not philosophers. If it were thought important to ground the law in a comprehensive moral view, judges could be required to familiarise themselves with such views in their judicial training or legal studies. And it would not be necessary for judges to construct a comprehensive

[9] Depending on one's comprehensive view, some or all intermediate principles might be regarded as foundational in the sense that they are not derived from a deeper principle. Fairness or dignity, for example, might be understood as 'bedrock' principles. But even if it turns out that fairness and dignity are bedrock principles, they are not comprehensive moral theories, at least as they are used by judges. Judges invoke these concepts to justify a relatively narrow range of legal rules.

[10] Not discussing comprehensive theories is not the same as defending the anti-theory view. To support the law on an anti-theory view, judges must do so explicitly.

[11] For a more detailed explanation of the practical objection, see Sunstein (n 1).

view from scratch: academics have already developed the most plausible candidates in detail and explained how they apply to the law. Further, not all judges would need to be equally familiar with the details of rival comprehensive moral views. Comprehensive moral views are mutually exclusive: one cannot be both a Kantian and a utilitarian.[12] The highest court would therefore need to decide upon 'the' comprehensive view for the law. In time, lawyers and judges would become familiar with this view; in particular, they would become familiar with its legal implications. Eventually, the view's contours and applications would become as commonplace to lawyers and judges as concepts such as 'contract' or 'property' are today.[13]

The main practical objection to judges invoking a comprehensive moral view to justify legal rules is that any such view would be controversial and, as such, fail to attract the support necessary for the law to operate effectively. If judges were to justify legal rules on the basis of a comprehensive moral view, the judges of the highest court would need to agree on which comprehensive moral view to adopt. Such an agreement would be difficult – to put the point mildly – to reach. The common law jurisdictions that are my focus are pluralist societies. Like the citizens, the judges in such societies hold a variety of comprehensive views. It is true that judges have special reasons to reach agreement on matters on which they may have initially been in disagreement. Judges are required to resolve the disputes before them and, more generally, to develop the law in a coherent fashion – and they must frequently do this as part of a group. But reaching agreement on a comprehensive view is different than reaching agreement on the kinds of issues that judges typically address, including (for reasons I explain in a moment), issues concerning intermediate principles. Legal academics, moral philosophers, theologians and ordinary citizens have disagreed about the merits of comprehensive views for hundreds if not thousands of years. These differences persist because disagreements over comprehensive views are typically more profound than ordinary disagreements. For most people, their comprehensive views reflect deeply held, foundational convictions. Traditionally (and still commonly) these convictions are religious, but even where they are not religious, they are usually based on deeply ingrained beliefs about the meaning of life. It is true that philosophers are often able to discuss amiably the respective merits of Bentham, Kant and so forth, in classrooms, at conferences and in their writings. But philosophers are not required to reach agreement on those merits, much less reach an agreement that will be enshrined in the law.

[12] It may be possible to construct a comprehensive theory that integrates principles drawn from both Kantianism and utilitarianism: see D Parfit, *On What Matters*, Volume 1 (Oxford, Oxford University Press, 2011). But the resulting theory is neither a Kantian theory nor a utilitarian theory.

[13] Closely related to the 'judges are not philosophers' objection is the objection that if judges justified legal rules on the basis of comprehensive moral views, their judgments, and the legal arguments that precede judgments, would become unduly long and complex. An increase in the length and complexity of judgments is a small price to pay if it is important in principle for the law to be justified using a comprehensive view.

It would be difficult, therefore, for judges to reach agreement on a comprehensive view. But even if judges could reach such an agreement, the controversial nature of comprehensive views creates a related problem. For a legal system to operate effectively, the judges, lawyers and other legal officials responsible for its operations must largely accept its rules. The rules must also largely be accepted by those who are their main subject – citizens. Of course, legal officials typically develop, follow and apply legal rules because their job requires them to do this. But the efforts they apply to these tasks are influenced by their acceptance, or lack thereof, of those rules. For their part, citizens usually comply with the law not because it is the law (the details of which they may be unaware), but because the law's directives coincide with their own inclinations. Still, citizens are sometimes inclined to act in ways that are contrary to the law. The law can, and does, impose sanctions to dissuade such acts, but effective sanctions are costly to implement and, largely for this reason, are often of limited effectiveness. In practice, legal rules are immeasurably more effective if their subjects are inclined to follow them, and they will be more inclined to follow them if they agree with the justifications offered to support them. The law is most effective where it is internalised both by those who apply it and those to whom it is applied.[14]

Thus, even if courts could reach agreement on a comprehensive moral view, many legal officials and citizens would have no allegiance towards that view. As a consequence, the law would become less effective. It is true that judicial decisions are often controversial; courts regularly reach decisions that significant numbers of legal officials and citizens disagree with. But in most cases, these disagreements are over the court's interpretation of the facts or its application to those facts of broadly accepted principles. Such disagreements typically have a limited effect on the disagreeing individuals' general support for the law. As already noted, disagreements that arise in respect of comprehensive moral views are different. They are both more common (because of the wide range of possible comprehensive views) and, typically, more profound (because of the importance that people attach to their comprehensive views).

The practical problems that would arise if judges attempted to invoke comprehensive justifications do not arise, or at least arise less often and less significantly, if judges confine themselves to intermediate justifications. It is easier for judges to agree on intermediate justifications, and, more broadly, easier for legal officials

[14] See, eg, R Cooter, 'Models of Morality in Law and Economics: Self-Control and Self-Improvement for the Bad Man of Holmes' (1998) 78 *Boston University Law Review* 903, 904. It might be thought that this explanation renders the law irrelevant. If legal rules are based on justifications that citizens accept, won't citizens do what those rules require regardless of whether they exist? The law remains relevant in this scenario for two main reasons. First, the law provides guidance in the many cases where it solves coordination problems or otherwise makes determinate indeterminate moral standards. Second, most of us are prone to moral weakness ('akrasia'): individuals frequently commit acts that they believe to be morally wrong (or that they would agree are wrong if they stopped to think about the morality of what they were doing). The existence of a law can remind of us our moral duties and provide a further reason for complying with those duties.

and citizens generally to support intermediate justifications because people who hold different comprehensive views can accept the same intermediate justifications. To be sure, not every possible intermediate justification is consistent with every possible comprehensive view. The broad definitions that I offered of these concepts allow for extreme examples. My claim is that the kinds of intermediate justifications that the courts invoke are consistent with the most commonly held comprehensive views. Indeed, if my arguments are correct, this overlap is exactly what we should expect. The reasons that (according to my arguments) judges justify the law on the basis of intermediate principles are also reasons for them to justify the law on the basis of intermediate principles that are widely accepted. Judges are unlikely to try to justify the law using an intermediate principle that is endorsed only by a narrow range of comprehensive views because few judges will agree with it, few citizens will accept it and (as I explain in the next section) it will not actually justify the rule that it purports to justify.

In practice, nearly every comprehensive view holds that it is wrong to lie, steal or carelessly injure others. Similarly, nearly every comprehensive view accepts that the law should generally be predictable, stable, prospective and so forth. This overlap explains why academics are able to offer prima facie plausible explanations of the law that are based on radically different comprehensive moral views. Utilitarians and Kantians give different explanations for why lying, stealing and carelessly injuring others is undesirable, but each agrees that they are undesirable. To be sure, academics who explain the law on the basis of utilitarian or Kantian comprehensive theories typically (though not invariably) argue that their theory alone can explain the law. But, at least in respect of the private law rules that I am familiar with, it is difficult to think of a single significant rule that it is explicable only on the basis of one of these theories. I cannot defend this claim here (though I have defended it elsewhere in respect of contract law rules).[15] However, the popularity and persistence of these rival legal theories (and their parallel popularity and persistence as explanations of conventional moral rules) suggests, at a minimum, that they overlap significantly at the level of intermediate principles.

There are exceptions. Judges sometimes rely on principles that appear to be tightly linked to a specific comprehensive view or a closely related set of comprehensive views. These exceptions arise most commonly in criminal law and constitutional law cases, particularly in criminal and constitutional cases that raise political issues such as abortion, euthanasia or animal rights. In such cases, almost any approach, including doing nothing, is likely to be inconsistent with some common comprehensive views (though even in these cases judges normally try to justify their decisions on grounds that, in principle, can be accepted by individuals with different comprehensive views, for example, on jurisdictional

[15] SA Smith, *Contract Theory* (Oxford, Oxford University Press, 2004) chs 5–11.

grounds). It is precisely for this reason that, today, it is typically the legislature, not the judiciary, that develops the law in these areas.[16]

Finally, the application of intermediate principles to particular cases is, of course, not a mechanical exercise. Different people have different views as to what 'fairness' requires in particular situations. It follows that individuals holding different comprehensive viewpoints who accept that, say, fairness is important, may nonetheless disagree with the courts' view of what fairness requires in a particular case. Still, when judges invoke concepts like fairness to justify the law, they do not purport to be invoking a special interpretation of the concept. They do not invoke fairness with quotation marks around the term. The concept that judges purport to rely upon is the shared concept. Successfully or not, they are attempting to justify the law on the basis of a concept that individuals holding different comprehensive views can in principle accept.

These observations could be expanded, but the substance of my argument should be familiar. If you want people who hold comprehensive views that differ from your own to agree with you, it is advisable to rest your arguments on the narrowest and least controversial propositions possible. More broadly, if you want to guide behaviour in a pluralist society, it is advisable to do so on the basis of low-level generalisations. It has long been recognised that social rules, both legal and non-legal, operate in this way.[17] The same observation applies to justifications for rules, at least insofar as authoritative institutions publicly endorse those justifications. In Cass Sunstein's words: 'When the authoritative rationale for the result is disconnected from abstract theories of the good or the right, the losers can submit to legal obligations, even if reluctantly, without being forced to renounce their deepest ideals.'[18]

B. The Principled Objection

There is a practical reason, then, for judges to limit themselves to intermediate justifications. But if this were the only reason, we would not expect the practice to

[16] Within private law, many of the rules that would be difficult to justify, except on the basis of a controversial intermediate principle, are legislative. However, courts do not need to invoke such principles to justify legislative rules: the justification for such rules, at least so far as the courts are concerned, lies in the democratic process by which they were created. As noted above, there remain situations where it is not possible to justify whatever decision a court makes, including making no decision, other than on the basis of a controversial intermediate principle. Such situations are relatively rare, particularly in private law litigation.

[17] '(The existence of social rules) enables people to unite in support of some "low or medium level generalizations despite profound disagreements concerning their ultimate foundations, which some seek in religion, others in Marxism or in Liberalism, etc. I am not suggesting that the differences in the foundations do not lead to differences in practice. The point is that an orderly community can exist only if it shares many practices, and that in all modern pluralistic societies a great measure of toleration of vastly differing outlooks is made possible by the fact that many of them enable the vast majority of the population to accept common standards of conduct.': J Raz, *The Morality of Freedom* (Oxford, Oxford University Press, 1986) 58.

[18] Sunstein (n 1) 1748.

be so uniform. If it were important in principle for judges to offer comprehensive justifications, we would expect some judges to do this or at least to explain why they are not doing it. And it might be thought that it is important in principle to ground legal rules in a comprehensive view. All else being equal, grounding a rule in a comprehensive view would seem to provide a more solid justification for the rule than grounding it only in an intermediate principle.

But all else may not be equal. A compelling argument can be made – I make no stronger claim here – that as a matter of principle judges should limit themselves to intermediate justifications for legal rules. The 'principled argument' is that justifications based on a comprehensive moral view cannot in fact justify legal rules. The idea underlying this argument is that to justify legal rules – rules that the state will coercively enforce – the justification must be one that those subject to the law could in principle endorse. The law should be justifiable to those subject to its coercive powers. This requirement does not mean, of course, that the law must be justifiable to every person. However, at a minimum, it should be justifiable to reasonable people. And whatever the boundaries of this category, in a pluralist society it must encompass individuals who hold different comprehensive views. Again, this does not require that the law be justifiable from every comprehensive view. However, at a minimum, it should be justifiable from a range of comprehensive views, including those that are most often advanced to explain and justify legal rules. Reasonable people hold utilitarian comprehensive views, Kantian comprehensive views and comprehensive views that reject comprehensive theories generally. The principled argument holds that a good justification for a legal rule should be acceptable to all of these people. And for the reasons explained in the previous section, the only kinds of justifications that are likely to satisfy this standard are intermediate justifications. By definition, a justification that is based on a single comprehensive view will only be acceptable to people who hold that view.

The principled objection to judges advancing comprehensive justifications is closely related to the practical objection. Each objection claims that a good justification for the law should be acceptable to the law's subjects, and each claims that comprehensive justifications fail this standard. However, they differ in three respects.

First, the practical objection focusses as much on the acceptability of judicial justifications to other judges as it does on their acceptability to the population at large. In contrast, the principled objection focuses exclusively on the acceptability of judicial justifications to those whom the law may coerce, which, in practice, means citizens. Exceptional cases aside, judges only fall into this group when they are acting as citizens. Second, while the practical objection focuses on whether judges could actually agree on a comprehensive justification and, in a similar vein, whether citizens could actually accept such a justification, the principled objection focuses on hypothetical acceptance.[19] The principled objection holds that

[19] Drawing, here, on a long tradition of 'social contract' theories of legitimacy: see generally J Waldron, 'Theoretical Foundations of Liberalism' (1987) 37(147) *The Philosophical Quarterly* 127, 138–40.

a justification for the law succeeds as a justification *if* citizens who have different comprehensive views could accept it. The objection therefore focusses on the substantive merits of judicial justifications, not on their effect in the world. It asks whether justifications for legal rules could be accepted by their subjects in order to assess the substance of those justifications, not because hypothetical acceptance matters in itself. This second difference leads directly to the third and most important difference. The practical objection reflects a concern for the *effectiveness* of legal rules; the principled objection reflects a concern for their *legitimacy*. The principled objection is that the legitimacy of legal rules depends on their being acceptable to individuals holding different comprehensive views.

In discussing the practical objection, I argued that citizens with different comprehensive views can nonetheless join in accepting the same intermediate justifications. More strictly, I argued that citizens who hold different reasonable comprehensive views can join in accepting the kinds of intermediate justifications that judges typically rely upon when they justify legal rules. If this argument is valid, the hypothetical consent to intermediate justifications that is required by the principled objection is also possible. If citizens can *actually* accept justifications invoked by the courts, they can also *hypothetically* accept them. Admittedly, judges do not try to prove that the intermediate justifications they invoke are acceptable from different comprehensive viewpoints. But it seems clear that they assume this consistency. By allowing intermediate principles to stand on their own, that is, by not offering further justifications for intermediate principles, the implication is that these principles are widely accepted. If it were not assumed that the principles are widely accepted, courts would provide justifications for them. This implication may be unwarranted, but, in practice, the kinds of intermediate principles that courts rely upon are familiar, widely shared and consistent with most comprehensive views. As I noted earlier, this overlap is not a coincidence: the reason that judges invoke intermediate principles in general (namely to provide widely acceptable justifications) is, at the same time, a reason to invoke widely accepted instances of such principles.

The fact that citizens who hold different comprehensive views can accept the same intermediate principles provides a principled reason, then, for judges to limit themselves to just such principles when they justify the law. It is also a familiar kind of reason. A standard method of justifying one's actions or views is appealing to principles that you believe you share with those you seek to convince.[20] But is the acceptability thesis a valid reason? Is it in fact the case that justifications for legal rules are only legitimate if they are acceptable to individuals holding different comprehensive views? As I noted earlier, a proper defence of the 'acceptability thesis' is outside this chapter's scope. Instead, I offer four comments.

[20] '(J)ustification is argument addressed to those who disagree with us, or to ourselves when we are of two minds … Being designed to reconcile by reason, justification proceeds from what all parties to the discussion hold in common': J Rawls, *A Theory of Justice* (Cambridge, MA, Harvard University Press, 1971) 580–81.

First, although the acceptability thesis is a general thesis about, broadly, the justification of state power, it is not a comprehensive moral view nor is it dependent on accepting such a view. Like intermediate principles, the thesis can be supported by citizens who hold different comprehensive views (though it may of course be rejected by some comprehensive views – which is why I offer these comments).

Second, the idea that coercive institutions should be justifiable to those whom they might coerce, and, in particular, that they should be justifiable to such people even when they hold different comprehensive views is a recurring theme in a wide range of contemporary political theories. Notably, this idea is a central theme in the work of John Rawls' and of many writers inspired by Rawls.[21] 'Our exercise of political power', Rawls wrote,

> is fully proper only when it is exercised in accordance with a constitution the essentials of which all citizens as free and equal may reasonably be expected to endorse in the light of principles and ideals acceptable to their common human reason.[22]

As in the acceptability thesis, in Rawls' model the aim is to identify principles that are acceptable to citizens who hold different comprehensive views. Rawls' model differs from the acceptability thesis in two main respects. First, for Rawls the object of the justificatory exercise is society's 'basic structure' (which in practice means its basic constitutional principles) rather than ordinary legal rules. Second, the hypothetical agreement – Rawls' 'overlapping consensus' – that justifies the basic structure is an agreement on higher-level abstract principles, not (as in the acceptability thesis) on lower-level intermediate principles. In theory, citizens with different comprehensive views might agree on both higher-order principles and intermediate principles, and, further, either form of agreement might be thought sufficient to justify the law. But it should be clear why judges focus on intermediate principles. Even assuming that it is possible to reach agreement on Rawls' higher-order abstract principles – principles that are more abstract than even the foundational principles that define comprehensive moral theories – these principles are unlikely to be of much help to judges trying to justify legal rules. Abstract principles might be capable of grounding a society's basic political structure, but to ground the kinds of detailed rules that judges use to resolve ordinary legal disputes requires narrower principles. There may be exceptions – the interpretation of a constitutional document or a basic constitutional principle might possibly be grounded directly on Rawls' abstract principles – but in the vast majority of cases, and certainly in the vast majority of private law cases, Rawls' principles are too abstract for judges. All that said, the basic idea motivating Rawls' approach – that

[21] J Rawls, *Political Liberalism* (New York City, Columbia University Press, 1993) Lectures 3 and 4. A sample of work by the other writers include Waldron (n 19); T Nagel, 'Moral Conflict and Political Legitimacy' (1987) 16 *Philosophy and Public Affairs* 218; J Cohen, 'Deliberation and Democratic Legitimacy' in A Hamlin and P Pettit (eds), *The Good Polity: Normative Analysis of the State* (Oxford, Basil Blackwell, 1989); A Gutmann and D Thompson, *Why Deliberative Democracy?* (Princeton, Princeton University Press, 2004).

[22] Rawls (n 21) 137.

state power should be justifiable in terms that citizens with different comprehensive views can accept – equally motivates the acceptability thesis.

The third comment is that if we reject the acceptability thesis, we must also reject judges' understandings of what they are doing when they justify the law and, more broadly, reject a central feature of the contemporary conception of law. Judges clearly presume that intermediate justifications are in principle sufficient and appropriate justifications. If we reject the acceptability thesis, this presumption becomes a puzzle. If intermediate justifications were only partial justifications, we would expect judges to go beyond them, or at least to try to explain (presumably on practical grounds) why they are not going beyond them. It is implausible to suppose that judges are involved in a massive conspiracy to misrepresent what they are doing, or that they are in the grip of an unseen force that compels them unwittingly to avoid comprehensive views.

It is of course possible that judges are simply confused. It is possible that they believe that they can justify the law using intermediate principles, but that they are mistaken. Clearly, judges, like anyone else, can be mistaken. But it is prima facie unlikely that judges are mistaken in their belief in intermediate justifications. The subject matter of this belief is a human activity (justifying the law), not a physical state of affairs; moreover, it is an activity in which judges themselves are central participants. Further, if the judges are mistaken in their belief in intermediate justifications, then they are mistaken not merely about what qualifies as a good justification in the abstract: they are also mistaken about what qualifies as a good justification for them. Judges offer justifications for legal rules not merely to convince the few citizens who read their judgments. They are also trying to justify the rules to other judges and, of course, to themselves. If they are mistaken about the acceptability thesis, then they are also mistaken in believing that they have justified the law to themselves. Again, this kind of mistake seems unlikely. Judges are sophisticated professionals; moreover, they are professionals whose job requires them to reflect constantly on the merits of legal rules. If we reject the acceptability thesis, we must assume that judges are collectively subject to a fundamental, persistent and pervasive cognitive error.

Finally, if we reject the acceptability thesis, we must also reject a central feature of the contemporary concept of law. The law is a self-reflective human practice. Our concept of law is in part a concept of that understanding.[23] Perhaps

[23] 'One feature of theories of law (common to philosophical accounts of action, morality and normative politics, among others) is that they deal with activities, attitudes, institutions and related phenomena which are themselves informed by some self-understanding, however imperfect. … In that way the theory of law is in part about the way those legal actors understand themselves and their actions. … And that is why we can say that the law makes certain claims for itself. Given that it is institutionalized, in that its norms can be changed and applied by institutions, and given that the institutions make certain statements and perform other speech acts in the course of their official actions, we can identify the presuppositions of those statements and actions': J Raz, *Between Authority and Interpretation* (Oxford, Oxford University Press, 2009) 2.

the most-discussed feature of law's self-understanding is its claim to authority.[24] Although the law may not in fact provide authoritative reasons for action, it necessarily purports to provide such reasons. If the law says we have a duty to do something, then, at least from the law's perspective, we necessarily have such a duty. As we have seen, however, the law not only claims to be justified; it also claims to be justified in a particular way. At least in the legal systems that are this chapter's focus, the law claims that it is justified on the basis of intermediate moral principles. And this claim is central to the concept of law in contemporary common law jurisdictions. Like other legal systems, the common law historically has been influenced by, and often intimately intertwined with, religious views, institutions and actors. However, it is central to the modern understanding of the common law that it is separate from religion. Part of our understanding of this separation focuses on institutional differences. The law is identified with coercion (though not, of course, only coercion), and the state has a monopoly on authorised coercion. In modern common law systems, only the state claims authority to imprison people or take away their property. But another, equally important, aspect of our understanding of the separation focuses on the law's normative commitments. Religious normative systems are nearly always expressions of comprehensive moral theories. The law's refusal to endorse a comprehensive moral theory is critical to its understanding of itself as separate from religion. The courts stand back from endorsing the comprehensive views that define religious normative orders. I am not suggesting that utilitarianism or Kantianism are religious theories (though I am tempted …). However, they are similar in their reliance on a single foundational idea (or small set of foundational ideas) and, of course, in their comprehensiveness. The courts' refusal to endorse these and other similarly comprehensive views is inseparable from our understanding of law as separate from religion. Stated differently, the acceptability thesis is closely related to the familiar idea that one of the central functions of the law, at least in its modern form, is to allow individuals with different religious convictions to live together. The acceptability thesis merely expands 'religious convictions' to include all comprehensive moral views.

III. Scholarly Justifications

Most legal scholarship does not seek to justify legal rules, much less to justify rules on the basis of a comprehensive moral view. Most legal scholarship focusses on non-justificatory tasks such as describing the law, tracing its history, uncovering its social roots or criticising it. Unlike judges, academics are at liberty to argue that legal rules are not justified. And when academics offer justifications

[24] See J Raz, 'Authority, Law, and Morality' in Raz (n 2).

for legal rules, they often offer the same kinds of arguments that courts offer. Like judges, academics frequently justify legal rules on the basis of intermediate justifications.[25]

However, some academics provide justifications for legal rules that invoke comprehensive moral views. In practice, the best-known and most developed comprehensive justifications are found in scholarship whose primary aim is to explain (or 'interpret') legal rules. For example, economist-lawyers such as Richard Posner (at least in his early work) have argued that most legal rules have a utilitarian foundation.[26] Posner clearly approved of this foundation, but his primary aim, it appeared, was to explain legal rules. Similarly, writers such as Charles Fried, Ernest Weinrib, Arthur Ripstein and Alan Beever have argued that most legal rules have a Kantian (or 'rights-based') foundation.[27] Like Posner, these writers clearly approve of this foundation, but, again, the primary aim of their best-known works is to explain legal rules, not to justify them. Nonetheless, these authors undoubtedly provide justifications for legal rules. Both utilitarianism and Kantianism are moral theories. Each provides standards that, assuming the theory is valid, can be used, inter alia, to develop and evaluate legal rules. The same is true of other comprehensive views that academics employ to explain legal rules. It is of course possible to argue that while the rules that we have reflect a particular comprehensive moral theory, this theory does not actually justify those rules. Academics often argue that legal rules are grounded in impoverished moral views. However, the best-known and most influential efforts to explain legal rules using comprehensive moral views do not take this stance. In particular, the academics who argue that the law reflects a utilitarian or Kantian morality invariably support that morality.[28]

Much more could be said about the kinds of justifications that particular authors offer (or do not offer) for legal rules. But whatever the outcome of such an exercise, it is, I trust, uncontroversial that at least some academics provide justifications for legal rules and, further, that some of these justifications invoke comprehensive moral views. The question is what we should make of this practice. In particular, what should we make of the fact that judges adopt a different practice?

Prima facie, the difference is puzzling. It is true that academics are not obliged even to consider justificatory questions. And when they consider them, they are

[25] See, eg: P Birks, *Unjust Enrichment*, 2nd edn (Oxford, Oxford University Press, 2005). Birks also criticised the law, but he grounded his criticisms in intermediate principles.

[26] 'The theory is that the common law is best (not perfectly) explained as a system for maximizing the wealth of society': R Posner, *Economic Analysis of Law*, 5th edn, (Boston, Little, Brown, 1998) 27.

[27] C Fried, *Contract as Promise* (Cambridge, MA, Harvard University Press, 1981); EJ Weinrib, *The Idea of Private Law* (Cambridge, MA, Harvard University Press, 1995); A Ripstein, *Force and Freedom* (Cambridge, MA, Harvard University Press, 2009); A Beever, *A Theory of Tort Liability* (Oregon, Hart Publishing, 2016). Non-Kantian rights-based theories include, A Brudner, *The Unity of the Common Law* (Oxford, Oxford University Press, 2013); Dworkin (n 1); P Benson, *Justice in Transactions* (Cambridge, MA, Harvard University Press, 2019).

[28] See nn 26 and 27 above.

free to conclude that legal rules are unjustified. However, insofar as academics provide justifications for legal rules, they are in the same position, at least so far as the principled objection to comprehensive justifications is concerned, as judges.[29] If judicial justifications for legal rules should be acceptable to citizens with different comprehensive views, then academic justifications for legal rules should be similarly acceptable. A justification succeeds or fails regardless of who offers it. The reasons underlying the acceptability thesis are not just reasons for judges: they are reasons for anyone trying to justify legal rules.

From the perspective of academics defending comprehensive justifications, the most straightforward explanation for this difference is simply that judges are mistaken. The strongest justifications for legal rules, in this view, are justifications grounded in a comprehensive view. For reasons that I have already explained, I have doubts about this view. I will not repeat those reasons here, but instead add one final comment.

As I mentioned above, the best-known and most developed comprehensive justifications for legal rules are found within theories whose overall aim is to explain legal rules. The academics defending such theories seek not only to justify legal rules, but also to explain why they have the features that they have. However, one of these features is the judges' practice of justifying rules using intermediate justifications, and only intermediate justifications. Admittedly, this practice, standing alone, does not raise an issue for explanatory theories that have rejected the acceptability thesis. The rejection of this thesis eliminates the principled explanation for the practice, but it leaves untouched the practical explanation. The practical importance of securing agreement amongst judges and support from the populace at large – considerations that apply primarily to judges – can explain why judges limit themselves to intermediate justifications. But these considerations cannot explain why judges do not explain the practice in this way. Judges do not present intermediate justifications as incomplete justifications; as justifications that they have curtailed for practical reasons. They present them as sufficient justifications. Moreover, that presentation, I have suggested, is closely tied up with our – judges and citizens alike – understanding of law as distinct from religious and other comprehensive normative systems. The hurdle for an explanatory theory of legal rules that rejects the acceptability thesis, then, is not just that one of the things it must explain is why judges are mistaken to endorse the thesis. The hurdle is that it must reject as mistaken a characteristic feature of the very thing that it is trying to explain. In other words, such a theory runs the risk that its explanation will show legal rules to be so different from our understanding of them that it ceases to be an explanation of legal rules at all.

[29] The practical objection has limited force in respect of academic writings. At least in the common law world, academic justifications for the law are unlikely to have much effect on judges and citizens' attitudes towards the law. And there is nothing equivalent in academia to the judicial need to reach actual agreement with other judges. Academics may want to convince other academics, but they are not required to reach a majority view on the issues they examine.

This comment only touches the surface of a large and complex issue. But if it is accepted that comprehensive justifications cannot adequately explain the law, what role can they play in contemporary legal theory? As we have seen, academics whose only concern is for the law's legitimacy are free to argue that the acceptability thesis should be rejected and, further, that legal rules are justified – and only justified – on the basis of a particular comprehensive theory. I have given some reasons to doubt that this approach will succeed, but it cannot be rejected out of hand. Beyond this, my comment suggests that attempts to justify legal rules on the basis of comprehensive theories must be understood as attempts to prove, not that the relevant theory is *the* justification for the rules in question, but, instead, that it is one of many possible justifications.[30] In other words, such scholarship must be interpreted as attempting to demonstrate that legal rules can be justified on the basis of different comprehensive views. Understood in this way, while such work cannot provide a complete justification for a legal rule, it can provide part of the justification.

IV. Conclusion

This chapter's thesis is admittedly provocative. I have suggested, albeit tentatively, that an entire category of legal theories may need to be rejected or significantly reframed, basically on the ground that they are too philosophical or at least too philosophical in a particular way. It may be useful to stress, then, that the thesis was motivated by a familiar feature of the legal landscape: the comprehensive justifications for legal rules which are defended by at least some academics are different in kind from the justifications offered by judges. Prima facie, this difference is puzzling. The merits of a justification do not depend on who is offering the justification.

My general approach to this puzzle should also be familiar, at least in broad outline. Reduced to its essentials, this chapter tries to take seriously a view that, while rarely articulated explicitly, is common amongst many lawyers, judges and legal academics. I refer to the view that certain academic accounts of the law employ concepts (or 'ideas', 'principles', etc) that are so foreign to the way that legal participants – judges, lawyers, citizens – understand the law that they seem not so much to be explaining the law as re-inventing it. The most common target of this view are economic theories of the law.[31] But if my arguments are correct, any theory that seeks to explain the law on the basis of a comprehensive moral theory is vulnerable to a similar objection. The objection is not merely that such theories explain the

[30] Most academics who invoke comprehensive theories in their work also critique other theories. But there are exceptions. Arthur Ripstein explicitly offers his Kantian account as *a* theory of the law, without commenting on alternative theories: A Ripstein, *Private Wrongs* (Cambridge, MA, Harvard University Press, 2016).

[31] See, eg: Weinrib (n 27) 46–48; Smith (n 15) 132–35.

law using ideas and concepts that would be considered odd and inappropriate for a judge. The more fundamental objection is to the basic orientation of such theories. It is central to the understanding of law in contemporary common law jurisdictions that the law provides a means for guiding and coordinating behaviour that citizens can accept without agreeing on a comprehensive moral view. The law, to this extent, is autonomous from morality: it makes it possible for individuals who may disagree deeply about foundational moral principles to live together. Theories that explain the law on the basis of comprehensive views must suppose that the law is something very different from what this understanding assumes.

5

Can We Be Wrong About Rights?

NICHOLAS J McBRIDE

I. Truth and Power

The encounter between Jesus and Pilate – as described in the Gospel of John – symbolises a deeper and daily confrontation that takes place all over the world: the confrontation between truth and power.[1] Jesus disclaims any interest in merely human power: 'My kingdom is not of this world. If my kingdom were of this world, my servants would have been fighting, that I might not be delivered over to the Jews. But my kingdom is not from the world'. He instead proclaims that, '[f]or this purpose I was born and for this purpose I have come into the world – to bear witness to the truth. Everyone who is of the truth listens to my voice'.[2] Pilate, the representative of earthly power, responds with puzzled indifference: 'What is truth?'[3]

The confrontation between truth and power looms very large for those who engage in activities – such as working in academia, as a journalist or for the police – that only make sense if they have truth-seeking as their goal and therefore have truth-seeking as their purpose, or *telos*. Those who engage in such truth-seeking activities will regularly be exposed to the temptation to 'sell out' the principles that underpin that activity in favour of obtaining greater power, in the form of money, popularity or promotion. Those who engage in activities that involve their attempting to acquire or retain power over others – most obviously, and centrally, through political campaigning – will also be regularly put to the test and asked how far they are prepared to 'sell out' the truth in the search for power. And even those who stand aside from engaging in either type of activity will often be exposed to the temptation to lie in order to preserve their position

[1] The confrontation between truth and power is replicated in Dostoevsky's legend of 'The Grand Inquisitor' in *The Brothers Karamazov* (1880) V.5. It was also a preoccupation of the novels of George Orwell (most obviously, *Nineteen Eighty-Four* (London, Secker & Warburg, 1949) – see, in particular, III.3) and Josephine Tey (in particular, *Brat Farrar* (London, Peter Davies, 1949) and *The Daughter of Time* (London, Peter Davies, 1951)).

[2] John 18:36–37.

[3] ibid 18:38.

or gain some advantage and will then have to decide whether it is truth or power that they are ultimately interested in.

The question that provides this chapter with its title asks whether (i) the *telos* of the activity of inquiring into the nature of rights is to seek out the truth about the nature of rights, or whether (ii) such inquiries are engaged in as a way of acquiring or retaining power over others. If (i) is the case, then we can be wrong about rights – there is a truth of the matter as to what rights are, and when we inquire into the nature of rights we are seeking to arrive at that truth. If (ii) is the case, then we cannot be wrong about rights – there is no truth of the matter as to what rights are, and people make claims about the nature of rights simply to advance particular power-seeking agendas.

Two reasons might lead us to believe that (ii) is very likely to be the case. The first is that the activity of *determining what legal rights we have* seems obviously aimed at acquiring and retaining power over others. That is why the issue of what legal rights we have *matters* – it makes all the difference in the world in terms of being able to appropriate the powers of the legal system to your side whether you do or do not have a legal right of some description. Given that the activity of determining what legal rights we have has power-seeking as its goal, it would be surprising if that same goal did not contaminate the activity of inquiring into the nature of legal rights.

Second, the intractability of debates over the nature of the rights makes little sense if the activity of inquiring into the nature of rights were truth-seeking in nature. There has been little to no progress in resolving debates over questions such as:

(1) Are rights best described as protecting the right-holder's interests (the 'Interest Theory' of rights), or as giving the right-holder the power to determine how someone else will behave (the 'Will Theory' of rights), or as combining these two functions in some way (the 'Hybrid Theory' of rights)?
(2) Are there such things as moral rights (as opposed to legal rights)?
(3) Are rights peremptory or not? In other words, does the existence of a right dictate to someone what they should do in a given situation, or does the existence of a right only affect what considerations someone should take into account in determining what they should do in a given situation?
(4) Are rights purely private in nature, held by and against individuals, or are there such things as distinctively public rights, held by or against the government?

Surely, it might be asked, if there were a truth of the matter in respect of these questions, we would have made some progress towards the truth by now? Instead, it might be thought, the intractability of debates on these questions shows that it makes no sense to think of the different views in these debates as being 'true' or 'false'. Rather, these different views must ultimately be rooted in different views as to which view of rights is more *politically advantageous*, in terms of advancing a particular power-seeking agenda.

Despite this, most theorists who debate questions such as (1)–(4), above, assume that (i) is the case, and that both sides of the debate on each question are seeking to penetrate to the truth of the matter in relation to that question.[4] But if (i) is true, how can we break the deadlock over what is the answer to questions (1)–(4), and arrive at the truth of the matter in relation to those questions? More argument over questions (1)–(4) cannot be the solution: we have not lacked for arguments over these questions, and deadlock has been the result.[5] One obvious alternative tactic would be to formulate *truth conditions* that have to be observed if one is to arrive at the truth in relation to questions (1)–(4). We can then see which side in the debate over one of those questions has more assiduously respected those conditions. Whichever side has done a better job of observing those conditions should be regarded (for the time being) as having won the debate, as their position is *more likely* to represent the truth than that taken by their more sloppy counterparts on the other side.

This tactic has been explored by Siegfried van Duffel, explaining in what respects a theory of rights has to be *extensionally* and *intensionally* adequate in order for us to accept it as a truthful account of the nature of rights. The *extensional* adequacy of a theory depends on how far 'it identifies as "rights" those normative incidents that we commonly regard as rights and does not classify as rights any normative incidents that are not commonly recognized as rights'.[6] The *intensional* adequacy of a theory depends on how far it identifies someone as having a right, for the right reasons.[7] Disappointingly – for our purposes – it is clear that it will not be possible to *apply* van Duffel's conditions in a non-controversial way to determine which of one of two sides in a debate over the nature of rights is more likely to be truthful. For example, what is 'commonly recognised' as being a right? And what are the 'right reasons' for recognising that someone has a right? More generally, it seems very likely that it will not be possible to *formulate* any truth conditions for a theory of rights without incurring further deadlock over what those conditions will be. This is because what truth conditions we will adopt for a theory of rights is very likely to depend on what sort of concept the concept of a right is. Is it a *descriptive* concept? – that is, one which simply seeks to capture some feature

[4] Exceptions are: NE Simmonds, 'Rights at the Cutting Edge' in MH Kramer, NE Simmonds and H Steiner, *A Debate Over Rights: Philosophical Enquiries* (Oxford, Oxford University Press, 1998) 115–41, and L Wenar, 'The Nature of Rights' (2005) 33 *Philosophy & Public Affairs* 223, 250–51, both of whom argue that – at least in their original forms – the Interest and Will Theories of rights emerged out of different political perspectives on the proper role of the state and its relationship with the individual. However, both then proceed to offer accounts of the nature of rights that purport not to be rooted in political considerations but instead capture something significant about the nature of rights: Simmonds, ibid 224–25; L Wenar, 'The Nature of Claim-Rights' (2013) 123 *Ethics* 202.

[5] L Wenar, 'The Analysis of Rights' in MH Kramer, C Grant, B Colbran and A Hatzistavrou (eds), *The Legacy of HLA Hart: Legal, Political, and Moral Philosophy* (Oxford, Oxford University Press, 2008) 267–68.

[6] S van Duffel, 'Adequacy Constraints for a Theory of Rights' in M McBride (ed), *New Essays on the Nature of Rights* (Oxford, Hart Publishing, 2017) 189.

[7] ibid 199.

of our institutions or our way of thinking about the world? Or is it an *interpretive* concept? – that is, a concept that emerges out of, and is informed by, an ongoing debate about the value of rights and what that implies for the nature of rights?[8] There seems to be no non-controversial way of answering these questions.[9]

Instead, I want in this chapter to explore a different tactic for resolving the deadlock in the debates over what is the right answer to questions (1)–(4). That is to ask: what position in these debates is *least likely* to have been adopted for reasons of political advantage, to advance a particular power-seeking agenda? If (i) is true, and there is a truth of the matter in relation to questions (1)–(4), then the side of the debate on any one of these questions that is *least likely* to have been adopted for political advantage is, correspondingly, the side that is *most likely* to have been adopted because it actually represents the truth of the matter on that question and is therefore the side that we should regard as correct, in the absence of any further argument indicating that that side is – in fact – incorrect. In implementing this tactic, three preliminary points should be noted.

First, Hohfeld's scheme for analysing the nature of rights is of no use to the project on which this chapter is embarked. As Andrew Halpin observes,[10] Hohfeld presents us with a 'neutral' scheme for understanding the nature of rights. Given this, one might think that Hohfeld's analysis of the nature of rights is least likely to have been advanced for reasons of political advantage and is therefore just what this chapter is looking for. However, it is precisely Hohfeld's neutrality that makes it of no use to us in seeking to break the deadlock in the debates over questions (1)–(4): his analysis takes no side on any of these debates, when it is precisely a side that we are seeking to take in each of these debates. Having said that, Hohfeld's analysis *will* prove useful in discussing questions (1)–(4) in one respect: it clarifies for us what *kinds* of rights we might be talking about in discussing these questions. In this chapter, the focus will simply be on what Hohfeld called 'claim-rights' – rights which correlate with someone else having a duty – and any reference below to 'rights' should be read as referring simply to claim-rights.

Second, I do not intend to suggest that those who take a particular side on questions (1)–(4) do so to advance a particular power-seeking agenda. Quite the contrary: the starting point of this chapter is the observation that *all* sides of the debates over questions (1)–(4) sincerely claim that their position represents the truth of the matter about the nature of rights, and therefore assume that it is possible to be wrong about rights. The point of this chapter is to capitalise on that rare point of agreement among parties to the debates over questions (1)–(4)

[8] On the nature of an interpretive concept, see R Dworkin, *Law's Empire* (Cambridge, MA, Harvard University Press, 1986) ch 2.

[9] cf Wenar (n 5) 252: 'The theorist of the nature of rights … cannot simply set a list of the phenomena to be explained – the rights that there are and could be – without making hotly contentious assumptions outside of his domains of inquiry.'

[10] A Halpin, 'The Value of Hohfeldian Neutrality When Theorising About Legal Rights' in McBride (ed), (n 6).

and identify positions on those questions that *all* sides in those debates can agree should be adopted (on the ground that those positions are *most likely* to represent the truth of the matter on those questions) unless it can be shown that adopting some other position would represent a clear and convincing epistemic gain.

Third, the tactic that this chapter seeks to pursue for resolving the deadlock in the debates over questions (1)–(4) has a lot in common with John Rawls' adoption of the 'original position' thought experiment to arrive at principles of justice for the basic structure of a democratic society.[11] Principles of justice that are agreed upon between individuals who are placed in a situation where 'no one knows his place in a society, his class position or social status' and where no one knows 'his fortune in the distribution of natural assets and abilities, his intelligence, strength, and the like' are *most likely* to be just because they are *least likely* to be affected by the vagaries of luck or venal self-seeking.[12] However, it is not possible to deploy the original position thought experiment to see which side of the debates over questions (1)– (4) is least likely to be adopted for reasons of political advantage. This is because someone who was placed in the state of ignorance that people in the original position 'enjoy' would be completely ill-equipped to take a side on the various debates around the nature of rights. So we cannot pursue the tactic suggested in this chapter for breaking the deadlock in these debates by delegating the job to someone in the 'original position': we have to do it ourselves.

II. Welfare and Control

Let us apply this method first to the vexed question of whether the Interest Theory or the Will Theory, or some kind of Hybrid Theory, best describes what is involved in having a claim-right against someone else.

While the distinction seems not to be generally noted, there are in fact two versions of the Interest Theory, which we can call the Interest-Ground Theory (or 'IG Theory' for short), and the Interest-Effect Theory (or 'IE Theory' for short). According to the IG Theory, A has a right against B if B is subject to a duty to do *x*, and that duty exists *because* B's doing *x* will (other things being equal) serve A's interests.[13] According to the IE Theory, A has a right against B if B is subject to a duty to do *x*, and B's doing *x* will (other things being equal) have the *effect* of serving A's interests.[14] In its classic formulation

[11] J Rawls, *A Theory of Justice*, rev edn (Cambridge, MA, Harvard University Press, 1999) §§3–4.

[12] ibid §3.

[13] The most well-known proponent of the IG Theory is Joseph Raz: J Raz, *The Morality of Freedom* (Oxford, Oxford University Press, 1986) 166.

[14] The most sophisticated proponent of IE Theory is Matthew Kramer: MH Kramer, 'Rights Without Trimmings' in Kramer et al (eds), (n 4); MH Kramer, 'Getting Rights Right' in MH Kramer (ed), *Rights, Wrongs and Responsibilities* (London, Palgrave, 2001); MH Kramer, 'Some Doubts About Alternatives to the Interest Theory of Rights' (2013) 123 *Ethics* 245; MH Kramer, 'In Defence of the Interest Theory of Right-Holding: Rejoinders to Leif Wenar on Rights' in McBride (ed), (n 6).

by HLA Hart,[15] according to the Will Theory, A has a right against B if B is subject to a duty to do *x*, and A has (i) the power to waive or extinguish that duty; (ii) the power to enforce[16] that duty if B breaches, or threatens to breach her duty to do *x*; and (iii) the power to waive or extinguish any obligation that B might owe A to pay compensation to B in the event that B breaches her duty to do *x*. According to Gopal Sreenivasan's Hybrid Theory, A has a right against B if B is subject to a duty to do *x* and A's measure of control over whether or not B performs that duty and what B is required to do if B breaches that duty is designed to match the measure of control that advances A's interests on balance.[17]

The debate between these different theories seems profoundly sterile in nature. The *only* thing that seems to turn on these debates is how we use the term 'right'. Interest Theorists point out that if we adopt the Will Theory, that seems to suggest that babies and the comatose do not have any rights, and that unwaivable duties not to be tortured or murdered or enslaved also do not give rise to any rights. Will Theorists point out that if we adopt the Interest Theory then in the case where C contracts with B for B to paint A's house while A is on holiday, the Interest Theory suggests that A has a right that B paint A's house when it was the case for centuries under English law – until the Contracts (Rights of Third Parties) Act 1999 was passed – that the only person who had a right that B paint A's house was C.

But does it *matter* what we say as to who has a right and who does not?[18] Saying that A has a right against B does not seem to tell us anything useful if we already know (i) that B is subject to a duty to do *x*; and (ii) what can or will happen if B breaches, or threatens to breach, that duty. Saying that A has a right against B merely tells us – for an Interest Theorist – something not very interesting about (i): why B has a duty to do *x*, or who will benefit from B's performing that duty (depending on whether you are an IG Theorist or an IE Theorist). Saying that A has a right against B is – for a Will Theorist – merely one way of telling us something about (ii) (that A has the power to determine what will happen to B if B breaches, or threatens to breach, her duty to do *x*); but we can say everything that needs to be said about (ii) without saying that A has a right against B.

The sterility of the debates between Interest, Will and Hybrid Theorists about rights may account for the protracted nature of those debates. But it also casts in doubt whether asking '[w]hat position in these debates is *least likely* to have been

[15] HLA Hart, 'Legal Rights' in his *Essays on Bentham* (Oxford, Oxford University Press, 1982) 184.

[16] This requirement is rendered problematic if we are talking about a *moral* right (if there is such a thing as a moral right) and would need to be modified by a Will Theorist in order to apply to that kind of right.

[17] G Sreenivasan, 'A Hybrid Theory of Claim-Rights' (2005) 25 *Oxford Journal of Legal Studies* 257, 271.

[18] *cf* Steiner, 'Working Rights' in Kramer et al (eds), (n 4) 261: 'What scintilla of a practical or analytical difference can it make if we construe the rights correlative to those protection duties [in relation to babies and the comatose] as … held by *those power-possessors* [those empowered to decide what is in the baby's or coma patient's best interests] rather than … held by unempowerable creatures? As far as I can see none'.

adopted for reasons of political advantage, to advance a particular power-seeking agenda?' will produce an answer. If it does not really matter whether one is an Interest Theorist, a Will Theorist or a Hybrid Theorist, then no one would adopt *any* of these positions to advance a particular power-seeking agenda. And this is correct, so long as these positions simply seek to *describe* what is involved in having a right against someone else. However, when it comes to the *normative* question of what rights *should we have* against other people, it makes a very big difference whether one is an Interest Theorist or a Will Theorist.

On the Interest Theory, there is a limit on what rights we *can* have against other people – I can only have a right against you if that serves my interests. On the Will Theory there is *no limit* on what rights we *can* have against other people – I will have a right against you any time you are subject to a duty and I have the ability to control you through the means of your being subject to that duty. So on the Interest Theory I *cannot* have a right that you climb Mount Kilimanjaro as your doing so will not serve my interests in any way. But on the Will Theory it is possible I could have a right that you climb Kilimanjaro: to have such a right, all I need is that the law imposes a duty on you to climb Kilimanjaro and leaves it up to me to determine whether or not you will be required to perform that duty. So in an Interest Theory world, my claim that I *should* be given a right that you climb Kilimanjaro would be regarded as bizarre and eccentric; in a Will Theory world, such a claim would be viewed as an interesting starting point for discussion. It is obvious, then, that as between the Interest Theory and the Will Theory, the Interest Theory is *less likely* to have been adopted for reasons of political advantage.

It might be argued against this that the Will Theory comes with Kantian baggage which means the range of rights we should be recognised as having in a Will Theory world will be far more restrictive than would be the case than in an Interest Theory world. The argument would go:

> The Will Theory is embedded in a particular understanding of what legal rights we can have against each other. The only rights we have against each other are rights that others not impair our independence as persons. This is why if I have a right against you in respect of your doing *x*, I get to control whether or not you do *x*. If I am happy for you to do *x*, then the right lapses because your doing *x* will no longer threaten my independence as a person. As a result, my having a right that you climb Kilimanjaro is ruled out under the Will Theory just as much as it is under the Interest Theory, as your not climbing Kilimanjaro does not threaten my independence as a person. And there are a lot of rights that might be regarded as possibilities under the Interest Theory that would simply be ruled out under the Will Theory as they do nothing to protect people's independence as persons. So, in fact, as between the Will Theory and the Interest Theory, it is the Will Theory that places more constraints on what rights we can argue we should have.

In support of this argument it may be noted that the foremost proponents of the Will Theory do show Kantian leanings in their other writings.[19] But against this,

[19] HLA Hart, 'Are There Any Natural Rights?' (1955) 64 *Philosophical Review* 175; NE Simmonds, *Law as a Moral Idea* (Oxford, Oxford University Press, 2007).

two points can be made. First, there is nothing in the Will Theory that *requires* that the only rights we can be recognised as having are rights that fit a Kantian template; 'the triumph of the will' is not, after all, a phrase we associate with Kantians. Second, the argument that the *only* legal rights that we can have against each other are rights that conform to Kant's Doctrine of Right is itself one which can be suspected of being designed to pursue a libertarian political agenda, under which protecting people's freedoms is given overriding priority over protecting people's welfare.[20]

Despite the objections made in the last but one paragraph, then, it seems that the Interest Theory is less likely than the Will Theory to have been adopted for reasons of political advantage, and under our method for determining which theory of what it means to have a right against someone else is most likely to be true, the Will Theory should fall for the time being, unless and until it can be revived by convincing arguments showing that it is clearly superior to the Interest Theory. And if the Will Theory falls, so does Sreenivasan's Hybrid Theory as that theory is designed as an upgrade on the Will Theory,[21] but it is not an upgrade that does anything to allay our fears that the Will Theory is more likely to have been adopted for political reasons than the Interest Theory.

That leaves us to adjudicate between the IG Theory and the IE Theory. As between these two, the IG Theory is more restrictive in what rights we *can* have against other people. Under the IG Theory, a claim that I should have a right that you do my shopping, make my meals, do my laundry and generally tidy up while I write about private law on my computer would be regarded as just as bizarre and eccentric as my claim that I should have a right that you climb Kilimanjaro. While your performing all these services for me will obviously be in my interests, my interests are not substantial enough to make it even remotely plausible that they justify your coming under a duty to do all these things for me. By contrast, under the IE Theory, it is entirely *possible* for me to have a right that you look after the rest of my life while I type away: for me to have such a right, all that needs to happen is that the law puts you under a duty to look after me in such a way. And the IE Theory, of and in itself, has nothing to say about whether I *should* have such a right against you: normatively, it is completely inert. So a claim that I should have a right that you look after the rest of my life while I write about private law would not be regarded as at all odd or bizarre under the IE Theory. As between the IG Theory and the IE Theory, then, the IG Theory is less likely to have been adopted to advance a particular power-seeking agenda, because it is so much tougher to

[20] See, eg, JR Otteson, 'Kantian Individualism and Political Libertarianism' (2009) 13 *Independent Review* 489.

[21] See Sreenivasan (n 17) 268: 'The correct theory [of right-holding] clearly has to be more general than the Will theory because there are important cases of claim-rights that the Will theory mishandles. One way of approaching the problem of a theory of claim-rights, then, is to look for a way of generalizing from the Will theory's treatment of the paradigm cases of contractual and property rights that manages not to over do it'.

make out claims that one should have a right against someone else under the IG Theory than under the IE Theory.

Our method therefore yields the conclusion that, in the absence of any further argument, we should accept – as most likely to be true – the position that on question (1), the particular version of Interest Theory that we have called the IG Theory best describes what it is to hold a right against someone else: A will have a right against B if B is under a duty that arose in order to protect a particular interest of A's.

III. Legal and Moral

Let's now turn to question (2) – are there such things as moral claim-rights, as opposed to legal rights? It might be thought that it is obvious that the answer is 'yes' – and, indeed, that would be the response of all the participants in the previous debate over the nature of right-holding.[22] As a result, the positions of modern-day thinkers like Alasdair MacIntyre – who insists that there are 'no natural or human rights … and belief in them is one with belief in witches and in unicorns'[23] – or Bernard Williams – who relegated rights, as a 'distinctive kind of ethical reason', to the lowly role of 'assuring expectations'[24] – can only arouse puzzlement among their contemporaries. However, what *should* puzzle us is that there is such a broad consensus nowadays in favour of the view that moral rights exist. After all, the one point on which Kant – the arch-deontologist – and Bentham – the arch-utilitarian – could agree on was that *moral rights do not exist*.

For Kant, the concept of a 'moral right' would have made no sense. In the realm of morality, I act according to a particular maxim or rule *because I will that everyone should act according to that maxim or rule*.[25] Only if this italicised 'internal' condition is satisfied can it be said that I am acting morally: if it is not, then my actions are of no moral worth at all.[26] So a shopkeeper who makes it a rule to give his customers the right change, but not because he wills that everyone should so act, but because he does not want to get a bad reputation cannot be said to be acting morally.[27] By contrast, in the realm of right, my motivations for acting do

[22] Kramer, 'Rights Without Trimmings' (n 14) 8: 'virtually every aspect of Hohfeld's analytical scheme applies as well, *mutatis mutandis*, to the structuring of moral relationships'; Simmonds (n 4) 231: 'legal and moral rights are more than simple homonyms. An acceptable analysis of legal rights must therefore at least imply appropriate ways of analysing moral rights, even if subtle adjustments are required to render the fit fully adequate'; Sreenivasan (n 17) 258, fn 6: 'Throughout the discussion, I shall ignore the distinction between moral rights and legal rights … [Doing this] conveniently enables me to concentrate on the core features of a claim-right, which hold in common between law and morals'.

[23] A MacIntyre, *After Virtue: A Study in Moral Theory*, 3rd edn (London, Bloomsbury, 2013) 82–83.

[24] B Williams, *Ethics and the Limits of Philosophy* (London, Routledge, 2006) 238, fn 20.

[25] I Kant, *Groundwork of the Metaphysics of Morals* (1785) 4:421, 390.

[26] ibid 4:397.

[27] ibid.

not matter at all.[28] I act rightly if I act according to a particular maxim or rule *that is compatible with everyone's enjoying the freedom to choose what to do with the means at their disposal.*[29] Whether I act rightly or wrongly depends simply on whether this italicised 'external' condition is satisfied: my reasons for acting are completely irrelevant.[30] So if I make it a rule to read a book a week, then I act rightly because my doing this does not deprive anyone else of their freedom to choose what to do with the means at their disposal. And I still act rightly whether my reason for doing this is to improve my mind or to be able to boast to my neighbours that this is something I do. If, on the other hand, I take a book to read from your library without your permission, I act wrongly because my doing this is not compatible with your enjoying the freedom to choose what to do with the means at your disposal. And it would be right for the law to coerce me to give the book back because coercing me in this way is compatible with everyone's (including me) enjoying the freedom to choose what to do with the means at their disposal.[31] Of course, in taking a book from your library without permission, I have *also* failed to act morally – but to say that because I have treated you in a way that is both not-right and not-moral, I have violated a *moral right* of yours is to confuse two completely different ways of evaluating my actions: the first according to the effects of my actions, and the second according to the goodness of my will.[32]

The concept of a 'moral right' made as little sense to Bentham as it would have to Kant: he famously declared that it amounted to 'nonsense upon stilts' in his eponymous 1795 essay on the 1791 French Declaration of the Rights of Man and the Citizen and its *sequelae.*[33] Instead, Bentham insisted, rights are 'the child of law'[34] and 'there are no such things as natural rights – no such things as rights anterior to the establishment of government – no such things as natural rights opposed to, in contradistinction to, legal' and '[w]e know what it is for men to live without government, and living without government is to live without rights'.[35]

Even modern-day thinkers on the nature of rights are prepared, from time to time, to concede that Kant and Bentham had a point and that there is something distinctively *legal* about the notion of having a right against someone else.[36] Given this, we should not regard the issue of whether there are such things as moral

[28] I Kant, *The Metaphysics of Morals* (1797) 6:219.

[29] ibid 6:230.

[30] ibid 6:231–32.

[31] ibid 6:231.

[32] ibid 6:220–21, 232.

[33] P Schofield, C Pease-Watkin and C Blamires (eds), J Bentham, *Rights, Representation and Reform: Nonsense Upon Stilts and Other Writings on the French Revolution* (Oxford, Oxford University Press, 2002) 330.

[34] ibid 400.

[35] ibid 329.

[36] cf Maitland, *A Historical Sketch of Liberty and Equality* (Indianapolis, Liberty Fund, 2001) 90: 'nothing we can do will ever deprive the word "rights" of its legal savour', quoted in NE Simmonds, 'Constitutional Rights, Civility and Artifice' (2019) 78 *Cambridge Law Journal* 175, 182. See also Simmonds (n 4) 231–32; Halpin (n 10) 28.

rights as settled, but instead apply our method to determine the issue by asking: which view of whether moral rights exist is less likely to have been adopted for reasons of political advantage, to advance a power-seeking agenda? At first sight, one might think that the denial that there are such things as moral rights is more likely to be made for political reasons than the assertion. The argument would go:

> It is no surprise that Bentham denied that there are such things as moral rights: if there are no moral rights then the government cannot be said to do anything wrong in sacrificing individual interests on the altar of promoting 'the greatest happiness of the greatest number'. And so it always goes – whenever the existence of moral rights are denied, it is always in the cause of allowing the powerful to do what they will with the weak.

However, two points can be made in response to this argument.

The first point is that what force this argument has rests on the fact that the resources available to us for evaluating our, or someone else's, actions are nowadays grotesquely impoverished. The idea that one cannot criticise or condemn the actions of a government unless there exist such things as moral rights and one can establish that the government's actions violate those moral rights would seem very strange to our predecessors, who had to hand a wide range of what Bernard Williams called 'thick ethical concepts'[37] that they could use to deplore someone's (including a government's) actions as, for example, 'corrupt', 'disgusting', 'inhuman', 'shameful', 'hypocritical', 'cowardly' and 'barbarous'.[38] However, we live in a flattened moral landscape where such 'thick ethical concepts' seem increasingly alien and the only language of moral judgement that we feel comfortable with is borrowed from law – the language of rights and duties.

This first point leads on to the second point, which is that the argument in the last but one paragraph shows that it is in fact those who *assert* the existence of moral rights who are more likely to be pursuing a power-seeking agenda. Thinkers like MacIntyre, who deny the existence of moral rights, simply want us to get back to where we once belonged – back to a moral landscape that is much thicker and richer than the one we currently inhabit.[39] By contrast, those who assert the existence of moral rights react to the flattening of our moral landscape with either

[37] Williams (n 24) 140–41.

[38] As it happens, Bentham's 'Nonsense Upon Stilts' essay is shot through with repeated condemnations of the French revolutionary government, which shows that denying that there are such things as moral rights does not necessarily result in one's adopting a '*laissez faire, laissez passer*' attitude to the world.

[39] See, most recently, A MacIntyre, *Ethics in the Conflicts of Modernity* (Cambridge, Cambridge University Press, 2016) 77–78: 'Another … fiction is the notion of a human right. Protagonists of this notion characteristically take it to be indispensable, if they are to be able to assert that there are some types of harm and wrong the infliction of which on others is unconditionally prohibited, prior to and independently of any particular system of positive law. My quarrel is not at all with their claim that there are such unconditional prohibitions. It is with their advancing the thesis that appeals to human rights … provide a justification for asserting and enforcing such prohibitions … [T]here were and are better arguments for doing what justice and the common good require than those appeals provide'.

terror or cupidity. Those who react with terror flail around, looking for something, anything that will provide protection from those who are no longer moved by the kind of thick ethical concepts detailed in the previous paragraph; they find what they need in the concept of a moral right.[40] Those who react with cupidity see, in the language of moral rights, an opportunity to bully you and me into doing what *they* want without their having to go to the trouble of changing the law to require us to act in the way: moral rights give them what the law could, but on the cheap. Either way, the adoption of the language of moral rights will be motivated by a desire for power – either the power to protect oneself from others, or the power to dominate others.[41]

Given these points, our method should lead us to take the side of those who deny that moral rights exist, in the absence of further and better arguments in favour of their existence.

IV. Peremptory and Non-peremptory

Turning now to question (3), as to whether claim-rights are peremptory or non-peremptory in nature, Nigel Simmonds insists that

> Rights have peremptory force. They bring an end to weighing and balancing. The question is not one of how my interests are balanced against yours, but of whether I am within or without the scope of my rights … If I demonstrate to the judge that I have a legal right to plant tall trees along the perimeter of my land, depriving your land of light,[42] we do not expect the judge to say: 'I accept that you have such a right and I will certainly take account of it when I decide whether you should be allowed to plant the trees.' Once the right is demonstrated, the question at issue is conclusively resolved.[43]

However, as Simmonds readily acknowledges with regret, such a view runs counter to modern trends in thinking about rights. Only a few of the rights that the European Convention on Human Rights recognises us as having are phrased in peremptory form (most notably the Article 3 right not to be 'subjected to torture or to inhuman or degrading treatment or punishment'): the rest simply insist that the state should not infringe on certain values (such as privacy or freedom of speech) unless other identified values demand that it does. Joseph Raz gives

[40] Though it will probably do them no good in the end. Bernard Williams is rightly scornful of the idea that morality might provide us with some refuge from those who wish us ill: see his *Ethics and the Limits of Philosophy* (n 24), speaking (at 23) of those who think 'that the justification of the ethical life could be a *force*. If we are to take this seriously, then it is a real question, who is supposed to be listening. Why are they supposed to be listening? What will the professor's justification do, when they break down the door, smash his spectacles, take him away?'

[41] This was (unsurprisingly) also Nietzsche's view: see his *Daybreak* (1881) Book II, §112 ('On the natural history of rights and duties').

[42] Strictly speaking, this is not a claim-right, but a Hohfeldian privilege/liberty. However, Simmonds' point about rights having peremptory force would apply just as much to a genuine claim-right.

[43] Simmonds (n 36) 183.

philosophical support to such an approach to rights, arguing that '[a] right of one person is not a duty on another. It is the ground of a duty, ground which, if not counteracted by conflicting considerations, justifies holding that other person to have the duty'.[44]

I have elsewhere framed the issue as to whether claim-rights are peremptory or non-peremptory in nature as an issue over where such rights are best characterised as 'rights that' or 'rights to …'.[45] 'Rights that …' are peremptory in nature. If I have a right that you take care not to run me over, then you must have a duty to take care not to run me over: nothing else could be implied by my having a right that you take care not to run me over. By contrast, 'rights to …' are non-peremptory in nature. If I have a right to life, it is very uncertain what that implies for other people. All we know from the statement that 'I have a right to life' is that my life is important and for that reason I enjoy some sort of legal protection against being deprived of my life – but what sort of protection is uncertain. The fact that I have 'a right to life' may mean that you have a duty (and I have a corresponding 'right that …') you take care not to run me over; but equally well it could mean that you have a duty not to run me over intentionally, or that you have a duty not to run me over *tout court*. All that has yet to be known, or worked out.

What view of claim-rights should we take? Applying our method, again, we ask: which view is least likely to have been adopted for reasons of political advantage, to advance a particular power-seeking agenda? At first sight, the view that claim-rights take the form of 'rights that …' would seem to be more likely to be motivated by a will to power. The peremptory nature of 'rights that …' gives them, in Simmonds' phrase, a 'cutting edge'[46] that 'rights to …' lack. A 'right that …' is like a red light at a junction: it is telling you in no uncertain terms to stop. A claim right that takes the form of a 'right to …' operates more like an amber light: it is warning you to be cautious in proceeding, but it is not exactly telling you to stop. So if you are interested in power – the argument would go – you will be interested in surrounding yourself with claim-rights that amount to red lights, not amber lights. As a result, you will be far more likely to think of claim-rights as 'rights that …' rather than 'rights to …' if your ultimate interest is in acquiring and maintaining power over other people. So the argument goes, but I take a different view.

'Rights to …' are shapeshifters. They insinuate themselves into our lives as amber lights, but once established, they have a habit of turning into red lights. Take the 'right to life'. Everyone accepts that there is such a thing as a 'right to life' because life is obviously hugely important and worthy of protection under the law. But once the notion of a 'right to life' is widely accepted, there is a perennial temptation to misuse that notion and turn the light cast by the 'right to life' from

[44] Raz (n 13) 171.

[45] Originally in NJ McBride, 'Rights and the Basis of Tort Law' in D Nolan and A Robertson (eds), *Rights and Private Law* (Oxford, Hart Publishing, 2012) 335–36, 343–46; and subsequently in NJ McBride, *The Humanity of Private Law, Part I: Explanation* (Oxford, Hart Publishing, 2019) 43–48.

[46] See text at n 4 above.

amber to red. For example, suppose A runs over and kills B, without any fault on A's part. If B's family wishes to sue A, they will have to show that A violated B's rights in acting as he did. Faced with the difficulty of showing any relevant red light 'right that …' which A violated in faultlessly running B down, B's family will be very tempted to argue: 'everyone accepts B had a right to life. A killed B. Therefore, A violated B's rights – B's right to life.' The fault in this argument is obvious: just because B had a 'right to life' does not mean that B had a right that A not faultlessly run B down. But this point will not be obvious to B's family, and it is not obvious either to a lot of academics who attempt to dispose of the argument made by B's family by resorting to devices like distinguishing between someone's 'right to life' being *violated* (which is always wrongful) and its being *interfered with* (which is not necessarily wrongful),[47] or even concede that B's family may have a point.[48]

The shapeshifting nature of 'rights to …' makes them very attractive to those who seek power over others. First I persuade you to accept that there is such a thing as a non-peremptory 'right to' something like a decent environment or access to the Internet, or a 'right to' be loved, on the (entirely correct) basis that things like a decent environment, or access to the Internet, or being loved, are very important for leading a good life. Once I have done that, it will be a relatively easy task to convince you (a) that my rights have been violated if I enjoy anything less than the full measure of whatever it is I persuaded you to accept I had a 'right to …'; and (b) that I am entitled to some kind of redress from someone for that violation of my rights. As Bentham observed:

> In vain would it be said that though no bounds are … assigned to any of these ['rights to …' that I have persuaded you to accept exist], yet it is to be understood as taken for granted … that they are to have bounds: viz: such bounds as it is understand will be set them by the laws. Vain, I say … for the supposition would be contrary to the plain words of the [rights themselves].[49]

Given the dangerously shapeshifting nature of 'rights to …', the view that claim-rights are best described as being 'rights that …' is *less likely* to have been adopted to advance a particular power-seeking agenda, than the view that claim-rights are

[47] See JJ Thompson, *Rights, Restitution, and Risk: Essays in Moral Theory* (Cambridge, MA, Harvard University Press, 1986) 10.

[48] See R Stevens, *Torts and Rights* (Oxford, Oxford University Press, 1997) 99, inferring from the fact that we have a 'right to bodily safety' that 'a producer's duty is … to refrain from manufacturing defective products which cause harm' with the result that '[i]t is not meaningless to describe the claim of a person harmed by a defective product as based upon a tort, although the manufacturer is without blame in any moral sense'. The same (illegitimate) move is made by RA Epstein, 'Towards a General Theory of Tort Law: Strict Liability in Context' (2010) 3 *Journal of Tort Law* 6; and Goldberg and Zipursky, 'The Easy Case for Products Liability Law: A Response to Professors Polinsky and Shavell' (2010) 123 *Harvard Law Review* 1919.

[49] Bentham (n 33) 333 (discussing art 2 of the 1791 Declaration of the Rights of Man, which describes the 'natural and imprescriptible rights of men' as being 'liberty, property, security, and resistance to oppression').

best described as 'rights to …'. As a result, we should adopt, as more likely to be true, the view that claim-rights are peremptory 'rights that …', in the absence of further arguments in favour of the view that at least some claim-rights must be described as taking the form of 'rights to …'.[50]

V. Private and Public

Finally, we turn to question (4), which asks whether claim-rights are exclusively private in nature – that is, held between individuals – or whether some claim-rights may be distinctively public in nature, in that they can be held by private individuals against the government, or held by the government against private individuals, and are very different from the claim-rights that private individuals might have against each other.

It might be thought that the answer to this question is obvious in that it is a matter of observable fact that English law recognises individuals as holding certain distinctively public claim-rights against the government. For example, under the European Convention on Human Rights (ECHR), as incorporated into English law by the Human Rights Act 1998, a private individual can have a claim-right against a government body (but not a government employee) that it take care in performing life-saving or cruelty-preventing functions that has no equivalent to the claim-rights that a private individual might have against another private individual.[51] And while the common law refuses to recognise the existence of distinctively public claim-rights against the government when it comes to claim-rights that a government body or employee *take care* in performing its functions,[52] it *does* recognise the existence of distinctively public claim-rights when it comes to cases where a government body or employee (D) has *misused* its powers in a way that harmed a private individual (C). In such a case C can argue that he had

[50] A variety of such further arguments are canvassed in NJ McBride, *The Humanity of Private Law* (n 45) 48–54, but none compel us to think of claim-rights in terms of being 'rights to …'. In particular, Razian rights, that ground duties, can be assimilated to Dworkinian principles, so that a Razian 'right to life' can be redescribed as a 'legal principle that life should be protected' (for the same suggestion, see C Webb, 'Three Concepts of Rights, Two of Property' (2018) 38 *Oxford Journal of Legal Studies* 246, 253–54). And while Kantians will not be able to give up the language of 'rights to …' as they need such language to denote the necessary connection between C and X that has to exist for C to be able to complain that D has violated C's Kantian right to independence by damaging or using X, that kind of 'right to …' is not a claim-right at all, but an *interest* in X.

[51] *Osman v United Kingdom* (App no 23452/94) ECHR 1998-VIII 3124, (1998) 29 EHRR 245; *Z v United Kingdom* (App no 29392/95) ECHR 31 May 2001, (2002) 34 EHRR 3.

[52] Under the common law, a private individual will only have a claim-right against a government body or employee that the body/employee take care in performing its functions if the general law on when private individuals will have claim-rights against each other indicates that such a claim-right exists: *Michael v Chief Constable of South Wales* [2015] UKSC 2, [2015] AC 1732 [101], [114]–[116]; *Robinson v Chief Constable of West Yorkshire* [2018] UKSC 4, [2018] AC 736 [32]–[35]; *Poole BC v GN* [2019] UKSC 25 [28], [74].

a claim-right that D not do what it did if (i) D intended to harm C; or (ii) D knew that he was misusing his powers and he knew that his doing so was likely to result in harm to C.[53] No such equivalent claim-right exists where a private individual is harmed by another private individual's misbehaviour.

However, it may be that *properly understood* claim-rights are exclusively private in nature, and that these examples of distinctively public claim-rights represent a misuse of the concept of a claim-right, a misuse that has been triggered by co-opting and distorting the concept of the claim-right for political ends. For example, suppose the law endowed me with a claim-right against the government that it set up a fully-functioning police station and hospital within five miles of where I live. If (as we are assuming is the case) the IG Theory best explains what is involved in having a claim-right against someone else, it looks, at first sight, like the concept of a claim-right has been misused here for political purposes – either I have bribed someone to provide me with this claim-right, or I have been provided with this claim-right because the people who gave it to me do not trust the government to decide for itself how best to deploy its resources in terms of crime-fighting and providing medical assistance to the sick. This is because the IG Theory seems not to support the existence of this kind of claim-right: my interests in remaining healthy and safe from crime are not important enough to ground a duty on the government to go to the lengths involved in setting up a fully-functioning police station and hospital within five miles of where I live.

Against this, Raz's version of the IG Theory might be taken as supporting the view that the law might justifiably endow me with such an ambitious claim-right. Raz's original version of the IG Theory supported the analysis in the previous paragraph: if my interest in remaining healthy and safe from crime, *counted alone*, is not enough to justify the government coming under a duty to set up a fully-functioning police station and hospital within five miles of where I live, then endowing me with a claim-right against the government to such things would amount to a misuse of the concept of a claim-right.[54] However, Raz later modified his IG Theory so that other people's interests *can* be taken into account in deciding whether my interests are sufficiently important to justify your (or the government's) coming under a duty. This will only be the case, however, 'when [those other people's interests] are served by serving [my] interests, only when helping [me] is the proper way of helping others'.[55] So if I am making huge progress in finding a cure for cancer, giving me a claim-right against the government that it set up a full-functioning police station and hospital within five miles of where I live may be appropriate and not involve a misuse of the concept of a claim-right: my interest alone in remaining healthy and

[53] *Three Rivers DC v Governor and Company of the Bank of England (No 3)* [2001] UKHL 16, [2003] 2 AC 1.

[54] Raz (n 13) 202–03.

[55] J Raz, 'Rights and Individual Well-Being' in J Raz, *Ethics in the Public Domain*, rev edn (Oxford, Oxford University Press, 2001) 51.

safe from crime may not be enough to justify the government's coming under a duty to do so much for me, but everyone else's interest in my remaining healthy and safe from crime should be more than ample to tip the balance.

Sreenivasan objects that endowing me with a claim-right on these grounds 'instrumentalizes' me: '[T]he vesting of an individual with a given claim-right … should reflect nothing apart from the *intrinsic* standing of the individual who is to possess it'.[56] Another objection – and one more germane to the project of this chapter – is that endowing me with a claim-right on these grounds allows *me* to instrumentalise *other people*. I am allowed to trade on the fact that other people have an interest in my interests being protected to appropriate government resources for my own ends. Given this, a version of the IG Theory that allows me to do this is far more likely to advance a particular power-seeking agenda, than a version of the IG Theory that only allows me to be endowed with a claim-right where my own interests, *counted alone*, warrant someone coming under a duty. Applying the method advanced in this chapter, we should therefore proceed on the basis that a narrower version of the IG Theory – where only the putative right-holder's interests count in favour of her being given a claim-right – is more likely to be true than a wider version of the IG Theory, where the putative right-holder's interests *and* the interests of those who have an interest in the right-holder's interests being served count in favour of her being given a claim-right.

On this narrower version of the IG Theory, the number of distinctively public claim-rights that can be plausibly recognised is drastically cut down. As we have just seen, giving me a claim-right that the government set up a fully-functioning police station and hospital within five miles of where I live would be ruled out as a misuse of the concept of a claim-right. As would any distinctively public claim-right held by the government against a private individual.[57] On the narrower version of the IG Theory, the interests of the *government* in your doing x, counting alone, could not warrant your coming under a duty to do x as those interests, of and in themselves, are very slight. It is only on the wider version of the IG Theory – where the government can invoke not only its own interests, but everyone else's interests in the government's interests being advanced, to support your coming under a duty to do x – that the government could plausibly be recognised as having a claim-right that you do x.

What about the less ambitious but still distinctively public claim-rights that English law currently recognises private individuals as having against the government? These are not ruled out by the narrower version of the IG Theory. *However,*

[56] Sreenivasan (n 17) 266.

[57] Against Wenar, 'The Nature of Claim-Rights' (n 4) 213: 'An army captain orders a corporal to peel potatoes. We are ordinarily inclined to say that … the captain [has] a right that the corporal do what she ordered'.

it is hard to avoid the impression that the distinctively public claim-right that corresponds to the tort of misfeasance in public office is no claim-right at all.[58] In other words, C's interest in not suffering whatever harm she suffered at D's hands is not the *real* reason why: (i) D had a duty not to abuse the powers of his office; and (ii) D is now liable to compensate C for the harm she suffered as a result of D's abusing those powers. (i) is true of D because the good administration of government demands it, and (ii) is true of D because holding D liable to C is a useful sanction against D's completely failing to respect those demands.[59] *Moreover*, the non-existence of ambitious claim-rights such as a right that the government put in place a police force to protect me from crime has the effect of creating paradoxes down the line should the law attempt (as it has under the law on human rights, but has refused to do so under the law of negligence) to endow me with claim-rights that the police take care to protect me from becoming a victim of crime. If I had no claim-right that the government create a police force in the first place, how can – absent special circumstances that would give rise to a claim-right between you and me – the government's creating a police force result in my having a claim-right that that police force take care to protect me from becoming a victim of crime?[60]

So while our best understanding of the nature of a claim-right does not rule out the possibility of there being distinctively public claim-rights (at least where those claim-rights are held by private individuals against the government), such rights will be rare and very difficult to make out without abusing the concept of a claim-right. The most natural territory for claim-rights is therefore between private individuals, from where they naturally extend to relationships between the government and a private individuals that are equivalent to the relationships that give rise to claim-rights between private individuals; when they go further and turn into distinctively public claim-rights, they are almost certainly out of their depth.

[58] See J Murphy, 'Misfeasance in a Public Office: A Tort Law Misfit?' (2012) 32 *Oxford Journal of Legal Studies* 51, 54–60; D Nolan, 'A Public Law Tort: Understanding Misfeasance in Public Office' in K Barker, S Degeling, K Fairweather and R Grantham (eds), *Private Law and Power* (Oxford, Hart Publishing, 2017) 196–98.

[59] As such the 'tort' of misfeasance in public office is not really a tort at all, and has a lot in common with the equally misnamed 'tort' of public nuisance, where those who suffer special damage as a result of a defendant's culpable failure to abide by the general demands of the common good are enabled to sue the defendant for compensation for that damage.

[60] To the same effect, see TC Grey, 'Procedural Fairness and Substantive Rights' in JR Pennock and JW Chapman (eds), *Due Process* (New York, New York University Press, 1977), arguing that if a given C has no right to a system to welfare benefits being set up in her favour, then she cannot have a right that any system of welfare benefits that is set up be administered with due process. See also *East Suffolk Rivers Catchment Board v Kent* [1941] AC 74 (HL) 87 (Viscount Simon LC).

VI. Conclusion

It may be that we cannot be wrong about the nature of rights. It may be that the different views about the nature of rights are rooted in different and irreconcilable political positions, and victory in the debate over the nature of rights will go (if it goes at all) to whichever side is able to hold out the longest against its rivals. But if (as everyone seems to assume) we can be wrong about claim-rights – if there is a truth of the matter about the nature of claim-rights – then we are least likely to go wrong in thinking about claim-rights if we think of them: (i) as arising because of the interests of the right-holder, considered in isolation; (ii) as being legal, not moral; (iii) as taking the form of 'rights that …', and as therefore being peremptory in nature; and (iv) as hardly ever being distinctively public in nature. This is the view of claim-rights that is least likely to have been adopted for reasons of political advantage, to advance a particular power-seeking agenda, and therefore the view that is most likely to be true, in the absence of further and better arguments establishing that one or more components of this view are incorrect.

6

Juridical Justification of Private Rights

PAUL B MILLER*

I. Introduction

Private law theory is on the rise in the United States. A wave of theoreticians, myself included, have been developing 'internal' theoretical perspectives on various facets of private law. As I have explained elsewhere, this group – gathered under the banner of the New Private Law (NPL) – tends to focus on interpretive theory.[1] And, while all legal interpretation of necessity blends conceptual and normative analysis, most NPL theorists prioritise fidelity in representations made by way of conceptual analysis of law over robust normative claims about the law's moral content or aims.

I have just described certain *tendencies* in a new way of thinking about private law, and for good reason. There is, refreshingly, no orthodoxy in the NPL, and so it is not possible to speak of it univocally. But the upsides of heterodoxy come with a downside: the NPL is characterised by a conflux of methodologies the mutual compatibility and orientation of which are yet to be analysed. NPL theorists have yet to engage in searching debate over what it means to interpret private law from an internal point of view, and why it might be necessary or important to engage in interpretation in this way.

I aim presently to frame and instigate debate over these and similar issues. I will do so by explaining the sense in which interpretive private law theory may be concerned with elucidation of the *juridical justification* of private rights, as reflected in *juridical reasons* for those rights. To some extent, this is a matter of elaborating and refining a methodology that informs my own work.[2] But it also,

* I am grateful for detailed comments from Michael Crawford, Hanoch Dagan, Avihay Dorfman, Stephen Smith and Ben Zipursky.

[1] PB Miller, 'Corporations' in AS Gold, et al (eds), *The Oxford Handbook of the New Private Law* (Oxford, Oxford University Press, 2020).

[2] See, eg: PB Miller, 'Justifying Fiduciary Duties' (2013) 58 *McGill Law Journal* 969; and PB Miller, 'Justifying Fiduciary Remedies' (2013) 63 *University of Toronto Law Journal* 570.

I think, offers one way in which to focus and defend methodological proclivities that characterise NPL.[3]

I have said that this chapter will address interpretive analysis of the juridical justification of private rights. As I will explain, the goal of interpretation, so framed, is to elucidate the justification of private rights in a manner consistent with understanding law as, at once, a set of *public practices of practical reasoning*, and a *product* of these practices. In other words, interpretation treats law as a set of reflexive, interlocking practices; practices that are generative of norms and focused on situating these norms relative to one another and goods to be promoted or secured by law in a given political community. Interpretive analysis of the juridical justification of private rights articulates practical reasons given in law for rights recognised at law. As I shall explain, it is important to distinguish interpretation, so understood, from analyses of private rights in terms of non-juridical practical reasons. It is also important to differentiate interpretive theory *tout court* from critical theory.

[3] These questions have been taken up sporadically in earlier writings. See especially EJ Weinrib, 'The Jurisprudence of Legal Formalism' (1993) 16 *Harvard Journal of Law and Public Policy* 583; BC Zipursky, 'Pragmatic Conceptualism' (2000) 6 *Legal Theory* 457; and H Dagan 'The Limited Autonomy of Private Law' (2008) 56 *American Journal of Comparative Law* 809. For more recent perspectives, see AS Gold, 'Internal and External Perspectives: On Methodology in the New Private Law' in AS Gold et al (eds), *The Oxford Handbook of the New Private Law* (Oxford, Oxford University Press, 2020); and F Jiménez, 'Two Questions for Private Law Theory' (unpublished manuscript on file with author). See also T Khaitan and S Steel, 'Theorising Areas of Law' (unpublished manuscript) < papers.ssrn.com/sol3/papers.cfm?abstract_id=3464432>.

Some of the arguments that I advance here resonate with those of Stephen Smith in his chapter in this volume (SA Smith, 'Intermediate and Comprehensive Justifications for Legal Rules'). Notably, we agree that interpretive private law theory ought to be oriented toward posited legal rules and reasons, and that the normativity of law as posited will rarely admit of persuasive foundationalist (in Smith's phraseology: 'comprehensive') interpretation. We also agree that legal or juridical justification tends to be relatively thin ('shallow', as Smith puts it).

However, our accounts also differ significantly. *First*, unlike Smith, I recognise three levels of abstraction in interpretive analysis (Smith's 'intermediate' category of justification runs together what are, in my account, 'juridical' and 'middle level' justifications, the former being wide enough to encompass mere assertions of value offered as justification for a single legal rule or framework of rules, with the latter encompassing principles of wider – regional, rather than merely local – extension). *Second*, I relate the importance of engagement with juridical reasons to the general jurisprudential literature on the nature and normativity of law, whereas Smith seems primarily concerned with political conciliation in societies characterised by moral relativism and religious division. *Third*, Smith does not differentiate general (content-independent) and particular (content-dependent) juridical reasons for legal rules. *Fourth*, Smith suggests that foundationalist interpretation is illegitimate. I agree that it tends to be suspect as interpretation but would not deny its potential legitimacy. In my view, the merits of interpretive theories turn on whether they provide faithful representation of legal rules and reasons. It is reasonable to infer that fidelity will falter in proportion to the complexity of the subject matter and the extent of abstraction in interpretation. But the failure of highly coherentist interpretation cannot be taken for granted. *Fifth*, and finally, Smith does not make much allowance for the value of critical theoretical analysis. He assumes that all theorists are, or should be, engaged in interpretation, and so bound by a norm of interpretive fidelity. But there is no reason to assume this. Critical theoretical analysis is a legitimate and important undertaking.

The argument will be developed as follows. Section I registers some stipulations about interpretive theory, contrasting interpretation with critique while emphasising that legal interpretation is inevitably concerned with law's normativity. Section II explains juridical justification, clarifying the nature of juridical reasons and their significance for practical reason, and distinguishing juridical from non-juridical practical reasons. Section III extends the analysis to private rights, showing how juridical reasons supply public justification for private rights, and contrasting characteristic features of juridical reasons for private rights embedded in legal forms from those that define isolated conduct rules. Section IV closes the loop by distinguishing interpretive theory oriented toward juridical justification of rights from that which articulates mid-level and foundational justifications. Section V comments on the value and limitations of juridical justification as an element of the public practices of practical reasoning that are central to law-making, adjudication and legal argument. It also explains the compatibility of respect for reason-giving as a focal point of these practices with postures of critique.

II. Interpreting Private Rights

I begin by registering several stipulations made here *arguendo*. They go to the nature of private rights, the nature of law and the differences between interpretive and critical legal theory.

A. Private Rights

This chapter, like the volume of which it is part, is focused on 'private rights'. But reference to private rights is potentially ambiguous given debate over what, if anything, makes rights 'private'. I will not here canvass points in debate or argue a position. Instead, I offer the following four comments in clarification of what I mean by 'private rights'.

First, an analytically robust basis for differentiating 'private' from 'public' rights has yet to found. For that reason, I lay no emphasis on the 'private' quality of the rights that I shall discuss. By 'private rights' I mean to refer to personal rights that obtain interpersonally and are enforced civilly. These rights are personal in that they protect an interest personal to the right-holder. They are interpersonal in that they establish terms of interpersonal interaction. And they are rights in respect of which the right-holder presumptively enjoys personal standing to seek vindication by civil suit.

Second, 'private rights' are held by, and regulate the interpersonal interactions of, all manner of persons, whether acquired or invoked in a personal or representative capacity. Private rights are, of course, held by natural persons acting in their own stead, and govern interactions between such persons in which each person acts on their own rights. But private rights can also be held by artificial persons and govern interpersonal interactions between two or more of them, or between natural and artificial persons. Furthermore, as experience with artificial persons makes plain, private rights can be held by natural persons acting in a representative capacity for others. The fact that groups or institutions may be treated in law as persons for public rather than private purposes gives further reason for ambivalence about the analytical significance of the 'private-ness' of 'private rights'.[4]

Third, while all 'private rights' establish terms of interpersonal interaction, they are structured differently. These differences appear to be rooted in the source of private rights: namely, in the exercise of personal powers by individuals (eg, in the acquisition, transfer or variation of rights) or in the exercise of prerogative powers by the state (eg, the power to make law, including fixing the specification of rights). Some private rights (those originating partly in an exercise of personal power(s)) are bilaterally structured, while others (those originating wholly in an exercise of prerogative power(s)) are held omnilaterally.[5] Rights held bilaterally govern the interaction of two individuals and define the normative contours of (part of) their relationship; the right-holder enjoys her right relative to the duty-holder and no one else, and likewise the duty-holder is obliged by virtue of her duty to the right-holder and no one else.[6] Private rights that have this quality – eg, those recognised in contract and fiduciary law – arise partly by virtue of the exercise of normative powers by, or for, a right- and/or duty-holder and presume privity in conditions requisite to the incidence of the right.[7] By contrast, omnilateral rights are held by the right-holder relative to all other persons; the duties correlative to these rights are general and assume nothing about pre-existing mutual involvements or interactions of the right- and duty-holder.[8] These rights – eg, as realised in tort law – are prescribed by the state and specify how each must treat others as a matter of general, reciprocal right and duty. Individuals will only ever enter into a relationship of direct interpersonal accountability if a duty-holder acts, or threatens to act, in breach of duty to a right-holder.

[4] As discussed in PB Miller and J Pojanowski, 'Torts Against the State' in PB Miller and J Oberdiek (eds), *Civil Wrongs and Justice in Private Law* (Oxford, Oxford University Press, 2020).

[5] Arguably, a third category of rights is structured multilaterally. Consider rights that obtain in associations and mediate relationships between members *inter se*, and between them and the entity.

[6] On bilaterality, see EJ Weinrib, 'Correlativity, Personality and the Emerging Consensus on Corrective Justice' (2001) 2 *Theoretical Inquiries in Law* 107.

[7] See generally N MacCormick and J Raz, 'Voluntary Obligations and Normative Powers' (1972) 46 *Proceedings of the Aristotelian Society, Supplementary Volumes* 59.

[8] As Keating explains, '[p]rimary responsibilities in tort are omnilateral and standing': GC Keating, 'Is the Role of Tort to Repair Wrongful Losses?' in D Nolan and A Roberston (eds), *Rights and Private Law* (Oxford, Hart Publishing, 2012) 367, 382.

Fourth and finally, by 'private rights' I mean to denote primary but not secondary (or remedial) rights. I also mean to refer to rights as such, rather than all manner of legal entitlements (rights, privileges and powers). Primary rights specify how a right-holder may insist upon being treated by a duty-holder. In turn, their content provides normative guidance. It might be hoped that the guidance will be abided by the duty-holder. But where it is not, the right-holder will have a cause of action for breach that may be asserted personally against the duty-holder. In pleading her case, she may assert a secondary 'right' to a particular remedy. But the relationship of rights and remedies is complex.[9] In some cases, remedies are available, doctrinally, on proof of a certain kind of wrong. They are available effectively as of right and seem grounded normatively in their responsiveness to practical reasons that underlie a primary right. However, in other cases they appear also, or instead, to be responsive to contingent features of the wrongful violation of the primary right, or to general considerations relating to the administration of justice.[10] However interesting, these puzzles are an unnecessary distraction and so I shall set them aside.

B. Law as Public Practical Reasoning

Given that this chapter is addressed to questions of methodology in interpretive legal theory, I ought to clarify how I understand law. As intimated earlier, I think that law is best understood as a set of interconnected practices of practical reasoning and as a product of a subset of these practices. More specifically, law encompasses reflexive public practices of practical reasoning that involve, most prominently, positing, arguing about, deciphering, deciding on, deliberating with and determining how to comport with rules of general application in a political community, as well as the products of a subset of these practices (the official practices of law-makers in giving, interpreting or otherwise pronouncing law).[11] This implies what leading general jurisprudes, notwithstanding their other differences, accept; namely, that law is inextricably bound up with practical reason and the exercise of that capacity (a) institutionally, in the governance of political communities and (b) personally, by individuals reflecting on what we owe to each other and/or our communities, and about how to act in light

[9] SA Smith, *Rights, Wrongs, and Injustices: The Structure of Remedial Law* (Oxford, Oxford University Press, 2019).

[10] As emphasised by N Cornell, 'What Do We Remedy?' in PB Miller and J Oberdiek (eds), *Civil Wrongs and Justice in Private Law* (Oxford, Oxford University Press, 2020); and C Webb, 'Duties and Damages' in PB Miller and J Oberdiek (eds), *Oxford Studies in Private Law Theory*, Vol 1 (Oxford, Oxford University Press, 2020).

[11] In thinking of law as a set of public practices of practical reasoning, I have been influenced by GJ Postema, 'Public Practical Reason: Political Practice' (1995) 37 *Nomos* 345; and GJ Postema, 'Public Practical Reason: An Archeology' (1995) 12 *Social Philosophy and Policy* 43.

of same.[12] One could, of course, say much, much more about the relationship between law and practical reason. Here, I must content myself with registering two assumptions that are reflected in the argument to follow.

The first is that law may be understood as a reflexive set of public practices of practical reasoning insofar as posited law is the *product* of public practical reasoning (ie, public deliberation and debate over, settled by public declaration of, law) and insofar as posited law, in turn, *structures* – by *enabling* and *focusing* – public practical reasoning (ie, it guides and directs those engaged in practical reasoning, whether in official or personal capacities). The reflexive quality of these practices is evident in reasoned engagement with law that accepts it as properly settled, as well as in that which critiques it as poorly or wrongly settled. To see the law in this way is to view it as a dynamic enterprise whereby a community subjects itself to rules in order to settle and thus enable, but not foreclose, effective practical reasoning.

The second assumption – also the subject of broad agreement – is that the primary function of law is that of providing normative guidance to those to whom it is addressed.[13] The guidance function of law is primary in that the law's other functions are contingent on its effectiveness in supplying guidance. Setting to one side, for now, the relationship between law and other sources of practical reason, I take it that law supplies normative guidance by giving practical reasons, and that it does so in issuing rules and in articulating reasons for these rules.[14] Finally, I share the view that the law will generally be suitable for (and thus, usually,

[12] A sampling: J Finnis, *Natural Law and Natural Rights* (Oxford, Oxford University Press, 1980); J Finnis, 'Foundations of Practical Reason Revisited' (2005) 50 *American Journal of Jurisprudence* 109; J Gardner and T Macklem, 'Reasons' in J Coleman and S Shapiro (eds), *The Oxford Handbook of Jurisprudence and Philosophy of Law* (Oxford, Oxford University Press, 2002); J Gardner, 'Nearly Natural Law' (2007) 52 *American Journal of Jurisprudence* 1; J Raz, *Practical Reason and Norms* (Oxford, Oxford University Press, 1999); and J Waldron, 'The Concept and the Rule of Law' (2008) 43 *Georgia Law Review* 1.

[13] Law's addressees being individuals acting in a personal capacity as well as legal officials acting in an official capacity. The modern *locus classicus* of analysis of the guidance function of law is HLA Hart, *The Concept of Law* (Oxford, Oxford University Press, 1961). See also J Raz, 'The Rule of Law and its Virtue' in J Raz, *The Authority of Law* (Oxford, Clarendon, 1979); and S Shapiro, 'Law, Morality and the Guidance of Conduct' (2000) 6 *Legal Theory* 127.

[14] In this, I depart from those legal philosophers (most of whom identify as hard positivists) who believe that the law gives practical reasons only by issuing rules – ie, directives – that figure in our practical reasoning by excluding our giving consideration or weight to other kinds of practical reason, including moral or prudential reasons that favour or disfavour a rule or an act in compliance with or contravention of a rule. I ally myself with those (many, but not all of whom, identify as natural law theorists) who think that the law can only be an exercise in public justification to the extent that it traffics in reasons as well as directives, and that law can generally serve as a (morally) suitable source of normative guidance on this basis. I say this while acknowledging that in some cases reasons may not be put for a rule on the basis of obviousness or in the belief that the justification for a rule is both patent and over-determined (perhaps even patently overdetermined), and that in other cases – as discussed in Section V.B, below – our law-makers might fail to give reasons – or to give good ones – for rules. I am grateful to Stephen Smith for encouraging me to clarify my views on these points.

more effective in) supplying normative guidance to the extent that the rules and reasons it articulates are practically reasonable.[15]

C. Interpretation and Critique

This chapter is, again, addressed to questions of methodology in interpretive legal theory. But, given the inherent normativity of law, and given that the normativity of law and its claim to authority are such as to invite reasoned assessment of the soundness as well as the nature of what the law permits or demands, it is important to distinguish interpretation from critique, or *interpretive legal theory* from *critical legal theory*.[16]

The task of *interpretive legal theory* is one of offering a simplified but faithful rendering of posited law that aims to make it more amenable to understanding. The rendering involves descriptive and normative elements, but the latter are supplied not by the theorist, but by law. The theorist aims at description of the posited law and elucidation of its *posited* normativity, the latter being a record of settled judgment reached for a political community on a normative issue.[17] The theorist might also point out gaps, discordant elements, or open questions about posited law and legal reasons, and they retain an interpretive posture provided they do so without critique. Finally, to the extent that interpretation of legal texts varies by interpretive methodology – for example, in the manner of construction of text and weight to be accorded non-textual evidence of the law – the theorist should explain their methodology, enabling others to evaluate their handiwork.

By contrast, the task of *critical legal theory* is avowedly, and properly unapologetically,[18] critical and, often, reformist in its orientation toward posited law.[19] Where the critical theorist believes the law, or reasons posited for it, to be deficient, they may advance the common good through argument for reform. Their argument will be an invitation that the community develop or revise

[15] See generally MC Murphy, 'Natural Law Jurisprudence' (2003) 9 *Legal Theory* 241.

[16] It is unfortunate – because obfuscating of the law, and our collective interest in reasoned scrutiny of what the law permits or demands, and whether its permissions and demands are justified – that interpretation and critique are so often run together in private law theory.

[17] See Postema, 'Public Practical Reason: An Archeology' (n 11) at 70–71, explaining that the 'point of justification is practical and public: it is to locate some form of common ground for action or assessment among rational agents who must live in close proximity to, and interact with, each other'. It is of no moment that the positing of law shows the issue to have been only contingently or imperfectly settled.

[18] cf Khaitan and Steel (n 3) at 2, who claim that 'the main purpose of theorisation is understanding the phenomenon [theorised]' and suggest that it may only 'incidentally have practical implications'.

[19] On the value of critique, and in exemplification of same, see H Dagan and R Kreitner, 'The Character of Legal Theory' (2011) 96 *Cornell Law Review* 671; and H Dagan and A Dorfman, 'Just Relationships' (2016) 116 *Columbia Law Review* 1395.

its settled judgment on a normative issue, or reframe it so as to provide better (ie, more practically reasonable) normative guidance.[20]

III. Juridical Justification Generally

I have promised to outline a methodology for interpretive analysis of the juridical justification of private rights. The elements relating specifically to private rights are set forth in Section III. But I shall first explain how juridical justification and reasons, respectively, are to be understood from a general jurisprudential perspective.

A. Juridical Reasons as Legal Reasons

Contemporary use of the word 'juridical' is sometimes thought an indulgence of the obscure. That may be because it is no longer in common use. But there is not any obscurity, nor does use of the word invite or imply mystical thinking. 'Juridical' is a synonym for 'legal', but emphasises that legal usage of language is technical, such that words and concepts – and actions and practices involving same – may not, in law, bear the meaning(s) that they have as a matter of general usage. So, for example, 'right', 'duty', 'wrong', 'remedy', 'care', 'cause', 'claim' and so on, have technical meanings in law that diverge from their other, more widely known, meanings. And law is laid down through, and taken up in, technical linguistic practices of lawyers, judges and others. Practical mischief and distortion of thought can arise if one fails to distinguish the technical from non-technical semantics of language in which law is expressed.[21] But adding the adjective 'legal' to a word that has a technical meaning in law distinct from its other, more familiar, meanings may not be sufficient to denote its technical usage because 'legal' is itself ambiguous (ie, not reserved for, and so a reliable marker of, legal semantics). There is thus value in substituting the adjective 'juridical' for 'legal', if only to clarify that one is invoking legal semantics and legal normativity.

In speaking of juridical reasons, then, I mean to denote *legal* reasons in a technical sense. The sense is that implied by recognition of the authority of legal

[20] It may be that the relative importance and prevalence of critique vis-à-vis interpretation varies depending on the level of stability of a community's settlement of a given normative issue or set of issues. In periods of social, cultural, religious or political tumult, the posited law might experience – and, indeed, be a site for – 'paradigm shifts', in which case critical theory will take on a special salience and interpretation is likely to become more fraught. I am grateful to Hanoch Dagan for emphasising this point and the Kuhnian language in comments on an earlier draft of this chapter. See also H Dagan, 'Doctrinal Categories, Legal Realism, and the Rule of Law' (2015) 163 *University of Pennsylvania Law Review* 1889.

[21] See J Finnis, 'Some Professorial Fallacies About Rights' (1972) 4 *Adelaide Law Review* 377.

officials to posit, interpret and enforce law, with juridical reasons being a matter of express or implied legal justification(s) for law, and for obedience to law.[22] I take juridical reasons to be of at least two kinds. *General juridical reasons* are content-independent reasons,[23] that obtain generally within legal systems and that call for obedience of legal rules as general matter (ie, irrespective of their content, because they were validly posited by legal institutions with a good claim to authority).[24] Content-independent reasons can be understood as reasons *for* obedience to law, and reasons given *by* law (ie, by the pertinence of a validly posited legal rule), in which case content-independence may be thought to indicate something important about their bearing on practical reasoning (eg, that one has a decisive reason to obey a legal rule, simply because it has been validly posited by an official or institution with a good claim to authority in relation to the rule). There is, unsurprisingly, considerable controversy over the normative significance of general juridical reasons.[25] I set this aside here. I take it that, whatever their significance, general juridical reasons are incomplete[26] in that they cannot account for the specificity of the normative guidance that the law provides; ie, they are not reasons for doing what this or that legal rule or framework of legal rules permits or requires. Such specificity is found only in the content of, and reasons for, particular legal rules. I shall thus focus here on *particular juridical reasons*, by which I mean posited reasons for a particular legal rule or framework of legal rules.

Particular juridical reasons are content-dependent; they are reasons offered in support of a legal rule or framework of legal rules, given the content and intended impact of the rule(s). For a content-dependent reason to be *juridical* – ie, one given in, and not merely for, law – it must be expressly articulated by a legal official with requisite authority, or be implied by law on the basis of the content or scheme of a rule or set of rules and/or objective evidence of the purpose or design of the lawmaker.

Reasons figure in the justification of something that stands in need of justification; here, a legal rule or framework of legal rules, or a decision or action taken in the face of the law. It follows that juridical reasons are legal reasons that figure in the juridical justification of law and actions that are, or should have

[22] Obedience being a matter of reasoned deference to the authority of law and, by extension, of legal institutions. Reasoned deference is usually shown in accepting and acting on the normative guidance supplied by law.

[23] HLA Hart, *Essays on Bentham* (Oxford, Oxford University Press, 1982); J Raz, *The Morality of Freedom* (Oxford, Oxford University Press, 1988).

[24] I will remain agnostic for present purposes on the conditions requisite to having a good claim to authority. On the relationship between the authority of law and legal officials or institutions, see A Marmor, 'Authorities and Persons' (1995) 1 *Legal Theory* 337.

[25] See, eg: P Markwick, 'Law and Content-Independent Reasons' (2000) 20 *Oxford Journal of Legal Studies* 579; L Valentini, 'The Content-Independence of Political Obligation: What it is and How to Test It' (2018) 24 *Legal Theory* 135.

[26] In Markwick's framing, they are, at best, 'partial' rather than 'complete' reasons. ibid.

been, responsive to law.[27] While reasons figure in justifications, it should also be remembered that their sufficiency as a matter of justification is a function of their weight, not just their public pronouncement and pertinence. A given juridical reason may make but a partial contribution to cumulative justification. Thus, juridical justification is a matter of the overall normative upshot of pertinent juridical reasons.

Juridical reasons are 'surficial'; they lie upon the surface of the law, in court opinions, transcripts, legislative records and statute books, and are usually relatively thin. In the common law tradition, they are thought to reflect the relative simplicity of conventional morality.[28] Juridical reasons are a kind of normative shorthand, offering the extent of justification that is apt for law considering its status as *authoritative public settlement* of normative issues within a political community. Consistent with rule of law values and the guidance function of law, it is important that juridical reasons be comprehensible to a layperson; one shouldn't need to be expert in ethics, economics or statecraft to be able to understand and make use of them. That is, one should not need to be practised in normative *longhand* to be able to understand the reasons that the law supplies for acting as the law permits or requires.

As I will explain in Section V, juridical reasons are not merely thin; they are also predictably imperfect. Imperfection is endemic, partly owing to concessions of analyticity to comprehensibility, but also because juridical reasons are developed through diffuse and/or uncoordinated law-making processes that introduce various institutional contingencies and that are often also politically charged. While we may have reason to regret these imperfections, we ought not to dismiss them. To do so is to miss the opportunity to discern whether the law is presently well suited to its guidance function.

B. Juridical Reasons as Practical Reasons

I have said that juridical reasons are legal reasons, and that they contribute importantly to the law's guidance function. But how ought we to understand the nature of legal rules and reasons, and the manner in which they provide guidance? Consistent with the convergence of views in general jurisprudence described in

[27] Smith suggests, plausibly in my view, that lawmakers (he has courts in mind) will tend to explicitly articulate reasons for a legal rule where that rule is new or is unsettled generally or when it is extended to a new set of circumstances. Judges applying settled law take the reasons for same to be settled, too, and so might say little about them. Smith, 'Intermediate and Comprehensive Justifications' (n 3) at 66–67.

[28] W Sadurski, 'Conventional Morality and Judicial Standards' (1987) 73 *Virginia Law Review* 339; GJ Postema, 'The Philosophy of Common Law' in J Coleman and S Shapiro (eds), *The Oxford Handbook of Jurisprudence and Philosophy of Law* (Oxford, Oxford University Press, 2002).

Section I.B, I take it that juridical reasons are a kind of practical reason, and thus fulcra for deliberative and discursive practices of practical reasoning, whether those practices relate to the positing, interpretation, civic utilisation or enforcement of law.

To say that juridical reasons are a kind of practical reason is to say that they figure in personal and public practical deliberations as reasons for the posited law to which they relate, and for, or against, action taken in the face of such law. Setting to one side their significance in, and to, law, general jurisprudes remain divided on whether juridical reasons are normatively distinctive in a *substantive* sense. I agree with those who hold that they are not.[29] Substantively, legal reasons are just moral or prudential reasons given in, and for, law.

As noted in Section II.A, juridical reasons are characteristically thin. And, as adverted to earlier, this might be a necessary concession to the difficulty of building consensus and compromise within political communities and, relatedly, the challenge of providing effective normative guidance in communities characterised by significant diversity of opinion and belief on matters of value. This is to say nothing of resource-related and other factors that favour economy in normative expression through law. But whatever might explain their characteristic thinness, it does not lend juridical reasons a substantively distinctive character.

To say that juridical reasons are *substantively* indistinguishable from moral and prudential reasons is not to say that there is no point in distinguishing them in *other respects* when engaging in practical reasoning. Indeed, one can and sometimes should take notice that reasons given in law are just that: posited as justification for what the law permits or requires. Analytically, there is value in recognising rules and reasons by their source.[30] And, pragmatically, there is value in recognising that reasons given in law are presented by legal officials as justifying rules subject to coercive enforcement, whether or not we think them sound or decisive.

IV. Juridical Justification of Private Rights

Thus far, I have said that juridical justification is a matter of the normative upshot of the *general* and *particular* juridical reasons for compliance with and/or reliance on a legal rule or framework of rules. Juridical reasons and justification are central to the discursive and deliberative practices that define law as a form of public practical reasoning and, likewise, to law's guidance function. It is partly through

[29] J Gardner, 'Legal Positivism: 5 ½ Myths' (2001) 46 *American Journal of Jurisprudence* 199; J Gardner, 'The Legality of Law' (2004) 17 *Ratio Juris* 168; L Green, 'Positivism and the Inseparability of Law and Morals' (2008) 83 *New York University Law Review* 1035; M Greenberg, 'The Moral Impact Theory of Law' (2014) 123 *Yale Law Journal* 1118; S Hershovitz, 'The End of Jurisprudence' (2015) 124 *Yale Law Journal* 1160.

[30] Hershovitz, ibid.

juridical reasons that the law supplies normative guidance. And it is primarily through reasoned engagement with juridical reasons that the law proves more and less fit in the provision of guidance.

Of private rights, I have noted that our focus will be on primary rights. I explained that these rights are an important means by which the law establishes terms of interaction for persons, whether natural or artificial. And I have noted that private rights are structured bilaterally or omnilaterally.[31]

In what follows, I comment on the juridical justification of private rights that have been posited in either of two ways. I turn first to private rights that are constitutive elements of a legal form of interaction. As one might expect, juridical reasons for these rights reflect the formal situation of the right. I then turn to stand-alone private rights. Stand-alone rights are (a) omnilateral and not connected to a form of interaction and, so, not conditioned by privity[32] or (b) arise in relation to a form of interaction but are protective rather than constitutive of the form (eg, rights against third party interference with the performance of a contract or fiduciary mandate). As we will see, it can be more difficult to identify juridical reasons for stand-alone rights because, absent formal context, one must seek direct indication of the interest(s) the right is meant to protect.

A. Juridical Reasons for Rights Embedded in Legal Forms

Private rights are often embedded within legal forms of interaction (hereinafter: legal forms). Legal forms are legally defined modes of interaction. The complex of rules that define legal forms delineate how parties to an association or relationship of that type may and/or must relate within its parameters. These rules may be predominantly power-conferring, or primarily duty-imposing. Where a given form consists predominantly of power-conferring rules and so is broadly *enabling*, the duty-imposing rules attached to it operate to ensure its effectiveness as an enabling device and to secure the integrity of the form. By contrast, where a form consists predominantly of duty-imposing rules and so is broadly *constraining*, the power-conferring rules attached to it often provide limited scope for private ordering (eg, for adjustment of the content, enforcement or directionality of duties), so far as is consistent with the integrity of the form.

Where embedded in legal forms, private rights contribute to the law's definition of discrete modes of interaction. In some cases, the general gist of a legal form corresponds to social modes of interaction. Thus, for example, contract may

[31] With an exception for rights structured multilaterally. See n 5 above.

[32] One should, however, not assume that legal forms are generally characterised by bilateral rules while stand-alone conduct rules are omnilateral. Certain legal forms are constituted primarily by omnilateral rules and supplemented by bilateral rules. Others are constituted primarily by multilateral rules. See n 5 above.

be understood to resolve, in legal form, a subset of social practices of promising.[33] Similarly, wills and other donative transfers are legal forms that correspond to and enable social practices of family provision and gift-giving.[34] However, legal forms, where based on social practices, abstract from those practices and often thoroughly re-work their normativity. And, in any case, legal forms make it possible for persons to interact *in a particular way* (ie, as adumbrated by rules constitutive of the form). Private rights contribute to legal forms by specifying what the right-holder may expect, and how the duty-holder must act, in relation to the subject matter of the right. But, in contrast with private rights that express stand-alone rules, the subject matter of a right embedded within a form must be understood in the context of other rules that constitute the form.[35]

Having described private rights embedded in legal forms, we may turn our attention now to juridical reasons for such rights. It may first be noted that the juridical reasons for private rights embedded in legal forms often reflect juridical reasons for the form. Indeed, it may often be that the juridical reasons for the right are derivative of those that support the form. In any case, interpretive analysis will be intricate, with the level of intricacy depending on the complexity of the form and the concatenation of rules constitutive of it. The second thing to be noted is that legal forms are not fixed constructs and so should not be taken to establish closed normative contexts for the positing of private rights or reasons for same.

Our account thus far has been abstract. We may now turn to some examples. For the sake of clarity, I will focus on simpler forms and focal rights within these forms: the right to performance in a conventional arms-length contractual relationship (here, we will assume a negotiated bargain between persons of equal bargaining power), and the right to loyalty in a fiduciary relationship (here, we will focus on the relationship between directors and a widely-held corporation).

We may begin with the right to performance in contract. Reciprocal rights and duties of performance supply mandatory terms of interaction for parties to a contract. The mere fact of their having been posited and made subject to coercive enforcement gives parties general juridical reasons for compliance. But these reasons are relatively weak and indeterminate. We understandably look to contract law for justification of rules peculiar to it. What reasons are found in contract law for the right to performance? Understandably, given the centrality of performance

[33] C Fried, *Contract as Promise: A Theory of Contractual Obligation*, rev edn (Oxford, Oxford University Press, 2015). See also S Shiffrin, 'The Divergence of Contract and Promise' (2007) 120 *Harvard Law Review* 709 and C Fried, 'The Convergence of Contract and Promise' (2007) 120 *Harvard Law Review Forum* 1.

[34] J Baron, 'Gifts, Bargains, and Form' (1988–89) 64 *Indiana Law Journal* 155; and EA Posner, 'Altruism, Status, and Trust in the Law of Gifts and Gratuitous Promises' (1997) *Wisconsin Law Review* 567.

[35] And, in turn, legal forms must be understood in terms of the wider operation of private law as a normative system. See Gold, 'Internal and External Perspectives' (n 3); Smith (n 3); and HE Smith, 'The Persistence of System in Property' (2015) 163 *University of Pennsylvania Law Review* 2055.

to contract, the reasons are complex and embed considerations of form, function and value. For example, the right to performance has been said to be justified morally on the basis that a valid contract is an exchange of promises. Court opinions often also emphasise trust in, or reliance on, contractual undertakings. One sometimes also sees mention of reasons that underlie contract generally as a form of interaction (eg, reasons rooted in the positive moral impact of contract law through its advancement of personal autonomy, interpersonal cooperation or social utility).

Turning to corporate law, one finds something similar. A director looking to the law for normative guidance will find not just indication of what they are required to do by way of compliance with their duty of loyalty, but also particular juridical reasons for compliance. Fiduciary duties being a species of voluntary obligation, the director will be reminded that they are bound partly because they willingly entered a relationship to which fiduciary impositions attach. Other reasons emphasise the relative positions of the parties and the centrality of the duty of loyalty to integrity of the form (eg, those that advert to expectations of trustworthiness implied by the entrustment of discretionary powers, or to the other-regarding character of fiduciary mandates). Still others point to reasons for enabling fiduciary relationships generally, or of a particular type, including reasons rooted in autonomy, interpersonal dependence and cooperation.

B. Juridical Reasons for Stand-Alone Rights

Private rights are not invariably embedded in legal forms; some rights are enjoyed by natural persons on the basis of status, and by some artificial persons on the basis of attribution. This appears to be especially true of omnilateral rights that prescribe universal rules of conduct. We may call these rights 'stand-alone rights' to emphasise their independence of specific legal forms of interaction.

Stand-alone rights are most prevalent in the law of torts. The stand-alone rights recognised in tort show their independence of form in their substantive plurality and resistance to unifying interpretation. One can catalogue rights in respect of which there are recognised civil wrongs (torts) as bases of liability, and one can perhaps group these rights in respect of their content (eg, fault elements) or referents (eg, personal or property interests); but it is difficult to convincingly arrange them as responsive to any one value or structured set of values.

The difficulty is, I think, a function of diversity in the interests that tort law protects.[36] Tort law is remarkable for its breadth. Many rights recognised in tort are responsive to the interests of persons, including interests in reputation, privacy, freedom of movement and physical security. Other tort rights protect interests in

[36] See J Murphy, 'The Heterogeneity of Tort Law' (2019) 39 *Oxford Journal of Legal Studies* 455.

acquired rights, including property and contractual rights. Here, tort leaves it to fields that govern the acquisition of rights to define those rights. Tort law simply reinforces (ie, secures) the legal forms that mediate the acquisition of property and contractual rights. And all of this is to say nothing of the complexities introduced by the recognition that tort law also protects certain interests of artificial persons.[37]

As one might expect, diversity in the rights that tort law recognises is reflected in a diversity of juridical reasons for its recognition of these rights. Sometimes the reasons given amount to assertions of the inherent moral value of human interests thought to underlie the right. In other cases, they reflect a rule-consequentialist logic, with the right being deemed rooted normatively in moral or policy considerations bearing on the social impact of behaviour controlled by the right.

Where a tort right provides omnilateral protection for interests in acquired rights, juridical reasons will usually refer to the legal form that enables acquisition and reasons for the form. In this sense, juridical reasons for a right recognised in tort law may be derivative of those engaged by values at stake in legal institution(s) that tort law protects (eg, many reasons for recognition of rights against interference with property are derivative of reasons for provision of forms of private property).

Furthermore, whether or not a given tort right secures interests in acquired rights, just like any other private right, the content of the tort right and/or its enforcement may be checked by other rights and limited by defences, justifications or excuses. In such cases, to understand the normative force of juridical reasons for a tort right, one must appreciate how those reasons are conditioned by other underlying rules or mechanisms that might adumbrate the right and/or the standing to enforce it.

In illustration, consider the torts of negligence and nuisance. Negligence provides omnilateral protection for interests in bodily integrity by recognising a right against negligent infliction of injury; nuisance provides omnilateral protection for interests in peaceful possession and use of real property by recognising a right of quiet enjoyment. Law-makers have posited a range of reasons for these rights. For example, the right at issue in negligence has been said to be grounded in the values of personal welfare and autonomy as well as a public policy of minimising the social costs of accidents. In turn, the right at issue in nuisance has been justified by reference to the autonomy interests of owners in quiet enjoyment, the welfare interests of owners put in issue by the psychological harms of nuisance-causing activity, and a public policy of incentivising owners to minimise negative externalities associated with their use of property.

[37] Miller (n 1); PB Miller and JA Pojanowski, 'Torts Against the State' in PB Miller and J Oberdiek (eds), *Civil Wrongs and Justice in Private Law* (Oxford, Oxford University Press, 2020).

Notice that, in respect of each of negligence and nuisance, one finds not just a plurality of juridical reasons for rights that tort law recognises, but also illustration of the importance of situating these rights and reasons contextually. Thus, the right at issue in nuisance, and the reasons for that right, are subject to a proportionality assessment that takes heed of the alleged tortfeasor's rights, including their right to use and enjoyment of their own property. Consider, too, the conditioning effect of reasons of public policy that support zoning laws, to say nothing of the effect of defences (eg, consent and necessity) and reasons for recognition of same.

V. Interpreting Private Rights, Revisited

I have argued that private rights and juridical reasons ought to be understood in light of the nature of law as, at once, a set of public practices of practical reasoning, and as the product of a subset of these practices. Reasons are given juridically for rights and other legal rules in order to more effectively guide the behaviour of beings endowed with practical reason. Private rights are legally binding to the extent that they are validly posited, but juridical reasons are only practically persuasive to the extent that they are practically reasonable.

I have also argued that central tasks of interpretive private law theory are those of: (a) elucidating private rights (and other jural statuses or relations); (b) explaining the juridical situation of particular private rights (and other legal rules), including, as appropriate, their incorporation within legal forms; (c) identifying posited reasons for private rights (and other legal rules); (d) identifying ways in which a given private right (or other legal rule) and reasons for it are cabined by legal or equitable conditions or limitations, including conflicting rights; and (e) highlighting any gaps, contradictions or inconsistencies in the content of a private right (or other legal rule) and the reasons posited for it.

It is in the nature of interpretive analysis of the juridical justification of private rights that it hews closely to posited law. It privileges the internal point of view in that it seeks to make the law more amenable to understanding. Again, this involves development of a simplified rendering of law. But, in contrast to those employing modalities of interpretation that abstract from the law to a greater extent, the interpretive theorist focused on the juridical justification of private rights will be especially concerned about the risk of interpretive over-simplification.

The distinction between interpretive and critical theory is, I think, relatively sharp. I shall therefore not comment on it further. However, recognising that (a) the law is inherently normative, and that interpretation therefore involves excavation of the law's normativity; and (b) the law is amenable of different levels of interpretation, depending how coherentist the interpreter is in isolating the nature and extent of its practical reasonableness, I shall here contrast interpretive analysis focused on *juridical justification* from that which articulates *foundational* and *mid-level justification* of private rights.

A. Contrasts, I: Foundational Justification of Private Rights

Interpretive theories that make foundationalist claims about the justification of private rights interpret them as manifesting a single value or system of values. Foundationalist interpretation often begins with an assertion or argument in favour of a value, or set of values, and an explication of a way of modelling private law in light of these value(s). The theorist will proceed, by way of interpretive exegesis, to show how all or part of private law comports with the model. Usually, the exegesis focuses on the content, effect and enforcement of private rights, and a selection of juridical reasons for them. Exegetical analysis of juridical reasons allows the theorist to claim that the normative foundations identified are those found in law (grounding the claim to engagement in interpretive theory) rather than a reflection of the value commitments of the theorist (which would require acknowledgement that the project is really one of critique).

Some of the most prominent theories of private rights articulate foundational justifications for them. Amongst these, notable is the work of Kantian theorists, Ernest Weinrib and Arthur Ripstein. Weinrib and Ripstein analyse the structure, content, effect, and enforcement of private rights as giving manifold expression of the value of equal freedom.[38] Systems of posited private law are modelled on Kant's abstract framework of private right.[39] Of course, the Kantians recognise gaps between abstract and posited rights; gaps implied in part by the fact that, as a normative matter, the entailments of equal freedom underdetermine the content of posited private rights. Nevertheless, they believe that Anglo-American private law can and should be interpreted in light of Kant's model, and understood as responsive to the value of equal freedom, with discordant parts of law being held out for critique.[40]

Theories such as these strike their critics as elaborate castles built at heady altitude. But they do aim at interpreting private law from an internal point of view. It is only that the perspective that they provide is shaped profoundly by model(s) of private rights associated with a particular value or system of value. Theorists who believe that it is possible and worthwhile to articulate foundational justifications of private law are strongly coherentist in their interpretation of private rights. The Kantians, for example, believe that private law manifests practical reasonableness in doctrine that coheres in its responsiveness to the value of equal freedom.

[38] EJ Weinrib, *The Idea of Private Law* (Cambridge, MA, Harvard University Press, 1995); EJ Weinrib, *Corrective Justice* (Oxford, Oxford University Press, 2012); A Ripstein, *Force and Freedom* (Cambridge, MA, Harvard University Press, 2009); A Ripstein, *Private Wrongs* (Cambridge, MA, Harvard University Press, 2016).

[39] Immanuel Kant, 'Doctrine of Right', in *Metaphysics of Morals* (Mary Gregor ed, New York, Colombia University Press, 1996).

[40] I am grateful to Avihay Dorfman for emphasising the prevalence of what is framed as 'internal' critique within foundationalist theory. It bears emphasis, though, that whether or not such critique is faithful to an internal point of view turns on the interpretive soundness of the normative story that the theorist tells about the pervasive immanence in the posited law of a particular foundational value or set of values.

Our exemplar of foundationalism analyses private rights in terms of a single value. But foundationalism, and the strong coherentism it implies, is not the preserve of normative monists preoccupied with analytic systematicity in practical affairs.[41] Foundationalism is, or could be, evident in interpretive analysis guided by any well-ordered theory of value. Thus, Lockean, Hegelian, consequentialist and classical natural law theories of private rights might each be foundationalist in the interpretation they inspire, depending how they account for the relationship between posited law and the demands of morality on practical reasoning.

Whether they espouse a monistic or pluralistic theory of value, foundationalist theories of private rights are associated with two kinds of interpretive excess. Each reflects downsides of undue preoccupation with coherence.

The first variety of interpretive excess is that whereby private rights and juridical reasons are interpreted apologetically, with analysis aiming to suggest conceptual and normative coherence in posited law, coupled with an implication that the package deal – the set or system of rights, shown to be coherent – is practically reasonable.[42] Implied is that it would be a mistake to revise or eliminate a given right or system of rights, or to reconsider whether reasons given for the right(s) are good reasons.

Where interpretation slides into apologetics, it is problematic to the extent that it ignores the frailty of practical reason, which is such as to introduce a significant probability of moral error in collective practices of public practical reasoning. It also problematic in that it elides the distinction between interpretation and critique. Apologetics are appropriate where the law and reasons given for it merit reasoned defence, but this is an exercise in critical analysis of law.

The second sort of interpretive excess is that whereby a theorist overlooks or discounts rights or reasons not readily amenable of interpretation through their preferred model or theory of value. It is entirely proper as a matter of critique to examine the practical reasonableness of a right and/or the reasons given for it. However, it is improper as a matter of interpretation to neglect those rights or posited reasons that they defy one's normative priors. This kind of excess, where indulged, produces interpretive infelicity in the form of partial or distorted representations of the law.

Whether or not these excesses can be avoided in foundationalist interpretive theory is an open question. They might well mark common tendencies rather than inherent biases of thought. But they are most readily avoided if one gives up on foundationalism in *interpretive* theory, reserving the normative aspirations that drive it for work of critical theory. By comparison, interpretation focused

[41] For critical assessment of monistic theories of private law, see H Dagan, 'Pluralism and Perfectionism in Private Law' (2012) 112 *Columbia Law Review* 1409.

[42] That is, that rights and juridical reasons for compliance supply sound normative guidance, insofar as they provide subjects with correct indication of what they ought, morally, to do. For critical perspective on apologetics in interpretive theory, see Dagan and Kreitner (n 19); and H Dagan, *Reconstructing American Legal Realism and Rethinking Private Law Theory* (Oxford, Oxford University Press, 2013).

on elucidating juridical justification is less prone to interpretive excess because it throws off strong coherentism.[43] It might be informed by expectations of moderate (usually local) coherence.[44] But the expectation is a default, readily ceded to recognition that law, being an artifice (a constructed normative system), will invariably bear the flaws[45] of human handiwork.

B. Contrasts, II: Middle Level Justification

There is a halfway house between the strong coherentism of foundationalism and the modest coherentism of work on the juridical justification of private rights. It is occupied by those who engage in 'middle level' interpretive theory.

The middle level theorist believes it to be possible and valuable to abstract from particular rights and juridical reasons a set of principles operative in particular areas of law. The invitation to, and scope for, abstraction is generated (and cabined) by doctrinal and other objective indicia of conceptual and/or normative links between various private rights, including such as might be suggested by their source, content or practical orientation. Thus, for example, a theorist might defend a supposition of intended systematicity in respect of the moral or policy design of a set of statutes, or between a statute and background law. Alternatively, a theorist might identify a moral or policy principle or set of principles in the content of, or posited reasons for, a limited subset of private rights.

For whatever reason, there have not been many takers on middle level theory. However, it has had prominent exponents, including Jane Stapleton.[46] Stapleton has repeatedly expressed concern over interpretive excesses characteristic of foundationalist theories of tort law.[47] And she has argued for, and offered, a middle-level approach to interpretive theory that suggests that different pockets of tort law are responsive to different values.[48] For instance, in tort law's response to economic loss, Stapleton finds concern for moral and social problems associated with indeterminate liability, as well as the value of self-protection balanced

[43] On problems with strong coherentism, see J Raz, 'The Relevance of Coherence' (1992) 72 *Boston University Law Review* 273. For wider discussion, see Khaitan and Steel (n 3) at 7–10.

[44] The expectation is rooted in the recognition that in giving law, political communities aspire toward coherence and systematicity, even as they predictably fail to achieve perfect coherence and totalising systematicity. See generally J Waldron, '"Transcendental Nonsense" and System in the Law' (2000) 100 *Columbia Law Review* 16.

[45] See C Sunstein et al, 'Predictably Incoherent Judgments' (2002) 54 *Stanford Law Review* 1153.

[46] See also, G Schwartz, 'Mixed Theories of Tort Law: Affirming Both Deterrence and Corrective Justice' (1997) 75 *Texas Law Review* 1801. For some acute reflections on the normative eclecticism of tort law, see S Hershovitz, 'The Search for a Grand Unified Theory of Tort Law' (2017) 130 *Harvard Law Review* 942.

[47] J Stapleton, 'Comparative Economic Loss: Lessons from Case-Law-Focused Middle Theory' (2002) 50 *UCLA Law Review* 533.

[48] ibid at 534: 'tort law cannot be explained by grand unitary theory but only by a rich "mixed" set of values that generate the complex boundaries of liability that interest practitioners and courts.'

by the moral importance of ensuring due protection of the vulnerable.[49] In other work, Stapleton has argued that commercial torts are responsive to values associated with trust, cooperation and commercial certainty.[50]

Whether middle level interpretive theory is illuminating or distorting will depend on whether the law admits of the representations made of it. That is, the cogency of middle level interpretation will depend on the level of congruence between a given set of private rights and associated juridical reasons on the one hand, and the principles that the latter are, on the other hand, said to reflect.

There is no inconsistency as a matter of principle between interpretive analysis focused on elucidating juridical, middle level and foundational justifications of private rights. However, a person drawn to foundationalism will often have ambitions that cannot be sated in appreciation of sound juridical or middle level analysis. And the person drawn to middle level or juridical analysis will worry about the impact of those ambitions on interpretive fidelity. Thus, a theorist will often choose between them. One drawn to foundationalism might think that others are unduly timid or cautious – and, ultimately, shallow – in the interpretive analyses that they provide. Their counterparts will resist the prodding because they don't believe that foundational justifications are availing and sound as an interpretation of the values to which private law is responsive.

VI. The Significance and Limits of Juridical Justification

I have already noted features of juridical justification that can limit the absolute and relative justificatory power of juridical reasons. I noted, in particular, that juridical reasons tend to be thin, relatively underdeveloped and eclectic. Even for a non-controversial right, juridical justification might appear little more than an ad hoc arrangement of crowd-sourced reasons.

Bearing this in mind, I wish now to comment on the significance of juridical reasons in, and for, legal argument and adjudication. As will become plain, some infirmities of juridical reasons are the product of exigencies of law as an embodiment of a distinctive set of public practices of practical reasoning – practices that must be open to, and understood by, a diverse public, and that are engaged in by lawyers and legal officials acting representatively for a political community.

Having established the significance of juridical reasons, I will also address their limits. In doing so, I will underscore the importance of rigorous assessment of the practical reasonableness of juridical reasons in public discussion of, and debate about, the law.

[49] ibid.

[50] J Stapleton, 'Tort Law's Cooperation Principle and Commercial Arrangements' (Clarendon Law Lectures, April 30 – May 2, 2018, University of Oxford Faculty of Law, 2018).

A. The Significance of Juridical Justification

Juridical reasons for private rights are sometimes not just thin but weak, providing incomplete or otherwise imperfect indication of moral or prudential bases for a right. They might be given in little more than a sentence in an otherwise prolix judgment or be set out in a tersely worded objects clause in a statute. Alternatively, a mesmerising array of reasons may be put for a right – or framework of rules in which a right is embedded – by countless judges in scores of cases, or by several legislators debating or speaking in support of legislation. Where reasons are articulated briefly, multitudinously and in haste, it can be hard to determine what to make of them.

Consider, for example, the assertion, oft repeated by judges, that one ought to perform one's contracts because they are a kind of morally binding promise. Consider, too, the common suggestion that self-dealing by fiduciaries involves immoral appropriation of power or property. And think of the familiar assertion that patents systems are justified on the basis of social utility, to the extent that they promote innovation and the dissemination of knowledge.

These examples serve well to illustrate the curt and often conclusory way in which juridical reasons are put. They strike many as intuitively plausible. But they are remarkably thin, and sometimes weak; an understandable reaction to weaknesses associated with the thinness of juridical reasons might be a desire for more or better – which is to say 'thicker' – public justification. Furthermore, again partly because of factors that also drive their thinness, juridical reasons sometimes are not just weak but flawed, whether because inapt, unsupported, incoherent or outweighed by countervailing reasons. But, setting to one side the recognition that juridical reasons are sometimes bad reasons, I want to focus on how and why their characteristic thinness might reflect and support their significance in law.

I should, however, first clarify that by 'thin' I mean that juridical reasons are usually unsupported by elaborate normative argument and are amenable of being understood as expressing different values. So, for example, references to 'trust', 'honesty', 'freedom', 'autonomy', 'good faith', 'reasonableness', 'equality', 'fairness', 'efficiency', 'social utility' and 'public good' signify a range of reasons capable of generating convergent acceptance within political communities notwithstanding that – indeed, *because* – their precise normative salience is understood differently by different people, including those who might wish to build up a thicker normative story about them by way of interpretation or critique.

Now, as for their significance, it may be observed that juridical reasons figure centrally in public justification undertaken by law-makers in support of laws that they have promulgated or recognised. It may be that they are thin because legal and political deliberative processes short-circuit extended reflection requisite to the development of thicker reasons. But the daily lives of legislators and judges are, in any case, usually not conducive to extended reflection; they work under practical imperatives that compress deliberation and favour parsimonious expression.[51] It might be, then, that the thinness of juridical reasons is, as a practical matter, overdetermined.

However, in addition to these observations are considerations of principle: the thinness of juridical reasons makes it more likely that they can serve as workable shorthand – a mode of normative argument or explication that is accessible to, and can be engaged in by, laypeople. Additionally, as intimated earlier, thin reasons are *ceteris paribus* more likely to reflect and/or attract agreement within diverse political communities.[52] It would thus appear that, as a general matter, the thinness of juridical reasons enables them to better instantiate the law's guidance function.

I should say a little more about the relationship between the thinness of juridical reasons and normative guidance. First, I observe that law is to guide most of the practices of lawyers and judges, including advice given to clients, transactional and other solicitor work, arguments made in and out of court, settlements, judgment and the preparation and issuance of public reasons for judgment. Legal issues and the factual circumstances in which they arise are often complex. All of this makes for a delicate real-world economy of practical reasoning that favours law and legal reasons that are clear and comprehensible. These familiar rule of law virtues are served by concision. It is easier, and in some cases only feasible, for lawyers to discern and make, and for judges to follow and develop, sound legal arguments where pertinent legal reasons are relatively simple; likewise, in reaching conclusions that are both right in law and defensible for their practical reasonableness. Equally, in turn, those who look to the law only for prospective guidance (ie, those not parties to a suit) are best served by relative simplicity in the public justification of law, even if that means that one gets little more than the gist of a justification.

Second, the thinness of juridical reasons renders the law more amenable to reform. It must be remembered that the law is ever a work in progress, legal texts being residue of a reflexive set of public practices of practical reasoning. The positing of law and juridical reasons are expected to reflect, and to produce, a settlement of normative issues for a political community, but the settlement is never permanent and is often openly tentative. Law does not always have the positive moral or prudential impact intended for it. And juridical reasons do not always hold up to scrutiny. As such, we are often best served by a relatively thin fabric of public justification, insofar as its thinness makes it more amenable to public scrutiny

[51] Admittedly, this is an unproven empirical point. But it enjoys plausibility. On factors that influence the kind and quality of moral reasoning typically engaged in by judges and legislators, respectively, see J Waldron, 'The Core of the Case Against Judicial Review' (2006) 115 *Yale Law Journal* 1346; J Waldron, 'Do Judges Reason Morally?' in G Huscroft (ed), *Expounding the Constitution: Essays in Constitutional Theory* (New York, Colombia University Press, 2008); and J Waldron, 'Judges as Moral Reasoners' (2009) 1 *International Journal of Constitutional Law* 2.

[52] *cf* Smith (n 3) at xxx: 'judges properly seek justifications that are acceptable to citizens who hold different [moral] theories or, indeed, who don't hold any [moral] theory' and xxx: 'if you want to coordinate behaviour in a pluralist society, it is advisable to do so on the basis of low-level generalisations'.

and deliberate revision. This is not to say that we are well served by shoddy or impressionistic normative assertion or argument. It is, rather, to say that clarity and progress are often best enabled through the relatively simple and fungible legal reasons.

B. The Limits of Juridical Justification

I have explained the characteristic thinness of juridical reasons, and the sense to their thinness. But I have also hinted at the limits of juridical reasons and, in turn, juridical justification. I noted that, being thin, juridical reasons are often given without extended normative argument of the sort that would, in an academic context, be taken to be necessary to situate them (ie, to determine what, precisely, the reason(s) claim) and to evaluate them (ie, to determine what weight they have given the value(s) they reflect). Thus, one limit of juridical reasons is amorphousness. One who subjects juridical reasons to careful scrutiny might find them irredeemably wanting, or, to the extent wanting but still apt, feel that they need still to be amplified, focused or refined.

When one considers, in a clear-eyed way, the legal and political processes through which laws are publicly contested, deliberated upon and posited, it should be unsurprising that juridical justification is eclectic and often flawed. The thinness and amorphousness of juridical reasons might be features rather than bugs. But there are plenty of bugs to go around. I have already noted that juridical reasons are usually weak. They are sometimes incomplete or missing in action. Otherwise, they might be incoherent or incapable of being reconciled with other reasons with which they should comport. Finally, they can reflect moral error or policy miscalculation.

Recognition that juridical reasons suffer from such shortcomings gives rise to some important lessons. The most important is that interpretive theorists should be wary of reading into the law a level and extent of practical reasonableness that simply is not there. As the product of, and fulcrum for, reflexive practices of practical reasoning, it would be surprising if the law were generally pervasively irrational. However, the fact that law manifests reason does not license one to paper over its defects. It is thus that I have argued here that interpretive theorists might profitably start with the reasons we have been given for the laws we have.

VII. Conclusion

This chapter is an effort to encourage wider engagement with questions of methodology in private law theory. It offers suggestions about how one might frame the tasks of interpretive and critical theoretical analysis of private law, respectively. The chapter situates these inquiries relative to the general jurisprudential literature on the relationship between law and practical reasoning, explaining how one ought to understand private rights and posited reasons for these rights. I have argued that, in explicating private rights and associated practical reasons as an interpretive matter, theorists ought to carefully distinguish those reasons that are posited from those that are arrived at through rational reconstruction involving the interpretive linking of posited reasons and higher-order practical reasons. Finally, the chapter explores the significance of juridical reasons in private law and more widely, as well as some common limits of, and deficiencies in, the practical reasonableness of juridical reasons.

7

Sources of Private Rights

LIONEL SMITH*

I. Introduction

Since the early days of law in the West, people have been thinking about the 'sources' of private rights and obligations. Indeed, thinking about this began before the emergence of the modern idea of a right. Rights – along with, we might say after Hohfeld, other fundamental jural conceptions[1] – are the currency of private law thinking and so it is not surprising that legal theory aims to understand, classify and categorise their sources. This chapter argues that one issue that has haunted all such discussions is that the idea of the source of a right is deeply ambiguous.

In the next part, I will explore some attempts to categorise sources, in both the common law and the civil law. The civil law story will help us to understand why still today, civilians tend to discuss the sources of 'obligations' rather than of 'rights'. The history of these attempts in both traditions will illustrate the confusion around the notion of 'sources'. Next, with the benefit of some recent scholarship in Quebec civil law, I will aim to unpack the ambiguity of 'source' in this context and set out a series of different kinds of source. I will then aim to relate this series to the schemes that have been proposed in common law and civil law, and to show what have been some consequences of the ambiguity of these ideas.

II. Some History

A. Civil Law

Our story begins, like many in law, with the second-century jurist Gaius. Peter Birks thought that Gaius was a genius who stood on a par with Darwin for his

* I thank Helge Dedek, Rebeca Fariña Fariña and Alexandra Popovici for helpful discussions.

[1] WN Hohfeld, *Fundamental Legal Conceptions as Applied in Judicial Reasoning*, 3rd printing with new foreword by AL Corbin (New Haven, Yale University Press, 1964).

role in the history of human understanding.[2] Even so, Birks liked to tell the story of how the brilliant jurist got into trouble with the sources of obligations, when it came to restitution. Gaius' *Institutes* were a relatively short overview of all of the law, intended for students.[3] When he started his discussion of obligations, Gaius began by saying: 'Let us now move on to obligations. The principal division of these puts them into two species: for every obligation arises either from a contract or from a delict'.[4] 'Delict' is a civilian word for an extracontractual wrong in private law.[5] Birks frequently pointed out that almost immediately after this division into two sources, Gaius noted that the obligation to repay a mistaken payment did not arise from contract;[6] and it went without saying that this obligation did not arise from a delict.

The *Institutes* of Justinian, promulgated in 533, were inspired by those of Gaius and were equally aimed at students. They included a four-fold classification of the sources of obligations that has echoed down the centuries:

> We turn to obligations. An obligation is a legal tie which binds us to the necessity of making some performance in accordance with the laws of our state. 1. They divide first into two: legal and praetorian. Legal obligations are those recognized by statute or, of course, by the state law. Praetorian obligations are those which the praetor recognized in the exercise of his own jurisdiction. These are also called honorarian. 2. The next classification is into four: obligations arise from a contract, as though from a contract, from a wrong, or as though from a wrong.[7]

We will return later to the twofold classification into 'legal' and 'praetorian'.

The fourfold classification of the sources of obligations made its mark in the French civil code, which has been immensely influential in other legal systems. Until 2016, that code divided obligations into those arising by agreement or otherwise. The latter category was divided into obligations arising entirely by

[2] 'Introduction' in Justinian, *Institutes*, trans P Birks and G McLeod (Ithaca, Cornell University Press, 1987) 18.

[3] 'Translated rather than anglicized, the name of the *Institutes* would be "Introduction" or "Basic Principles"': ibid 12. Tony Honoré sometimes translated *Institutes* as 'Teaching Manual': eg T Honoré, *Ulpian: Pioneer of Human Rights*, 2nd edn (Oxford, Oxford University Press, 2002) 243, 282.

[4] G.3.88; this translation is from P Birks, *The Roman Law of Obligations*, E Descheemaeker (ed), (Oxford, Oxford Univeristy Press, 2014) 17.

[5] F Allard et al, *Private Law Dictionary and Bilingual Lexicons – Obligations* (Cowansville, Les Éditions Yvon Blais, 2003) sv 'delict'. All of the bilingual civil law dictionaries of the Crépeau Centre are available online at www.mcgill.ca/centre-crepeau/.

[6] G.3.91. See Birks, *Obligations* (n 4) 17 and P Birks, 'Definition and Division: A Meditation on *Institutes* 3.13' in P Birks (ed), *The Classification of Obligations* (Oxford, Clarendon Press, 1997) 1, 18; also Birks, 'Introduction' (n 2) 18.

[7] Justinian (n 2), 105 (J.3.13); for slightly different translations, see Birks, 'Meditation' (ibid) 6 and Birks, *Obligations* (n 4) at 19. Birks noted that Gaius himself seems to have developed his original classification in this direction in a book that he wrote after his *Institutes* and that is only known insofar as it was extracted in Justinian's *Digest* (in this respect, at D.44.7.1, D.44.7.5): Birks, 'Introduction' (n 2) at 14 note 28; Birks, *Obligations* (n 4) at 18–19 (noting the possibility that Justinian's compilers modified the texts attributed to Gaius in the *Digest*). The possibility that J.3.13 reflects a later Gaian scheme has also been suggested by French Romanists: B Moore, 'La classification des sources des obligations: courte histoire d'une valse-hésitation' (2002) 36 *Revue Juridique Thémis de l'Université de Montréal* 275, 278.

operation of law – to which I will return immediately below – and those arising from the act of the person who became obliged. That latter sub-category was further divided into three: quasi-contracts, delicts and quasi-delicts.[8]

The bilingual Civil Code of Lower Canada (CCLC) was in force in Quebec from 1866 to 1993; it provided in its article 983:

Les obligations procèdent des contrats, des quasi-contrats, des délits, des quasi-délits, ou de la loi seule.	Obligations arise from contracts, quasi-contracts, offences, quasi-offences, and from the operation of the law solely.

Both codifications reveal a decision to add a fifth wheel to Justinian's coach, one which seems to imply that obligations arising from delicts or quasi-delict are *not* obligations arising from the law alone.[9] The fivefold classification comes from the work of Robert-Joseph Pothier, which was an important source for the codifiers in both jurisdictions.[10] The idea was that some obligations did not arise from anyone's act and for this reason, not from any of the four parts of Justinian's classification. Article 1057 CCLC gives examples, including the obligation of a tutor (guardian) or other like person who could not refuse the role; the obligation of children to support their parents if in need; and the obligations that may be owed between owners of adjacent properties.

The classifications of Gaius and Justinian were of the sources of obligations, not of rights. Roman law did not have a modern idea of 'right' in the sense of an individual right held by one person against another; *ius* was the law, or what was right or rightful, and the idea of an individual right as a prerogative was developed only during the Middle Ages.[11] Obligations, famously defined in the extract from Justinian's *Institutes* set out above, were well understood and of course we now see them as corresponding to individual personal rights, seen from the other end. Theophilus, one of the compilers of Justinian's *Institutes*, famously said that 'obligations are the mothers of actions'.[12] This was a way of explaining the relationship between the two, although it faces the difficulty that some actions were 'real' actions which did not arise from obligations. Roman law had rules on the original acquisition of ownership, but those rules were not brought within the fourfold classification of the sources of obligations; they were understood, rather, as rules on how we acquire things.

[8] Art 1370, which was repealed in 2016 (see below).

[9] Criticised, for example, by D Lluelles and B Moore, *Droit des obligations*, 3rd edn (Montreal, Thémis, 2018) 32–33.

[10] Moore (n 7) 281–82.

[11] M Villey, 'Les Institutes de Gaïus et l'idée de droit subjectif' in M Villey (ed), *Leçons d'histoire de la philosophie du droit*, 2nd edn (Paris, Dalloz, 1962) 167; by the same author and in the same volume, 'Les origines de la notion de droit subjectif', 221.

[12] Theophilus, *Paraphrase*, 3.13, discussed in E Metzger, 'Actions' in E Metzger (ed), *A Companion to Justinian's Institutes* (Ithaca, Cornell University Press, 1998) 208, 217; HF Jolowicz, 'Obligatio and Actio' (1952) 68 *LQR* 469, 473; R Zimmermann, *The Law of Obligations: Roman Foundations of the Civilian Tradition* (Cape Town, Juta & Co, 1990) 28.

There is no such noun as 'quasi-contract' in Justinian's text, only a phrase translatable as 'as though from a contract'. In France, as used to be the case in Quebec, 'quasi-contract' became a noun, referring to situations in which obligations arise from the facts without wrongdoing and without agreement or intention.[13] The substantive law to which this concept relates, or related, was not that different from the Roman origins.[14] The story of 'quasi-delict' is more obscure; for Justinian, the obligations that arose 'as though from a wrong' were a miscellany of liabilities for damage caused without fault, in which it was difficult to see a unity.[15] In French and Quebec law, quasi-delict simply came to mean delictual liability that was based on carelessness rather than intentional action.[16] But since in the modern civil law of delictual liability nothing usually turns on degrees of fault, this was a distinction without a purpose.

In both France and Quebec there was dissatisfaction in legal scholarship with the codal classifications. Many alternatives were proposed.[17] The dominant approach in modern doctrine distinguishes simply between 'juridical acts' and 'juridical facts'. A juridical act is a 'manifestation of intention of one or more persons in a manner and form designed to produce effects in law'.[18] This can include a contractual offer or acceptance, the making of a will or the abandonment of property.[19] A juridical fact is a fact, or sequence of facts, that has juridical

[13] My translation of the (rather obscure) French civil code, art 1300, as amended in 2016: 'Quasi-contracts are wholly voluntary events that create an obligation owed by the one who benefits therefrom without right, and sometimes an obligation owed towards another by the one who brought the situation about./The quasi-contracts governed by this sub-title are management of the business of another, performances that are not legally owing, and unjustified enrichment'. ('Les quasi-contrats sont des faits purement volontaires dont il résulte un engagement de celui qui en profite sans y avoir droit, et parfois un engagement de leur auteur envers autrui./Les quasi-contrats régis par le présent sous-titre sont la gestion d'affaire, le paiement de l'indu et l'enrichissement injustifié'.) The definition in the first paragraph can probably be traced to Pothier's definition: Moore (n 7) 282. This is reinforced by the consideration that the implication in the second paragraph – that there may be other quasi-contracts than those that appear in this part of the code – is also found in Pothier (Moore ibid).

[14] The law on management of the business of another and undue performances is fairly closely based on the Roman law. What is called unjustified enrichment in France and Quebec is based on developments from Roman sources that took place during the *ius commune* period; see for example Zimmermann (n 12) 878–84.

[15] For one attempt to describe the unities of the 'quasi categories' in a principled way, see Birks, *Obligations* (n 4) 259–63, suggesting that quasi-delicts arose in the context of pre-existing relationships, so that one might say that the duty breached by the defendant, even though it may in some cases have been owed *to* everyone, was not owed *by* everyone (although Roman law, like much of the civilian tradition today, did not necessarily articulate wrongs in terms of breaches of duty). See also Zimmermann (n 12) 16–18, suggesting that quasi-delictual liabilities were imposed on those in control of certain situations.

[16] See for example *Driver v Coca-Cola Ltd.* [1961] SCR 201; *Private Law Dictionary and Bilingual Lexicons – Obligations* (n 5) sv 'quasi-delict'.

[17] Moore (n 7) 289–91.

[18] *Private Law Dictionary and Bilingual Lexicons – Obligations* (n 5) sv 'juridical act'.

[19] I am less familiar with German law but a similar concept in that system is the *Rechtsgeschäft*, which could be translated as 'juridical act', and which is implemented by one or more *Willenserklärungen* or 'declarations of intent', which are regulated by BGB paras 116–44; see BS Markesinis, W Lorenz, and G Dannemann, *The Law of Contracts and Restitution: A Comparative Introduction* (Oxford, Clarendon Press, 1997) 31–34.

consequences without regard to anyone's manifestation of intention.[20] In the law of civil responsibility, which corresponds to tort law, the practice in legal doctrine is to refer to the *fait générateur*: the 'generative fact' that creates the obligation to pay damages, assuming that there is fault on the part of the defendant (or something that stands in its place) and a resultant loss to the plaintiff.

This approach has of course attracted its share of criticism. Some authors have noted that the line between the two categories is often difficult to draw.[21] It also lumps together obligations arising from wrongs with those arising neither from wrongs nor consent, such as those arising from mistaken payments; these are also produced by juridical facts. Peter Birks took the view that we should aim to identify sources in such a way as to order them rationally, while trying to leave as little as possible in a residual category of 'others', even though such a category is probably always necessary.[22] On that view, the classification between juridical acts and juridical facts is going the wrong direction: from Gaius's contract and wrongs, to which an 'others' category was an essential addition, we have moved effectively to two categories: 'consent' and 'others'.

It has also been observed that we should not confine our inquiry to the *sources* of obligations; juridical acts may also transfer rights or extinguish or abandon them.[23]

The Civil Code of Québec (CCQ), which came into force in 1994, seems clearly to have been influenced by the wide acceptance of the distinction between juridical acts and juridical facts. This bilingual code abandoned the 'quasi' categories, and provides in its article 1372:

L'obligation naît du contrat et de tout acte ou fait auquel la loi attache d'autorité les effets d'une obligation.	An obligation arises from a contract or from any act or fact to which the effects of an obligation are attached by law.[24]

The doctrinally-developed distinction between juridical acts and juridical facts is reflected here, but in a confusing and illogical way, since both are seemingly presented as an alternative to 'contract'. But contracts arise from juridical acts, so the classification treats two of its entries (contract and juridical acts) as alternatives, when their relationship is actually that one (contract) is an example or sub-category of the other (juridical acts). On one reading, the article practically

[20] *Private Law Dictionary and Bilingual Lexicons – Obligations* (n 5) sv 'juridical fact'.

[21] eg B Moore, 'De l'acte et du fait juridique ou d'un critère de distinction incertain' (1997) 31 *Revue Juridique Thémis de l'Université de Montréal* 277. For other criticisms, Moore (n 7) 291.

[22] P Birks, *Unjust Enrichment*, 2nd edn (Oxford, Oxford University Press, 2005) ch 1.

[23] Lluelles and Moore (n 9) 35.

[24] The CCQ has dispensed with the CCLC's use of the word *délit* and, in English, 'offence': see (in French) N Kasirer, '« Délit » interdit! No « Offence »!' in Quebec Research Centre of Private and Comparative Law (ed), *Colloque du trentenaire: Regards croisés sur le droit privé / Thirtieth Anniversary Conference: Cross-Examining Private Law* (Cowansville, Éditions Yvon Blais, 2005) 203.

says that an obligation arises whenever the law says it does.[25] The headings of the codal chapters that follow afterwards tell a slightly different story: 'Contracts', 'Civil liability' and 'Certain other sources of obligations', the latter including management of the business of another, undue performances and unjustified enrichment (in the very narrow version of that idea which is particular to the French legal tradition and those derived from it).[26]

Finally we can notice the French reform of 2016. Three new articles, under a new title 'The Sources of Obligations', provide in part as follows:

> 1100. Obligations arise from juridical acts, from juridical facts, or by the pure operation of law.[27] …
>
> 1100-1. Juridical acts are manifestations of intention aimed at producing legal effects. They may be part of an agreement or unilateral.[28] …
>
> 1100-2. Juridical facts are actions or events to which the law attaches legal effects.
>
> Obligations arising from juridical facts are governed, as the case may be, by the sub-title on extracontracual liability or the subtitle on other sources of obligations.[29]

As with the CCQ, the section of the code that follows is organised into contractual obligations, extracontractual liability and 'other sources of obligations'. Strangely perhaps, in the light of these changes, the French code still uses the category of quasi-contracts, and still refers to quasi-delicts.[30]

Just as in the CCLC, the need was felt to add the category of obligations arising by the operation of the law alone to juridical acts and juridical facts. The logic of this seems to be that obligations may arise in some situations which, at least on some views, cannot be described in terms of juridical facts.[31]

[25] Lluelles and Moore (n 9) 39. Moore (n 7) 294 also aims to make sense of art 1372 by noting that it refers to 'acts' and 'facts', not to 'juridical' acts and facts.

[26] Arts 1491–92, derived from the Roman *condictio indebiti*, are called by the CCQ 'de la réception de l'indu'/ 'receipt of a payment not due', and in the French code (arts 1300, and the heading before art 1302) 'paiement de l'indu'. I have translated these in terms of 'performance' since the civilian sense of 'payment' includes the performance of a non-monetary obligation (eg CCQ art 1553). To this extent the concept is wider than the *condictio indebiti*.

[27] My translation of: 'Les obligations naissent d'actes juridiques, de faits juridiques ou de l'autorité seule de la loi'.

[28] My translation of: 'Les actes juridiques sont des manifestations de volonté destinées à produire des effets de droit. Ils peuvent être conventionnels ou unilatéraux'. There was disagreement in legal doctrine as to whether there could be unilateral juridical acts, which this article resolves for French law.

[29] My translation of: 'Les faits juridiques sont des agissements ou des événements auxquels la loi attache des effets de droit. / Les obligations qui naissent d'un fait juridique sont régies, selon le cas, par le sous-titre relatif à la responsabilité extracontractuelle ou le sous-titre relatif aux autres sources d'obligations'.

[30] At art 1300 (n 13), under the heading 'Other sources of obligations', the only other sources listed are the three named quasi-contracts. They are described as 'voluntary actions' (*faits purement volontaires*) though one might have thought that quasi-contracts are what *arise from* the relevant voluntary actions. There is a reference to 'quasi-delicts' in art 1417.

[31] Moore (n 7) 293.

B. Common Law

When the old forms of action were abolished in the 1850s, the common law of obligations began to develop somewhat more conceptually, with the appearance of books on tort law and contract law that benefited from civilian learning.[32] The law of restitution, or unjust enrichment, was somewhat left out of this development;[33] since at common law it had generally been pleaded using *assumpsit*, which was the same sub-species of trespass that had been used for contract law, it was long treated under the headings of implied contract or quasi-contract.[34] In the US, civilian thinking on unjust enrichment was influential beginning in the late nineteenth century, although this was only accepted much later in other common law jurisdictions.[35]

The sources of obligations – or in fact of private law rights – was a special preoccupation of Peter Birks. Inspired by the Roman efforts, he was convinced that a sound understanding of private law needed a sound classification of sources.[36] He did not, however, frame the question in terms of sources but in terms of 'causative events'. Much of his work was built around an argument that these could be organised into (1) consent; (2) wrongs; (3) unjust enrichment; and (4) others. The residual miscellany was always needed, for such things as judgments of courts (when they are understood to create new rights) and the creation of new rights by events such as the first acquisition of a previously unowned thing.

Birks's classification has been very influential in the common law world. The recognition of a law of 'restitution' in addition to other categories was certainly not his creation, but it was part of his project to insist that 'restitution' did not belong in a classification by causative events, because it was not a causative event but a legal response.[37]

Birks was aware that this classification concealed the distinction between secondary rights (which arise via the infringement of another right) and primary rights (which do not).[38] This may have been a more serious issue than he realised.

[32] L Smith, 'Common Law and Equity in R3RUE' (2011) 68 *Washington & Lee Law Review* 1185, 1187–93.

[33] So too was Equity, having no direct civilian counterpart (ibid).

[34] JH Baker, 'The History of Quasi-Contract in English Law' in WR Cornish et al (eds), *Restitution: Past, Present and Future: Essays in Honour of Gareth Jones* (Oxford, Hart, 1998) 37; JH Langbein, 'The Later History of Restitution' in WR Cornish et al (eds), *Restitution: Past, Present and Future: Essays in Honour of Gareth Jones* (Oxford, Hart, 1998) 57.

[35] A Kull, 'James Barr Ames and the Early Modern History of Unjust Enrichment' (2005) 25 *Oxford Journal of Legal Studies* 297.

[36] A monograph-length statement of this credo is at P Birks, 'Equity in the Modern Law: An Exercise in Taxonomy' (1996) 26 *University of Western Australia Law Review* 1–99. Almost everything he wrote expresses a preoccupation with classification.

[37] P Birks, 'Misnomer' in WR Cornish et al (eds), *Restitution: Past, Present and Future: Essays in Honour of Gareth Jones* (Oxford, Hart, 1998) 1.

[38] Birks, 'Equity' (n 36) 10–12.

We will return to this later.[39] For now, I observe that manifestations of consent are facts; wrongs and unjust enrichments are legal characterisations of facts, or juridical conclusions from facts. It may be that by 'consent' he meant 'right-engendering manifestations of consent'.[40] This would make the category of consent also into a legal conclusion from facts. Still the classification cannot in my view rightly be called one based on 'causative events'. All three of the nominate categories are not categories of events, but of the outcome of applying legal rules to events.[41] Events happen in the world, but 'wrongs', 'unjust enrichments' and 'right-engendering manifestations of consent' are conclusions that we reach in our minds about events in the world.[42]

What was Birks classifying? He started from Gaius, who was classifying the sources of obligations, but Birks wanted also to classify the sources of rights, including real rights in the civilian sense, namely what a common lawyer might call proprietary rights.[43] Such rights do not correspond to obligations in the civilian sense. But he did not aim to classify the sources all rights: rather, 'rights realizable in court'.[44] Thus he was not concerned with my right to my reputation, but only with my right to sue for damage caused by an infringement of my right to my reputation. In civilian terms, he aimed to classify all patrimonial rights.[45] The other rights (such as the primary right to one's reputation, or to bodily integrity) he sometimes called 'superstructural': they are not realisable in court, though their infringement might create new rights that are.[46]

Transfers of rights have a very low profile in Birks's scheme, since he was mainly preoccupied with the creation of rights.[47] Quite apart from transfers, we might observe, as some civilians have, that a scheme might rightly take notice of

[39] Section IV.C.

[40] Birks, 'Equity' (n 36) 61.

[41] I disagree with Birks's claim (*Unjust Enrichment* (n 22) 9–10): 'Unjust enrichment at the expense of another – unjust enrichment for short – is no more than a generic name for the receipt of a mistaken payment'. The receipt of a mistaken payment is a fact. Unjust enrichment is the legal characterisation of that fact.

[42] At the seminar at which this chapter was presented, James Penner disputed this point with the example of a goal in a game of football: the ball goes into the net in the world. I think the example serves to illustrate and strengthen my point. The ball goes into the net in the world, but whether it makes a goal is a conclusion we reach in our minds. Imagine that the play is reviewed by the 'video assistant referee' (VAR) and the conclusion is that a player was offside so that the goal is disallowed. The ball went into the net, but as a result of the ruling of the relevant official, we now must change our *minds* about whether a goal was scored.

[43] Birks, 'Equity' (n 36) 8.

[44] Birks, *Unjust Enrichment* (n 22) 28–30.

[45] *Private Law Dictionary and Bilingual Lexicons – Obligations* (n 5) sv 'patrimonial right'. A right is patrimonial because it forms part of the holder's patrimony, which means that in principle it is available to his creditors to meet his obligations (although the civil law also makes some assets exempt from seizure). One characteristic of such rights is that they are capable of pecuniary evaluation.

[46] Birks, 'Meditation' (n 6) 11–12, 24–25; Birks, *Unjust Enrichment* (n 22) 30. In the French tradition these are called 'extrapatrimonial': *Private Law Dictionary and Bilingual Lexicons – Obligations* (n 5) sv 'extrapatrimonial right'.

[47] He occasionally suggested, however, that transfers fall under consent: Birks, 'Equity' (n 36) 10; Birks, *Unjust Enrichment* (n 22) 21.

how rights can be extinguished.[48] In every system, if you owe me money, I can forgive and thus eliminate the debt. Systematising the end of obligations seems equally interesting as systematising their inception.

III. Moore's System

Benoît Moore is a Quebec judge who for many years was a professor of law, being for 11 years the inaugural holder of the Chaire Jean-Louis Baudouin en droit civil at the Université de Montréal.[49] An expert in family law as well as the law of obligations, he has taken a special interest in the question of the sources of obligations.[50] In an important article, he describes the deeply ambiguous nature of much civilian discourse about 'sources'.[51]

His argument is developed partly by showing the confusions that have resulted from this ambiguity. Some scholars, for example, have said that all obligations arise from the law, because a legal obligation is a creature of the law. This is true, in a way, but it is also true in an important way that some obligations (or more generally legal relations) arise from consent.

Moore distinguishes four different senses of the idea of source. In each case, in my sub-headings I have added my own understanding of a precision as to what each source is an immediate source of. All four are sources of obligations, but there is a sense in which only the last one is an *immediate* source of *particular* obligations; the others are sources only mediately, by being sources, for example, of general legal rules or by being sources not of the particular obligation that arises but of a class of obligations that arise in comparable circumstances.

A. Justificatory Principle (of One or Many Legal Rules)

One is the 'justificatory principle'. A justificatory principle is not a legal rule, but a principle that is capable of justifying legal rules. 'Seriously made promises should be kept' would be an example, and the unpacking of that into legal rules can be seen to lie behind rules of offer and acceptance, along with inquiries into consideration (in the common law) and perhaps into object and cause (in the civil law, depending on the system). In the common law, the same justificatory principle might underlie some rules that are outside of the main body of contract law, such

[48] n 23.

[49] He was appointed to the Quebec Superior Court in 2017 and to the Court of Appeal in 2019.

[50] In addition to the article about to be discussed, see Moore (n 21) and Moore (n 7).

[51] B Moore, 'La théorie des sources des obligations: éclatement d'une classification' (2002) 36 *Revue Juridique Thémis de l'Université de Montréal* 689. The English reader can read 'éclatement' as 'explosion' or 'blowing up', but ideally he or she also bears in mind the image of the 'exploded view diagram', a notional explosion that exists only to reveal the inner structure of some complex artefact.

as the law of promises under seal, and certain aspects of estoppel.[52] 'Those who induce reasonable reliance should make reasonable efforts to fulfil it' could be seen as justifying other aspects of estoppel in the common law.[53] A similar principle may underpin other rules in a civilian order.[54] And the principle that no one should be unjustly enriched at the expense of another may also be the basis of a number of legal rules in different legal systems.[55]

It is important to see that a justificatory principle (which I will sometimes call a justifying principle) can underlie many legal rules, not just one. Thus, the justificatory principle related to the importance of serious promises lies behind the law of contract, with its requirement of consideration in the common law, and the law of promises under seal, which has no such requirement but has requirements of form. Conversely, one might find that some legal rules implement more than one justificatory principle. Legal rules on estoppels arising from promises could be seen to be underpinned by the justificatory principle related to the importance of serious promises, and also by the justificatory principle related to the importance of protecting induced reliance.

B. Formal Source (of any Particular Legal Rule)

A second sense of source is the 'formal source'. The formal source is that which allows us to conclude that the rule in question is a legal rule, rather than (for example) a moral or religious precept. Every legal rule has a formal source, which is exactly what makes it a *legal* rule. Consider these two rules: 'every natural person has a legal right to bodily integrity'; 'the cause of action in battery consists of the intentional infliction upon the body of another of a harmful or offensive contact'.[56] These two rules probably have the same justificatory principle, but it is quite possible that they have different formal sources. One might be in a statute or a constitution, and the other might be found in case law.

Civilian systems have a 'theory of sources of law' that stands apart from any debates about the sources of obligations or of rights. The theory of sources of law aims at producing an account of where legal rules can be found; that is, a

[52] B McFarlane, *The Law of Proprietary Estoppel* (Oxford, Oxford University Press, 2014), [1.15], arguing that the most practically important element of proprietary estoppel in English law is based on promises which do not have effect as contracts.

[53] M Spence, *Protecting Reliance* (Oxford, Hart, 1999); compare B McFarlane, 'Understanding Equitable Estoppel: From Metaphors to Better Laws' (2013) 66 *CLP* 267 (arguing that multiple principles are at play in equitable estoppel).

[54] ADP Heeney, 'Estoppel in the Law of Quebec' (1930) 8 *Canadian Bar Review* 401, 500.

[55] This seems to be what Birks meant when he referred to the 'weakly normative' sense of unjust enrichment (Birks, *Unjust Enrichment* (n 22) 274–75), which is a 'constant reminder of the conclusion which the rules aim to reach'. He said it is needed for the development of the law in new situations; were this justificatory principle not needed, 'one might just as well speak of pink enrichment'. In other words, when it is considered as a justificatory principle, a label like 'pink enrichment' would not be very useful.

[56] *Bettel v Yim* (1978) 20 OR (2d) 617 (Co Ct).

list of formal sources in Moore's terms. This list always includes statute law, often includes doctrine (in the civilian sense of learned commentary), sometimes includes custom and general principles, and may or may not include jurisprudence in the civilian sense of that word (that is, case law).

Here we can recall the division of obligations in Justinian's *Institutes* into legal and praetorian (or honorarian).[57] The Roman praetors, the officials who authorised the bringing of most legal proceedings, had the ability to create new remedies through a document called the praetor's edict.[58] Although of course the label is not literally accurate, in France and Quebec jurists still today often describe as 'praetorian' a legal rule that arises from case law.[59] When jurists in the common law tradition describe a rule as either 'Equitable' or as 'common law' in the sense that is opposed to Equity, they are making a claim about its formal source; and when they apply those labels to rights or obligations, they are making a claim about the formal source of the legal rule that is the normative source of those rights or obligations.[60]

It may seem obvious that every legal rule has a formal source, but it can lead to confusion. Common law jurists may think that any rule arising from case law needs to be explained and understood in terms of its justificatory principle (mentioned above) and analysed in relation to normative and material sources (discussed below); and yet they may think that none of these inquiries are relevant to legislated rules. I will take one example, not meaning to be invidious, but only intending to isolate the role in the analysis of the idea of formal source. James Edelman published an argument that all fiduciary duties arise out of undertakings given by the person who owes them.[61] In a later text, he noted that his argument had nothing to say about situations where such duties arise under a statute. He noted that 'Parliament can create new duties which in equity would not be considered "fiduciary," and can attach the same remedial consequences upon those duties'.[62] He went on to expand on Parliament's sovereignty. But what if Parliament enacted a Fiduciary Relationships Act which aimed to codify the understanding of fiduciary relationships that Edelman himself has set out? Assuming his understanding were correct (and I think it is incomplete),[63] the law would not have changed at all. The justificatory principle, and the normative and material sources of fiduciary duties, would remain unchanged. The only

[57] Text at n 7.

[58] P du Plessis, *Borkowski's Textbook on Roman Law*, 5th edn (Oxford, Oxford University Press, 2015) 33–35.

[59] *Private Law Dictionary and Bilingual Lexicons – Obligations* (n 5) sv 'praetorian law', sense 1: 'Rules of judicial origin'; Mathieu Devinat, *La règle prétorienne en droit civil français et dans la* common law *canadienne: Étude de méthodologie juridique comparée* (Aix en Provence, Presses universitaires d'Aix-Marseille, 2005).

[60] Normative sources are discussed in the next section.

[61] J Edelman, 'When Do Fiduciary Duties Arise?' (2010) 126 *Law Quarterly Review* 302.

[62] J Edelman, 'The Role of Status in the Law of Obligations' in AS Gold and P Miller (eds), *Philosophical Foundations of Fiduciary Law* (Oxford, Oxford University Press, 2014) 21, 23.

[63] L Smith, 'Fiduciary Relationships: Ensuring the Loyal Exercise of Judgement on Behalf of Another' (2014) 130 *Law Quarterly Review* 608.

thing that would have changed is the formal source: although the rules would be all the same, they would now find their source (in the sense of their status as *legal* rules) in a statute and not in case law.

Common lawyers often view the case law as giving the base line and legislation as generally exceptional, perhaps even suspect. The world looks different in a codified civilian system, where all or almost all of private law is in statutory form. Common lawyers are right to think that where the rules are in a statute, there is less room for argument about what the rules are, or, what is almost the same thing, how they should rightly be developed. But it is not the case that there is no room at all. Like any text, a civil code needs to be interpreted, and sometimes this leads to the conclusion that it is incomplete, or that it does not mean what one might think on a first reading. Whether in common law or civil law, a modern approach to interpretation needs to pay attention to the legislative purpose, which often means finding (and this, often by inference) the justificatory principles for enacted norms. This is why, in the civil law just as in the common law, people argue about why promises are enforced, what kinds of loss should be recoverable, and so on.

C. Normative Source (of Many Individual Rights, Obligations and Other Jural Relationships)

Every obligation, every right, every liability – in short, every particular juristic relationship – has a 'normative source' in the legal rule that is apt to create it. Above it was said that every legal rule *has* a formal source, that makes it count as a legal rule; it also has one or more justificatory principles. Every legal rule in its turn can *be* a normative source, that can create (for example) obligations and rights.

The general rule that 'every natural person has a right to bodily integrity' is the normative source of my particular legal right to bodily integrity, and also of yours. If someone punches me without reason, the rule that 'the cause of action in battery consists of the intentional infliction upon the body of another of a harmful or offensive contact' is the normative source of my particular legal right to claim damages from that particular person, and it is also the normative source of the cognate right of anyone who has been the victim of this tort.

D. Material Source (of Any Particular Right, Obligation or Other Jural Relationship)

All of the legal rules that are capable of creating obligations and other juridical relationships will only do so when the relevant facts are proved to have occurred. These facts are the material source of the obligation (or whatever juridical relationship is created). Thus while a normative source is a general rule that can create unlimited numbers of obligations, the material source of an obligation is the set of facts that creates a particular obligation.

Material sources may include manifestations of consent, as they certainly do in cases of power-conferring rules. But they need not do so in other contexts, such as negligent harm to person or property.

IV. What can we Learn from Moore's System?

The system described in the previous section is not intended as a modification of the system proposed by Gaius (which in turn was modified by Birks), nor of that of Justinian, nor of the systems of the CCLC or the CCQ or the French code, whether in its original or its post-2016 form, nor of the division (sometimes viewed as exhaustive) between juridical acts and juridical facts. Moore's multiple layers do not compete with those systems, although they bid fair to replace them. When someone says that every obligation ultimately arises from the law and not from consent, the Moorean response is that this person is correct if they are referring to the formal source of the rule that created the obligation, but not if they are referring to the material source of the particular obligation, since material sources include manifestations of consent and other facts in the world that are not legal norms. If someone says that every obligation arises either from juridical acts or juridical facts, the Moorean response is that the material sources of an obligation sometimes have juridical acts as necessary (but perhaps not sufficient) elements, while in other cases the material sources of an obligation have no relationship to juridical acts.

A. Juridical Acts and Juridical Facts

This distinction, a creation of French legal doctrine, has been very influential. Sometimes, as we have seen, it is treated as exhaustive of all sources, and at other times (as in the codifications of Quebec and the French reform) these are treated as two categories among a larger set.

One significant ambiguity about juridical acts is whether they create the obligations or whether they also determine the content of the obligations so created. Take contract law as the paradigm of obligations created by juridical acts. Here, in the main, the intention of the parties not only creates the relevant obligations but determines their content. But there are many situations that are importantly different. Take the case of marriage, which is a kind of contract requiring capacity and consent, but which obviously has other constituent elements including formalities. You have to consent to get married; the giving of that consent is a juridical act; but no one contends that the obligations that arise from marriage are created and shaped by the consent, even the objective manifestations of consent, of the particular parties. They are set by the law. This is the kind of situation which seems to have led many civilian classifications to include a category for obligations arising from the law alone, even though in another sense they arise from a juridical act. They depend upon a juridical act, but they are not shaped by it.[64]

On Moore's scheme, the material sources of an obligation (or other legal relationship) may include a juridical act, whether or not the juridical act shaped the particular obligation (or other legal relationship). When a juridical act was part of the creation of a legal relationship, one can ask whether the juridical act was vitiated. This indeed is part of the conceptual function of the reasoning category of juridical acts. A person may be able to resile from their contractual offer if they were mistaken or under duress; but they may also be able to resile for similar reasons from making a will, forgiving a debt, adopting a child or abandoning property. In each case and context, protections for others who relied on objective appearances may be necessary. When a juridical act is made by the use of a power held for and on behalf of another, it may be subject to being set aside if it was used for an improper purpose.[65]

Juridical acts therefore have this conceptual unity: they are elements of material sources that are dependent on someone's volition and therefore subject to challenge when that volition was imperfect. Those obligations that arise from juridical acts may have in common a justifying principle, or more than one related justifying principles, such as freedom to bind oneself and freedom to dispose of one's entitlements.

Moore's scheme however suggests that we do not necessarily need an independent category of juridical facts. Juridical facts, in the end, are material sources that are *not* juridical acts.[66] One lesson of the long story related in this chapter is that whenever a category is defined by something it is not, it is revealed to be a kind of leftover miscellany lacking a conceptual unity. It is certainly interesting that while German civil law has a concept that corresponds to juridical act, it has never adopted a category of juridical fact.[67]

B. The Ambiguity of 'Causes of Action'

Moore's scheme provides an insight into the ambiguities of the common law's idea of 'cause of action'. This is because these ambiguities correspond rather closely to the ambiguities of 'sources' identified by Moore. Some well-known judicial

[64] This distinction has been made by Moore (n 51) 722–24; see also P Jestaz, 'Une révolution inaperçue' [2014] *Revue Trimestrielle de Droit Civil* 67, 70, summarising the argument in P Amselek, 'L'acte juridique à travers la pensée de Charles Eisenmann' (1995) 39 *Archives de Philosophie du Droit* 31, and J Raz, 'Voluntary Obligations and Normative Powers' (1972) 46 *Proceedings of the Aristotlean Society, Supplementary Volumes* 79, 97. I am grateful to Michelle Cumyn and Sandy Steel for references.

[65] For some discussion of the common law, see Smith (n 63) 619–21; Quebec civil law: M Cantin Cumyn and M Cumyn, *L'administration du bien d'autrui*, 2nd edn (Cowansville, Éditions Yvon Blais, 2014) 333–36, 347.

[66] This is what the usual definitions come down to (nn 20, 29).

[67] n 19.

definitions of cause of action refer to facts: 'A cause of action has traditionally been defined as comprising every fact which it would be necessary for the plaintiff to prove, if disputed, in order to support his or her right to the judgment of the court …'[68]

On the face of it, this definition refers to a collection of particular facts that have happened. I will call this 'cause of action^{a}'. This definition is important when, for example, you have to know where or when a cause of action arose, as you might for jurisdictional reasons or in relation to concerns about the limitation of actions. Facts have a 'where' and a 'when', but legal rules do not. Cause of action^{a} corresponds to the material source in Moore's system.

The first ambiguity is foreshadowed by the words 'it would be necessary for the plaintiff to prove' in the definition above. Necessary according to what or to whom? According to a legal rule, which is the second sense of the phrase. 'The cause of action in battery consists of the intentional infliction upon the body of another of a harmful or offensive contact': that is a description of a general rule, which can be satisfied by an infinite number of factual scenarios, and which, when satisfied, creates a liability to pay damages. I will call this 'cause of action^{b}'. It is clearly very different from a cause of action^{a}, because a cause of action^{a} is a collection of facts while a cause of action^{b} is a legal rule. It has no 'where' or 'when'. Being a liability-creating rule, it is a normative source in Moore's system.

Although causes of action^{b} are normative sources, many rules are normative sources of rights and obligations without being causes of action (in any sense). Being born, getting married, having children, making a contract of sale, being the first possessor of a previously wild animal: all these events create rights and obligations under legal rules that are not causes of action.

We can identify a third sense of cause of action. If I go to my lawyer and explain that someone has punched me without justification, she might say, 'you have a cause of action in battery against that person'. She is not describing the relevant facts, nor the legal rule which they activate, but the outcome: she is saying, 'that person is liable to you in damages'. She is making a claim that a particular liability exists, although her expression in terms of a cause of action also names the normative source that created that particular liability. I will call this third and most particular sense a 'cause of action^{c}'. In Moore's scheme, it is not any source; it is the obligation that has been created, whose source we may inquire after.

In earlier work I noted these three senses of 'cause of action'.[69] It now seems necessary to add a fourth sense. Andrew Burrows has argued that although there are multiple causes of action (what I am calling causes of action^{b}) in tort, it is

[68] *Danyluk v Ainsworth Technologies Inc.* [2001] 2 SCR 460, 2001 SCC 44, [54].

[69] L Smith, 'Defences and the Disunity of Unjust Enrichment' in A Dyson, J Goudkamp, and F Wilmot-Smith (eds), *Defences in Unjust Enrichment* (Oxford, Hart, 2016) 27. In that chapter I aimed to explain (35–36) how the same ideas are named with less ambiguity in German legal thinking: the individual claim (cause of action^{c}) being called an *Anspruch*, the general norm (cause of action^{b}) that may create such a claim is called an *Anspruchnorm* or *Anspruchgrundlage* (claim-foundation).

possible to say, 'A has a cause of action against B in tort for damages'.[70] He describes this as expressing the idea of cause of action in more general terms as opposed to more specific terms. And so it is also with unjust enrichment: he claims that '[u]njust enrichment is a cause of action', even while unjust enrichment contains multiple 'more specific causes of action which have significantly different normative explanations'.[71] To me, this only underlines that he is talking about two different things and giving both the same name. It is fine to say that one is speaking at a higher or lower level of generality, but it is inviting confusion to give *the same name* to a category of tests for liability that are claimable in court, and to each of those particular claims.[72] He argues that his more general sense of unjust enrichment is 'a single normative principle', and also that it is not a legal test that can be pleaded in court like the elements of the tort of battery.[73]

Burrows' more general sense of 'cause of action' does not correspond to any of the three senses of that expression that have been identified above. Let us call it cause of action^{d}. It seems to me that this must refer to what in Moore's system is called a justificatory principle. It fits the definition of a justificatory principle: it is not pleadable in court, but it explains the legal rules that are pleadable in court. This interpretation is reinforced by Burrows' discussion of claims to restitution arising out of wrongs: his reasons for excluding those claims from unjust enrichment (in his wide sense) are purely pragmatic and not conceptual.[74] The implication is that were it not for those pragmatic considerations, Burrows would be content to treat those claims as part of unjust enrichment.[75] Those claims to restitution arising out of wrongs are clearly *not* based on the same cause of action^{b} as are claims to restitution that are not founded on wrongs, which Burrows does include in unjust enrichment. What those wrong-based claims *do* have in common with the claims that Burrows does include in unjust enrichment is that all of these claims may be said to be based on the same justifying principle: a principle against unjust enrichment. Thus, Burrows' more general sense of cause of action – that is, cause of action^{d} – is what Moore means by a justificatory principle.[76]

[70] A Burrows, 'In Defence of Unjust Enrichment' (2019) 78 *Cambridge Law Journal* 521, 526.

[71] ibid 529, 530.

[72] To use a Birksian biological analogy, it would be as if, instead of distinguishing between genus and species, we called a genus a species in a more general sense, while saying that a species is a species in a more specific sense. But it is worse than that, because genus and species are larger and smaller sets of the same contents (organisms); a justificatory principle is not simply a *set* of normative sources but is an explanation for why normative sources exist. Moreover, justificatory principles are not tests for liability to be applied to the proven facts, but normative sources are exactly that.

[73] Burrows (n 70) 529, 527.

[74] ibid 529: 'in order to stop duplication with other established causes of action in English law.' See also footnotes 35–37.

[75] Just as many common law books on restitution do indeed include restitution for wrongs, on the ground that these claims are based on the same justificatory principle as restitution claims that do not depend on wrongdoing. See for example P Maddaugh and J McCamus, *The Law of Restitution*, looseleaf edn (Toronto, Canada Law Book, 2004); American Law Institute, *Restatement of the Law Third: Restitution and Unjust Enrichment*, 2 vols (Philadelphia, ALI, 2011).

[76] Burrows (n 70) 529 fn 38 also makes clear that Burrows is talking about a justificatory principle.

It is intriguing, but perhaps not surprising, that the ambiguities of 'cause of action' track so closely to the ambiguities of 'sources of obligations'.

C. Birks's Classification and the Travails of Unjust Enrichment

Birks had an abiding admiration for the achievements of Roman legal science.[77] He purported to be open to any new system of classification that could improve on that of Gaius, but took the view that none had so far been proposed.[78] His project, however, was exactly to propose an improvement. Gaius's named categories were contracts and wrongs, but Gaius realised that there had to be a residual category of 'others'. Birks saw his proposal of adding unjust enrichment as one that would withdraw from that miscellany a group of cases which could properly be unified as arising from a third 'causative event'.[79]

For all his richly deserved renown, Gaius was only human. His classification of 'things' into corporeal and incorporeal things, the latter including (among others) obligations, inheritances and usufructary rights over tangible things, has been characterised as 'illogical' by the Romanist Barry Nicholas, and as 'lame' by the Belgian civilian Henri De Page.[80] We must remember that the classical Roman jurists did not have a modern conception of individual rights.[81] This can help to explain why Gaius lined up 'obligations' with such things as usufructs and inheritances, which are not obligations but rights.[82] Much more seriously, when it is viewed with a modern conception of rights, Gaius's approach can be seen to mix haphazardly rights and physical things, which are not rights but the objects of our rights. Robustly rejected by civilians in Germany and in South Africa,[83] this rather naïve scheme has the effect of unconsciously demolishing the fundamental distinction between real rights and personal rights, with predictable confusion as to the meaning of equally fundamental concepts such as ownership.[84] One scholar

[77] L Smith, 'Peter Birks and Comparative Law' (2013) 43 *Revue de Droit de l'Université de Sherbrooke* 193.

[78] P Birks, 'Introduction' in P Birks (ed), *English Private Law*, 2 vols, vol 1 (Oxford, Oxford University Press, 2000) xxxv, xlvi–xlvii.

[79] For example, Birks, 'Meditation' (n 6) 19–20.

[80] Both cited by G Gretton, 'Ownership and its Objects' (2007) 71 *Rabels Zeitschrift* 802, 806. Gretton translates De Page's 1941 pronouncement that 'cette classification est boîteuse' as 'this classification is gimcrack', though the literal translation of 'boîteuse' is 'lame'. Villey, 'Les Institutes de Gaïus' (n 11) 175 said in 1962 that Gaius's scheme is traditionally characterised as 'boîteuse'.

[81] n 11.

[82] Discussed in Birks, *Obligations* (n 4) 7–8; Birks, 'Meditation' (n 6) 7–9.

[83] In German civil law, only 'things' can be owned, and only tangible things are things (BGB § 90). For the same approach in South Africa, see CG van der Merwe and M de Waal, *The Law of Things and Servitudes* (Durban, Butterworths, 1993) 13.

[84] In both Quebec and France, ownership is understood as the largest and most fundamental real (or proprietary) right that can be held (French Civil code, art 544; CCQ art 947); in this sense, it stands apart from all personal rights. And yet in both places, many scholars argue that 'incorporeal

has argued that in proposing this classification of things, Gaius was only trying to help his students and was not making any deep claim about jural concepts.[85]

Perhaps the same was true of his classification of the sources of obligations: it was a way of breaking up the law to help the student to understand it. It is not at all clear that Gaius thought that there were important shared characteristics among all obligations arising from contracts, or among all obligations arising from wrongs, beyond their belonging to those broad categories which might help students to keep an overview.[86]

Birks claimed that his own classification was of 'causative events', but we have already seen that it is a classification of the legal characterisation of events that take place in the world. His classification was actually into 'events that the legal system characterizes as wrongs', 'events that the legal system characterizes as unjust enrichments' and 'manifestations of consent to which the legal system attaches the consequences of creating obligations'.[87]

Birks rightly said that some obligations arise from manifestations of consent. Consent can also be essential for their transfer or extinguishment. Birks's category of consent has the same unity as that of juridical acts: the legal relation created has, as one of its material sources, a manifestation of intention. This may also create a regime, which may or may not be perfectly unified, allowing the setting aside of the results of such manifestations for vices of consent. Birks was aware of

property' (such as personal claims) can be owned (Y Emerich, *La propriété des créances: approche comparative* (Cowansville & Paris, Les Éditions Yvon Blais and LGDJ, 2006 and 2007); for discussion of the evolution of this thinking, see Gretton (n 80) 810–15). The concept of 'ownership' ('propriété') is thus used sometimes to refer to one particular real (or proprietary) right, and sometimes to refer to titularity or 'mineness', whether or not involving any real or proprietary right. This is precisely the logical defect in Gaius's work to which Nicholas and De Page (among many others) drew attention. For one common lawyer who seems to continue this tradition, see J Penner, *The Idea of Property in Law* (Oxford, Clarendon Press, 1997), esp ch 5.

Another way to try to make sense of Gaius's attempt to line up rights and things has a longer history in French legal thought; this is to argue that full ownership of a thing is somehow equivalent to the physical thing itself: see citations in Gretton (n 80) 809–10, who observes that this idea 'is metaphysically so bizarre that one can hardly believe that is [sic] could be accepted'. And yet a similar position is apparently taken in P Birks, 'The Roman Concept of Dominium and the Idea of Absolute Ownership' [1985] *Acta Juridica* 1, 20–21. In my view, this again relates to the fact that Gaius and his contemporaries were not reasoning in terms of rights (n 11); as explained by Birks in the passage just cited, it is only when your rights in a thing are less than full ownership that you are *forced* to distinguish between the rights you hold and the things in which you hold rights (even though it is always clearer so to distinguish).

[85] F Giglio, 'Pandectism and the Gaian Classification of Things' (2012) 62 *University of Toronto Law Journal* 1 esp 24–28. Compare Villey, 'Les Institutes de Gaïus' (n 11) 172–79, suggesting that Gaius's goal was to articulate how the world looks when seen through the eyes of a jurist who did not think in terms of rights.

[86] 'Gaius, and to a lesser extent Justinian, is concerned far more with methods of acquisition and loss (of status in the law of persons, of the various types of things elsewhere) than with the nature and content of what is being acquired and lost': B Nicholas, *An Introduction to Roman Law* (Oxford, Oxford University Press, 1962) 99 note 1. See also Villey, 'Les Institutes de Gaïus' (n 11) 173, arguing that Gaius's aim was to provide a *description* of how the things important to jurists (persons, things and actions; not rights) come into being and disappear.

[87] n 41.

the distinction mentioned earlier, that some rights arise from consent but are not shaped by the particular consents of the particular parties.[88]

When we come to Birks's category of wrongs, however, we have more difficulty in identifying the unity. A wrong is an unexcused infringement of a right. Rights can arise from consent or from the law, and the category of wrongs includes breaches of trust, breaches of contract, breaches of rights granted to all by the law (such as the right of bodily integrity), breaches of proprietary rights held by only some (such as the rights of property in a particular asset), and more besides. There is no unity in the law of wrongs by material source, nor by normative source (cause of action[b]); rather there is plurality. There is no unity as to justifying principle, as these many rights have many justifying principles.[89] We could posit an intermediate justifying principle that says that any unexcused infringement of a right should create one or more remedial rights, although it is not clear that this would really be a different justifying principle from that which justifies the original right. What we see is that the unity in this category seems to be one of form: the claims arising from wrongs are remedial secondary rights, that is rights arising from infringements of other rights. This is not the same kind of unity that one sees in a category of juridical relationships that arise from manifestations of consent, namely a unity by justifying principle. Since there is no unity as to justification among wrongs, it is not surprising that there is not much unity among the regimes governing the different kinds of wrongs.

Finally we come to unjust enrichment. Running all through Birks's work, during his whole career, was a project to add unjust enrichment to Gaius's categories of 'consent' and 'wrongs'. This was often the avowed purpose of his writing, and even when it was not, it was just below the surface.[90]

Birks's view was that this classification had relevant consequences for the features of the obligations with which it dealt. He very often argued that it is a fundamental principle of justice that like cases be treated alike.[91] His classification project was tied to this. All the obligations arising from unjust enrichment should have similar characteristics, such as not requiring the proof of any wrongdoing, such as depending upon showing an enrichment of the defendant, and such as allowing the defendant the defence of change of position since they were prima facie liable on only 'very slight facts'.[92] Obligations arising from other sources have no reason to have such characteristics.

[88] n 64; see Birks, 'Meditation' (n 6) 19, where he notes that 'becoming a parent' is a causative event in the miscellany, implying what must be correct, that the obligations so arising cannot be said to arise from consent even where becoming a parent is consensual.

[89] If there is a unity as to formal source, that is only accidental and of little interest. Most common law jurisdictions have at least some statutory wrongs.

[90] Birks often suggested that Gaius came close to recognising unjust enrichment as a separate category (n 7).

[91] Birks, 'Equity' (n 36) 5, 17, 27, 35, 38, 95; see also Birks, 'Meditation' (n 6) 34 and Birks, 'Misnomer' (n 37) 29.

[92] The phrase appears twice at Birks, *Unjust Enrichment* (n 22) 7.

My reading of Birks's project is thus that he wanted to pay homage to Gaius, to improve his system within its own logic and spirit, but also (consciously or not) to carry it further than Gaius ever seemed to do. Birks started with a classification which purported to be descriptive. He almost always used analogies from biology, whose taxa aim to be based on nothing more nor less than facts. Birks wrote as if his classification was of facts;[93] he aimed to turn his classification into a normative tool, using it to argue for improvements in the law through the requirement that like cases be treated alike. But since his classification was actually of legal characterisations of facts, his category of 'unjust enrichment' was the creature of an argument: that everything within it had something in common. So his arguments for law reform were not, as he sometimes implied, necessary implications from existing facts, but rather implications from his own views of the nature and particularly of the scope of unjust enrichment.

It seems to me that he overplayed his hand in two distinct but related ways. First, he took an enormously wide view of what are the obligations and rights that arise from unjust enrichment. It is not totally clear what criteria he applied in this respect, but by inference they were (i) that the obligation or right did not depend on wrongdoing nor directly on consent; (ii) that it could be described as linked to the defendant's being better off (including through acquiring rights, getting rid of liabilities, or getting something the defendant subjectively wanted even if it made the defendant financially poorer); and (iii) that there was a reason to treat the plaintiff as having a jural connection to the defendant's being better off.[94] When questions were raised by other scholars as to the coherence of the very wide range of claims that he included within unjust enrichment, his response was to argue that the characteristics of unjust enrichment needed to be reinterpreted precisely to admit all of the claims he wished to bring in.[95] In this sense, what he presented as a descriptive category was very much the product of his own convictions.

Here is one striking example. In his early work he went out of his way to distinguish 'restitution for wrongs' from 'subtractive unjust enrichment', precisely on the basis that the cause of action[b] is different in the two cases: the first is based on a wrong, the second is not. There are still books that treat them together; the basis for this might be that the common (non-legal) justifying principle is one that aims to remedy unjust enrichment. But Birks's final vision of unjust enrichment seemed to treat any case of profitable infringement of another's rights as a case of unjust enrichment (even if such a case could also be analysed through wrongdoing).[96] Yet his original argument remains persuasive: there is very little in common, at the level of normative source, between liability to repay a mistaken payment and liability to give up the benefit one acquires through infringement of another's

[93] ibid 10.

[94] ibid 10–11.

[95] Discussed in detail in L Smith, 'Tracing' in A Burrows and Lord Rodger of Earlsferry (eds), *Mapping the Law: Essays in Memory of Peter Birks* (Oxford, Oxford University Press, 2006) 119.

[96] Birks *Unjust Enrichment* (n 22) 78–86.

right, where that infringement caused no loss. The latter case can only succeed if there is an infringement, while the former has nothing to do with infringement. Whether Birks realised it or not, the only thing that could possibly be common to all of the cases he called unjust enrichment was the justifying principle, not the normative source.

There is nothing wrong with a classification based on justifying principles. We have already seen that this appears to be the position taken by Burrows, who in many ways has always remained committed to Birks's earlier work.[97] We have also seen the consequences of that approach: for one, since it accommodates many normative sources, it is impossible to insist on uniformity across the whole category.[98] Thus, a classification based on a justifying principle could never be made to do the work that Birks wanted it to do. Justifying principles do not strongly demand uniformity among all of the normative sources which they may underpin (especially since a given normative source may be underpinned by more than one justifying principle).

The second way in which he overplayed his hand was that his project seems to have blinded him to the fact that the different claims with which he was working do not actually have all that much in common (except, again, their justifying principle, which he acknowledged as unjust enrichment in the 'weakly normative' sense).[99] In his early work he seems to have operated on the principle that there were multiple causes of action^{b} in unjust enrichment. These are normative sources in the Moorean scheme. He proposed a 'generic conception' of unjust enrichment, and since he liked biological analogies, it is not surprising to see that this was because he thought it was a genus that contained more than one species.[100] The 'generic conception' therefore was *not* a cause of action^{b} or a normative source. But he sometimes rather acted as if it were. He abstracted a series of three 'high-level questions' from the claims. The implication was that if all three of these elements could be satisfied, a claim was made out, even if the ways in which they were satisfied revealed a configuration that had not previously been recognised in the law.[101] But this only follows if these elements were elements of a cause of action^{b}. A good example lies in his arguments that a recipient of an unauthorised transfer of trust property should be personally liable to the beneficiary in unjust enrichment, without proof of fault.[102] This was not a descriptive argument, since it was not based on any claim known in the law; it was based rather on the idea that such a claim must

[97] n 70.

[98] Indeed, as we noted in relation to Burrows' argument, a category of unjust enrichment that is based on a justifying principle is liable to include some normative principles (causes of action^{b}) that are wrongs.

[99] n 55.

[100] P Birks, *An Introduction to the Law of Restitution*, rev edn (Oxford, Clarendon Press, 1989) 16–19.

[101] ibid 21.

[102] eg Birks, 'Equity' (n 36) 67–72.

logically exist – if his implicit generalisation was justifiable, that the known claims are actually particular examples of a cause of action[b].[103]

I have already mentioned that Birks responded to the objections of others by modifying his understanding of the elements of unjust enrichment, going so far as to propose, for example, that a plaintiff could sue a defendant in unjust enrichment by choosing to transfer the plaintiff's rights to that defendant so that the defendant was enriched as the claim required.[104] But he went further, realising perhaps that the law reform part of his project could never be achieved if there are multiple normative sources in unjust enrichment. There are lots of torts, and it is quite impossible to reason directly from one tort to another, insisting that they all be identical because they are all torts. Torts are infringements of rights, and the rights have different sources, and the consequences of breaches of different rights can be different, and may permit different defences.[105] Birks's category was 'wrongs', which of course includes breach of contract and breach of trust, which are substantively different again in many dimensions. Even 'manifestations of consent' reveals important diversity at the level of normative sources: no one would argue that because parol contracts need consideration, justice demands that promises under seal need consideration, nor would they argue the converse. Such an argument could be made, of course, as an argument for law reform, but not simply on the ground that like cases must be treated alike. Birks did not want that degree of diversity in unjust enrichment, since otherwise it would not be possible to reason from one claim situation to another as he wished to do. The only way that the claims he was concerned with could all be sufficiently similar to allow that kind of reasoning was if, after all, they were just examples of liability based on the same cause of action[b] or normative source.

More importantly, the substantive part of his project, that there is a 'causative event' of unjust enrichment alongside 'consent' and 'wrongs', could not be achieved if there are multiple normative sources (causes of action[b]) in unjust enrichment. This is because rights arising from unjust enrichment are primary rights and so do not share a unity in arising from wrongs.[106] If they have no unity either as to normative source, their only possible unity is by justifying principle, which cannot be a source in Birks's understanding of the Gaian classification because a justifying principle cannot be a 'causative event'. This seems to be why, ultimately, he argued that there is only one normative source in this category.[107] The genus had only one

[103] For some objections to these strategies of generalisation, see L Smith, 'Unjust Enrichment, Property, and the Structure of Trusts' (2000) 116 *Law Quarterly Review* 412; W Swadling, 'Ignorance and Unjust Enrichment: The Problem of Title' (2008) 28 *Oxford Journal of Legal Studies* 627.

[104] Smith (n 95) 120–24.

[105] The principles of causation may also be applied differently: Lord Hoffmann, 'Causation' (2005) 121 *Law Quarterly Review* 592.

[106] Earlier (text at n 38) we noted that Birks thought that it mattered not that rights arising from 'wrongs' were secondary rights while rights arising from 'consent' and 'unjust enrichment' were primary rights. But it did matter in relation to his goal to have a unified and not a plural law of unjust enrichment.

[107] Birks, *Unjust Enrichment* (n 22) 16–17 and chs 5–6.

species. The 'generic conception' became a single cause of action[b] as otherwise it had nowhere else to go but up and out of reach.

V. Conclusion

The desire to classify obligations by sources is old and understandable. But every classification only makes sense in relation to some goal or goals. Moore's classification helps us to see the ambiguities in the idea of 'source'. That is its goal, and it is, in a sense, a classification of meanings of the word 'source'.

A justificatory principle is a non-legal ideal or aspiration or value. A normative source is a legal rule that is capable of creating or modifying particular rights, liabilities and other legal relationships between citizens. A material source is one of the factual events that activate a normative source. A formal source is simply that which qualifies a rule as rule of law.

It is striking to observe that the phrase 'cause of action' in the common law is sometimes used to mean a material source, sometimes a normative source, sometimes a justificatory principle, and sometimes to mean the obligation that arises when the material source has activated a normative source.

Inevitably, a category of law that is unified by justificatory principle may reveal diversity in the normative sources that it contains. Different normative sources may have different features that relate to their different concrete instantiations of legal liability. The law of contract, the law of covenants, the law of express trusts, and the law of estoppel give effect in quite different ways to the principle that people should honour their serious commitments. The shared justificatory principle does not justify ironing out their differences.

Every legal relationship is created (or extinguished or modified) by one or more material sources. All legal relationships that have a juridical act as the (or a) material source do have something important in common. It is not necessarily the case that the principles allowing such acts to be set aside will be identical in every case, but we can reasonably start from a presumption of some uniformity and expect variations to be justifiable. In my view, the common law needs to pay more attention to the concept of juridical act.

The category of wrongs does not reveal much unity, either by justificatory principle or by normative source. Thinking about that category, however, requires us to think about the sources – in all four senses that we have seen – of the rights protected by the law of wrongs.[108] It requires us also to think about why some rights are protected differently from others. For some wrongs, punitive damages or nominal damages may be available, but not for others; for some, a claim may only lie if the plaintiff has suffered consequential loss. Contract rights may be

[108] R Stevens, *Torts and Rights* (Oxford, Oxford University Press, 2007) 350.

specifically enforceable, or not, while in the common law the obligations of a trustee in relation to administration of the trust are always specifically enforceable where this is possible, and are specifically enforced by substitution in money where it is not. The law of wrongs is a glorious miscellany, just as is the law of rights.

If 'unjust enrichment' is a category organised by justificatory principle, we can expect it to relate to diverse normative sources, some of which may well be wrongs.[109] Beyond wrongs, there is a wide range of situations in which defendants may become responsible to plaintiffs without having consented or having done anything wrong. Some of these cases may be described as assumption of responsibility, waiver or estoppel. Some of them involve defendants acquiring rights which must be returned, in specie or in value. Some involve defendants having to pay the value of work that they asked for. Among all these normative sources of obligations, some may have in common a justifying principle against unjust enrichment. That commonality, however, does not justify ignoring the differences of detail among the different normative sources. It is not surprising that civilian systems have multiple and diverse normative sources in the area of law that may be described as unjust enrichment.[110] The common law does too.

[109] For a well-known example of the formulation of unjust enrichment as a justificatory principle, but not as a normative source, see D.12.6.14, translated in A Watson (ed), *The Digest of Justinian*, 4 vols, revised edn (Philadelphia, University of Pennsylvania Press, 1998) as: 'For it is by nature fair that nobody should enrich himself at the expense of another.' The (unpaginated) preface of the work indicates that Book 12 was translated by Peter Birks. See also D.50.17.206 (Pomponius): 'By the law of nature it is fair that no one become richer by the loss and injury of another' (trans M Crawford). These principles can certainly be understood to justify gain-based claims arising out of wrongs.

[110] L Smith, 'Restitution: A New Start?' in P Devonshire and R Havelock (eds), *The Impact of Equity and Restitution in Commerce* (Oxford, Hart, 2018) 91, 103–04. Nor is it surprising that, as in the common law, uncertainty about whether unjust enrichment is a justificatory principle or a normative source has led to disagreement and confusion: N Jansen, 'Farewell to Unjust Enrichment?' (2016) 20 *Edinburgh Law Review* 123; J du Plessis, 'Long Live the Law of Unjustified Enrichment – A Response to Jansen' [2019] *Acta Juridica* 371.

PART II

Particular Private Rights

8

Justifying Possession (or How We Get from Here to There)

MICHAEL JR CRAWFORD*

I. Introduction

After a journey of many months requiring ceaseless toil and privation, two pioneers clamber over a ridgeline and are greeted with the sight of a fertile valley stretching into the distance. A, a farmer, wishes to use the land to raise crops. B, a grazier, wishes to run cattle instead.[1] Because the cattle would trample and eat the crops, their use preferences are incompatible. How, then, should their conflict be resolved? Perhaps the valley could be declared a commons, in which case A and B will be left to negotiate some cooperative solution to their problem.[2] An alternative, winner-takes-all, solution would be to designate either A or B as the 'owner' of the valley and allow him to have the first and final say about the use to which it is to be put. The second solution describes a system of private property, the advantages of which are well known.[3]

Noting the many benefits of a system of private property tells us nothing, however, about who ought to be the decision maker or the rule by which such a person is to be chosen.[4] So how does the law pick the owner? The answer is that it does so by the outcome of a race.[5] The first person to take possession of an object

* Previous versions of this chapter were presented at the Justifying Private Rights workshop at UNSW Law and the Herbert Smith Freehills Law & Economics Initiative, Work in Progress Series. I would like to thank all participants for their comments. For particularly helpful comments, I would like to thank Rosalind Dixon, Ben McFarlane, James Penner, Timothy Pilkington, Stephen Smith and Nicholas Tiverios. The usual caveats apply.

[1] The oft-used farmer and rancher example comes from RH Coase, 'The Problem of Social Cost' (1960) 3 *Journal of Law & Economics* 1.

[2] Or perhaps not.

[3] For a familiar list see TW Merrill, 'The Property Strategy' (2011) 160 *University of Pennsylvania Law Review* 2061, 2081–94.

[4] I here follow Merrill in identifying decentralised decision making as the essence of the 'property strategy': ibid 2063.

[5] For the race analogy, see TW Merrill, 'Accession and Original Ownership' (2009) 1 *Journal of Legal Analysis* 459, 463.

of property becomes its owner. If A, being the faster runner, can enclose the valley with temporary fencing before B arrives, then A will become owner and B will be obliged to respect his decision to use the land to grow crops.

As the parable of the pioneers sought to make clear, the effect of rights of private property is to exclude duty-bearers from valuable resources. Given this, it is only natural that we should want the basic allocative rule at the heart of our system of private property to be morally satisfactory.[6] It is unsurprising that many commentators are unconvinced by the moral desirability of an allocative rule that depends on the outcome of a race.[7] How would we feel if, for example, it turned out that A was an extremely wealthy farmer with several properties, whilst B was an impoverished grazier brought to his knees by drought? Why should A benefit at the expense of B simply because he is the faster runner? What is more, whilst we might defend, for instance, a labour-based theory on desert or incentive grounds, the possession rule does not actually require that the possessor do anything useful with the object over which she claims a right.[8] A does not forfeit his right to the land if, after enclosing it, he lets it lie fallow.[9]

Given these sorts of criticisms, can we mount a normative defence of the possession rule? Epstein has offered a famous 'qualified defense'[10] of possession that centres on its incumbency. His argument is that, given the difficulty of determining who gets what, the best mechanism for creating property rights is the mechanism that we have.

The argument made in this chapter goes further than this. Drawing on insights from game theory and the spontaneous order tradition, it is argued that, because no allocative mechanism can reliably pick deserving winners, a basic allocative rule will be tolerably fair so long as it treats everyone as equally deserving, in the sense that no one is systematically excluded from benefitting from it. Although the possession rule not only appears to be, but in fact is, morally arbitrary,[11] it satisfies this minimal requirement of fairness. If the argument advanced below is correct, incumbency is not the possession rule's only virtue. It is also a tolerably fair mechanism for creating rights to scarce things.

[6] Indeed, Waldron argues that this makes private property a prima facie morally objectionable institution that, like punishment, requires special justification. See J Waldron, 'Property Law' in D Patterson (ed), *A Companion to Philosophy of Law and Legal Theory* (Chichester, John Wiley & Sons, 2010) 14.

[7] JW Singer, 'Original Acquisition of Property: From Conquest & Possession to Democracy & Equal Opportunity' (2011) 86 *Indiana Law Journal* 763, 763. See also A Ripstein, *Force and Freedom* (Cambridge, MA, Harvard University Press, 2009) 96–97.

[8] As his own acorn example demonstrates, Locke's nominally labour-based theory did not actually draw a distinction between possession and labour. John Locke, *Two Treatises of Government: And a Letter Concerning Toleration* (first published 1689, Ian Shapiro ed, New Haven, Yale University Press, 2003) 112 §28. This point is also noted in RA Epstein, 'From Natural Law to Social Welfare: Theoretical Principles and Practical Applications' (2015) 100 *Iowa Law Review* 1743, 1756.

[9] It should be noted that the law of adverse possession does not actually require owners to do anything productive or useful with their land.

[10] RA Epstein, 'Possession as the Root of Title' (1979) 13 *Georgia Law Review* 1221, 1238.

[11] 'Arbitrary' is not intended to mean 'not susceptible to justification'. Rather, it means that the possession rule's moral dimension is incidental to its emergence and ultimate triumph as the basic rule for determining who owns what. I thank Timothy Pilkington for raising this issue.

II. Getting Started: A Dilemma

A. Acquisition and the Problem of Unilateralism (with Some Doubts)

Waldron has written that:

> [i]n a private property system, a rule is laid down that, in the case of each object, the individual person whose name is attached to that object is to determine how the object shall be used and by whom. His decision is to be upheld by society as final.[12]

Every system of private property must have a rule that determines how those entities that count as 'persons' acquire rights to those objects that count as 'things'. To adapt Waldron's explanation, there must be some means of 'allocating names to things'.

Although the need for such an 'allocative' rule is plain, selecting the appropriate mechanism places the law on the horns of a dilemma, for the following reason. Systems of private property involve claims to exclusivity. At common law, A, an owner, has the exclusive ability to determine the use of some object of property because B, C, D, E … owe him a duty, instantiated by the tort of trespass, to refrain from physically interfering with it.[13] If, as Locke insisted,[14] the earth belongs to mankind in common, then, so goes the argument, any act by which A incorporates an object into her exclusive domain of decision-making authority must violate the rights of the other commoners who, being subject to a duty of non-interference, now have fewer objects over which they can exercise their own decision making authority. Any allocative rule that turns on a non-consensual act thus appears to run headlong into the problem of 'unilateralism', according to which, as a general philosophical matter, it seems impossible to explain why any duty-imposing act should bind others in the absence of their consent.[15] The basic position is outlined by Epstein, who writes that:

> [t]he essence of any property right is a claim to bind the rest of the world; such cannot be obtained, contra Locke, by [any] unilateral conduct on the part of one person without the consent of the rest of the world whose rights are thereby violated or reduced. First possession runs afoul of this principle; so does the labor theory. Indeed the point

[12] J Waldron, *The Right to Private Property* (Oxford, Oxford University Press, 1988) 39.

[13] The canonical text being JE Penner, *The Idea of Property in Law* (Oxford, Clarendon Press, 1997). Even those who criticise what they regard as the over-emphasis on exclusion agree that an owner's 'agenda-setting' authority is fundamental to her position. See, eg: L Katz, 'Exclusion and Exclusivity in Property Law' (2008) 58 *University of Toronto Law Journal* 275, 277–78.

[14] Locke (n 8) 111 §25.

[15] See generally L Wenar, 'Original Acquisition of Private Property' (1998) 107(428) *Mind* 799, 806–07. For the Kantian view see LM Austin, 'Possession and the Distractions of Philosophy' in JE Penner and HE Smith (eds), *Philosophical Foundations of Property Law*, 1st edn (Oxford, Oxford University Press, 2013) 182, 191–92; NW Sage, 'Original Acquisition and Unilateralism: Kant, Hegel, and Corrective Justice' (2012) 25 *Canadian Journal of Law & Jurisprudence* 119, 121–22.

> is a matter of principle perfectly general, and it applies moreover to any and every theory that uses individual actions as the source of entitlements against the collectivity at large. Property may look to be an individualistic institution, but the very nature and definition of the right seems to require some collective social institution to lie at its base. No 'natural' act can legitimate a social claim to property.[16]

One may question the degree to which 'unilateralism' is actually a problem for the creation of property rights. Gibbard, to take a prominent example, commences his article with the assertion that, '[i]f a person owns a thing, his ownership enhances his liberty, but it does so at the expense of others. Ownership of a thing gives a person the right to exclude others from its use, and that right, though it adds to the freedom of the owner, detracts from the freedom of others'.[17] If unilaterally constraining people's liberties by placing them under duties were always illegitimate then, as others have noted,[18] this would be a fatal objection to *all* non-consensual rights, whether proprietary or otherwise.[19]

In order to avoid this problem, Gibbard posits a more demanding requirement, arguing that, whilst A does not need B's permission to change the world physically, A does need B's permission in order to 'bring him under new moral constraints'.[20] He writes that:

> [a] distinction must be made between depriving someone of opportunities and depriving him of rights. To deprive someone of an opportunity is to make a physical change in the world; to deprive someone of a right is to change what it is morally permissible for him and others to do. What I am supposing is that it is morally permissible, in certain cases, to deprive someone else of an opportunity without his consent, but that it is impossible to deprive someone of a right unless he himself gives up or loses that right through a voluntary act.[21]

Whilst this stronger formulation, predicated on the existence of a 'right', prevents the problem of unilateralism from becoming a universal solvent, it also raises others. First, as Gaus and Lomasky observe,[22] a serious problem is caused by the ambiguity in Gibbard's use of the term 'right'. If, by 'right', Gibbard means a Hohfeldian claim-right,[23] then it is incumbent on him to demonstrate why, in a pre-civil condition, we have rights, as tenants in common, to the world's resources. Assuming this is what Locke, for instance, meant when he wrote that 'the earth, and all inferior creatures, be common to all men',[24] then it is an assertion that

[16] Epstein (n 10) 1228.

[17] A Gibbard, 'Natural Property Rights' (1976) 10 *Noûs* 77, 77.

[18] GF Gaus and Loren E Lomasky, 'Are Property Rights Problematic?' (1990) 73 *The Monist* 483, 487–88.

[19] The entire law of tort, for instance, would become highly problematic on this basis.

[20] Gibbard (n 17) 78.

[21] ibid.

[22] Gaus and Lomasky (n 18) 489. Their analysis neatly demonstrates why a careful understanding of the concept of a 'right' matters in both legal and political/moral philosophy.

[23] WN Hohfeld, 'Some Fundamental Legal Conceptions as Applied in Judicial Reasoning' (1913) 23 *Yale Law Journal* 16, 31–32.

[24] Locke (n 8) 111 §27.

requires some justification. If, unlike Locke, one is not content to base the truth of this claim in scripture,[25] then one needs some other reason that explains why we have such a claim-right, as opposed to nothing at all.[26]

Alternatively, if, by 'right', Gibbard instead means a Hohfeldian 'liberty' or 'privilege',[27] then a different problem arises, namely that the idea of a global commons of mankind is essentially incoherent. As Ostrom has emphasised,[28] what is significant about a successful commons, as opposed to an 'open-access' regime, is not simply that the commoners have a *liberty* to use a common pool resource, but that non-commoners have a *duty* to keep out.[29] So far as a non-commoner is concerned, a commons is simply private property. However, if all of mankind has a liberty to use any and all resources, then we do not have a 'commons' but Hobbes's 'warre, as is of every man, against every man'.[30] Because liberties correlate to 'no-rights',[31] exercising one's liberty to appropriate a resource in a global commons does not raise a problem of unilateralism because it is, by definition, impossible to breach the 'no-right' that everyone has against everyone else.[32] To the extent that we are concerned that a system of property transforms hitherto *liberties to x* into *duties not to x*, we have not identified a problem that is peculiar to property law but, as noted above, have simply encountered an issue that plagues all systems of non-consensual rights.

B. The Cost of Consent

There are, as discussed above, reasons why one may question the degree to which unilateralism really is an obstacle in getting from the 'here' of anarchy to the 'there' of a system of property rights. However, proceeding on the assumption that unilateralism is a problem, it follows that any legitimate allocative rule must turn on the consent of those whose erstwhile liberties have become duties.

[25] ibid 111 §25.

[26] See also Gaus and Lomasky (n 18) 489.

[27] A Hohfeldian liberty or 'privilege' describes conduct that one may engage in because such conduct does not breach duties owed to others. Hohfeld (n 23) 32–33.

[28] E Ostrom, *Governing the Commons: The Evolution of Institutions for Collective Action* (Cambridge, Cambridge University Press, 1990) 91–92.

[29] Although Rose has argued that resources, such as roads and waterways, can be successfully held in common by the 'unorganized public' because problems of over-consumption can be managed by the existence of strong customs. She also argues that, in some cases, resources might be more efficiently managed by common rather than private property because the former is less costly to administer. See C Rose, 'The Comedy of the Commons: Custom, Commerce, and Inherently Public Property' (1986) 53 *University of Chicago Law Review* 711, 743–47. Rose's emphasis on a shared 'custom of civic care' makes one wonder whether her argument applies to large and culturally heterogeneous populations whose members do not necessarily share such norms, in which case Ostrom was right after all.

[30] Thomas Hobbes, *Leviathan* (first published 1651, London, Penguin Books, 1968) 185.

[31] Hohfeld (n 23) 33.

[32] As Penner has remarked, '[t]he liberty-no-right correlation is a description of the absence of any legal norm, not the institution of one'. JE Penner, 'Hohfeldian Use-Rights in Property' in JW Harris (ed), *Property Problems: From Genes to Pension Funds* (London, Kluwer Law International, 1997) 169.

If property rights could be created by consent then, contrary to the claim above, there would not be much of a dilemma. The dilemma arises because the consent model collides with three, seemingly insuperable, objections. First, and perhaps most obviously, bargaining presupposes that people have something to bargain with. The problem is that, under conditions of anarchy, a starting position is precisely what people do not have. One might note, as does Buchanan,[33] that an equilibrium, or 'natural distribution', will naturally emerge when the marginal benefits derived from each additional unit of some resource equals the marginal costs incurred in acquiring and defending it from predation. However, whilst such an equilibrium provides a default position from which parties can bargain, because it is ultimately based on violence, or the threat of violence, it does not overcome the objection from unilateralism.[34]

Even if Buchanan's 'natural distribution' provides an initial position from which the parties can bargain, two further problems remain. In a community of more than a handful of members, the path to agreement, which would require the consent of every community member, would be blocked by enormous transaction costs and the strategic behaviour of those holding out for a disproportionately large share of the gains from trade. Indeed, Epstein has gone so far as to argue that any such society would likely replace the philosophical problem of unilateralism with the very real problem of starvation.[35] Finally, in the unlikely event that these problems could be overcome, the final nail in the coffin of the consent model is that, because consent can only bind those who give it, any initial distribution created by consent could not bind the unborn, and would thus require renegotiation every time a new member of the political community attained the age at which she could hold rights and bear duties.[36]

C. Unilateralism by Necessity

If the foregoing is correct, the law appears to be left in the following, invidious, position. It can either choose a morally pristine solution that, due to insuperable transaction costs, turns out to be no solution at all or, assuming unilateralism is a problem worth worrying about, it can create a viable system of property rights that, being based on a unilateral act, creates duties that no one has any moral obligation to obey.

[33] JM Buchanan, *The Limits of Liberty: Between Anarchy and Leviathan* (Chicago, University of Chicago Press, 1975) 24–25.

[34] As Umbeck argues, force is the only allocative mechanism that does not, in the final analysis, depend on any form of consent. See J Umbeck, 'Might Makes Rights: A Theory of the Formation and Initial Distribution of Property Rights' (1981) 19 *Economic Inquiry* 38, 39–40.

[35] RA Epstein, 'Holdouts, Externalities, and the Single Owner: One More Salute to Ronald Coase' (1993) 36 *Journal of Law & Economics* 553, 562.

[36] See generally D Hume, 'Of the Original Contract' in *Essays Moral, Political and Literary* (London, Liberty Fund Ed, 1777) 471.

When the options are framed in these terms, it is obvious that, in all but the smallest and most hermetically sealed communities, there is only one choice. Epstein is thus surely correct to conclude that,

> [i]t may be an unresolved intellectual mystery of how a mere assertion of right can, if often repeated and acknowledged, be sufficient to generate the right in question. As an institutional matter, however, it is difficult in the extreme to conceive of any other system.[37]

Proceeding on the assumption that no system of consent is viable, the next question is, which unilateral mechanism should perform the allocative function of attaching 'names to things'? The answer to this question depends on where you start. As a matter of practical legal theory, and not the *tabula rasa* of moral philosophy, it seems legitimate to start with the system that we have. Within our legal system, the basic mechanism for creating original rights to objects of property is take possession of them. Possession is, to borrow Pollock's famous phrase, 'a root of title'.[38]

Adopting this justificatory approach, Epstein gives the following, minimalist, defence of the possession rule:

> [w]ithin this viewpoint it is possible to show the unique place of first possession. It enjoyed in all past times the status of a legal rule, not only for the stock examples of wild animals and seashells, but also for unoccupied land. In essence the first possession rule has been the organizing principle of most social institutions, and the heavy burden of persuasion lies upon those who wish to displace it.[39]

Taking the present as the appropriate baseline for analysis, Epstein's defence of the possession rule is, essentially, 'if it ain't broke don't fix it' or, given the fearsome institutional constraints of doing anything else, 'the best rule you can get is the rule that you have'. Building on insights from game theory and the spontaneous order tradition, the remainder of this chapter investigates whether it is possible to go beyond Epstein's minimal defence.

III. Possession and the Spontaneous Order Tradition

A. Coordination and Convention

Although largely disregarded in his own lifetime,[40] Hume's *A Treatise of Human Nature* anticipated, with remarkable accuracy, developments in modern biology

[37] Epstein (n 10) 1242.

[38] F Pollock and R S Wright, *An Essay on Possession in the Common Law* (Oxford, Clarendon Press, 1888) 22. Though possession is not the only event that creates original property rights, there are, as McFarlane also notes, only two others; mixing and natural increase. See B McFarlane, *The Structure of Property Law* (Oxford, Hart Publishing, 2008) 163.

[39] Epstein (n 10) 1241.

[40] See, eg: DC Rasmussen, *The Infidel and the Professor: David Hume, Adam Smith, and the Friendship That Shaped Modern Thought* (Princeton, Princeton University Press, 2017) 201–02.

and evolutionary game theory.[41] In particular, Hume's genius was to appreciate that many basic property rules are not the product of conscious design but are conventions that emerge spontaneously and unconsciously as the aggregate product of the innumerable interactions of self-interested actors. In the most famous passage in his discussion of property, Hume wrote that:

> I observe that it will be for my interest to leave another in the possession of his goods, *provided* he will act in the same manner with regard to me. He is sensible of a like interest in the regulation of his conduct. When this common sense of interest is mutually express'd, and is known to both, it produces a suitable resolution of behaviour. And this may properly enough be called a convention or agreement betwixt us, tho' without the interposition of a promise, since the actions of each have reference to those of the other, and are perform'd upon the supposition that something is to be performed on the other part. Two men who pull the oars of a boat do it by an agreement or convention, tho' they have never given promises to each other. Nor is the rule concerning the stability of possession the less deriv'd from human conventions, that it arises gradually, and acquires a force by a slow progression and by our repeated experiences of the inconveniences of transgressing it.[42]

Conventions solve problems of interdependent decision-making, known as 'coordination problems', in which, as Ullmann-Margalit explains, 'the best choice for each depends upon what he expects the others to do, knowing that each of the others is trying to guess what he is likely to do'.[43] The archetypal, if threadbare, example of a coordination problem is that of deciding on which side of the road to drive. Unlike in other forms of social interaction, the 'problem' in any given coordination problem is not the need to reconcile inconsistent preferences. To the contrary, in 'pure' coordination problems such as the 'driving game', any given player's only preference is that his choice be held in common with everyone else. The challenge posed by coordination problems is instead that, where there are multiple potential solutions, or 'equilibria', but no particular reason to choose any one of them, it is, in the absence of prior agreement, very difficult to know which solution others will choose.

Given that there is, for instance, no uniquely rational reason for supposing that people will drive on the left rather than the right, or vice versa, one's choice about whether to steer to the right or the left in the presence of oncoming traffic can only depend on one's beliefs about others people's beliefs. My decision to keep to the left-hand side of the road is ultimately based on my belief that other people believe that I believe, that other people believe that I believe … that people in Australia drive on the left hand side of the road. In other words, what is required in order to solve a coordination problem is a notorious belief that people in fact drive on the

[41] See, eg: P Vanderschraaf, 'The Informal Game Theory in Hume's Account of Convention' (1998) 14 *Economics and Philosophy* 215.

[42] D Hume, *A Treatise of Human Nature* (first published 1739, DF Norton and MJ Norton eds, Oxford, Oxford University Press, 2000) 315 [3.2.2.10].

[43] E Ullmann-Margalit, *The Emergence of Norms* (Oxford, Clarendon Press, 1977) 78.

left.[44] The existence of such a belief, upon which people condition their behaviour, is known as a convention. A convention solves a coordination problem because, as Postema explains, it '"anchors" free-floating, mutually conditional preferences or expectations to a single equilibrium'.[45]

The perfect coincidence of interests between people playing the 'driving game' neatly illustrates why conventions can emerge spontaneously and why, once they have emerged, they are self-enforcing in the absence of a central authority with coercive powers. When faced with a 'pure' coordination problem, conformity is its own reward. However, most problems of social interaction are not like this because they involve some degree of both cooperation and conflict.[46] It does not require much imagination to realise that a society that solves the 'driving game' will also need a solution to the problem caused by the simultaneous arrival of two vehicles at an intersection. Unlike players in the driving game, players in the 'intersection game' are not indifferent to the solution chosen for the obvious reason that each would prefer that the other driver yield to them. However, whilst they have diverging interests, it remains true that, if we proceed on the uncontroversial assumption that each party regards a collision as the worst outcome, the intersection problem is still one that requires the participants to coordinate their decisions. No matter the degree of divergence between the interests of the participants, a problem of social interaction will be a 'coordination problem' if the attempt by each party to pursue his most favoured outcome, irrespective of the choice of the other party, results in the worst outcome for both.

B. Property as a Coordination Problem

Although disputes over scarce resources are characterised by a stronger divergence of interests than are interactions between drivers at an intersection, they are not zero-sum interactions in which neither party has any incentive to cooperate because the loser's loss is precisely equal to the winner's gain. Nor is the basic structure of such interactions captured by the pernicious logic of the more famous 'Prisoners' Dilemma', in which a decision to cooperate, though mutually beneficial, is never in either party's individual best interest.[47] Disputes over scarce resources are coordination problems

[44] In game theory, such a belief is described as 'common knowledge'. See generally M Suk-Young Chwe, *Rational Ritual: Culture, Coordination, and Common Knowledge* (Princeton, Princeton University Press, 2013) 13–16.

[45] GJ Postema, *Legal Philosophy in the Twentieth Century: The Common Law World* (London, Springer, 2011) 490.

[46] These sorts of interactions are, following Schelling, known as games of 'mixed-motive'. TC Schelling, *The Strategy of Conflict* (Cambridge, MA, Harvard University Press, 1960) 89.

[47] The Prisoners' Dilemma is a two person, non-zero-sum game that famously highlights an *apparent* paradox of human rationality. Though mutual 'cooperation' represents a better outcome than mutual 'defection', the payoff structure of the game is such that each player will nevertheless choose to defect. In game-theoretic terms, the choice to defect is 'strictly dominant'. The qualification 'apparent' is used advisedly. At least in its 'one-shot' form, the unfortunate truth is that it *is* irrational to cooperate in an interaction that shares the payoff structure of the Prisoners' Dilemma.

because the worst outcome, as viewed by the participants, is not merely that the vanquished must concede the resource to the victor. Rather, it is that, if the dispute degenerates into violence, the disputants may either destroy the resource or suffer an injury, the costs of which exceed the value of the disputed resource.[48]

If we assume some level of abundance,[49] and rough parity in fighting ability,[50] then each has an incentive to develop norms that restrain the otherwise anarchic competition over scarce things. This insight explains why animals resolve many resource disputes by an appeal to ownership rather than force.[51] It also explains why Hume, writing in 1738, was correct to theorise that the basic building blocks of property emerge spontaneously from the bottom-up, and are not imposed from the top-down by the state or some other central authority. As Sugden has observed:

> [p]erhaps the most important lesson to be learned from the study of conventions is that a society can be ordered without anyone ordering it. In many significant cases, the coordination of individuals' actions can be brought about by self-reinforcing expectations, which evolve spontaneously out of the repeated interaction of self-interested individuals.[52]

That a population will unconsciously create solutions to the most basic problems caused by the imbalance between 'wants and things' tells us little, however, about what those solutions are likely to be. In particular, it tells us nothing about whether those solutions, when assessed against some exogenous standard, such as fairness, will be desirable.

IV. Conventions and the Simplicity Imperative

A. Property Rights and Game Theory

In evolutionary biology, disputes over scarce resources are often modelled on the so-called 'Hawk-Dove' or 'Chicken' game,[53] the latter being a reference to

[48] A fatal injury, being the most obvious example.

[49] This assumption is necessary because, as resources reach exhaustion point, the consequence of deferring to one's opponent will be certain death by starvation. J Maynard Smith, *Evolution and the Theory of Games* (Cambridge, Cambridge University Press, 1982) 96.

[50] For the obvious reason that, if A were in no position to injure B, there would, so far as B was concerned, no need to coordinate. The coordination analysis thus follows the Hobbesian assumption that, '[n]ature hath made men so equall, in the faculties of body, and mind; as that though there bee found one man sometimes manifestly stronger in body, or of quicker mind then [sic] another; yet when all is reckoned together, the difference between man, and man, is not so considerable, as that one man can thereupon claim to himselfe any benefit, to which another may not pretend, as well as he': Hobbes, *Leviathan* (n 30) 183.

[51] Maynard Smith (n 49) 98.

[52] R Sugden, 'Conventions' in Peter Newman (ed), *The New Palgrave Dictionary of Economics and the Law*, vol I (New York, Macmillan Reference, 1998) 460.

[53] The classic work here is Maynard Smith (n 49). For a useful overview see also JE Krier, 'Evolutionary Theory and the Origin of Property Rights' (2009) 95 *Cornell Law Review* 139.

the boneheaded game of nerve, popularised in movies such as *Rebel Without a Cause*,[54] in which adolescent males simulate a head-on car accident and demonstrate their *bravura* to the gawping bystanders by being the last to take evasive action or 'chicken out'. To use the standard nomenclature, 'Hawk' describes a belligerent strategy. Someone who adopts this strategy will invariably fight for mastery of a disputed resource. 'Dove', on the other hand, is a submissive strategy. Someone who adopts this strategy may feign aggression but will defer to his opponent at the first sign of conflict. Assuming more-or-less equal fighting ability, the payoffs for these various outcomes are represented by in Figure 1, below.

Figure 1

		Player A	
		Dove	**Hawk**
Player B	**Dove**	*1*,1	*0*,2
	Hawk	*2*,0	*-2*, -2

As is represented by the payoffs in Figure 1,[55] whilst everyone would prefer to play Hawk in a world of Doves, no one will play Hawk if he believes that his competitor will play Hawk too. So, if it is clear in advance that Player B will play Hawk, then, even though it is not Player A's most preferred outcome, it is in Player A's interest to play Dove and, in effect, treat Player B as the de facto owner of the resource.

Given each player's desire to avoid the worse possible 'miscoordination event' of a Hawk-Hawk confrontation, it is obviously important to know whether one's opponent will play Hawk or Dove in any given encounter. The problem is that, as with the 'Driving Game', mere knowledge of each participant's payoffs provides no clue as to which strategy one's opponent will adopt. In 'symmetric contests',[56] contests in which neither player has any information that is exogenous to the structure of the game, the best that each can do is to adopt a randomised strategy. On the payoffs in Figure 1, a stable equilibrium will emerge when each plays Hawk with the probability 1/3 and Dove with probability 2/3.[57]

[54] I am informed by Dr Tiverios that the 'tractor scene' in the movie *Footloose* is, culturally speaking, an equally seminal example. Whether or not this is a notorious fact, I am happy to accept the point.

[55] There is nothing special about the value of the payoffs selected in Figure 1. In selecting payoffs, all that matters is that their ordinal ranking reflects the subjective preference ranking of the nominal players. The cardinal value of the payoffs becomes important when, as is discussed immediately below, the players begin to randomize their strategies, because it determines the frequency with which they will choose each strategy.

[56] Maynard Smith (n 49) 22.

[57] In decision-theory terms, the players have only succeeded in replacing 'uncertainty' with 'risk'.

Although stable, an equilibrium that consists of randomised strategies could hardly be described as a nascent convention of property. Nor is this arrangement particularly desirable. On the payoffs in Figure 1, one in nine encounters will result in the least preferred Hawk-Hawk confrontation. This question is, how do we get from this sort of anarchy to a settled system of property rights? The answer lies in the concept of an 'asymmetry'.

B. Asymmetry Selection

In game theory, anything that differentiates the players in any pairwise contest is known as an 'asymmetry'. To illustrate with the 'intersection game', the relative size of two cars, their contrasting direction of travel, that one has arrived from a large road and the other a small road, and so on, are all 'asymmetries' in this sense.

A remarkable insight of evolutionary game theory is that almost any asymmetry, no matter how apparently unrelated to the structure of the game, can provide the foundation for a convention.[58] For instance, Hargreaves Heap and Varoufakis have demonstrated that, in an iterated Hawk-Dove game, randomly labelling members of a population either 'red' or 'blue' will create a convention the turns on the asymmetry of colour.[59] Because, in their experiment, the colours were randomly assigned, there was no reason to believe that the 'reds' were, for instance, more ferocious than the 'blues'. Nevertheless, once the reds acquired their earned or unearned reputation for belligerence, the outcome 'reds take the prize' became a self-fulfilling prophecy.

One can appreciate that, once such a 'bandwagon' gets rolling, a convention can be stable even though it is based on an apparently arbitrary distinction between the players. Once the convention 'reds play Hawk' becomes common knowledge, it will not pay for any blue player to unilaterally deviate from it and play Hawk. The more mysterious question is why such an obviously arbitrary asymmetry should provide the basis for a nascent convention in the first place. Hargreaves Heap and Varoufakis explain that:

> [i]n interactions (like Hawk-Dove) in which there is rational indeterminacy in the conventional game theoretic sense, people try to condition their behaviour on any information that comes to hand, even meaningless information … It is a simple psychological response to uncertainty. Indeed there is much evidence to support the idea that people look for 'extraneous' reasons to 'explain' what are in fact purely random types of behaviour. Of course, once they do so, an initial, random difference in the behaviour of the 'reds' and the 'blues' gets a bandwagon rolling, leading to a stable discrimination

[58] Biologists describe these sorts of asymmetries as 'uncorrelated' because there is no reason why the distinguishing trait in question should correlate to greater success in the game. See JM Smith and GA Parker, 'The Logic of Asymmetric Contests' (1976) 24 *Animal Behaviour* 159, 163–64.

[59] S Hargreaves Heap and Y Varoufakis, *Game Theory: A Critical Text*, 2nd edn (Abingdon, Routledge, 2004) 232–34.

> that succeeds in minimising costly conflict despite being non-rational ... So ex post, it will seem to make sense as each player does take the best action given that chosen by the other, even though there is no reason ex ante for this selection of actions.[60]

Psychologists and behavioural economists delight in demonstrating our statistical illiteracy and tendency to find patterns in distributions that are nothing more than manifestations of randomness.[61] It is almost certainly not true that, in Hargreaves Heap's and Varoufakis's experiment, players from one colour group were uniformly more bellicose or fearsome than players from the other colour group. However, in the circumstances, the inductive validity of their collective inference is of no importance. When faced with a coordination problem, what matters is that people notice, or fancy that they notice, the *same* pattern, even though they are almost certainly witnessing the random perturbations of chaos.[62]

C. The 'Simplicity Imperative'

The benefits of coordination explain why a convention can be perfectly stable even though it is based on a distinguishing feature that is arbitrary in the sense that, in the absence of that particular convention, it would not enhance any player's chances of prevailing in a dispute. Although *any* asymmetry present in any pairwise contest would seem to allow for coordination, evolutionary forces shape conventions in such a way that there are conventions that we would *not* expect to emerge spontaneously.

This is because asymmetries function as, in effect, labelling devices that tell each player how he or she ought to behave in a given situation. As a consequence, one essential feature of any convention is that the asymmetry on which it turns must be one that can be reliably applied by the players whose actions require coordination. A convention that left any player in any doubt as to whether she is to play Hawk or Dove would cause costly miscoordination events and, for this reason, would be superseded by one that was simpler to apply and, consequently, yielded a higher average payoff.

Sugden illustrates this point with the example of a hypothetical convention that turns on the asymmetry of beauty, such that the more beautiful of the two contestants plays Hawk and takes the prize.[63] Because beauty is famously 'in

[60] ibid 233–34.

[61] A notable example being the famous 'gambler's fallacy'. See A Tversky and D Kahneman, 'Judgment under Uncertainty: Heuristics and Biases' (1974) 185 *Science* 1124, 1125. See generally D Kahneman, *Thinking, Fast and Slow* (London, Penguin, 2011).

[62] In Hargreaves Heap's and Varoufakis's experiment, it is perhaps not entirely surprising that a convention arose based on colour labelling. This is because, whilst the colour asymmetry was plainly arbitrary, the experimenters' act of labelling the players either 'red' or 'blue' most likely made it focal.

[63] R Sugden, *The Economics of Rights, Co-Operation, and Welfare* (Oxford, B Blackwell, 1986) 100–01.

the eye of the beholder', no convention could turn on a subjective assessment of beauty. Importantly, however, this is not how the relevant population of players would approach the problem. Recall that, when confronted with a coordination problem, each player asks himself, 'what do I think the other party thinks that I think?'. Neither player is asking what sort of features he *personally* finds attractive. Rather, each player is attempting to guess what sorts of features *the other* player is likely to find attractive, knowing that everyone else is asking himself the same question. Sugden argues that what we would expect to see evolve is a convention for applying the convention, such that 'more beautiful' simply becomes, for instance, the 'taller' of the two competitors. A convention based on height would rapidly supersede the original because, though height is obviously a crude approximation of beauty, it is simple to apply and thus avoids inadvertent and unwelcome miscoordination events.[64]

Sugden's insight is important for two reasons. First, it demonstrates the 'competitive advantage' of the possession rule. Because the underlying convention turns on an observable physical connection between a person and a thing, it generates, at least in most cases, little interpretive confusion.[65] Second, it demonstrates why no convention that answers elementary questions of 'mine and thine' could turn on a criterion of 'need', 'desert' or 'fairness'.[66] Whilst there will be pairwise contests in which, due to strongly held beliefs in a particular population, a consensus will exist as to which of the two contestants has the best claim,[67] there are simply too many borderline cases for such a convention to survive. As a consequence, the population of players would evolve a convention for applying the convention. As with Sugden's beauty example, the concept of 'desert' or 'need' would be replaced by a crude proxy that bears little resemblance to the original asymmetry but has the virtue that it can be reliably applied.

[64] It should be noted that Sugden's example is a mere thought experiment. Unless imposed by state fiat, no such convention could ever 'get going' in the first place.

[65] Sugden (n 63) 101. For further discussion see MJR Crawford, *An Expressive Theory of Possession* (Oxford, Hart Publishing, 2020) ch 4.

[66] This argument also forecloses on the possibility of a 'Lockean' convention that turned on the application of 'useful' labour, however morally attractive such a convention may be. On the general acceptance of 'Lockean-type' arguments, see E Hoffman and ML Spitzer, 'Entitlements, Rights, and Fairness: An Experimental Examination of Subjects' Concepts of Distributive Justice' (1985) 14 *Journal of Legal Studies* 259.

[67] I am not making a normative claim about which of two players actually has the better distributive claim. I am simply observing that, in certain circumstances, a consensus on such questions will exist. So, for example, there might be a consensus that the elderly woman ought to have a seat on the train in preference to the young man. Presumably, at the margins, these sorts of comparisons would fall afoul of the problem of interpersonal comparisons of utility. For further discussion of this point see Sugden (n 63) 100.

V. Morally Repugnant Conventions

A. Efficiency and Distributive Concerns

Conventions, including conventions of property, arise and thrive at the expense of other alternatives, not because they are uniquely fair or just, but because they turn on an asymmetry that is salient, simple to apply and, as a consequence, yields a superior average payoff to the population of players confronted with a coordination problem. As with all evolutionary phenomena, conventions are strictly amoral. That conventions are *amoral* does not, of course, entail the conclusion that they are therefore *immoral*.[68] Although there is no reason to believe that a convention of property will be fair or morally appealing, it may well be that, through sheer luck, it is. The relevant question is whether this is true of the possession convention.

Determining whether the possession convention is a tolerably fair way of allocating 'names to things' raises an anterior question. That is, why should we care whether the mechanism is fair, so long it is effective? One might plausibly argue that distributive patterns are, in the final analysis, a matter of personal preference and, consequently, that all that any system should concern itself with is defining rights at minimum cost and ensuring that those rights can be traded from lower to higher-valuing users.[69] Given such an imperative then, as Coase famously demonstrated,[70] any initial allocation will do so long as transaction costs are sufficiently low. Precisely this argument has been advanced by Epstein, who has written that:

> [i]n this zero transactions cost world, it is difficult to form any strong intuitions of what the law should or should not do, how rights should or should not be defined, precisely because nothing of consequence appears to attach to the choices that are made … Where there are no social effects (save perhaps for some purely distributional consequences), our instincts about the merits of legal rules ebb in a sea of indifference.[71]

Because, as Coase emphasised,[72] we do not live in a frictionless world so that decisions about initial allocation can, on occasion, become decisions about final allocation, the efficiency goal demands that the law develop rules that replicate the outcome that would have been reached in the absence of transaction costs.[73]

[68] It might also be noted that all conventions have a *de minimis* moral value in so far as they enable social coordination.

[69] This has been the standard approach of many economists, particularly those of a positivist bent. See, eg: N Kaldor, 'Welfare Propositions of Economics and Interpersonal Comparisons of Utility' (1939) 49 *The Economic Journal* 549, 551–52.

[70] Coase (n 1) 10.

[71] Epstein (n 35) 555–56.

[72] Coase (n 1) 15–16, 19.

[73] Epstein (n 35) 556.

The law can, for instance, replicate the frictionless universe by imposing a duty, or 'no-right', on the party who can solve the particular problem at least cost.

Though Epstein is perhaps unduly dismissive of the distributive consequences of decisions about initial allocations,[74] it is important to appreciate any legal solutions to problem of scarcity will have distributive effects.[75] In a Coasean world of zero transaction costs, any rule will distribute income from the person with the duty, or no-right, to the person with the right, or liberty, by the amount of the least-cost solution to the problem.[76] Take Calabresi and Melamed's example of a society in which the social problem created by noise is resolved in favour of those who prefer loud music at the expense of those who prefer silence.[77] Even if that society begins in a position of perfect equality, those who prefer music will, *ceteris paribus*, become wealthier than those who prefer silence because the latter will have to pay the former to, for instance, listen to their music through headphones. Whilst such a society may decide to redistribute some of the music-lovers' gains to the silence-lovers, some initial distributive effect is inevitable, whatever rule is chosen.

What is more, attempting to fashion an allocative rule that is sensitive to the immediate distributive consequences of its own application is doomed to failure. This is demonstrated, perhaps most famously, by Locke's infamous 'proviso'. Locke's aim in the *Second Treatise* was 'to show how men might come to have a property in several parts of that which God gave to mankind in common, and that without any express compact of all the commoners'[78] by appealing to an axiom of self-ownership.[79]

According to Locke, because one's labour is 'the unquestionable property of the labourer, no man but he can have a right to what that is once joined to, *at least where there is enough, and as good left in common for others*'.[80] For present purposes, what is significant about the most famous apology for private property in the liberal tradition is not its author's full-throated *moral* justification for the unilateral acquisition of property rights, but the fact that, in the final analysis, he could not quite stomach its immediate distributive consequences.

[74] As Waldron rightly observes, the lack of interest in the distributive consequences of particular rules is, to the non-economist, a striking omission in the work of 'Law and Economics' scholars: Waldron (n 6) 12.

[75] This is not to say that all legal rules have distributive effects. For instance, the costs of imposing strict liability on the producer of some product may simply be passed on to the purchasers in the form of higher prices. See AM Polinsky, *An Introduction to Law and Economics* (London, Wolters Kluwer Law & Business, 2011) 156–57.

[76] See generally ibid 14.

[77] G Calabresi and AD Melamed, 'Property Rules, Liability Rules, and Inalienability: One View of the Cathedral' (1972) 85 *Harvard Law Review* 1089, 1098–99.

[78] Locke (n 8) 111 §25.

[79] In particular, Locke aimed to demonstrated that it was possible to move from state of nature communism to a settled system of private property without relying on agreement or, in contrast to Sir Robert Filmer, the notion that the earth was the patrimony of Adam who gifted it by bequest. See T Mautner, 'Locke on Original Appropriation' (1982) 19 *American Philosophical Quarterly* 259, 259–60.

[80] Locke (n 8) 111–2 §27. Emphasis added.

Locke's 'proviso', indicated in italics, has spawned a veritable cottage industry in political philosophy.[81] Some have defended it as a prerequisite for any just system of property rights.[82] Others have argued that the proviso is irrelevant because the transition from anarchy to civil society makes everyone better off.[83] Yet others have turned the proviso on its head, making the case that privatisation is a moral necessity because, if resources are not reduced to private ownership, the inevitable over-exploitation of any common-pool resource will ensure that there is not 'enough and as good' left for *anybody*.[84]

Though it might be relevant to *redistribution*, the fundamental reason why Locke's proviso cannot limit *appropriation* is that acts of appropriation that satisfy the proviso could only exist in a fairy-tale world of superabundance. Take the following example. If A exhausts the supply of firewood in a given copse then B will have to walk to the next copse to collect more. Whilst this might be considered a mere irritation, it is also a cost, measured in time and energy expenditure, that B would not have incurred but for A's act of appropriation. Although A's act of appropriation did not exhaust the supplies of firewood, it nevertheless made B worse off. So long as there is *some* demand for, but a finite supply of, a given resource and its substitutes, any act of appropriation will impose a cost on others.[85]

As a resource becomes scarcer, there will come a point at which it will become rational for B, rather than walking many miles for firewood, to risk injury and attempt to take A's wood by force. So long as resources are so plenteous that acquisition by A does not make B any worse off, we simply do not need property rights.[86] It is only once resources become scarce that, as Rose notes, 'a property regime begins to matter, as a way of deciding who has what'.[87] The irony of Locke's proviso is that, by conditioning the legitimacy of a unilaterally acquired property

[81] See generally R Nozick, *Anarchy, State, and Utopia* (New York, Basic Books, 2013) 175–82; Waldron (n 12) 209–18.

[82] Nozick, for example, argued that any sound theory of justice in acquisition requires some version of Locke's proviso. Nozick (n 81) 178. See also Singer (n 7) 764, 775.

[83] Rose argues that, so long as we own our labour, a system of private property actually makes everyone better off because it increases the value of everyone's labour. See C Rose, 'Enough, and As Good of What' (1986) 81 *Northwestern University Law Review* 417, 430, 432–33. Thus, on Rose's account, systems of private property not only meet the Pareto criterion, they also satisfy Rawls's difference principle. For a different argument that draws on specialisation and the division of labour, see JE Penner, 'Rights, Distributed and Undistributed: On the Distributive Justice Implications of Lockean Property Rights, Especially in Land' in JE Penner and M Otsuka (eds), *Property Theory: Legal and Political Perspectives*, 1st edn (Cambridge, Cambridge University Press, 2018) 155.

[84] See D Schmidtz, 'When Is Original Appropriate Required?' (1990) 73 *The Monist* 504, 508. Schmidtz makes the point that, '[i]t is not true that appropriation of land inevitably decreases the amount of land available to others. It only inevitably decreases what is available for original appropriation by others, which is not the same thing at all': at 512.

[85] As Rose notes, the 'congestion' point does not arise when the last piece of firewood has been burned. Rose (n 83) 426–27.

[86] As Merrill notes, '[p]roperty does not attach to things that are so plenteous [that] they are not scarce, or to things no one wants': TW Merrill, 'Property and the Right to Exclude II' (2014) 3 *Brigham-Kanner Property Rights Conference Journal* 1, 4.

[87] Rose (n 83) 426.

right on its distributive consequences, it undermines the legitimacy of the right precisely when it is needed most. To borrow from Wenar, '[a]s for "enough and as good" provisos, they will prevent potentially onerous duties being generated only at the price of prohibiting the acquisition of any scarce good'.[88]

B. When Efficiency Meets Morality

Epstein is right to dismiss distributive concerns in so far as, first, any rule will have distributive effects and, second, 'privatising' a resource that was previously held in common cannot help but to make others worse off.[89] Indeed, property rights are needed precisely *because* unilateral appropriation by A makes B, C, D and E … worse off. However, it does not follow that we should therefore be completely indifferent about the mechanism by which initial entitlements are created, even if that mechanism provides the basis for welfare-increasing trades that ultimately result in an efficient allocation of resources.[90]

The way in which moral commitments ultimately constrain welfarist and other utilitarian analyses of legal duties is best illustrated by the limits of Coase's reciprocal and morally inert conception of causation.[91] A central plank of Coase's argument was that our intuitive notions of causation distract us from the real issue in any social conflict. Take Coase's oft-repeated example of a rancher's cows trampling a farmer's crop.[92] Because cows, though sedentary beasts, are more dynamic than crops, we intuitively regard the cows as the cause of the trampled crops. However, from a welfarist perspective, causation is purely reciprocal.[93] Each of the cows and the crops are necessary, but not independently sufficient, causes of the damage. The relevant question is not, 'who *caused* damage to what?' but, 'what allocation of rights, given transaction costs, will maximise social welfare?'.

Whilst, from a moral perspective, we might be indifferent as to whether a rancher has a 'liberty' to trample, or a 'duty not to', there are many situations in which, to paraphrase Epstein, our instincts about the merits of legal rules *do not* ebb in a sea of indifference. Though, in a frictionless world, starting with either a 'liberty' to punch or a 'duty not to' will lead to an efficient number of 'fist to nose interactions', our beliefs about the inviolability of our bodies prevents us from

[88] Wenar (n 15) 810.

[89] As others have noted, assuming some scarcity, it is impossible to satisfy the proviso. Schmidtz (n 84) 504–05. See also Epstein (n 35) 561–62.

[90] By which I mean that rights to those resources end up in the hands of those who value them most.

[91] Coase (n 1) 13.

[92] ibid 2.

[93] Demsetz has remarked that, '[t]he use of words such as "blame", "responsible" and "fault" must be treated with care by the economist because they have no useful meanings in an economic analysis of these problems other than as synonyms for the party who could have most easily avoided the costly interaction.' H Demsetz, 'When Does the Rule of Liability Matter?' (1972) 1 *Journal of Legal Studies* 13, 28.

accepting the legitimacy of a starting point in which B must pay A *not* to exercise his Hohfeldian liberty to break his nose.[94]

Similar, non-distributive, considerations can be applied to the mechanism that determines who acquires rights to scarce resources and who is subjected to correlative duties. Accepting that any such rule will have distribute effects, we may still object to the differentiating feature, or 'asymmetry', that a convention uses in order to label people as winners or losers in a property dispute.

To reiterate the point made above, conventions, like all evolutionary phenomena, are *amoral*. Whether a convention flourishes or perishes does not depend on whether it is morally attractive, but whether, when compared to alternative mechanisms, it returns a higher average payoff to those confronted with a coordination problem. As a consequence, it is perfectly possible that a convention will pick up on a salient, but morally unattractive, asymmetry. Hargreaves Heap and Varoufakis explain that:

> evolutionary theory predicts that the slightest asymmetries will engender a convention even though it may not suit everyone, or indeed even if it short-changes the majority. It may be discriminatory, inequitable, non-rational, indeed thoroughly disagreeable, yet some such convention is likely to arise when antagonistic social interaction (like *Hawk-Dove*) is repeated.[95]

To illustrate this point, McAdams gives the example of a property convention that turns on the asymmetry of sex, according to which, in a dispute between a man and a woman, the man is always assigned the role of Hawk and thus accorded the status of owner.[96] McAdams explains that:

> [w]hether you are a male or a female, if all other players play the strategy specified for their sex, your best response is to play the strategy specified for your sex. As with all conventions, once it arises, it will not pay for an individual to deviate. If a woman tries to play Hawk against men, who expect women to play Dove, she will simply endure the worst outcome (as will the men with whom she interacts). The result is a convention in which all property winds up in the hands of men. The same point can be made by using race roles instead of or in addition to sex roles, or any other immediately observable distinguishing traits.[97]

When compared to anarchy, such a convention is welfare-increasing. Moreover, its distributive effects could, presumably, be corrected via transfers to women.[98] Nevertheless, we would object to such a convention for the same reason that we

[94] See also TW Merrill and HE Smith, 'The Morality of Property' (2007) 48 *William and Mary Law Review* 1849, 1861.

[95] Hargreaves Heap and Varoufakis (n 59) 247.

[96] RH McAdams, 'Beyond the Prisoners' Dilemma: Coordination, Game Theory, and Law' (2008) 82 *Southern California Law Review* 209, 247.

[97] ibid.

[98] Note that redistribution need not occur formally through transfers such as welfare payments. It could equally occur informally through norms of, for instance, sharing within the family.

would object to an initial position in which people have to pay others not to punch them in the nose.

Lest McAdam's example be dismissed as a strawman, it should be emphasised that, as Hargreaves Heap's and Varoufakis's colour experiment demonstrates, conventions that track easily verifiable physical characteristics *are* the very sorts of conventions that are likely to emerge spontaneously. Though plainly morally arbitrary and, in many cases, of no obvious predictive value in any given dispute, evolutionary processes latch onto these sorts of asymmetries because, by minimising the interpretive confusions that cause costly miscoordination events, they deliver a higher payoff in the long run. What is more, as McAdams emphasises in the passage above, the fact that the convention is obviously morally objectionable, and seen to be so, does not make it any less stable a solution to a coordination problem. Once a convention becomes established, it becomes resistant to individual acts of rebellion because everyone, including those whom it selects to play Dove, does better by conformity than contravention.[99]

VI. (Tolerably) Fair Conventions

A. Constraints on Conventions

What, then, makes for a fair convention? Before answering this question, it important to briefly note two unavoidable constraints on any convention that solves a highly impure coordination problem. First, as noted above, the 'simplicity imperative' dictates that no convention can turn on a genuine asymmetry of 'need' or 'desert'. This is not to deny that, in particular interactions, the existence of a sufficiently strong social consensus about the requirements of fairness may enable people to coordinate their actions. Rather, it is to say that, given the huge number of borderline cases, no such convention could ever survive. As with Sugden's beauty example, such a convention would ultimately be 'need' or 'desert-based' in name only.[100] So, whilst basing a system of property rights on the outcome of a race may be morally unattractive, the simplicity imperative places a hard limit on the creation of a more morally sophisticated alternative.[101]

[99] Such a convention could only be changed by concerted, collective action. Hargreaves Heap and Varoufakis (n 59) 246.

[100] The reality is, of course, that no such convention could have emerged spontaneously in the first place.

[101] As the institution of queueing demonstrates, the sheer ubiquity of the 'first in, best dressed' principle demonstrates the difficulty of operationalising a more morally attractive system for distributing resources or benefits. This does not, of course, prohibit private acts of virtue and charity. Someone who has acquired a right through an arbitrary mechanism, such as queuing, can always forego it in favour of someone whom he regards as more deserving.

The second constraint concerns the inevitability of unequal distribution in individual interactions. As the payoffs in Figure 1 demonstrate, one possible outcome in the Hawk-Dove game appears to be equal division. This would seem to be the best solution to the problem for two reasons. First, if there are no distributive reasons for favouring one party over another, and neither party can demonstrate that they are the highest valuing-user, the most morally defensible solution would be to divide the prize in two. Second, as a pacific solution to an antagonistic problem, equal division has the virtue of delivering the same aggregate payoff as Dove-Hawk/Hawk-Dove, but avoids that which Hobbes described as, 'worst of all, [the] continuall feare, and danger of violent death'.[102]

Whilst it has much to commend it, equal division is not a possible convention of property because it is not a stable, or 'Nash',[103] equilibrium. It is not stable because, given one party's decision to play Dove, the other party can, and will, improve her position by switching to Hawk. Inequality in the division of spoils is not a defect of the applicable convention but, in a highly impure coordination problem, is an inevitable consequence of the player's preferences.[104]

B. 'Cross-Cutting' Asymmetries

Given the foregoing limitations, how might we determine whether a convention of property is morally acceptable or tolerably fair? One way might be the following. Because no convention can turn on relative merit or desert, it must treat everyone as equally deserving. Consequently, a convention of property can be said to be 'unfair' if the asymmetry along which it breaks means that some people are systemically excluded from benefitting from it because, due to some salient but morally irrelevant characteristic, be it race, sex, or whatever, they are forever doomed to be assigned the role of Dove.

This basic idea can be formalised by adapting Sugden's concept of a 'cross-cutting' asymmetry.[105] A convention will be 'cross-cutting' if the asymmetry along which it breaks allows any given member of a population to be selected as 'Hawk' at least some of the time. A convention will be 'perfectly cross-cutting' if any given individual has the same probability as any other individual of being assigned the role of Hawk or Dove in any given encounter. To return to the intersection game,

[102] Hobbes (n 30) 186. Although, as Rose observes, such a solution misses out one of the greatest benefits of private property; exclusive resource management. C Rose, 'Psychologies of Property (and Why Property Is Not a Hawk/Dove Game)' in JE Penner and HE Smith (eds), *Philosophical Foundations of Property Law* (Oxford, Oxford University Press, 2013) 281.

[103] On which see DG Baird, RH Gertner and RC Picker, *Game Theory and the Law* (Cambridge, MA, Harvard University Press, 1994) 310.

[104] This is not to say that people never share, but simply that they will not on the preference ordering that defines the Hawk-Dove game. In other words, when people share, they are not playing Hawk-Dove. See further McAdams (n 96) 231.

[105] Sugden (n 63) 157.

a rule such as 'cars give way to buses' is not cross-cutting because those who travel exclusively by car must always give way to buses. By contrast, a convention such as 'give way to the right' is cross-cutting because there is nothing to prevent any given driver from arriving at an intersection to the right of any other driver.

Sugden uses the concept of a 'cross-cutting' asymmetry to explain why emergent conventions, though rooted in self-interest, eventually come to have the status of accepted social norms.[106] For present purposes, that a convention turns on a cross-cutting asymmetry is significant for a different reason. The argument made below is that a convention that turns on such an asymmetry also satisfies a minimalist standard of fairness.

C. Cross-Cutting Asymmetries and Fairness

As noted above, because conventions are necessarily blind to distributive merit and cannot pick 'deserving' winners,[107] a desirable feature of any convention is that it treats all members of a given population as equally deserving. To put the same point another way, a convention that *systematically* favoured one sort of individual over another because of some simple and salient, though morally arbitrary, characteristic, would be unfair. So, for instance, the nascent convention of property, witnessed by Hargreaves Heap and Varoufakis, that picked owners by favouring one colour group over the other would count as an unfair convention according to this basic moral intuition.

Conventions that turn on a cross-cutting asymmetry, such as two people's spatial relationship at a roundabout, avoid this sort of unfairness because, unlike the players in Hargreave Heap's and Vaoufakis's game, there is nothing to prevent any given individual from being selected to play Hawk in any given encounter.[108] As noted above, a convention of equal distribution is attractive, not only because it banishes the lingering spectre of violence, but also because, in the absence of any reason for favouring one party over the other, it treats each as equally deserving. Given that equal division is not a viable convention of property, a convention of unequal division that turns on a cross-cutting asymmetry is the next best thing.[109]

For present purposes, what is significant about the possession convention is that it turns on an asymmetry that depends, not on *who a person is*, but on what on *he or she does*. Unlike potential conventions that turn on sex, colour attribution, or any other readily observable and easily verifiable trait, the possession rule does not label players 'Hawk' or 'Dove' by reference to some characteristic that is personal

[106] ibid 157–59.

[107] Or if they do, it will be entirely accidental.

[108] The resource at stake in the 'intersection game' being, at least principally, time.

[109] In iterated play, a 'perfectly cross-cutting asymmetry' will also replicate the distributive outcome of a convention of equal division.

to them. Instead, it requires that they themselves create the labelling asymmetry by being first to unambiguously perform the act that, within a particular community, counts as 'possession' of some object of property. Rose has written that:

> [p]ossession as the basis of property ownership, then, seems to amount to something like yelling loudly enough to all who may be interested. The first to say, 'This is mine,' in a way that the public understands, gets the prize, and the law will help him keep it against someone else who says, 'No, it is mine.'[110]

Possession is a 'cross-cutting', and thus tolerably fair, convention because there is no formal restriction that prevents any given individual from being first to make that announcement by performing the appropriate act and, in doing so, taking the prize. This absence of any formal or status-based bar to the acquisition of rights to property is desirable because it is, at the very least, consistent with a basic commitment to the moral equality of all persons.

This is not to deny that there are objections to the possession convention. Because possession requires some sort of physical interaction between a person and an object of property, it will favour some more than others. To borrow Sugden's term, it is not 'perfectly cross-cutting'. In many cases the physical act required will be undemanding. If I see a $50 note lying the gutter, the simple act of picking it up and placing it in my wallet will count as a sufficient act of possession. Nor is it necessary that I perform the act myself. If I wish to take possession of a parcel of land, I can pay someone else to place fencing around it.[111] However, whilst unlike the principle of accession, the possession rule does not necessarily make the rich richer,[112] there are instances in which performing the possessory act is physically onerous and will favour some over others. Although the existence of state-enforced remedies makes a system of property rights a great physical leveller, it remains true that mortally wounding a fleeing fox,[113] successfully harpooning a whale,[114] or gathering driftwood from a beach after a storm,[115] are physically demanding acts of possession that favour the able-bodied over the disabled, and those with sight over the blind. Because possession is not, for this reason, perfectly cross-cutting, it departs from our ideal of equal division in which morally indistinguishable parties are treated without distinction.

[110] C Rose, 'Possession as the Origin of Property' (1985) 52 *University of Chicago Law Review* 73, 81.

[111] Acts of enclosure, such as fencing, being the primary means of demonstrating possession of real property. See the discussion in *Buckinghamshire County Council v Moran* [1990] Ch 623, 641–42 (Slade LJ).

[112] Because accession works by means of a prominent connection between owned and unowned objects of property, those who have more get more. For discussion of this point see Merrill (n 5) 499.

[113] *Pierson v Post* 3 Cai R 175 (NY Sup Ct 1805).

[114] For a discussion of possessory norms in the whaling industry, see RC Ellickson, 'A Hypothesis of Wealth-Maximizing Norms: Evidence from the Whaling Industry' (1989) 5 *Journal of Law, Economics & Organization* 83.

[115] R Sugden, 'Spontaneous Order' (1989) 3 *Journal of Economic Perspectives* 85, 85.

Importantly, however, the concept of a 'cross-cutting asymmetry' is not employed in order to highlight the possession convention's distributive shortcomings, and nor should it. The primary virtue of the possession rule is not that it guarantees equality of resources or a perfectly level playing field. Rather, as Hume appreciated, it benefits everyone, though not necessarily equally, by preventing the social implosion that would otherwise occur if Hawk-Hawk interactions over resources were the rule rather than the exception.[116] As the discussion of Locke's 'proviso' sought to make clear, attempts to create a rule that both creates an initial entitlement and addresses its distributive consequences misunderstands the task that allocative mechanisms, such as possession, must perform. Given that, at 'Day 0', people neither bargained behind a veil of ignorance[117] nor participated in a one-time auction of resources using clamshells as a rudimentary currency,[118] the point of any theory of distributive justice is not to start from the beginning, but to design institutions that, taking the world as it is, replicates some ideal distribution, whatever that happens to be.[119]

Consistently with Epstein's argument about the virtue of incumbency, if the distribution created by the possession rule offends some notion of distributive justice because, for example, it discriminates against the blind, then the appropriate response is not to dispense with the possession rule, but to design redistributive institutions that redress this injustice.[120] The point of deploying the concept of a 'cross-cutting' asymmetry is simply to demonstrate that, irrespective of any redistributive mechanism, a convention that allows any given person to be selected as a Hawk is desirable because it treats people as equally deserving and, in doing so, avoids the moral pitfall of, in effect, telling certain people that they must forfeit some resource because of who they are.

VII. Conclusion

The defence of the possession rule offered above will not satisfy those who object to a system in which rights to scarce things are allocated according to the outcome of a race. Nor does the argument advanced in this chapter deny that possession is a

[116] Hume (n 42) 330 [3.2.4.1].

[117] J Rawls, *A Theory of Justice* (Cambridge, MA, Harvard University Press, 2009) 118–19. Presumably, those bargaining in Rawls's original position would prefer a convention of property that is 'perfectly cross-cutting'.

[118] R Dworkin, 'What Is Equality? Part 2: Equality of Resources' (1981) 10 *Philosophy & Public Affairs* 283, 286–87.

[119] A point neatly demonstrated by Dworkin's own comments on his fictitious auction. See ibid 291. I make precisely no comment about the preferred distribution.

[120] Amongst economists, the consensus is that redistributive goals are better achieved through transfer payments than by fine-tuning the rules that determine the initial allocations of entitlements. See generally Polinsky (n 75) 158–62; S Shavell, *Foundations of Economic Analysis of Law* (Cambridge, MA, Harvard University Press, 2009) 654–55.

morally and distributively arbitrary way of determining who gets what.[121] Instead, it stresses that, due to both the impossibility of basing a system of property on consent and the constraints on any convention that must solve an impure coordination problem, so is every other viable alternative to the possession rule.

Given this, satisfaction of the minimalist, non-distributive conception of fairness, discussed above, is the most that we could hope for. If this is correct, then we can go further than Epstein's argument that the principal virtue of the possession rule is that, as the incumbent convention, it allows for socially beneficial coordination. Because the possession convention turns on a cross-cutting asymmetry, we can also conclude that, though it may be morally arbitrary, it is tolerably fair.

[121] This is strikingly demonstrated when the possession rule confers enforceable property rights on thieves. On which see *Costello v Chief Constable of Derbyshire Constabulary* [2001] EWCA Civ 381. See further R Hickey, 'Possession Taken by Theft and the Original Acquisition of Personal Property Rights' in N Hopkins (ed), *Modern Studies in Property Law*, Vol 7 (Oxford, Hart Publishing 2013); Crawford (n 65) ch 7.

9

Understanding the Tort of Deceit

ANDREW BOTTERELL*

The tort of deceit is mostly unloved. Compared with other torts deceit has not received much scholarly attention, and what attention it has received has often been critical. Over a century ago, for example, Edward Jenks argued that the tort of fraud (ie, deceit)

> cannot be fitted into the scheme (now usually adopted) which classifies torts according to the rights or interests they infringe; for, apparently, damage of any kind caused by fraud gives rise to an action, if the other essentials of the action are present.[1]

Finding incoherent the idea that *any* kind of damage could give rise to an action Jenks suggested that the tort of deceit should be dispensed with entirely. But this seems to me to be a mistake. Once we do some conceptual ground-clearing we will see that the tort of deceit fits comfortably with the commonplace idea that it is wrong to intentionally deprive somebody of something to which they have a pre-existing normative entitlement. Or in plainer English: you shouldn't trick somebody into giving up what is theirs.

I have three aims in this chapter. First, I want to sketch an account of private law based around the idea that private law is a system of reciprocal norms that protects certain things that are mine from certain sorts of interferences by others. (I'll explain below what I mean by 'certain things that are mine' and 'certain sorts of interferences by others'.) Second, I want to show how the tort of deceit fits with this general picture of private law. And third, I want to suggest that showing that the tort of deceit fits with this general picture provides us with additional reasons for thinking that this general picture is true.

My plan is as follows. After describing the tort of deceit in more detail I consider some unsuccessful attempts to make sense of the underlying normative basis of the tort. Next, I sketch an account of private law based around the idea that no person is naturally in charge of any other person. And finally, I indicate how the

* Many thanks to Jason Neyers for extensive discussion of these issues, and to the participants at the Justifying Private Rights Workshop at UNSW for helpful comments. This work was supported by the Social Sciences and Humanities Research Council of Canada; I am grateful for its support.

[1] E Jenks, 'On Negligence and Deceit in the Law of Torts' (1910) 26 *Law Quarterly Review* 159, 166.

tort of deceit fits with this approach to private law. If I am right, the tort of deceit is not puzzling, but is instead pedestrian: it is another manifestation of the idea that it is up to you, and you alone, how your means are to be used and your purposes pursued.

I. The Tort of Deceit

The classic statement of the elements of the tort of deceit can be found in Viscount Maugham's reasons in *Bradford v Borders*:[2]

> First, there must be a representation of fact made by words or, it may be, by conduct … Secondly, the representation must be made with a knowledge that it is false. It must be wilfully false, or at least made in the absence of any genuine belief that it is true. Thirdly, it must be made with the intention that it should be acted upon by the Plaintiff or by a class of persons which will include the Plaintiff in the manner which resulted in damage to him … Fourthly, it must be proved that the Plaintiff has acted up on the false statement and has sustained damage by doing so.[3]

Not surprisingly, the standard interpretation of the tort of deceit conceives of it as a tort based on financial or pecuniary loss. As stated in *McGregor on Damages*, the 'principal, and generally the only, recovery in deceit is for pecuniary loss'.[4] As a result, the tort of deceit is often included alongside the economic torts in textbooks, and is regularly discussed in the context of pure economic loss cases.[5] As John Murphy summarises, '[a]ccording to conventional wisdom, deceit is an economic tort concerned with the protection of economic interests and its gist is usually portrayed as being the infliction of economic loss'.[6]

There are two ways to understand the emphasis placed on the requirement of economic loss in the tort of deceit.[7] Some have argued that this emphasis shows that loss is constitutive of the tort. On this 'constitution' view, nothing wrong has happened – that is, no tort has been committed – until somebody has suffered a loss as a result of reliance on a fraudulent or deceitful representation. Prior to that point the tort is inchoate. As Peter Eggers puts it: 'From the earliest development of the tort [of deceit] it was the combination of fraud and damage (or *iniuria* and *damnum*) that distinguished the case of action at common law'.[8]

[2] *Bradford v Borders* [1941] All ER 205 (HL).

[3] ibid 222.

[4] J Edelman (ed), *McGregor on Damages*, 20th edn (London, Sweet & Maxwell, 2018) 1653.

[5] See J Neyers, 'Form and Substance in the Tort of Deceit' in A Robertson and J Goudkamp (eds), *Form and Substance in the Law of Obligations* (Oxford, Hart Publishing, 2019) 311–330.

[6] J Murphy, 'Misleading Appearances in the Tort of Deceit' (2016) 75 *Cambridge Law Journal* 301, 316. As Murphy points out, however, this standard view is almost certainly false; see his discussion at 321–22.

[7] For a more extensive discussion of the economic loss requirement in the tort of deceit, see Neyers (n 5).

[8] PM Eggers, *Deceit: The Lie of the Law* (London, Informa, 2009) 1.10. See also 8.109–8.111 for Eggers' discussion of *Latker v General Guarantee Finance Ltd* [2001] EWCA Civ 875.

Others, however, have argued that in the context of the tort of deceit the element of loss goes not to wrongfulness but rather to *actionability*. On this view the idea is that the tort, or wrong, is complete once an individual has detrimentally relied on a fraudulent representation, from which it follows that the wrong complained of is separable from any loss suffered. As it was put by Lord Tucker in *Briess v Woolley*:[9]

> The tort of fraudulent misrepresentation is not complete when the representation is made. It becomes complete when the misrepresentation … is acted upon by the representee. Damage giving rise to a claim for damages may not follow or may not result until a later date, but once the representation is acted upon by the representee the tortious act is complete.[10]

However, each view faces problems. The problems faced by the first view are nicely summarised by Donal Nolan. This 'constitution view' fails, says Nolan, because it is conceptually impossible:

> The structure of my argument could not be simpler. It rests on two independent claims, from the truth of which the conclusion follows as a matter of logic. The claims are: (i) that a wrong (in other words, the violation of a right) occurs in a moment of time; and (ii) that whether or not a person has suffered loss as a result of another's conduct cannot be determined at any given moment in time. It follows that the causing of loss cannot be a wrong, and hence a right not to suffer loss is impossible.[11]

Nolan relies in part on the famous story of a farmer, a horse and his son to make his point,[12] but he also helps himself to an example of Ernest Weinrib's. Suppose, says Weinrib,

> … that as Smith is travelling to the airport to catch a plane, she is negligently injured by Jones's careless driving. The incident causes Smith to miss her plane. In the course of its flight to Smith's desired destination, however, the plane crashes, killing everyone on board.

[9] *Briess v Woolley* [1954] AC 333 (HL).

[10] ibid 353.

[11] D Nolan, 'Rights, Damage, and Loss' (2017) *Oxford Journal of Legal Studies* 255, 262.

[12] See ibid 255. On Nolan's telling, the story goes as follows:

> A farmer had a horse, which ran away. Upon hearing the news, his neighbours sympathized, saying, 'This is such bad luck. Without a horse, your work will be much harder.' The famer replied, 'Maybe good, maybe bad. We shall see.'
>
> The next day, the farmer's horse returned, bringing with it three wild horses. 'How lucky you are,' his neighbours said, 'With four horses, the work on your farm will be much easier'. The farmer replied, 'Maybe good, maybe bad. We shall see.' The next day, one of the wild horses kicked the farmer's only son, breaking his leg. His neighbours said, 'This is terrible. Now you will have to make do without your son's help until his leg recovers.' The farmer replied, 'Maybe good, maybe bad. We shall see.'
>
> Shortly afterwards, a war broke out, and officials came to the farmer's village to draft all the young men into the army. Seeing that the farmer's son had a broken leg, they passed him by. The farmer's neighbours said to him, 'You are so fortunate! All the other young men will surely die.' The farmer replied, 'Maybe good, maybe bad. We shall see.'

> It is as certain as anything can be that Smith too would have died in the crash, had she not been injured by Jones. Can she recover in tort for the injuries Jones inflicted on her?
>
> The paradox of this situation is that Smith has benefited from Jones's tortious conduct. Although Jones did not so intend it, his negligence has resulted in a net gain to Smith. Had it not been for Jones's negligence Smith would have reached the plane on time with limbs intact, only to die shortly thereafter. It would seem that Smith has no basis for complaint, since she owes her life to Jones's carelessness. Yet Jones has violated her rights.[13]

The conclusion of Weinrib's story is that there is a fundamental difference between committing a wrong and causing somebody loss. This is because the concept of loss is a comparative concept – whether it makes sense to say that I have suffered loss at some time *t* depends on comparing my status at *t* with my status at some other time *t**. The concept of a wrong, however, is not comparative in the same way. That is because it is possible to know at time *t* that I have been wronged without knowing what the future might bring. It is clear in Weinrib's example that Smith has been wronged by Jones's negligent driving; what is unclear is whether at the time of the accident Jones's negligent driving has made Smith worse off. As Nolan notes, 'we might *think* in the immediate aftermath of the accident that [Jones's] conduct had made [Smith] worse off, but a later event (the plane crash) would falsify that belief'.[14] So the idea that until there is loss the tort of deceit is incomplete seems problematic.

Unlike the constitution view, however, the actionability view *is* conceptually possible. As Nolan argues, although there cannot be a general right not to be caused loss – I cannot prevent a competing business from setting up shop across the street and diverting customers away from me:

> there is nothing to stop the law from making the *actionability* of a wrong depend on whether at a given moment it looks as if the wrong has caused the claimant loss. Indeed, there are familiar examples of the law limiting the actionability of a wrong in this way, such as the rule that to sue in deceit you must show that the deceit has caused you loss.[15]

The problem, however, is that without a better account of the normative basis of the tort of deceit the actionability view is hard to understand. To be coherent, a theory must display its subject as constituting a unitary whole, not 'a collection of discrete dooms but a systematic union of norms'.[16] The actionability view runs into problems because the justification for the imposition of liability (that the plaintiff has detrimentally relied on the fraudulent representation of the defendant) is limited by the unrelated requirement that the claimant suffer some form of consequential loss as a result of that reliance. Put most simply, to be

[13] E Weinrib, 'Right and Advantage in Private Law' (1989) 10 *Cardozo Law Review* 1283, 1283–84.
[14] Nolan (n 11) 263.
[15] ibid 266.
[16] E Weinrib, 'Private Law and Public Right' (2011) 61 *University of Toronto Law Journal* 191, 197.

coherent the reasons for *imposing* liability must at the same time be reasons for *limiting* liability. But what is the conceptual link between detrimentally relying on the deceitful or fraudulent representation of another, and requiring that that reliance result in actual loss?

II. Rationalising the Tort of Deceit

In short, we have a puzzle. The 'constitution' view of deceit appears to be a non-starter, and the 'actionability' view seems conceptually fragmented. What is needed, then, is a better understanding of the underlying normative contours of the tort. Happily, a number of theorists have attempted to provide precisely such an account. Unhappily, however, in my view each of them goes wrong. So what I would like to do now is consider three accounts of the tort of deceit – that of Robert Stevens; that of John Goldberg, Tony Sebok and Benjamin Zipursky; and that of John Murphy – and show why their accounts fail to adequately capture the tort's underlying normative basis. I will then present a different – and, I believe, better – account.

A. Stevens

Let me begin with Robert Stevens. As presented in his *Torts and Rights* the normative basis of the tort of deceit is straightforward: the tort protects our right not to be lied to.[17] Recognising, however, that such a right is too broad – it would be 'unacceptable for the law to make actionable all of the minor deceptions that we practice upon one another'[18] – Stevens argues that the plaintiff must also show that her reliance on the lie or other deceitful conduct of the defendant caused her loss.

The problem with this view should be clear. As with the actionability view of the tort of deceit discussed above, there is a gap between the right that the tort seeks to protect and the requirement of proving loss: the reasons for imposing liability do not seem to be connected in the right way with the reasons for limiting liability. It could of course be argued that the requirement of loss is needed because if there were no such requirement the courts would be overwhelmed with actions involving deceit. This is what is often dubbed a floodgates argument. But two points can be made.

[17] R Stevens, *Torts and Rights* (Oxford, Oxford University Press, 2007) 8.

[18] ibid 89. As Stevens also notes in 'Rights and Other Things', '[i]t has not been suggested by anyone that lies which are believed should be actionable without more': R Stevens, 'Rights and Other Things' in D Nolan and A Robertson (eds), *Rights and Private Law* (Oxford, Hart Publishing, 2012) 129.

First, in *Torts and Rights* Stevens explicitly disclaims any reliance on policy-based arguments in private law, and floodgates-based arguments, at least as they are typically presented, are policy-based arguments *par excellence*.[19] But a second observation is also relevant. Floodgates concerns are usually understood as limiting the scope or operation of a right that has been independently identified as forming the basis of a private law cause of action. That is, we identify a right – in Stevens's telling, the right not be lied to – and then limit the unfettered application of that right by appealing to floodgates-based considerations. When courts do this, they often invoke Cardozo J's famous quotation about 'liability in an indeterminate amount for an indeterminate time to an indeterminate class'.[20] But floodgates was not Cardozo's point in *Ultramares Corporation v Touche*. Rather, his point was that if the invocation of a right carries in its wake liability in an indeterminate amount for an indeterminate time to an indeterminate class, then that should lead us to question whether we have identified a coherent right at all. As Cardozo J went on to say, '[t]he hazards of a business conducted on these terms are so extreme as to enkindle doubt whether a flaw may not exist in the implication of a duty that exposes to these consequences'.[21] That is, if auditors owed a duty of care to all individuals who in fact relied on their representations then nobody would engage in the business of preparing audits, since the financial and legal hazards of doing so would be unjustifiable. The solution, however, is not to arbitrarily limit the scope of such a duty; rather, says Cardozo J, we should question whether imposition of such a duty makes sense in the first place.

To return to the tort of deceit, the worry again is that unless there is a clear conceptual connection between the underlying normative basis of the tort and the doctrinal requirement that economic loss be established, the normative basis of the tort will remain incoherent. This is the challenge faced by Stevens' view.

B. Goldberg, Sebok and Zipursky

Consider next the analysis offered by John Goldberg, Anthony Sebok and Benjamin Zipursky in their helpful article 'The Place of Reliance in Fraud'.[22] Goldberg, Sebok and Zipursky argue that the right or interest protected by the tort of deceit is not the right not to be lied to but is instead a right not to have one's decision-making autonomy fraudulently interfered with. The right they identify is therefore a right

[19] For further discussion, see Murphy (n 6) 317.

[20] *Ultramares Corporation v Touche* 174 NE 441, 444 (NY 1932) (New York Court of Appeals). For contemporary invocations of the spectre of indeterminate liability see, eg, *Cooper v Hobart* 2001 SCC 79 (Supreme Court of Canada); *Deloitte & Touche v Livent Inc (Receiver of)* 2017 SCC 63 (Supreme Court of Canada); *Pioneer Corp v Godfrey* 2019 SCC 42 (Supreme Court of Canada).

[21] *Ultramares Corporation v Touche* (n 20) 444.

[22] J Goldberg, A Sebok and B Zipursky, 'The Place of Reliance in Fraud' (2006) 48 *Arizona Law Review* 1001.

that protects one's 'interest in making certain kinds of choices in certain settings free from certain forms of misinformation'.[23]

Murphy raises several concerns with this general approach, the most prominent of which is that the basis of the right as stated is murky. He notes that the right

> is far too opaque, since the references to 'certain kinds of choices', 'certain settings', and 'certain forms of misinformation' do little, if anything, to elucidate the precise scope and concern of deceit. Instead, defining its gist and province in this way merely causes us to wonder: What kinds of choices? Which settings? What kinds of misinformation?[24]

But there is, I think, a deeper problem with appeals to a right to autonomy in this context, and that is the fact that the law in general is not particularly concerned with protecting autonomy. A prominent example concerns fraud or deceit in matters having to do with sexual relations. The standard rule is that deception does not negate consent to sexual relations unless the deceit goes to the nature or quality of the act,[25] the identity of the complainant's sexual partner,[26] or imposes on the complainant a significant risk of serious bodily harm.[27] As Larry Alexander and Emily Sherwin explain, 'if a woman consents to sex with a man impersonating her husband, he has raped her; but if she consents to sex with a man who falsely swears that he loves her, her consent is effective'.[28] In other words, liability due to fraud in matters having to do with sexual relations is limited.

On the whole, then, the law does not seem to be particularly interested in protecting the right of individuals to make decisions free from deception. And where it does show such an interest, it appears that the deception must be egregious, or the stakes high. As Alexander and Sherwin argue, 'courts do not regularly protect a free-standing autonomy-based right not to be deceived'.[29] Rather, 'the pattern of legal regulation betrays an ambivalent attitude toward deception … Legal rules attempt to remedy significant concrete harms that follow from lies and deception … At the same time, they fall short of consistent, principled

[23] ibid 1011.

[24] Murphy (n 6) 318–19.

[25] See, eg, *R v Maurantonio* [1968] 1 OR 145 (Ontario Court of Appeal). But compare *Bolduc v The Queen* [1967] SCR 677 (Supreme Court of Canada).

[26] See, eg, *R v Crangle* 2010 ONCA 451 (Ontario Court of Appeal).

[27] See *R v Cuerrier* [1998] 2 SCR 371 (Supreme Court of Canada); *R v Mabior* 2012 SCC 47 (Supreme Court of Canada); *R v Hutchinson* 2014 SCC 19 (Supreme Court of Canada); and *PP v DD* 2017 ONCA 180 (Ontario Court of Appeal).

[28] L Alexander and E Sherwin, 'Deception in Morality and Law' (2003) 22 *Law and Philosophy* 393, 406. There is a growing philosophical literature on the relationship between fraud and consent in sexual assault and battery. For a very incomplete list see T Dougherty, 'Sex, Lies, and Consent' (2013) 123 *Ethics* 717; J Rubenfeld, 'The Riddle of Rape-by-Deception and the Myth of Sexual Autonomy' (2013) 122 *Yale Law Journal* 272; and T Dougherty, 'No Way Around Consent: A Reply to Rubenfeld on Sex by Deception' (2013) 123 *Yale Law Journal Forum* 321.

[29] Alexander and Sherwin (n 28) 432.

condemnation'.[30] Now, to be fair to Goldberg, Sebok and Zipursky, their claim is that deceit protects the right to make *certain* kinds of choices in *certain* settings free from *certain* forms of misinformation – they are not claiming that the tort protects a bare right to decisional autonomy, a 'free-standing autonomy-based right not to be deceived'.[31] But this just takes us back to Murphy's point: *why* do Goldberg, Sebok and Zipursky qualify the right in the manner in which they do? More discussion is needed.

C. Murphy

With that in mind, let me turn to Murphy's analysis of the tort of deceit. To this point I have followed Murphy in considering the analyses of Stevens and Goldberg, Sebok and Zipursky; but what does Murphy offer in their place? According to Murphy: Goldberg, Sebok and Zipursky were on the right track. According to Goldberg, Sebok and Zipursky: the tort of deceit protects an interest in (1) making certain kinds of choices in (2) certain settings (3) free from certain forms of misinformation. Murphy's proposal is that we make this statement less vague by being very clear about the choices, settings and forms of misinformation at issue. This yields the following: the 'gist of deceit is an interference with the victim's decision-making autonomy that occurs by virtue of one of the established types of misinformation (laid down in *Derry v Peek*) and which results in a recognized form of harm'.[32]

This is, I think, an improvement on the account offered by Goldberg, Sebok and Zipursky, for precisely the reasons that Murphy gives: it is clearer, and better reflects legal doctrine (at least in England). Still, it is difficult to square the gist of the tort as Murphy understands it with the requirement that the interference with the victim's decision-making autonomy must result in some form of harm or loss to the plaintiff.[33] Again, if the tort is designed to protect the ability to make decisions free from fraud or deception, why is harm required? Murphy is correct that the law in fact requires proof of damage. But the question remains: why does it insist on that requirement?

Given what seems to be a sort of argumentative stalemate, what I would like to do next is turn to a fairly abstract discussion of the nature of and justification for private rights. I will then return to the tort of deceit and argue that the tort of deceit protects the right not to be intentionally deprived of something to which you have a pre-existing normative entitlement.

[30] ibid 433.

[31] As Alexander and Sherwin (n 28) contend.

[32] Murphy (n 6) 321. According to *Derry v Peek* (1889), 14 App Cas 337 (HL), only a misrepresentation that has been made knowingly, or without belief in its truth, or recklessly, will give rise to liability in deceit.

[33] For a much more detailed discussion of Murphy's approach to the tort of deceit, see Neyers (n 5).

III. The Canberra and Toronto Plans

In a recent article, Christopher Essert has suggested that we might use the term 'The Toronto Plan' to describe the particular approach to understanding private law championed by, among others, Ernest Weinrib and Arthur Ripstein, both at the University of Toronto.[34] The phrase 'The Toronto Plan' is intended to call to mind the so-called 'Canberra Plan', which is an approach to philosophy developed by David Lewis and Frank Jackson at the Australian National University.[35]

A. The Canberra Plan

The basic idea underlying the Canberra Plan is this. (Note to readers: if you are already familiar with the Canberra Plan, or if you are not familiar with the Canberra Plan and have no desire to become familiar with it, feel free to skip the next five paragraphs.) Assume that we want to provide a philosophical analysis of some domain of inquiry X (involving, say, free will, consciousness, morality or colour). Canberra Planners tend to employ a two-step procedure.[36] Step one involves collecting together those 'folk' platitudes that characterise the domain in question. (What counts as a platitude is something that needs further refinement, but at a minimum, basic or core beliefs about X will count as platitudinous.) So in the case of colour, for example, we might include among the folk platitudes the belief that some scarlet red things really are scarlet red; that something's being scarlet red sometimes causally explains our perceptual experience of scarlet red things; that we are justified in believing that something is scarlet red simply on the basis of its appearing that way to us; and, more controversially, that the intrinsic

[34] See C Essert, 'Thinking Like a Private Lawyer' (2017) 68 *University of Toronto Law Journal* 166. The list of relevant publications is voluminous, but for representative samples see A Ripstein, *Private Wrongs* (Cambridge, Massachusetts, Harvard University Press, 2016); P Benson, 'Misfeasance as an Organizing Normative Idea in Private Law' (2010) 60 *University of Toronto Law Journal* 731; E Weinrib, *The Idea of Private Law*, revised edn (Oxford, Oxford University Press, 2012); and E Weinrib, *Corrective Justice* (Oxford, Oxford University Press, 2012).

[35] As D Stoljar reminds us: 'The story of Canberra, the capital of Australia, is roughly as follows. In 1901, when what is called 'Federation' occurred – that is, when the six colonies then occupying the territory of Australia decided to join forces and become one colony – it was naturally felt that there should a be a capital city. But the rulers of the two most powerful cities, Sydney and Melbourne, could not agree on which of them it was to be. (Nobody took seriously the claims of any other city.) So it was decided to build a completely new city more or less midway between them'. That city was Canberra. See D Stoljar, 'The Argument from Revelation' in D Braddon-Mitchell and R Nola (eds), *Conceptual Analysis and Philosophical Naturalism* (Cambridge, MA, The MIT Press, 2009) 113.

[36] See, eg, D Lewis, 'How to Define Theoretical Terms' (1970) 67 *Journal of Philosophy* 427; D Lewis, 'Psychophysical and Theoretical Identifications' (1972) 50 *Australasian Journal of Philosophy* 249; and F Jackson, *From Metaphysics to Ethics: A Defence of Conceptual Analysis* (Oxford, Oxford University Press, 1998).

nature of scarlet red is fully revealed to us by standard visual experiences of scarlet red things.[37]

Here is where things get tricky. Once we have our set of platitudes or core beliefs we combine all those platitudes into a long conjunctive sentence. Next, we replace the theoretical terms in that long conjunctive sentence (the *T*-terms) with existentially bound *t*-variables (that is, variables ranging over the *T*-term), and we replace the central observational or other terms (the *O*-terms) with existentially bound *o*-variables (again, variables ranging over the *O*-terms). This gives us something like the following sentence *S*: there exists a *t1*, a *t2*, and a *t3*, and an *o1*, an *o2*, and an *o3*, such that … *t1* & *o1* … *t2* & *o2* … *t3* & *o3* … (where the ellipses are filled in by claims about how entities satisfying the specification of the *t*-variables are related to each other and to entities that satisfy the specification of the *o*-variables).

This brings us to step two. At this stage we engage in empirical investigation to see what in the world satisfies our complex existentially quantified sentence *S*. Suppose, to make what is surely a very long and very complicated story very short, we learn that Property *F* – the property of having a particular surface spectral reflectance, say – plays the role associated with the variable that, according to our platitudinous account, occupies the 'scarlet red' role. Then we will have learned what scarlet red *is*. In other words, from an analysis of the folk concept of colour via an empirical investigation of the world we arrive at a conclusion about what scarlet red is.

A slightly less abstract example might be useful; here is one suggested by David Lewis.[38] Suppose we are detectives trying to solve a crime. We collect evidence and learn that there were three individuals involved in the crime; for simplicity, we call those individuals *X*, *Y* and *Z*. Now, suppose we learn that *X* did such-and-such, while *Y* did so-and-so, and *Z* did this-and-that. Based on this information we come up with a story about what it is that *X*, *Y* and *Z* did. What we know about *X*, *Y* and *Z* is therefore defined by their roles in the story: *X* is the one who did this, *Y* is the one who did that, and so on. In short: *X*, *Y* and *Z* are our *T*-terms.

Next, we replace *X*, *Y* and *Z* in our story with existentially bound variables, to yield the following sentence *S**: there exists an *x*, a *y*, and a *z* such that *x* did such-and-such, *y* did so-and-so, and *z* did this-and-that. And finally, we look to see whether there is a triple of individuals who satisfy our existentially quantified sentence *S**. If we determine that Able, Baker and Charlie uniquely satisfy *S** then Able, Baker and Charlie are the culprits. (And if Able, Baker and Charlie uniquely but only imperfectly satisfy *S**? Then either our sentence *S** was incorrect, but Able, Baker and Charlie satisfy enough of *S** to be our culprits; or our original story was wrong.)

So much for the Canberra Plan. To be clear: I am *not* suggesting that you have to endorse the Canberra Plan in order to find the Toronto Plan attractive.

[37] See M Johnston, 'How to Speak of the Colors' (1992) 61 *Philosophical Studies* 221; and D Lewis, 'Naming the Colors' (1997) 75 *Australasian Journal of Philosophy* 325.

[38] See Lewis, 'Psychophysical and Theoretical Identifications' (n 36).

The two plans are clearly distinct, and although (as I will discuss below) they share certain similarities they are doing different things. The Canberra Plan is about finding a place for apparently problematic facts or properties (mental, non-natural or evaluative facts or properties) in a world composed of less problematic (physical, natural, non-evaluative) facts or properties. We believe that some objects are coloured, and that coloured objects have certain features. But if the world is composed entirely of physical things, how can it also contain colours? And if it does, what physical properties are colours identical with? That is the general sort of puzzle that Canberra Planners aim to solve, and it is clearly not the preoccupation of Toronto Planners. But what is instructive about the Canberra Plan is how it attempts to do what it does: it begins with a recipe of sorts, combines it with a set of fundamental facts, properties, concepts, or phenomena, and then tries to show how we might find room for other non-basic facts, properties, concepts, or phenomena in that story. That is why it pays to think about the Canberra Plan in this context.

B. The Toronto Plan

So let me turn to the Toronto Plan. At its core the Toronto Plan hinges on the claim that private law is a unified system of norms governing the reciprocal conduct of individuals. Although there are variations between specific views, all Toronto Planners are committed to a core organising idea, namely that the norms governing private law are relational, bilateral or correlative – that, as Weinrib has memorably put it, defendant and plaintiff in a private law action are always related as doer and sufferer of the same wrong.[39] I am going to try to explain the Toronto Plan twice, once with Kantian terminology, and once without. My hope is that by doing this we will be in a better position to see what it is that Toronto Planners are trying to accomplish.

First the Kantian gloss. In the *Doctrine of Right* Immanuel Kant discusses the 'only original right belonging to every man in virtue of his humanity'.[40] Kant calls this right '*Freedom* (independence from being constrained by another's choice), insofar as it can co-exist with the freedom of every other in accordance with a universal law'.[41] Following others, I will call this conception of freedom *external freedom*, since it articulates the idea that to be free is to be independent of the

[39] See, eg, E Weinrib, 'Corrective Justice in a Nutshell' (2002) 52 *University of Toronto Law Journal* 349.

[40] M Gregor (ed), Immanuel Kant, *The Metaphysics of Morals* (Cambridge, Cambridge University Press, 1996) 6:237. There is much that I am going to leave out in what follows, including the transition from a state of nature, where rights are provisional, to a civil condition, where rights are guaranteed. For discussion of Kant's views about the differences between the two states, see A Ripstein, *Force and Freedom: Kant's Legal and Political Philosophy* (Cambridge, Massachusetts, Harvard University Press, 2009).

[41] Kant (n 40) 6:237.

constraining choices or actions of others.[42] I am free if nobody else is in a position to tell me what to do. I am unfree if what I am able to do is subject to the choice of somebody else. Importantly, however, Kantian external freedom also has a relational aspect. To establish that I am free it is not enough to show that I am unconstrained by another's choice. What must also be shown is that the manner in which I act – my freedom or independence – is consistent with everybody else acting in the same way.

According to Kant, from this innate right to external freedom flow various other rights or authorisations. First, there is the right to equal treatment under the law (what Kant calls innate *equality*, that is, 'independence from being bound by others to more than one can in turn bind them');[43] second, there is the right to legal independence (which Kant glosses as the quality of being one's *own master* (*sui juris*));[44] third, there is the right to be presumed innocent until proven otherwise (as he puts it, the quality of being a *human being beyond reproach*);[45] and fourth, there is the right or authorisation 'to do to others anything that does not in itself diminish what is theirs'.[46] Following B Sharon Byrd and Joachim Hruschka, I will call this fourth right the right to freedom of expression. On this Kantian view, then, there is one original, innate and fundamental right – the right to external freedom – from which flow various other rights, and these other rights reflect some of the ways in which a right to be free from the constraining choices of others generates private rights and obligations.

In addition to the original right to external freedom, however, Kant also proposes the following *Postulate of Practical Reason with Regards to Rights*:

> [i]t is possible for me to have any external object of my choice as mine, that is, a maxim by which, if it were to become a law, an object of choice would *in itself* (objectively) have to *belong to no one* … is contrary to rights.[47]

So in addition to the original right to freedom there are also *acquired rights*. To make something external to me mine might involve acquiring (rights to) a thing, as in the case of property; or acquiring another's choice to perform an

[42] See, eg, BS Byrd and J Hruschka, *Kant's Doctrine of Right: A Commentary* (Cambridge, Cambridge University Press, 2010).
[43] Kant (n 40) 6:238.
[44] ibid.
[45] ibid.
[46] ibid.
[47] ibid 6:246. Concludes Kant, '[i]t is therefore an *a priori* presupposition of practical reason to regard and treat any object of my choice as something which could objectively be mine or yours'. But of course, it must also be possible to have as yours or mine something that you and I possess, but that is not in our physical possession; that is, it must be 'possible for any external object of my choice to be reckoned as rightfully mine if I have control of it (and only in so far as I have control of it) without being in possession of it': ibid 6:252. Kant allows, however, that there is 'no way of proving of itself the possibility of non-physical possession' – this claim simply follows from the Postulate of Practical Reason with Regards to Rights. In this sense the Postulate of Practical Reason with Regards to Rights is in Kant's view 'a postulate incapable of further proof'.

action, as in the case of contract.[48] Armed with this distinction between the original right to external freedom and acquired rights to external things, we can understand different ways in which the law protects these rights. I am in charge of my body; consequently, if somebody touches me without my consent, I have been wronged: that person is not allowed to do that to me. This is what we call in private law a battery, and in criminal law an assault.[49] Similarly, I am in charge of my property; consequently, if somebody takes my property without my say-so, or uses or damages it in ways that I have not authorised, I have been wronged: that person isn't allowed to do that to my things. This is what we call trespass to chattels, or conversion.

Why are these forms of interaction inconsistent with the right to external freedom, or with rights to things external to me? The answer is, I think, simple: if touching me or using my things without my consent were permissible then I would *never* be free, and *nothing* would properly be mine: my body and my property would always be subject to somebody else's decisions, and that sort of situation is not something that could be normalised as part of a system of reciprocal norms.

This story will strike some as resting on dubious metaphysical and epistemological premises – transcendental nonsense, as it might be put.[50] So let me try to sketch the same general story without employing explicitly Kantian terminology. For simplicity I will focus on Ripstein's idea in *Private Wrongs* that no person is in charge of any other person. This idea – which has obvious affinities with Kant's idea that we are *sui juris*, that is, that we are our own masters – is simple yet powerful: I get to decide what I do with my person and with my things, so long as I do not interfere with the ability of other people to do the same with themselves and their things. It also entails a particular conception of a private wrong: 'a private wrong consists in pursuing purposes in a way that is inconsistent with some other person's entitlement to do so'.[51] Note, again, that this is a *relational* conception of a private wrong: you wrong another if you act in a way that is inconsistent with that person doing the same. We cannot understand what makes your conduct wrong without considering how it affects the conduct of others.

You are able to do the things you do because you have a body, and because you have things of your own. You can swim in a pool; you can write letters to friends; you can bike to work. You set purposes – you determine what it is that you would like to do – and you use your body and your things to pursue the purposes that you set. This is how you act in and on the world. But this also means that I am limited in what I can do with or to you or your things. I cannot touch your body or move

[48] According to Kant, another person's *status* in relation to me can also be a possible external object of my choice: see Kant (n 40) 6:247. I set status aside for present purposes.

[49] For a Kantian discussion of consent, see H Stewart, 'The Limits of Consent and the Law of Assault' (2011) 24 *Canadian Journal of Law and Jurisprudence* 205.

[50] See, eg, F Cohen, 'Transcendental Nonsense and the Functional Approach' (1935) 35 *Columbia Law Review* 809.

[51] Ripstein (n 34) 30.

your things without your say-so since to allow me to do that would be to allow me to interfere with your ability to pursue your own purposes – and that would mean that I would be in charge of you, since it would be up to me what you can and cannot do with your body and with your things. Ripstein therefore suggests that there are

> two basic ways in which one person can interfere with another person's means, corresponding to the familiar distinction between torts that are intentional and those that are not. I can wrong you by using what is yours without your authorization, or I can wrong you by damaging what is yours.[52]

Both kinds of wrongs involve preventing you from using what is yours to pursue the purposes that you are entitled to pursue.

Note that I can also *frustrate* your purposes by preventing you from acquiring things that you need in order to accomplish your purposes. But it does not follow that I wrong you in doing so. If I take something that you need, but to which you have no entitlement, then I do not wrong you because I do not interfere with something to which you already have a right. As Ripstein explains:

> I might buy the last lettuce at the supermarket, effectively preventing you from making a salad. My act prevents you from acquiring something that you could have used to do something, but it does not deprive you of any powers you had. It just stops you from using the powers you have – in this case, money – to acquire new ones. If I pick the last wild lettuce in a wilderness area, I do not deprive you of means either. Here too, I simply eliminate an opportunity for you to use your powers – in this case, your hands – to acquire something useful. Although I could have produced the very same effect by pushing you out of my way, I produced it without interfering with your possession of your means. You can still use your money or hands to do other things. All I have done is change the world in which you can now decide what to do.[53]

This is obviously *very* quick. Still, on this way of thinking about private law the key ideas are the following: you, and you alone, are in charge of your person; you have a right to set your own purposes, so long as you do not interfere with the ability of others to do the same; and I wrong you if and only if I use or damage (in some proscribed way) something to which you already have a right. Again, on this view private wrongs link plaintiffs and defendants together through the prism of what the defendant has done to the plaintiff, and in terms of what the plaintiff has a right that the defendant not do to her.

I pointed out above that the Canberra and Toronto Plans are distinct. But they share some common features. Two in particular are worth emphasising in this context. The first is the role played by common sense. Canberra Planners are explicit about this: they begin by collecting all those folk platitudes about domain

[52] ibid 43.
[53] A Ripstein, 'As If It Had Never Happened' (2007) 48 *William and Mary Law Review* 1957, 1975.

of inquiry X, this on the not unreasonable assumption that what it means to offer a *philosophical explanation* of X must be responsive to what people commonly think X is about. But it seems that Toronto planners are also committed to platitudes. As Ripstein says, in discussing the social policy approach to private law endorsed by Oliver Wendell Holmes Jr, among others,

> I believe that these [social policy] modes of thinking are the product of losing sight of a simple way of thinking about private wrongs, one that is both morally and legally familiar. When a plaintiff brings a tort action against the defendant, the basic form of the complaint is "the defendant is not allowed to do that to me" … The plaintiff goes to court seeking a remedy, but the ground of the remedy is what the plaintiff contends is a wrong. On this simple and familiar picture, the point of the remedy is to make up for the wrong; the remedy is meant as a substitute for some right that was infringed.[54]

So both plans share a commitment to common sense thinking. But there is something else that (critics, at least, say) both plans share, and that is a kind of austerity: both plans seem to downplay or ignore various core phenomena. As David Braddon-Mitchell and Robert Nola remark in connection with the Canberra Plan:

> [s]ince Canberra is a planned city founded originally as the seat of the Federal Government of Australia, its detractors complain that it lacks the features that arise in cities that grow organically and have diverse inhabitants who are not government bureaucrats.[55]

For simplicity, call this the 'Lack of Diversity' objection. In the case of the Canberra Plan, the criticism typically highlights some overlooked role played by language – the worry being that there are many things that we do with language, only some of which are descriptive in nature. In the case of the Toronto Plan, on the other hand, the 'Lack of Diversity' objection operates somewhat differently. Here the concern is that by emphasising (over-emphasising?) private law's relational structure, and by focusing on correlative rights and duties, Toronto Planners overlook various other important aspects of private law doctrine, such as principles of distributive justice, broad concerns about the role and importance of public policy, and the availability of non-compensatory justifications for private law remedies, such as deterrence and punishment.[56] Another mode of attack is to claim that the Toronto Plan is unable to account for torts that do not ostensibly share these

[54] Ripstein (n 34) 3–4.

[55] D Braddon-Mitchell and R Nola, 'Introducing the Canberra Plan' in D Braddon-Mitchell and R Nola (eds), *Conceptual Analysis and Philosophical Naturalism* (Cambridge, MA, The MIT Press, 2009) 1.

[56] For an example, see S Hershovitz's review of Ripstein's *Private Wrongs*, where Hershovitz argues that Ripstein's view cannot account for some of the most basic kinds of private wrongs, such as battery, and fails to provide a satisfying account of the rationale for private law remedies: see S Hershovitz, 'The Search for a Grand Unified Theory of Tort Law' (2017) 130 *Harvard Law Review* 942.

formal structures, such as the unlawful means tort, vicarious liability, passing off, or injurious falsehood.[57]

One response to the Lack of Diversity objection is to argue that it is no part of the Toronto Plan to show that its preferred approach to private law is able to explain every corner of legal doctrine. Rather – goes this response – the goal of the Toronto Plan is to show what private law would look like if we took seriously the basic principles that Toronto Planners propose.[58] But another response to the Lack of Diversity objection is to meet it head on and demonstrate that various apparently problematic private law doctrines can in fact be understood in terms of the simple (and austere) idea that freedom consists in independence from the constraining choices of others, that nobody is in charge of anybody else. This is what I propose to do with the tort of deceit.

IV. Applying the Toronto Plan to the Tort of Deceit

Let me recap the argument to this point. I have described the elements of the tort of deceit and provided reason to think that some recent attempts to characterise the underlying normative structure of the tort are incomplete. I then sketched a picture of private law – the so-called Toronto Plan – and indicated how individuals should relate to one another if we are indeed governed by such a reciprocal system of norms. What I would like to do now is show that liability for the tort of deceit follows directly from the simple idea that, as I put it above, it is always wrong to intentionally deprive somebody of something to which they have a pre-existing normative entitlement.

Earlier I described Kant's idea that from the right to external freedom flows the right to freedom of expression. To illustrate this right Kant remarks that a person does no wrong in merely communicating his thoughts to another person, in 'telling or promising them something, whether what he says is true and sincere or untrue and insincere; for it is entirely up to [the other person] whether they want to believe him or not'.[59] In other words, on Kant's view lying to another person is not contrary to the innate right to external freedom – is not a legal wrong – because

[57] For recent statements of this sort of argument, see J Goudkamp and J Murphy, 'The Failure of Universal Theories of Tort Law' (2015) 21 *Legal Theory* 47; and J Murphy, 'The Heterogeneity of Tort Law' (2019) *Oxford Journal of Legal Studies* 1. For Weinrib's views on vicarious liability, see *The Idea of Private Law* (n 34) 185–87. For an account of the unlawful means tort that is compatible with the Toronto Plan, see J Neyers, 'Causing Loss by Unlawful Means: Should the High Court of Australia follow *OBG Ltd v Allan*?' in S Degeling, J Edelman and J Goudkamp (eds), *Torts in Commercial Law* (Pyrmont, New South Wales, Thomson Reuters, 2012) 117–40.

[58] As C Essert puts it, '[t]hinking about private law first and foremost in terms of the nature of our relations with others provides an important and illuminating standpoint on what it would be for us to live together as moral agents': see Essert (n 34) 185.

[59] Kant (n 40) 6:238.

it is ultimately the other person's choice whether to believe or act on what is said. Simply telling somebody something that is untrue does not diminish or interfere with anything that that person already has.

Does it follow that on this view there can never be legal liability for intentionally deceiving another person? It does not. But it does follow that only certain sorts of untruths or lies will attract liability. Thus, says Kant:

> [t]he only kind of untruth we want to call a lie, in the sense *bearing upon rights* … is one that directly infringes upon another's right, e.g., the false allegation that a contract has been concluded with someone, made in order to deprive him of what is his[.]

Kant calls these intentional untruths *juristic lies*, as distinct from *ethical lies*.[60] Thus, while there is in general no *legal* prohibition on deceiving another person, such deception wrongs another person when it is done with the intention of infringing or interfering with another's right, and when that right is in fact interfered with. *This* is the gist of the tort of deceit. What then does the tort protect? Not freedom from being lied to, nor freedom from interferences with autonomy. Rather, the tort of deceit protects *everything to which you have a normative entitlement*, and it does so by preventing the non-consensual dispossession of those things as a result of another's fraud. Because such a transaction 'involves another in something to which he or she in principle cannot consent' the transaction would be by definition non-consensual 'since the scheme requires that he or she doesn't know what is going on'.[61] As Ripstein notes:

> [f]raud is distinctive because the willful misrepresentation of the situation *guarantees* that there can be no united will; the fraudster does not suppose he shares a united will with his dupe. Of course the dupe thinks there is a united will and that there is an agreement. That is why he's a dupe.[62]

In sum, the right that forms the basis of the tort of deceit is not the right to make decisions free from deception but rather the right not to be deceptively dispossessed of what is rightfully yours. It is similar to the difference between having your means interfered with and being denied something that would enable you

[60] As J Mahon very helpfully explains, Kant distinguishes three kinds of lies: lies in the *ethical sense*, lies in the *juristic sense*, and lies in the *sense of right*. A lie in the ethical sense is the making of an untruthful statement with the intention that it be believed to be true. A lie in the juristic sense is the making of an untruthful statement to a particular person intending that the person believe the statement to be true and intending that the person be harmed by believing that it is true. Here harm simply means violating a right. And finally, a lie in the sense of right is the making of an untruthful statement intending that others believe that the statement is true and intending that 'humanity generally' be harmed by those others believing that statement to be true. See J Mahon, 'The Truth About Kant on Lies' in C Martin (ed), *The Philosophy of Deception* (Oxford, Oxford University Press, 2011) 208–12.

[61] O O'Neill, 'The Moral Perplexities of Famine Relief' in T Regan (ed), *Matters of Life and Death* (Philadelphia, PA, Temple University Press, 1980) 287. This is why, on O'Neill's *interpretation* of Kant, '[a] person who promises falsely treats the acceptor of the promise as a prop or a thing and not as a person'.

[62] Ripstein (n 40) 131–32.

to use your means to pursue your purposes. The first is wrongful; the second is merely unfortunate.

As James Mahon says, on Kant's view,

> [h]arming a person by depriving that person of what is rightfully hers or his is wrong insofar as it is a violation of her or his property rights, her or his contract rights, and so on. The wrongness of telling a lie in the juristic sense, therefore, just is the wrongness of intending to violate a person's property rights, rights based on contract, and so on.[63]

Ripstein makes essentially the same point when he says, in connection with fraud and deceit, that

> [t]he right at issue is not against being lied to, but rather against being deprived of what you have through deceit. The protection of that right is a structural requirement of the system in which each person is entitled to use his or her means consistent with the entitlement of others to do the same.[64]

In short, if private law is indeed a system of reciprocal norms that protects what is mine from wrongful interferences by others, then it must protect what is mine from *all* forms of wrongful interference or dispossession, including interference or dispossession by deceit or fraud. Otherwise I would not be secure in what is mine since somebody else could always trick me into parting with it, even if they could not take it directly from me. And again, that is not a right that could be consistently systematised.

Let me turn now to the second puzzling feature of the tort of deceit that I mentioned at the outset, viz, the apparent necessity of proving loss. To understand how that feature of the tort of deceit fits in with the general picture of private law set out above we need to return to the distinction between loss and damage. As we saw earlier, loss is a comparative concept: whether a person has suffered a loss at a time t depends on what happens at some later time $t+1$. Damage, on the other hand, is not comparative in the same way: we should be able to say, at a given time, whether somebody has suffered damage from the perspective of private law. As Nolan puts it, 'if a violation of right happens in a moment of time, then whether or not a person suffered damage must be determinable at a particular moment in time if a requirement of damage is to be integral to a rights-based analysis' of private law.[65]

How then *should* we understand damage in the tort of deceit? Using the Toronto Plan, the way forward is to view it as being nothing over and above the fact that one has been intentionally dispossessed of one's rights through the fraudulent representation of another. On this view, then, damage – but not, importantly, loss – is essential to deceit, since without damage in the sense of a dispossession

[63] Mahon (n 60) 218.
[64] Ripstein (n 34) 50 at n 32.
[65] Nolan (n 11) 272.

of rights there is no wrong to which the plaintiff can point. This is not to deny, however, that in many cases plaintiffs will also suffer losses as a result of being disposed of their normative entitlement and that these losses will be recoverable if they are consequential on that dispossession.[66] Rather, the point is to make it clear that loss is neither a constitutive element of the tort nor a criterion for the tort's actionability.

V. Conclusion

In this chapter I have argued the tort of deceit is best understood as a manifestation of some simple ideas about how people should treat one another. Deceit is wrongful because it interferes with people's normative entitlements to things that are theirs. Such deceptive conduct is what Kant would call a lie in the juristic sense. The tort of deceit does not protect a right not to be lied to, nor does it protect a right to decisional autonomy. Rather, it protects everything that is rightfully ours – anything to which we have a normative entitlement to – from dispossession due to fraud.

I have also suggested that this view is consistent with the approach to private law that I have called the Toronto Plan, and provides an additional reason for thinking that that approach to private law may very well be correct. This is because it suggests that the Toronto Plan is not too austere and has the resources to explain the normative foundations of a tort that many have found perplexing. If, as Toronto Planners suggest, a private wrong consists in pursuing purposes in a way that is inconsistent with some other person's entitlement to do the same, then deceit is a private wrong: for by tricking another person into giving up what is theirs, you are pursuing your purposes in a way that requires you to violate the rights of others. And that is precisely what the Toronto Plan says you are not entitled to do.

[66] For a classic example, see *Doyle v Olby (Ironmongers) Ltd* [1969] 2 QB 158 (CA).

10

Justifying Liabilities and Duties

ANDREW ROBERTSON*

What is it that calls for justification in the law of obligations, and what features of the law should be taken into account in considering questions of justification? While this volume is focused on the justification of rights, this chapter argues that a thorough consideration of the justifications for the law of obligations requires close attention to liability and duties. Liability provides an important frame of reference for any justificatory exercise in the law of obligations for two reasons. The first is that, historically and as a matter of practice, the common law of obligations begins with, and focuses primarily on, liability rather than rights and duties. The common law is explicated through judgments, and in private law cases those judgments mostly take the form of justifying liability or justifying the denial of liability. A second reason to consider liability as a frame of reference is that important questions of justification arise in relation to primary liabilities. Those questions will be left out of account in an analysis that focuses exclusively on rights and duties.

The first part of this chapter will consider liability as a justificatory frame of reference and its connection with conventional morality and broader considerations of public interest. The chapter will then consider the need to justify primary liabilities, sketching some ideas about possible justifications for particularly controversial forms of primary liability: vicarious liability and equitable estoppel. This chapter uses the examples of equitable estoppel and the right to performance of a contractual promise to explore the difficulty that is encountered in determining the existence and significance of rights in the common law of obligations, and the difficulty that is encountered in drawing the boundary between right/duty relationships and power/liability relationships. In light of those difficulties, it is important to question the utility of the distinction between right/duty relationships and power/liability relationships, and to question the value of analysis of justification in the law of obligations by reference to rights.

* I am grateful to Anne Orford and participants in the 'Justifying Private Rights' workshop for helpful comments.

The second part of the chapter discusses the need to take account of duties in the analysis of justification in private law. The duty perspective draws attention to the idea of behaviour guidance as a possible justification for private law. As we will see, however, it is not only through the announcement and explication of duties that private law guides behaviour: the courts also guide behaviour through judgments on primary liabilities. John Goldberg and Ben Zipursky have suggested that there is a choice to be made between duty-based and liability-based understandings of the law of torts, arguing that: 'Tort law is better understood and explained as a law of guidance rules than a scheme of liability rules'.[1] But, as Goldberg and Zipursky's own work shows, private law is *both* a law of guidance rules and a scheme of liability rules. Duties can only be understood in the context of rights and liability. The chapter therefore concludes that a full understanding of justification in the law of obligations can only be gained by integrating analysis of liability, duties and rights.

I. Liability

A. Liability as a Frame of Reference

The phenomenon of liability provides an important frame of reference for a consideration of justification in the law of obligations. That is because deciding whether one person is or is not liable to another – and justifying that decision – is primarily what the courts do in this area of the law. Even where courts are giving effect to what might be understood to be rights and correlative duties in the Hohfeldian scheme,[2] the context in which those rights and duties arise for consideration and are explicated is, in the vast majority of cases, in relation to questions of liability. The common law in this field is primarily articulated and developed in the course of, and for the purpose of, explaining why liability does or does not arise in particular circumstances. Lawyers and judges think primarily in terms of causes of action, which are ultimately broken down into factual elements that justify liability. Private law in this sense 'takes the form not of forward-looking legislation or regulation, but of backward-looking attributions of liability by judges'.[3] This does not mean that we should adopt an exclusive focus on liability to the exclusion of rights and duties, but it does mean that liability must be one of the lenses through which we consider questions of justification in private law.

[1] JCP Goldberg and BC Zipursky, 'Seeing Law from the Internal Point of View: Holmes and Hart on Legal Duties' (2006) 75 *Fordham Law Review* 1563, 1577.

[2] WN Hohfeld, 'Some Fundamental Legal Conceptions as Applied in Judicial Reasoning' (1913) 23 *Yale Law Journal* 16.

[3] Goldberg and Zipursky (n 1) 1588 (arguing that this does not render tort law 'ineligible for treatment as a home for primary rules of conduct').

Stephen Smith has suggested that:

> The law imposes itself upon its subjects in three principal ways. First, lawmakers announce substantive rules: rules that stipulate general legal duties ('Everyone has a duty to perform their contractual promises') or that tell individuals what they must do to create or modify such duties ('A contract is created by an offer, acceptance, and consideration'). Second, courts issue rulings: they order individuals to do or not do specific things ('It is ordered that the defendant pay the claimant £100') or grant them specific powers or immunities ('Title to Blackacre is hereby vested in the claimant'). Third, legal officials impose sanctions: examples include imprisonment and the seizure of property.[4]

While Smith's second and third categories are familiar to common lawyers, his first is not. While it is possible, through careful study, to identify rights and duties in the common law, the common law is not imposed on us through the announcement of general rights or duties.[5] Because the common law is explicated through judgments, and judgments are primarily concerned with the attribution of liability, substantive rules are rarely announced in the form of general duties. When a substantive rule is, exceptionally, announced in the form of a general duty, the statement of the general duty is necessarily at a high level of abstraction from the liability issue with which the court is dealing. Even those of us who take seriously the judges' own reasons for their decisions could very rarely understand the statement of a general duty as part of the ratio decidendi of a case. That leaves the existence and significance of any general duties open to question. To take Smith's example: is there a general duty to perform contractual promises and, if so, what is its significance? Oliver Wendell Holmes famously denied the significance of any such general duty, asserting that: 'The duty to keep a contract at common law means a prediction that you must pay damages if you do not keep it, – and nothing else'.[6] The accuracy of Holmes' claim can be assessed only indirectly, by considering the common law's treatment of relevant liability issues.[7]

In Australian law, for example, it is possible to find occasional statements of high authority to the effect that there is a right to performance of a contractual promise, and from that we can draw the conclusion that there is a correlative duty. In the course of a lengthy analysis of the nature of the tort of interference with contractual relations for the purpose of identifying the scope of the defence of justification in *Zhu v Treasurer of NSW*, the High Court of Australia observed

[4] SA Smith, *Rights, Wrongs, and Injustices: The Structure of Remedial Law* (Oxford, Oxford University Press, 2019) 1.

[5] An exception is the 'duty of care' in the tort of negligence, which is not a duty in the Hohfeldian sense because the legal duty is 'not a duty to be careful but a duty not to cause damage by carelessness': *Leigh and Sillivan Ltd v Aliakmon Shipping Co Ltd* [1985] 1 QB 350, 375 (Oliver LJ), discussed and explained by D Nolan, 'Deconstructing the Duty of Care' (2013) 129 *LQR* 558, 560.

[6] OW Holmes, 'The Path of the Law' (1897) 10 *Harvard Law Review* 457, 462.

[7] Cf Smith (n 4) 167 ('the law says that contracting parties have duties to perform their contractual promises').

that 'subject to the established limits on the grant of specific performance and injunctions, in Australian law each contracting party may be said to have a right to the performance of the contract by the other'.[8] The court explicitly rejected Holmes' view that a duty to perform a contract means no more than a prediction that damages must be paid if the promise is not kept.[9] The availability of equitable remedies in some cases and the existence of the tort of interference with contractual relations clearly show that there is something more to contractual rights and duties than Holmes allowed.[10] How much more remains open to question. The idea that there is a duty to perform a contract and a correlative right to performance is supported in other ways, such as the recognition that a threat to breach a contract constitutes illegitimate pressure for the purpose of duress, both as a vitiating factor in contract and as an unjust factor in the law of unjust enrichment. The Court in *Zhu v Treasurer of NSW* approved Windeyer J's statement in his dissenting judgment in *Coulls v Bagot's Executor and Trustee Co Ltd* that:

> It is … a faulty analysis of legal obligations to say that the law treats a promisor as having a right to elect either to perform his promise or to pay damages. Rather … the promisee has 'a legal right to the performance of the contract'.[11]

The announcement in passing in the context of an exploration of the tort of interference with contractual relations (or, for that matter, in the context of assessing an application for specific performance)[12] of a duty to perform a contract and a correlative right to performance leaves the existence and significance of such rights and duties open to question in other contexts. In assessing detriment for the purpose of promissory estoppel and in the context of the consideration requirement for contract variation, contracting parties have been understood to exercise a choice as to whether or not to perform a contractual obligation. In *Je Maintiendrai Pty Ltd v Quaglia*, a tenant who continued to observe the covenants of a lease on the faith of the landlord's promise to accept a reduced rent was held to have suffered a detriment in the form of the loss of an opportunity to abandon the shop 'and to have taken his chances about being sued for breach of contract'.[13] Similarly, in *Musumeci v Windadell Pty Ltd* a tenant who stayed in occupation under a lease 'rather than walking away at the cost of damages' was held to have thereby provided consideration for the landlord's promise to

[8] *Zhu v Treasurer of NSW* [2004] HCA 56; (2004) 218 CLR 530 [128] (Gleeson CJ, Gummow, Kirby, Callinan and Heydon JJ). See also *Mann v Paterson Constructions Pty Ltd* [2019] HCA 32; (2019) 373 ALR 1 [195] (Nettle, Gordon and Edelman JJ), where the point was again of peripheral relevance to the decision.

[9] Holmes (n 6) 462.

[10] *Zhu v Treasurer of NSW* [2004] HCA 56; (2004) 218 CLR 530 [128].

[11] *Coulls v Bagot's Executor and Trustee Co Ltd* (1967) 119 CLR 460, 504 quoting *Alley v Deschamps* (1806) 13 Ves Jun 225, 228; 33 ER 278, 279 (Lord Erskine, mentioning a party's legal right to performance of a contract in passing in the course of dismissing an application for specific performance).

[12] *Alley v Deschamps* (1806) 13 Ves Jun 225, 228; 33 ER 278, 279.

[13] *Je Maintiendrai Pty Ltd v Quaglia* (1980) 26 SASR 101, 115.

accept a reduced rent.[14] However much one might wish for cases such as these to be resolved by reference to broad, consistent, clearly announced rules about the rights and duties of contracting parties, the fact is that liability questions are not generally dealt with in that way. Even in cases raising basic questions about rights and duties, the focus of common law adjudication is on liability issues arising in the case at hand. It is in the nature of the common law that the existence, nature and significance of rights and duties cannot be definitively laid down by announcement but can only be deduced and assessed through analysis of the treatment by the courts of particular liability questions.

Although liability-focused analysis tends to be associated with a utilitarian, loss-distribution model of law,[15] viewing private law from the perspective of liability does not necessitate a commitment to any particular view about justification. Rather, it simply makes questions about the grounds of liability more visible and opens up a wider range of possible answers. In cases where liabilities arise from the infringement of rights, thinking about justification from the point of view of liability keeps open certain questions which are obscured if we approach the law only in terms of rights or duties. John Goldberg and Ben Zipursky have, for example, explained the phenomenon of liability on the basis that the state owes a duty to its citizens to provide an avenue of civil recourse for the redressing of wrongs.[16] They have justified the state's duty to provide an avenue of civil recourse as an obligation owed by the state in return for taking away the liberty that individuals enjoyed in the state of nature to seek recompense for injuries by way of violent or disorderly means of self-help.[17] Goldberg and Zipursky have also explained the state's duty to empower citizens to act against those who have wronged them as a manifestation of the state's duty to treat individuals with respect and to respect their equality with others.[18]

Civil recourse can also be justified from a consequentialist perspective: private law liability might derive some justification from the idea that providing civil recourse for wrongs is desirable in the interests of maintaining social harmony.[19] That explanation connects with the historical roots of the law of obligations in buying off blood feuds, assuaging passions for vengeance through the payment of compensation, and maintaining the King's peace.[20] However far removed that might seem from the contemporary law, the idea that private law remains concerned to maintain civil peace finds some expression in the contemporary case law.[21]

[14] *Musumeci v Windadell Pty Ltd* (1994) 34 NSWLR 723, 749.

[15] Goldberg and Zipursky (n 1) 1566–72.

[16] eg JCP Goldberg and BC Zipursky, 'Torts as Wrongs' (2010) 88 *Texas Law Review* 917, 974.

[17] See, eg: BC Zipursky, 'Philosophy of Private Law' in J Coleman and S Shapiro (eds), *The Oxford Handbook of Jurisprudence and Philosophy of Law* (Oxford, Oxford University Press, 2002) 623, 642.

[18] Goldberg and Zipursky (n 16) 974.

[19] R Pound, *Law and Morals* (Chapel Hill, University of North Carolina Press, 1924) 77 described it as a concern 'to maintain the social interest in the general security, to prevent conflict and to set up a legal order in place of private war'.

[20] See eg: OW Holmes, *The Common Law* (Boston, Little, Brown & Co, 1881) 1–38; D Ibbetson, *A Historical Introduction to the Law of Obligations* (Oxford, Oxford University Press, 1999) ch 1.

[21] See, eg: *See Toh Siew Kee v Ho Ah Lam Ferrocement (Pte) Ltd* [2013] SGCA 29; [2013] 3 SLR 284 [87].

A notable feature of the maintenance of civil peace or social harmony as a justification for liability is that it assumes some connection between the substance of private law and a collective community understanding as to what justice requires in particular circumstances. Such a connection in turn assumes the existence of conventional understandings as to how people should behave and as to when and how the law should intervene when there are departures from those behavioural norms. It also assumes some consistency between such views and the rules of private law. Arthur Goodhart has helpfully distinguished between three sources of moral ideas at play in the development of the law: first, 'the will of God', second, reasoning from fundamental premises and, third, simple intuition.[22] Conventional morality represents a fourth source or way of thinking about moral or ethical ideas.[23] It involves intuiting what Ames has called 'the moral sense of the community' or what are understood to be widely held views in the community as to how people should behave and when the law should provide a remedy.[24] It is famously exemplified by the notion identified by Lord Atkin in *Donoghue v Stevenson* of a 'general public sentiment of moral wrongdoing for which the offender must pay'.[25]

This notion of 'conventional morality' or 'ethical custom' has played an significant role in the development of private law, though it would seem to have been motivated, underpinned, shaped and qualified by the public interest, and to have been filtered through and constrained by the accumulated baggage of the law's past.[26] Oliver Wendell Holmes has suggested that, while the substance of the law depends on convenience and necessity, its 'form and machinery, and the degree to which it is able to work out desired results, depend very much upon its past'.[27] Whatever motivates judges to develop the common law, their capacity to do so is limited by the doctrine of precedent, the recognised 'form and machinery of the law', and its inherent conservatism, all of which require that any change must be incremental.

Holmes acknowledged the role of conventional morality in the development of the law, but expressed the hope that it would be eliminated through the development of objective standards:

> It remains to be proved that, while the terminology of morals is still retained, and while the law does still and always, in a certain sense, measure legal liability by moral standards, it nevertheless, by the very necessity of its nature, is continually transmuting those

[22] See, eg: AL Goodhart, *English Law and the Moral Law* (London, Stevens & Sons, 1953) 30–37 (suggesting that 'moral law based on reason' rather than intuition has been most influential in English law).

[23] cf KN Llewellyn, 'The Normative, the Legal, and the Law-Jobs: The Problem of Juristic Method' (1940) 49 *Yale Law Journal* 1355, 1359 (rejecting the notion of 'custom' as 'too blunt and confused to serve in careful analysis').

[24] JB Ames, 'Law and Morals' (1908) 22 *Harvard Law Review* 97, 98, 101 and 105.

[25] *Donoghue v Stevenson* [1932] AC 562, 580.

[26] See Holmes (n 20).

[27] ibid 1–2.

> moral standards into external or objective ones, from which the actual guilt of the party concerned is wholly eliminated.[28]

James Barr Ames, on the other hand, argued that the common law was not moving away from moral ideas, but towards them. Ames argued that judges had spent the previous 600 years 'bringing our system of law more and more into harmony with moral principles'.[29] He did not, however, suggest that the law did or should seek perfect harmony with conventional moral principles. Ames observed that, on the one hand, there 'are and always will be' situations in which liability attaches for policy reasons to those who are 'morally blameless' (such as an employer held vicariously liable for a wrong committed by a carefully chosen employee).[30] And on the other hand, the necessary denial of liability in certain instances on policy grounds means that there are cases in which 'the innocent suffer and the wicked go unpunished': 'The law is utilitarian. It exists for the realization of the reasonable needs of the community. If the interest of an individual runs counter to this chief object of the law, it must be sacrificed'.[31]

An interesting question for legal scholars is the extent to which those influences that have shaped the development of the law of obligations continue to constrain or shape analysis of its justifications. A well-known observation made by Oliver Wendell Holmes was that when the reason for a rule disappears, a new justification may be found, and the rule gradually moulded to suit the new rationale:

> A very common phenomenon, and one very familiar to the student of history, is this. The customs, beliefs, or needs of a primitive time establish a rule or a formula. In the course of centuries, the custom, belief, or necessity disappears, but the rule remains. The reason which gave rise to the rule has been forgotten, and ingenious minds set themselves to inquire how it is to be accounted for. Some ground of policy is thought of, which seems to explain it and to reconcile it with the present state of things; and then the rule adapts itself to the new reasons which have been found for it, and enters on a new career. The old form receives a new content, and in time even the form modifies itself to fit the meaning which it has received.[32]

If Holmes is right, then we can legitimately distinguish between the *reasons why we have* a particular legal doctrine, which is an interpretive/historical/normative question, and *the justification* for a legal doctrine, which could properly be treated as a more purely normative or interpretive/normative question. A purely normative justification is unlikely to gain much traction, however, if it is seen to be imposed from the outside. An interpretive approach to justification

[28] ibid 38. Compare, though, Holmes' later statement in 'The Path of the Law' (n 6) 459 that 'The law is the witness and external deposit of our moral life. Its history is the history of the moral development of the race'.

[29] Ames (n 24) 113.

[30] ibid 109.

[31] ibid 110.

[32] Holmes (n 20) 5.

of a common law doctrine is more likely to gain the support of scholars and judges, and that requires engagement and the drawing of connections with the law's past. Moreover, Holmes' idea that some new 'ground of policy' can be found for an existing rule is grounded on his assumption that the connection between legal rules and conventional morality is purely historical. To the extent that conventional ideas about how people should behave towards one another retains an influence on the law, that, along with the inherent conservatism of the common law, limits the capacity for new justifications to supplant old reasons.[33] Whether one finds Holmes' or Ames' account of the relationship between the law of obligations and moral ideas more persuasive as a matter of interpretation – or more normatively appealing – there can be no doubt that the law in this field remains concerned with notions of how people should behave in relation to one another. Nor can there be any doubt that the focus on conventional morality is deeply entangled with concerns about broader community interests.

To the extent that the maintenance of social harmony remains a justifying force in the law of obligations, this might therefore require the law to maintain some connection with conventional morality, as opposed to, say, moving toward a rule that is solely concerned to encourage efficiency-enhancing behaviour at the expense of interpersonal justice.[34] That is subject to two qualifications. First, even if social harmony is accepted as a goal or justification for the law of obligations, liability (in the form of civil recourse) may not always be needed. In some subject areas, or on some issues, the existence of clear rules may be enough to avoid and resolve disputes. Moreover, as Roscoe Pound has suggested, the rules required to avoid disputes need not always be grounded in social conventions: the mere existence of a clear rule may be effective to quell controversies, whatever its content.[35] In general, though, Pound has suggested that 'law cannot depart far from ethical custom nor lag far behind it'.[36] The reason he gives is that law is enforced by human beings, and people will be inevitably be guided by ethical custom in their selection and interpretation of legal materials.[37]

[33] As Ibbetson (n 20) 299 has observed: 'In a system so heavily dependent upon case law, it is change that needs to be explained, not continuity'. cf BH Bix, 'The Promise and Problems of Universal, General Theories of Contract Law' (2017) 30 *Ratio Juris* 391, 398: 'To be sure, the history of why doctrines arose is at best only half the historical story. The question is not only why a doctrine is introduced, but also why it lasts – why it is not replaced in time by other and better rules (however one defines "better")'.

[34] See, eg: A Robertson, 'The Failure of Economic Analysis of Promissory Estoppel' (1999) 15 *Journal of Contract Law* 69.

[35] cf Pound (n 19) 77, (suggesting that in some instances in the law of property and commercial transactions 'the law might require either of two alternative courses of action with equal justice' and in those cases all that is needed to prevent conflict is for the law to 'choose one and prescribe it in order to insure certainty').

[36] ibid 122.

[37] ibid 122–23.

B. Justifying Primary Liabilities

A second reason to take liability seriously in a consideration of justification in private law is that, as Stephen Smith has shown, some significant private law relations are not right/duty relationships in the Hohfeldian scheme, but power/liability relationships.[38] In a number of important instances, the law recognises that one person incurs a liability to another without that second person ever having a right against the first, in the sense of a legally recognised entitlement that the first person behave in a particular way or bring about a particular state of affairs. The most notable example is the relationship that arises from an unjust enrichment, which gives rise to a liability to make restitution. Smith has made a compelling argument that the liability to make restitution arises as a response to an injustice rather than any infringement of the plaintiff's rights.[39] What needs to be justified in that situation is the liability to make restitution and the notion of injustice that underlies it, rather than any right of the plaintiff or duty on the part of the defendant.

i. Vicarious Liability

An obvious example of a liability which is primary in the relevant sense is vicarious liability, the justification for which is one of the more intractable issues in the law of obligations. The liability is secondary in the sense that it arises only when a wrong is committed, and therefore only where there is a right/duty relationship between the victim and the primary wrongdoer. But it is a primary liability as between the victim and the employer, who – at least on the dominant servant's-tort theory – owes no duty to the victim and commits no wrong. Why an employer should be liable for an employee's wrongs is a longstanding justificatory question. Holmes, for example, suggested that the employer's responsibility arose because the wrongful acts 'were likely to happen in the course of the service',[40] while Ames proposed that since the business is carried on for the employer's benefit, the employer should bear the risk of the employee's misconduct rather than having it fall on a stranger.[41] Despite the vast attention devoted to the topic by scholars and judges, we do not seem to be much closer to justifying the current law of vicarious liability than that rather loose notion that the employer is in some sense responsible for the existence of the risk of wrongdoing by the employee, and that

[38] Smith (n 4) ch 8; SA Smith, 'The Restatement of Liabilities in Restitution' in C Mitchell and W Swadling (eds), *The Restatement Third: Restitution and Unjust Enrichment – Critical and Comparative Essays* (Oxford, Hart Publishing, 2013) 227.
[39] Smith (n 4) 237–49.
[40] Holmes (n 20) 5.
[41] Ames (n 24) 109.

it is therefore a risk that should, in fairness, be borne by the employer rather than the victim.[42]

If vicarious liability can be justified, it is *as* a liability, based on a broader sense of responsibility not involving notions of fault or wrongdoing.[43] While scrutiny and critique of contentious doctrines such as vicarious liability is important, it may also be helpful to approach the grounds of such a doctrine simply as a question of justification. It may be useful to ask how best to justify a principle of long standing,[44] which seems firmly entrenched in the law.[45] It may, for example, be thought to serve the interests of social harmony that, as far as possible, someone answers for wrongdoing.[46] If that cannot be the wrongdoer, then the purpose may be served through the imposition of liability on someone who is responsible for the existence of the environment in which the wrong was committed, and bears a broader responsibility through the capacity to exert some control over the risk that such a wrong might be committed.[47]

What is interesting about the realm of primary liabilities, as distinct from primary rights and duties, is that because liability arises without any wrongdoing on the part of the person who is liable, broader notions of responsibility come into play.[48] That is also true of equitable estoppel, although here the responsibility for harm is more directly attributable to particular risk-creating conduct on the part of the defendant.

ii. Equitable Estoppel

In contrast with vicarious liability, a substantial question arises as to whether equitable estoppel gives rise to primary rights and duties or whether, as Ben McFarlane

[42] See, eg A Gray, *Vicarious Liability: Critique and Reform* (Oxford, Hart Publishing, 2018) chs 5–8 (rejecting all justifications and proposing a recasting and narrowing of the principle); N McBride and R Bagshaw, *Tort Law*, 6th edn (Harlow, Pearson Education, 2018) 852–56 (concluding that 'vicarious liability is a bit of a mystery … the existence of which has no rational justification') and C Beuermann, *Strict Liability for the Tort of Another* (Oxford, Hart Publishing, 2019).

[43] Smith (n 4) at 230 treats vicarious liability as a response to an 'injustice', which he suggests 'is used to identify undesirable consequences of behaviours' rather than a wrong which 'is used to identify undesirable behaviour'.

[44] See, eg, Holmes (n 20) 15–18; Ibbetson (n 20) 69–70.

[45] W Swain, 'A Historical Examination of Vicarious Liability: "A Veritable Upas Tree"' (2019) 78 *CLJ* 640, 659 has observed that 'Despite the struggle to find a coherent justification, vicarious liability has proved to be remarkably resilient'.

[46] See the related suggestion of HJ Laski, 'The Basis of Vicarious Liability' (1916) 26 *Yale Law Journal* 105, 121 that 'the promotion of social solidarity' may provide the underlying justification. Laski's contribution is discussed by Swain (n 45) 649.

[47] cf Smith (n 4) 268: 'If you have engaged someone to work on your behalf, it is fair to attribute their actions to you when they are engaged in that work. It follows that, if the employee's actions are tortious, the liability for the tort is fairly attributed to the employer'.

[48] As Smith observes, ibid 267, 'responsibility for bad outcomes is not limited to cases where those outcomes are a consequence of bad behaviour'.

has argued, it gives rise to a primary liability.[49] The principle operates, relevantly, where one person (the inducing party) leads another (the relying party) to adopt an assumption as to the existing legal rights of the relying party or the future conduct of the inducing party, and the relying party acts on the assumption in such a way that the relying party will suffer detriment if the inducing party behaves inconsistently with that assumption.[50] The scope of the principle is a matter of some uncertainty – and differs between jurisdictions – but it is uncontroversial in proprietary estoppel cases involving reliance on an assumption that the inducing party will, at some point in the future, grant or transfer an interest in land to the relying party.[51]

If this form of equitable estoppel does create a primary duty, it is best characterised as a duty not to cause harm through inconsistent conduct.[52] There are two potential difficulties with the idea that there could be such a duty (and correlative right), the first apparent and the second real. The apparent problem is that there is never a point at which the relying party can be understood to have an entitlement that the inducing party act in any particular way. The inducing party's freedom of action might be constrained, but he or she always has multiple options. When an assumption of the relevant kind has been induced, the inducing party may resile from it, adhere to it or issue a warning that it should not be acted upon. Even after the relying party has changed his or her position, the inducing party is not necessarily under an obligation to adhere to the assumption or fulfil the expectation. The inducing party may be able to give notice to the relying party which allows the relying party to resume his or her position, may be able to take other steps to ensure that the relying party suffers no detriment, and if sued may only be required to compensate the relying party for harm suffered as a result of reliance on the assumption.

[49] B McFarlane, 'Understanding Equitable Estoppel: From Metaphors to Better Laws' (2013) 66 *Current Legal Problems* 267, 293–94 and B McFarlane, 'Equitable Estoppel as a Cause of Action: Neither One Thing Nor One Other' in S Degeling, J Edelman and J Goudkamp (eds), *Contract in Commercial Law* (Sydney, Lawbook Co, 2016) 359, 376–77. Smith (n 4) 270–71 also takes the view that equitable estoppel is a response to injustice rather than a wrong.

[50] For a fuller statement of the principle and discussion of its scope of application, see A Robertson, 'The Form and Substance of Equitable Estoppel' in A Robertson and J Goudkamp (eds), *Form and Substance in the Law of Obligations* (Oxford, Hart Publishing, 2019) 249. cf McFarlane, 'Understanding Equitable Estoppel' (n 49) and 'Equitable Estoppel as a Cause of Action' (n 40).

[51] See, eg, *Thorner v Major* [2009] UKHL 18; [2009] 1 WLR 776; *Giumelli v Giumelli* [1999] HCA 10, (1999) 196 CLR 101; *Sidhu v Van Dyke* [2014] HCA 19; (2014) 251 CLR 505.

[52] cf M Spence, *Protecting Reliance: The Emergent Doctrine of Equitable Estoppel* (Oxford, Hart Publishing, 1999) 2 (arguing that equitable estoppel creates a primary 'duty to ensure the reliability of induced assumptions') and YK Liew, *Rationalising Constructive Trusts* (Oxford, Hart Publishing, 2017) ch 7 (offering a defence of Spence's view against McFarlane's primary-liability conception). KFK Low, 'Nonfeasance in Equity' (2012) 128 *Law Quarterly Review* 63, has asserted that a concern to prevent the prevention of harm resulting from inconsistent conduct is not a distinctive concern of the principles of estoppel by conduct because the law of contract may also be described as being concerned to prevent harm resulting from inconsistent conduct. That is incorrect. The harm with which the law of contract is concerned is that which results from the non-fulfilment of bargained-for promises. Harm is only caused by inconsistent conduct if action is taken in reliance on the position initially adopted. Reliance is not, of course, required for contractual liability.

Although a 'right' in the Hohfeldian sense is sometimes described in the form of a legal entitlement that another person act or refrain from acting in any particular way,[53] a right need not take that form, and routinely consists of an entitlement to a '*state of affairs* … that is specified in the imposition of a duty on someone else'.[54] Contractual duties, for example, often take the form of an obligation to bring about a particular state of affairs which could be achieved in a number of different ways. The duty created by the law of negligence is a duty *not* to bring about a particular state of affairs in a particular way, namely a duty 'not to harm others as a result of acting negligently towards them'.[55] A non-delegable duty requires the duty-holder to procure a particular state of affairs: namely that care is taken in the discharge of certain responsibilities or at least that no injury is caused through a want of care by those who discharge those responsibilities.[56] Returning to equitable estoppel, one could, therefore, in theory owe a duty not to cause harm through inconsistent conduct.

The real problem with such a duty, however, is that it is not one that the supposed duty-holder is generally capable of fulfilling. Stephen Smith has made a powerful argument that a wrongdoer must be understood to be under a liability to pay compensatory damages, rather than a secondary duty to do so, because, inter alia, a duty to pay damages would be 'an unknowable duty'.[57] The existence of a duty to pay damages may be doubted because 'it would normally be impossible for wrongdoers to satisfy such a duty (or at least impossible for them to know that they had satisfied it) because the duty's content could not be determined prior to a judicial decision'.[58] A wrongdoer may be unaware that they have committed a wrong and will usually be unaware of the victim's losses, the victim may have a choice of remedies, and courts exercise considerable discretion in the determination of some categories of damages such as for pain and suffering.[59] Smith has made a similar argument for the notion that there is no duty to make restitution for unjust enrichment, but only a liability, because it would be impossible for the

[53] Hohfeld (n 2) 30–32; G Williams, 'The Concept of Legal Liberty' (1956) 56 *Columbia Law Review* 1129, 1145 ('every right in the strict sense relates to the conduct of another'); MH Kramer, 'Rights without Trimmings' in MH Kramer, NE Simmons and H Steiner (eds), *A Debate about Rights: Philosophical Enquiries* (New York, Oxford University Press, 1998) 7, 13–14; Smith (n 38) 233.

[54] Kramer (n 53) 32 (emphasis added).

[55] S Perry, 'The Role of Duty of Care in a Rights-Based Theory of Negligence Law' in A Robertson and HW Tang (eds), *The Goals of Private Law* (Oxford, Hart Publishing, 2009) 79, 101 (although Perry was describing a moral duty, it is also an accurate characterisation of the legal duty).

[56] See, eg, *Woodland v Swimming Teachers Association* [2013] UKSC 66; [2014] AC 537 [5] and [7], where Lord Sumption JSC, with whom Lord Clarke, Lord Wilson and Lord Toulson JJSC agreed, characterised a non-delegable duty as a duty to procure the careful 'performance of work delegated to others' and noted that the defendant bears 'legal responsibility *for the proper performance of a duty* which is in law his own' (emphasis added). See also *D&F Estates Ltd v Church Commissioners for England* [1989] 1 AC 177, 208.

[57] Smith (n 4) 197 and also, more tentatively, SA Smith, 'Duties, Liabilities, and Damages' (2012) 125 *Harvard Law Review* 1727, 1743–44.

[58] Smith (n 57) 1743.

[59] Smith (n 4) 197–99.

enriched party to know whether such a duty has arisen or its extent.[60] Whether a payment was made under a mistake, for example, depends on facts known only to the payer.[61]

Ben McFarlane has pointed out that Smith's argument extends to equitable estoppel and that a party against whom an equitable estoppel can be asserted is best understood to be subject to a liability rather than under a duty.[62] The inducing party cannot be under a duty not to cause harm through inconsistent conduct because what that requires of the inducing party depends on: (a) the action taken by the relying party, (b) the likely effect on the relying party of that action if the assumption is not adhered to, and (c) what steps would be required to allow the relying party to resume his or her position.[63] These are all matters concerning the position of the relying party, and the inducing party may have little or no knowledge of them.[64] An authoritative determination of those facts is needed before it can be said what is necessary to prevent harm resulting from reliance on the assumption, and therefore before it can be said what is required of the inducing party. If the inducing party cannot know what good conscience requires in the circumstances, then it cannot be said that the inducing party is under a duty at this stage either to act in any particular way or to bring about a particular state of affairs.[65]

Sandy Steel and Robert Stevens have argued, against Smith, that the common law does recognise a secondary duty to pay compensatory damages for wrongdoing.[66] They argue that unknowability is not a bar to recognition of a legal duty: 'ought' does not necessarily imply 'can' and '[t]here are good reasons to doubt that private law insists upon a stringent version of the ought-implies-can principle'.[67] In the common law, 'obligations that can be breached without fault' are commonplace.[68] Steel and Stevens suggest that obligations that can only be performed with the cooperation of another are also commonplace: an obligation to pay a liquidated sum also 'requires the cooperation of the obligee'.[69] Even if one accepts for the

[60] ibid 243–49.

[61] ibid 244.

[62] McFarlane 'Understanding Equitable Estoppel' (n 49) 294.

[63] As B McFarlane, 'Proprietary Estoppel: The Importance of Looking Back' in P Davies and J Pila (eds), *The Jurisprudence of Lord Hoffmann* (Oxford, Hart Publishing, 2015) 331, 345 has pointed out, it may also be necessary to consider whether any countervailing benefits have been received by the relying party.

[64] cf McFarlane, 'Understanding Equitable Estoppel' (n 49) 294.

[65] Smith (n 4) 243–245; Smith (n 57) 1743–44. cf Liew (n 52) (arguing that a duty need not be '*immediately ascertainable* and *immediately dischargeable*' and drawing a false analogy with a trustee's duty to invest or to distribute assets among a large class of discretionary beneficiaries, neither of which require an authoritative determination of matters that may be unknowable to the trustee before he or she can discharge his or her duty).

[66] S Steel and R Stevens, 'The Secondary Legal Duty to Pay Damages' (2020) 136 *LQR* 283. See also, J Gardner, 'Damages without Duty' (2019) 16 *University of Toronto Law Journal* 412.

[67] Steel and Stevens (n 66) 285.

[68] ibid.

[69] ibid 286.

sake of argument that there are legal duties that can only be performed with the cooperation of the obligee – and which are not conditional on such cooperation – there is a fundamental difference between a duty that requires cooperation for its performance and a duty the very content of which is dependent on facts that are either unknowable or are entirely within the hands of another party. However common it is in practice to compromise damages claims without adjudication, our understanding of the law must recognise an obligor's entitlement to have those facts authoritatively determined.

When it is argued that in routine situations parties are under legal duties to do things they cannot do, and are subject to legal obligations with unknowable content, one might begin to wonder whether the idea of a private law 'right' is a meaningless fiction, and whether we should, as Holmes suggested, concern ourselves only with 'what the courts will do in fact'.[70] The idea of a private law right does, however, have meaning to the extent that it informs other legal rules. The right to performance of a contractual promise is meaningful and does valuable work in the law to the extent that it informs the law on interference with contractual relations, and to the extent that it determines what constitutes illegitimate pressure for the purpose of duress and what constitutes detriment for the purpose of the consideration requirement and reliance-based estoppels.[71] Whether equitable estoppel should be understood to create primary duties or primary liabilities might well, however, be considered to be much less important than the question of whether and how it can be justified.

Justifying equitable estoppel is not a straightforward exercise due to uncertainty as to its core features, such as whether a promise is required.[72] The justification of equitable estoppel is, however, a particularly interesting question because there is such a longstanding division of opinion as to whether the law should impose such liability even with the most stringent requirements. The notion of liability arising from reliance by one party on an assumption as to the future conduct of another has a long and chequered history in English law.[73] The principle seems to lie at the outer limits of what people are entitled to expect from one another. A possible justification, which assumes that a promise is not required, is that a person (the inducing party) who induces an assumption in another person (the relying party) as to the future conduct of the inducing party creates the risk of a certain kind of harm, namely harm resulting from a change of position by the relying party which proves detrimental if the inducing party

[70] Holmes (n 6) 461.

[71] See above, text accompanying nn 6–14.

[72] Compare B McFarlane, *The Law of Proprietary Estoppel* (Oxford, Oxford University Press, 2014) 47–65 and B McFarlane and P Sales, 'Promises, Detriment and Proprietary Estoppel' (2015) 131 *LQR* 610, 612–15 (arguing that a promise is required) with Robertson (n 50) 264–71 (arguing that a promise is not required).

[73] See A Robertson, 'Revolutions and Counterrevolutions in Equitable Estoppel' in S Worthington, A Robertson and G Virgo (eds), *Revolution and Evolution in Private Law* (Oxford, Hart Publishing, 2018) 161.

does not fulfil the assumption.[74] If the inducing party should reasonably have expected the change of position then that party bears a significant measure of responsibility for the harm because of the role they played in inducing it, and because of the control they had or have over the risk of harm. That measure of responsibility justifies a liability on the inducing party to do what is necessary to prevent the harm, either: (a) by giving sufficient notice to the relying party to enable the relying party to resume his or her original position, (b) by behaving consistently, or (c) by compensating the relying party for the resulting detriment.

What both justifies such liability and calls it into question is the extent to which the inducing party controls the risk of harm, and the degree of trust that the relying party therefore places in the inducing party. The degree of trust placed by the relying party in the inducing party may be seen as a reason to impose liability on the party whose conduct – in inducing the assumption – created the risk of harm. But that degree of trust can also, under an ethos more heavily weighted towards individual responsibility, be seen as a reason to blame the relying party for his or her fate. In placing such trust in the inducing party, the relying party may 'be deemed morally unworthy of recompense due to their foolishness'.[75]

II. Duties

Having helpfully highlighted and foregrounded a liability-focused understanding of private law in *The Common Law*, Oliver Wendell Holmes took his thinking about the importance of liabilities one step further in his lecture 'The Path of the Law'.[76] In that lecture, Holmes applied some sceptical pressure to the idea of a legal duty, with a particular determination to dispel confusion between legal and moral ideas. The problem with 'the notion of a legal duty', Holmes suggested, is that we 'fill the word with all of the content which we draw from morals'.[77] Holmes famously suggested that, 'to a bad man', to be subject to a legal duty means little more that 'a prophecy that if he does certain things he will be subjected to disagreeable consequences by way of imprisonment or compulsory payment of money'.[78] If the idea of a legal duty were merely a prediction that certain consequences will result from specified behaviour, then there would be no point considering justification in private law from the point of view of legal duties. The duty perspective would simply be an indirect and potentially confusing version of the liability perspective.

[74] See Robertson, ibid 161–62 and Robertson (n 50) 253–54.

[75] MB Metzger and MJ Phillips, 'The Emergence of Promissory Estoppel as an Independent Theory of Recovery' (1983) 35 *Rutgers Law Review* 472, 502: 'Perhaps … there was an ethical dimension to classical contract law's suppression of reliance-based claims. In a time when individualism tended to assume "rugged" forms, promisees who relied without the protection of an enforceable bargain might have been deemed morally unworthy of recompense due to their foolishness'.

[76] Holmes (n 6) 461–62.

[77] ibid 461.

[78] ibid.

Goldberg and Zipursky have criticised Holmes for 'collapsing the idea of legal duty into the idea of threat of sanction'.[79] They argue, following HLA Hart, that to say that someone is subject to a legal duty to do something is not to say that the person will be subject to a legal sanction if the thing is not done, but rather it is to say that a valid legal rule directs the person to do the thing.[80] Whether the law imposes a duty can be understood independently of the question whether a sanction or liability will follow from a failure to comply. The existence of a legal duty is an interpretive question which depends on how lawyers, officials and citizens talk and act, and on whether they routinely use the rules as guides to conduct and as the basis of claims, demands, admissions and criticism.[81] Goldberg and Zipursky argue that the language, concepts and practice of tort law suggest strongly that it is 'a law of genuine duties rather than pseudo-duties'.[82]

Hart concluded his discussion of the idea of obligation in *The Concept of Law* by stressing that there is likely always to be tension between the perspective of those who accept rules and see their own and others' behaviour in light of them, and those who are concerned only with the consequences of non-compliance. Hart emphasised the importance of keeping in mind both of these points of view and not adopting a theory that defines one of them out of existence.[83] Goldberg and Zipursky, however, set up a stark choice between duty-based and liability-based understandings of the law of tort, arguing that: 'Tort law is better understood and explained as a law of guidance rules than a scheme of liability rules'.[84] The idea of a choice between a guidance-rules view and a liability-rules view of the law of torts, and the law of obligations more broadly, raises important issues. In the first place, it is difficult to see why a choice needs to be made, and why private law cannot be both. It would seem that both are required to provide a full understanding of private law, and that both need to be considered when considering questions of justification. Second, to see the law of torts or the law of obligations as *only* or even *primarily* a set of guidance rules would be a serious distortion. It is essential to take account of the rights and liability perspectives in order to understand private law duties.

It is helpful to view private law from the perspective of duties because private law does – albeit mostly indirectly – tell people how to behave, people do act on the basis of those directives for reasons that are unrelated to the sanctions attached to them, and this undoubtedly yields social benefits.[85] If we want to consider behaviour-guidance in the justification of obligations, then it is necessary to frame the analysis in terms of duties rather than legal sanctions and liability

[79] Goldberg and Zipursky (n 1) 1566.
[80] ibid 1574.
[81] ibid 1575; HLA Hart, *The Concept of Law*, 3rd edn (Oxford, Oxford University Press, 2012) 90.
[82] Goldberg and Zipursky (n 1) 1575.
[83] Hart (n 81) 91.
[84] Goldberg and Zipursky (n 1) 1577.
[85] SA Smith, 'The Normativity of Private Law' (2011) 31 *OJLS* 215.

consequences, and also to frame the analysis in terms of duties rather than rights. Not only is it the duty-bearer whose conduct is guided, but it is the language of duties that is used to express guidance as to how people should behave: how the pursuit of self-interest is restricted, and how and when it must be sacrificed in the interests of others.[86] A focus on duties tells us what we owe others, a focus on rights tells us what we can demand from others, and a focus on liability reminds us of the role of the state and the context in which rights, duties and liabilities are identified, explicated, developed and enforced.

Where primary rights and duties are involved, the guidance provided by the law is best understood from the perspective of legal duties. It is noteworthy, though, that behaviour guidance is not only provided in the context of right/duty relationships, but also through the case law relating to primary liabilities. Some of the most detailed behaviour guidance provided in the obligations case law in recent decades has concerned the steps a bank should take when put on notice of the risk that a guarantee has been procured through undue influence or other conduct on the part of the borrower that would render the guarantee voidable. The steps described in detail by Lord Nicholls in *Royal Bank of Scotland v Etridge (No 2)*[87] are not required to discharge any legal duty a bank owes to a guarantor, but are necessary for a bank to avoid exposing itself to a primary liability which is correlative to the guarantor's power to rescind the transaction. Lord Nicholls described the prescribed course of action as the steps that a bank '*must* take if it is to avoid having constructive notice of the [surety's] rights'.[88] Lord Nicholls also provided detailed guidance to a solicitor advising a guarantor as to the advice that a solicitor retained to advise a guarantor 'can be expected to provide' and other steps the solicitor 'should' take to discharge his or her duty to the guarantor.[89] Lord Nicholls noted that the precise content of a solicitor's duty would depend on the circumstances of the transaction, but thought it was necessary to educate solicitors in order to improve standards:

> As already noted, the advice which a solicitor can be expected to give must depend on the particular facts of the case. But I have set out this 'core minimum' in some detail, because the quality of the legal advice is the most disturbing feature of some of the present appeals. The perfunctory nature of the advice may well be largely due to a failure by some solicitors to understand what is required in these cases.[90]

Royal Bank of Scotland v Etridge provides a particularly clear example of the way in which even an uncodified law of obligations can be directed towards guiding behaviour. Even if we accept that behaviour guidance is important, however, that does not mean that the law of obligations can be understood as a 'law of guidance

[86] Hart (n 81) 87.
[87] *Royal Bank of Scotland v Etridge (No 2)* [2001] UKHL 44; [2002] 2 AC 773.
[88] ibid [70] (emphasis added).
[89] ibid [64]–[74].
[90] ibid [68].

rules'. The problem with Goldberg and Zipursky's claim that 'tort law is better understood and explained as a law of guidance rules than a scheme of liability rules'[91] is that, while tort law is not best understood simply as a scheme of liability rules, nor can it adequately be understood as a scheme of guidance rules. Goldberg and Zipursky's own work has made this abundantly clear, and their conclusion that tort law 'is a law of genuine duties of conduct'[92] better reflects their argument and their broader contribution to the private law literature. It is in the nature of private law duties that they are not simply or even primarily legal directives or guides to behaviour.[93] Their defining features are: that they are relational, that they are owed to others, and that they are correlative to rights held by those others.[94] The person to whom a private law duty is owed controls the duty, not only through a capacity to choose whether to sue, but also through a power to consent to non-performance or release the obligor from the duty.[95] This can be seen most obviously in the contractual context.[96] To the extent that the law directs contracting parties to perform, it is a qualified directive which can only be understood in light of the obligee's correlative right and consequent powers with respect to it. The directive is conditional upon the possibility of an accommodation being reached with the person to whom the contractual duty is owed, and some concession being granted by that rights holder. This is obviously true as a matter of law, but would also seem to accord with the way in which business people view contractual obligations: as fundamentally relational and contingent.[97]

To the extent that Holmes is right that '[t]he business of the law of torts is to fix the dividing lines between those cases in which a man is liable for harm which he has done, and those in which he is not',[98] this begs the question as to how the dividing lines are determined and why they fall where they do. For the reasons discussed in the first part of this chapter, the law of obligations *can* be seen as a system of liability rules. As Goldberg and Zipursky make clear, however, the danger of viewing the law of torts exclusively through the lens of liabilities is that that can make it seem that the law of torts 'is about *allocating losses*' rather than 'an

[91] Goldberg and Zipursky (n 1) 1577.

[92] ibid 1591.

[93] This was recognised by Hart (n 81) 87–88, who observed that the chain of obligation is sometimes entrusted 'to a private individual who may choose whether or not to insist on performance or its equivalent in value to him. [This] situation typifies the duties or obligations of … the civil law where we think of private individuals having rights correlative to the obligations'.

[94] Goldberg and Zipursky have done more anyone to illuminate these aspects of private law; see, eg Goldberg and Zipursky (n 1) 1580–81 (on the idea that private law empowers rights holders, who control the right to sue) and 1583 (on the relationality of private law duties).

[95] R Stevens, 'Private Law and the Form of Reasons' in A Robertson and J Goudkamp (eds), *Form and Substance in the Law of Obligations* (Oxford, Hart Publishing, 2019) 249.

[96] There are of course many non-contractual relationships – including those giving rise to routine negligence claims – in which it is not practical for an obligee to release the obligor or consent to non-performance.

[97] See eg, S Macaulay, 'Non-Contractual Relations in Business: A Preliminary Study' (1963) 28 *American Sociological Review* 55.

[98] Holmes (n 20) 79.

injurer being held to account for having breached *an obligation to conduct herself in certain ways toward the victim*'.[99] The perspectives of duties and rights and wrongs provide essential corrections to the misleading abstraction of the notion that torts is a system of loss allocation, which allows it to be seen, wrongly, as a 'regulatory scheme for deterring and compensating'.[100] The rights perspective reminds us that the guidance rules provided by the law of obligations are guidance rules of a particular kind: they are rules about how to behave towards and in relation to others. For that reason, even if the law of obligations is best understood to be justified by community welfare goals such as maintaining social harmony, guiding behaviour and preventing and resolving disputes, it is primarily shaped by – or at least kept consistent with – what are understood to be widely accepted ideas as to what we owe each other.

III. Conclusion

The justification of liability provides a good starting point for the consideration of justification in private law because private law is driven by questions of liability. As explicated by judges, the law of obligations primarily takes the form of a set of justifications for liability. To focus exclusively on liability, however, raises the potential for serious misunderstanding. Analysis of the role of duties provides a useful corrective by reminding us of the central role of duties in setting the dividing lines in cases of liability for wrongs. The duty framework itself requires correction to the extent that it can be seen to present private law as a set of guidance rules. Duties cannot be considered in isolation from rights or liability. We can then see that a full understanding of the nature of private law, and a solid platform for consideration of its justification, can only come from an integrated analysis of liability, rights and duties.

[99] Goldberg and Zipursky (n 1) 1563 (emphasis added).
[100] ibid 1576.

11

Equity and the Justification of Private Rights

BEN McFARLANE*

I. Overview

Attempts to justify private rights are, it may seem, complicated by the enduring importance of rules and principles based on those originally developed in courts of Chancery. First, the very existence of distinct equitable rules multiplies the number of entities in need of justification. For example, an attempt to explain the law of assignment will have to account for both common law and equitable rules; an examination of the circumstances in which an agreement can give rise to legal rights will have to refer not only to the law of contract, but also to equitable estoppel.[1] Second, more significantly, the courts' willingness to recognise a distinct set of equitable rules can compromise justifications offered for the common law position. For example, given the possibility of equitable assignment, it may be thought that only weak justifications were available for the common law's general refusal to allow the transfer of choses in action.[2] Similarly, if seeking to defend traditional requirements of contract law, such as the need for consideration, or for an intention to

* I am grateful for comments received from the editors, and at the Justifying Private Rights workshop at UNSW, and also at the Equity Workshop hosted by Notre Dame Law School in 2019 and the 2020 Oxford-Edinburgh Private Law Workshop.

[1] In England, the effect of a clause imposing a consequence on the breach by B of B's contract with A may have to be considered under both the common law rule against penalties, and the equitable doctrine of relief against forfeiture; in Australia, further complication may arise if the rule against penalties is regarded as having both a common law and an equitable strand. For discussion, see J McGhee and S Elliott (eds), *Snell's Equity*, 34th edn (London, Sweet and Maxwell, 2019) ch 13 and NA Tiverios, *Contractual Penalties in Australia and the United Kingdom: History, Theory and Practice* (Sydney, Federation Press, 2019) ch 8.

[2] See, eg: E Peel, *Treitel on the Law of Contract*, 14th edn (London, Sweet & Maxwell, 2015) 15-002, stating that the common law prohibition derives from 'early lawyers' finding it 'hard to think of a transfer of something intangible like a contractual right' and that later 'the rule was based on the fear that assignment of choses in action might lead to maintenance.' For a more persuasive conceptual justification of the common law's stance, see CH Tham, *Understanding the Law of Assignment* (Cambridge, Cambridge University Press, 2019) ch 3.

make a legally binding agreement, one must account for the ability of equitable estoppel to give rise to a cause of action in circumstances where both those features are absent. Indeed, commentators may point to such equitable claims precisely as a means to challenge the validity of the common law rules.[3] Conversely, it is of course equally possible to rely on the common law rules to dispute the justification, and hence call for reform, of their apparent equitable analogues.[4] Partly as a result of such complications, calls have regularly been made to limit the distinct role of equity in private law and to move towards a unified system.[5]

The purpose of this chapter is to argue that, when it plays its distinctive role of mitigating the effects on a particular party, B, of a private right held by A,[6] equity is crucial not only in justifying the specific right held by A, but also in justifying the very existence of a system of private rights. The chapter makes three points about the distinctive form of equitable intervention, and then two points as to its function.

A. Form

In seeking to justify private rights, we need to be aware of the diverse forms of the different legal relations that fall into the general category of private rights. As clearly demonstrated by Hohfeld,[7] a failure to differentiate such forms severely hampers attempts to understand or justify particular private law claims.

[3] In relation to equitable estoppel, see, eg: PS Atiyah, 'When is an Enforceable Agreement Not A Contract? Answer: When it is an Equity' (1976) 92 *Law Quarterly Review* 174.

[4] A move adopted, for example, by P Birks (in another area where the relationship between common law and equitable rules has caused difficulty) in calling for the equitable knowing receipt claim to conform to the common law personal restitutionary claim by imposing a strict liability subject to defences, see eg: 'Receipt' in P Birks and A Pretto (eds), *Breach of Trust* (Oxford, Hart Publishing, 2002).

[5] See, eg: J Austin, *Lectures on Jurisprudence*, 1st edn (London, J Murray, 1863) i, 38–39: 'the distinction [between common law and equity] is utterly senseless'; Z Chafee, Foreword to ED Reed, *Selected Essays on Equity* (New York, Oceana Publications, 1955) iii, iv: it would be 'absurd' to continue with a distinction 'put up by historical accident in 14th century England'.

[6] It is not argued that each and every part of modern equity has the characteristics emphasised here: first, this chapter focusses on rights rather than remedies, and does not seek to explain eg the availability of specific performance; secondly, some equitable doctrines have developed beyond their traditional confines and now seem to impose primary duties on A to B that are not related to any specific right of A (the extension of breach of confidence to deal with invasions of privacy provides an example: for discussion of the role of equity in expanding the boundaries of tort law, see J Goldberg and H Smith, 'Wrongful Fusion: Equity and Tort' in PG Turner et al (eds), *Equity and Law: Fusion and Fission* (Cambridge, Cambridge University Press, 2019) 309, esp at 327–28). Nor is it argued here that the characteristics emphasised here are never present at common law. The argument is rather that the characteristics are much more significant when considering equitable doctrines and it may indeed be the case that the characteristics are seen together only in relation to equitable doctrines (so for example waiver is a common law example of a rule which has the function of regulating A's assertion of a right against B, but its effect is simply that A's right ceases to exist, and so (unlike e.g promissory estoppel as applied in a case such as *Hughes v Metropolitan Rwy Co* (1877) 2 App Cas 439 or *Legione v Hateley* (1983) 152 CLR 406) it does not have the characteristically equitable form of controlling A's exercise of an existing right.

[7] WN Hohfeld, 'Some Fundamental Legal Conceptions as Applied in Judicial Reasoning' (1913) 23 *Yale Law Journal* 16, (1917) 26 *Yale Law Journal* 710.

Three points as to the form of equitable intervention are crucial to the analysis in this chapter. The first, echoing points made by, for example, Stephen Smith[8] and Andrew Robertson,[9] is that not all private law claims consist of the enforcement of a pre-existing duty, or of a response to a breach of such a duty. For example, where equitable estoppel operates as a cause of action in B's favour, a court does not respond to a pre-existing duty of A to B, arising as soon as A makes a promise to B; it rather recognises a primary liability of A to B.[10] This reveals that, even if it is based on a promise made by A to B, the liability arising where equitable estoppel operates as a cause of action is quite different from that arising where A and B make a contract. This point will be examined in Section II.A.

Of course, the need to pay attention to the specific form of legal relations is a general one, and arises even when considering only common law doctrines.[11] This first point, however, links to a second, wider point specific to the examination of equity, which will be discussed in Section II.B. It is that, when considering an equitable doctrine, one may be misled, for example by its name or its function, into assuming that it operates in the same way, and involves the same legal relations, as its common law 'equivalent'. So, whilst equitable estoppel may, and often does, have the effect, or function, of enforcing an agreement between A and B, that does not mean that it should be regarded either as part of, or as an illegitimate threat to, the law of contract. Recognising the distinct nature of the legal relations arising from an equitable estoppel claim, as opposed to a contractual claim, preserves space for distinct justifications for those two different means of acquiring a private right: simply put, different types of private right (one correlating to a liability of A arising in equitable estoppel, another correlating to a duty of A arising a result of a contract) may require different types of justification. Similarly, terms such as 'equitable assignment', or 'equitable property', should not prevent a careful examination of the legal relations involved in such cases, which may show, for example, that an equitable assignment in fact differs in significant ways from a simple transfer of a right,[12] and that a beneficiary's interest under a trust may have a quite different impact on third parties than a legal property right.[13]

[8] See, eg: SA Smith, 'Duties, Liabilities, and Damages' (2012) 125 *Harvard Law Review* 1727; SA Smith, 'The Restatement of Liabilities in Restitution' in C Mitchell and W Swadling (eds), *The Restatement Third: Restitution and Unjust Enrichment* (Oxford, Hart Publishing, 2013).

[9] A Robertson, 'Justifying Liability', ch 10 in this volume.

[10] See Robertson, ibid; B McFarlane, *The Law of Proprietary Estoppel*, 2nd edn (Oxford, Oxford University Press, 2020); B McFarlane, 'Equitable Estoppel as a Cause of Action: Neither One Thing nor One Other' in S Degeling et al (eds), *Contract in Commercial Law* (Sydney, Thomson/Law Book, 2016).

[11] See, eg: the discussion below of *Glencore International AG v Commissioner of Taxation* [2019] HCA 26.

[12] As shown most clearly in the comprehensive treatment of the topic by Tham (n 2); as noted by eg B McFarlane, *The Structure of Property Law* (Oxford, Hart Publishing, 2008) 212–14; B McFarlane and R Stevens, 'The Nature of Equitable Property' (2010) 4 *Journal of Equity* 1, 6–8; J Edelman and S Elliot, 'Two Conceptions of Equitable Assignment' (2015) 131 *Law Quarterly Review* 228.

[13] See, eg the discussion in Sections II.B and II.C below of *Akers v Samba Financial Group* [2017] UKSC 6, [2017] AC 424.

The third point as to the form of equitable intervention is related to this second point and is also exemplified by an examination of equitable assignment and of equitable interests, as will be seen in Section II.C. It is that, in many cases, equitable doctrines have a distinctive formal feature: they give B a right which relates, in some sense, to a right of A.[14] So, for example, where B's equitable right is a claim-right against A, and so correlates to a duty owed by A to B, the content of that duty may relate to a specific right held by A.[15] This is the case, it can be argued, where A makes an equitable assignment in favour of B, and also where A holds on trust for B.[16] In such a case, the fact that A's duty relates to a specific right held by A means that B's correlative equitable right operates differently from each of: (i) a right arising where A's duty is simply to act in a particular way unrelated to any specific right of A (as where A is under a duty to pay B £100); and (ii) a right arising where A's duty relates to a specific physical resource owned by B (as where A is under a duty to B not deliberately or carelessly to damage or otherwise physically interfere with B's bicycle). Where A's duty thus relates to a specific claim-right or power held by A,[17] it can be said that B thus has more than a purely personal right against A, but instead has an 'equitable property right'.

The same general model can apply even where B's right is not a claim-right. Where, for example, B has an equitable power to set aside a contract entered into as a result of A's innocent misrepresentation, B's power again relates to specific rights of A: the rights acquired by A under the contract, which B has a power to avoid. Unless and until the contract is thus set aside, A is not under an equitable duty to B, and so it cannot be said that B's right operates in quite the same way as a standard equitable property right;[18] but, as B's power does again relate to specific rights held by A, it is clear that B has more than a purely personal right against A.[19]

[14] See, eg: L Smith, 'Unravelling Proprietary Restitution' (2004) 40 *Canadian Business law Journal* 317; R Chambers, *An Introduction to Property Law in Australia*, 4th edn (Sydney, Thompson Reuters, 2018) 3.90; McFarlane (n 12); McFarlane and Stevens (n 12); J Edelman, 'Two Fundamental Questions for the Law of Trusts' (2013) 129 *Law Quarterly Review* 66; B McFarlane, 'Form and Substance in Equity' in A Robertson and J Goudkamp (eds), *Form and Substance in the Law of Obligations* (Oxford, Hart Publishing, 2019); B McFarlane and R Stevens, 'What's Special About Equity? Rights About Rights' in D Klimchuk et al (eds), *Philosophical Foundations of the Law of Equity* (Oxford, Oxford University Press, 2020).

[15] It is not claimed here that *all* equitable doctrines give B a right that relates to a right of A: an equitable estoppel, for example, may result in A's simply being ordered by a court to pay a sum of money to B (see eg *Jennings v Rice* [2002] EWCA Civ 159, [2003] 1 P &C R 8) in which case A's liability does not relate to any specific right of A.

[16] See, eg: McFarlane and Stevens (n 12).

[17] See, eg: ibid at 12–15. See text at n 80 below.

[18] See, eg: *Phillips v Phillips* (1861) 4 De G F&J 208; *Latec Investments Ltd v Hotel Terrigal Pty Ltd* (1965) 113 CLR 265; *Mortgage Express Ltd v Lambert* [2017] Ch 93. For a detailed analysis, see A Reilly, 'Is the "Mere Equity" to Rescind a Legal Power? Unpacking Hohfeld's Concept of "Volitional Control"' (2019) 39 *Oxford Journal of Legal Studies* 779.

[19] See, eg: McFarlane, (n 12) 224–27.

B. Function

The argument to be made here as to the function of equitable intervention is linked to the arguments as to its form, as it also depends on the distinct character of equity as a supplement to, or gloss on, the primary rules established by common law.[20] It can be argued that the key contribution of equity is to modify, and mitigate, the effects on B of the primary, (usually) common law rules which initially determine the parties' legal relations.[21] This has an impact on the form of equitable intervention: equity can often modify the effect of those primary rules without formally denying or contradicting the legal relations they involve. For example, where A is found to have made an equitable assignment to B of A's contractual right against X, equity does not contradict the common law position that A retains that right; it rather finds that A is now under a duty to B in relation to that right of A.[22] Similarly, where equity gives relief against forfeiture, it does not deny that A has a valid contractual right against B; it may rather prevent A's enforcing that right in such a way as to allow A to acquire a benefit, or to impose a burden on B, which goes beyond the purpose of that right as a form of security.[23] It can also be seen where B's claim does not specifically relate to a right of A. So, for example, an equitable estoppel claim (which may result in A's

[20] For accounts of the supplementary nature of equity, see, eg: FW Maitland, *Lectures in Equity* (Cambridge, Cambridge University Press, 1929); PB Miller, 'Equity as Supplemental Law' in D Klimchuk et al (eds), *Philosophical Foundations of the Law of Equity* (Oxford, Oxford University Press, 2020).

[21] See McFarlane and Stevens, (n 14). H Smith, 'Fusing the Equitable Function in Private Law' in K Barker et al (eds), *Private Law in the 21st Century* (Oxford, Hart Publishing, 2017) and in 'Equity as Meta-Law' *Yale Law Journal* (forthcoming 2021), identifies equity as characteristically having a more targeted function of dealing with problems of polycentricity, conflicting rights, and opportunism, which are more effectively dealt with in a supplementary system, rather than in a fused single system. The analysis here is largely consistent with that of Smith, although the focus in this chapter is on equity's role in dealing with problems that arise specifically from having a system of private rights: see text at n 79 below.

[22] As noted by Tham (n 2) ch 4, the effect of an equitable assignment is thus similar to (although not the same as) the effect of a declaration of trust: see n 59 below. As noted by Edelman and Elliot (n 12), this traditional model of equitable assignment has been challenged by a more recent model in which an equitable assignment is said to involve a transfer of a right: see, eg: G Tolhurst, *The Assignment of Contractual Rights*, 2nd edn (Oxford, Hart Publishing, 2016) [1.02], [3.04–3.10].

[23] For a recent example, see *Manchester Ship Canal Co Ltd v Vauxhall Motors Ltd* [2019] UKSC 46, [2019] 3 WLR 852. This is also true of the equitable rule against penalties, as applied in Australia: see, eg *Andrews v Australia and New Zealand Banking Group Ltd* (2012) 247 CLR 205; [2012] HCA 30. In contrast, the English rule, now seen as a common law rule following *Cavendish Square Holding BV v Makdessi* [2015] UKSC 67; [2016] AC 1172, does not allow for *pro tanto* enforcement of A's right, but rather finds that A's right is, as a matter of public policy, wholly unenforceable. For discussion, see NA Tiverios and B McFarlane, 'Controlling Private Punishment in Three Dimensions: Penalties and Forfeiture in England and Australia' in E Bant et al (eds), *Punishment and Private Law* (Oxford, Hart Publishing, 2020).

simply being ordered to pay a sum of money to B)[24] does not contradict the point that the parties' informal, non-contractual agreement does not in itself impose an immediate duty of performance on A.

The secondary nature of equity has an impact not only on the justification of the equitable intervention, but also, perhaps more significantly, on the justification of the primary legal relations whose practical effect is modified. For example, the possibility of an equitable assignment lessens the practical impact on A of the common law's general prohibition on transfers of choses in action; the cause of action based on equitable estoppel softens the potentially harsh effects on B of the rules which determine when an agreement is contractually binding. The possibility of relief against forfeiture ensures that, where the parties have agreed to confer a power of termination on A for the specific purpose of securing a particular outcome (eg B's payment of rent), A cannot then undermine the basis on which the power was created by using it for a different purpose (eg to terminate B's right even though B is offering to pay the rent due and to compensate A for any delay in payment). This mitigating function of equity has been noted as a matter of prospective legislative design in England,[25] and can also be observed in hindsight: the rigour of the doctrine of consideration, for example, is easier to justify if there is the possibility, in at least some cases, of a claim for a party who has reasonably relied to his or her detriment on a non-contractual promise.[26]

Equity here can be seen as functioning in both a negative and a positive way. Negatively, equity can also be seen as mitigating some of the risks that inevitably arise not only from particular primary legal doctrines, but more generally from having a system of private rights *at all*.[27] Any such system, founded on correlative legal relations, creates a risk. For example, once we say that, rather than B simply being liable to a sanction for acting in a particular way, B is instead under a duty *to A* not to act in that way, a system of private law places A in a very powerful position, both practically and normatively.[28] Justifying such bilateral relationships may then require mechanisms which deal with the risk of abuse. Equity as

[24] See n 15 above.

[25] When proposing what is now s 2 of the Law of Property (Miscellaneous Provisions) Act 1989, the Law Commission (of England and Wales) expressly noted that, whilst operating to mean a non-complying agreement would not have any contractual effect, the provision would not rule out an equitable estoppel claim: Law Com No 164 (1985) at 5.2.

[26] There is some element of prospectivity to this point in the United States, as shown by the arguments between eg Williston and Corbin in the American Law Institute as to the proper scope of §90 of the Restatement of Contract: S Williston and A Corbin, *Restatement of Contracts*, 1st edn (St Paul, American Law Institute, 1932).

[27] See too, B McFarlane, 'Equity' in A Gold et al (eds), *The Oxford Handbook of the New Private Law* (Oxford, Oxford University Press, forthcoming).

[28] The two are separate because even if A cannot enforce a duty owed by B (for example because of the lapse of a limitation period), A's ability to waive the duty or not may still be significant (e.g an unenforceable duty remains relevant as a potentially justifying basis of an enrichment received by B's mistaken performance of the duty): see R Stevens, 'Defences' in A Gold et al (eds), *The Oxford Handbook of the New Private Law* (Oxford, Oxford University Press, forthcoming).

an institution is clearly not the only means of dealing with such a risk,[29] but equitable doctrines often have the aim of preventing A from acquiring or enforcing a right against B 'where it would be inequitable having regard to the dealings between the parties'.[30]

Positively, as a result of recognising consensually created legal relations that relate to a right of A, equity enhances the autonomy of private parties in a specific way. The benefits to A of having a claim-right or power are thus magnified: for example, the value to A of a chose in action against Z are increased by the possibility of making an equitable assignment of that right in favour of B. Hanoch Dagan, for example, has argued that enhancing the autonomy of parties by providing a diverse range of legal relationships which they may enter is an important function of each of contract law and property law,[31] and the argument made in this chapter is that equity makes a particularly significant contribution to that wider function of private law.

To return to form, it is notable that equity performs both these negative and positive functions whilst still operating within the conventional boundaries of private law. The *in personam* nature of equitable intervention has often been emphasised, and it is certainly true that its effect, like that of the primary legal rules it mitigates, can be described in terms of correlative legal relations. So, where equitable estoppel operates as a cause of action, it is a specific liability of A to B that is recognised, which B can waive or, if necessary, enforce by an application to court. Similarly, when it is said, for example, that A, a trustee or fiduciary, lacks the power to acquire a right in breach of duty to B, what is meant that, *as against B*, A cannot claim the benefit of that right.[32] At the same time, however, in order to perform this function effectively, equitable doctrines cannot simply replicate the structure of the primary rules they seek to affect. If, for example, equitable estoppel, when operating as a cause of action, were merely another means of allowing a promise of A to B to impose an immediate duty on A, then it would simply become part of contract law, rather than existing as a supplement to, or means to mitigate, contract law. If, as is argued here,

[29] eg, a contract is voidable at common law on the grounds of fraud or duress.

[30] See Lord Cairns in *Hughes v Metropolitan Rwy Co* (n 5) 488: '[the] first principle upon which all Courts of Equity proceed [is that] … the person who might otherwise have enforced those rights will not be allowed to enforce them where it would be inequitable having regard to the dealings between the parties'.

[31] See H Dagan and M Heller, *The Choice Theory of Contracts* (Cambridge, Cambridge University Press, 2017) and H Dagan, 'Autonomy and Property' in H Dagan and B Zipursky (eds), *Research Handbook on Private Law Theories* (Cheltenham, Elgar, forthcoming) and *A Liberal Theory of Property* (Cambridge, Cambridge University Press, 2020).

[32] So in *Keech v Sandford* (1726) Sel Cas Ch 61, for example, the trustee clearly did have the power to acquire a lease, and validly exercised that power, thereby gaining the lease, but that lease was then held on trust, as the trustee did not have the power, *as against the beneficiary*, to take the lease for his own benefit free from any duty to the beneficiary. See too, J Hudson, 'One Thicket in Fraud on a Power' (2019) 39 *Oxford Journal of Legal Studies* 577, considering the disability of a trustee, as against a beneficiary, imposed by the fraud on a power doctrine.

equitable estoppel as a cause of action imposes a liability, rather than an immediate duty, then it has a form which is distinct from contract law in a specific way. As shown by Stephen Smith's work,[33] the court has a more active role to play in turning that initial liability of A into a specific duty owed by A to B.[34] A court can, for example, consider the current position of the parties, taking into account circumstances occurring after the parties' initial dealings,[35] and can consider the impact of its rulings on third parties.[36] This fits both with the common understanding of equity as particularly identified with remedial questions,[37] and with the idea that at least some rules of equity reflect the executive and prerogative-based origins of the jurisdiction.[38] It may also help to explain why a doctrine such as equitable estoppel can take account of a practical notion such as detriment (which may not involve any interference with a claim-right of B) whereas tort law, on one view at least, is focussed not on losses as such, but rather on infringements of rights.[39] Even if, therefore, one were to take a narrow view of what may count as a justification for primary claim-rights (and hence of private law duties) it may be that maintaining such a view is plausible only because equitable doctrines can mitigate the potentially harsh practical consequences of having such a narrow set of claim-rights, by supplementing them with a wider set of liabilities.

[33] See, eg: Smith, 'Duties, Liabilities, and Damages' (n 8) and *Rights, Wrongs, and Injustices* (Oxford, Oxford University Press, 2019). Note that Smith's arguments that a breach of duty by A gives rise not to a duty to pay damages but to a liability to be ordered to pay damages have been disputed: see eg: J Gardner, 'Damages Without Duty' (2019) 69 *University Toronto Law Journal* 412; S Steel and R Stevens, 'The Secondary Legal Duty to Pay Damages' (2020) 136 *Law Quarterly Review* 283. Those responses in relation to damages are not however addressed to the point made in this chapter, which is rather that some forms of equitable intervention impose a primary liability on A, rather than any primary duty.

[34] In discussing a party's statutory liability to serve as a juror, for example, Hohfeld (n 7) 53, explains that the 'enactment imposed only a *liability* and not a *duty*. It is a liability to have a duty created. The latter would arise only when, in exercise of their powers, the parties litigant and the court officers, had done what was necessary to impose a specific duty to perform the functions of a juror.' (emphasis in original). Similarly, in the case of a liability arising in equitable estoppel, action by the court, as well as by B, is required to turn A's liability to B (and also to the court) to a duty owed to B (and also to the court).

[35] For recent examples in relation to equitable estoppel, see, eg: *Moore v Moore* [2018] EWCA Civ 2669, and *Habberfield v Habberfield* [2019] EWCA Civ 890.

[36] In relation to equitable estoppel, see, eg: *Giumelli v Giumelli* (1999) 196 CLR 101.

[37] See, eg: S Bray, 'The Supreme Court and the New Equity' (2015) 68 *Vanderbilt Law Review* 997. In a contractual case, for example, the content of A's duty to B is set by the contract, and so matters occurring later, and the position of third parties, are generally relevant to the different question of what remedy to give in response to A's breach of duty. In an equitable estoppel case, in contrast, the content of A's duty itself is not fixed until a court order, as until then A is only under a liability to B: see further McFarlane (n 10) ch 8.

[38] See, eg: L Katz, 'Pathways to Legal Rights: The Function of Equity' in D Klimchuk et al (eds), *Philosophical Foundations of The Law of Equity* (Oxford, Oxford University Press, 2020).

[39] See, eg: R Stevens, *Torts and Rights* (Oxford, Oxford University Press, 2007); EJ Weinrib, *Corrective Justice* (Oxford, Oxford University Press, 2012).

II. The Formal Diversity of Private Rights

A. Beyond Duties

The first step in justifying a private right is to be clear about the particular legal relations constituted by that right. As a result, Hohfeld's seminal work continues to be important. One of its most basic propositions is that, whilst invocations of a right in B necessarily also presuppose a correlative position of A with respect to B, that position of A does not always consist of a duty. In *Glencore International AG v Commissioner of Taxation*,[40] for example, the High Court of Australia considered the claim of B (companies within the global Glencore group) that A, the Commissioner, return documents which formed part of the 'Paradise Papers' taken from a law practice's file management systems. The claim was not based on breach of confidence,[41] but was rather said to arise solely from the fact that the documents, as they had been held by a practice providing legal advice to B, were covered by legal professional privilege. That argument was forcefully rejected by the court, which noted that it rested upon:

> an incorrect premise, namely that legal professional privilege is a legal right which is capable of being enforced, which is to say that it may found a cause of action. The privilege is only an immunity from the exercise of powers which would otherwise compel the disclosure of privileged communications[42] … [B's argument] seeks to transform the nature of the privilege from an immunity to an ill-defined cause of action which may be brought against anyone with respect to documents which may then be in the public domain.[43]

The court thus adopted the consciously Hohfeldian analysis and terminology used by counsel for the Commissioner in resisting B's argument.[44] The essential point, accepted by the court, is that the presence of a right of B does not equate to a duty of A: it may instead mean that some other form of legal relation exists between the parties. Equally however, the fact that B may have a right other than a claim-right, such as a liberty, power or immunity does not *in itself* mean that there cannot simultaneously be some other form of allied legal relation between A and B, which *does* involve A's being under a duty to B. Indeed, the justification of some such duties may lie in the protection they afford to a liberty, power, or immunity

[40] *Glencore International* (n 11).

[41] Such a claim would have been problematic, given that the documents were in the public domain, and the potential public interest in the Commissioner's retaining such documents.

[42] Reference was made here to *Daniels Corporation International Pty Ltd v Australian Competition and Consumer Commission* (2002) 213 CLR 543, 553 where legal professional privilege was described as an 'important common law immunity'.

[43] *Glencore International* (n 11) [9] and [12]–[13].

[44] See counsel's submissions at [17]: '[B's] argument is also flawed as a matter of legal theory. As Hohfeld demonstrated, the word "right" is ambiguous and can be used to describe any one of a number of legal interests and relations and their jural correlatives'.

of B. For example, B's liberty, as against A and (prima facie) all other parties, to make use of B's bicycle is not inconsistent with, and indeed is protected by, the claim-right of B, as against A and (prima facie) all other parties, that correlates to the duty of A and others not deliberately or carelessly to damage or otherwise physically interfere with B's bicycle. Indeed, the practical role of such a claim-right in protecting B's liberty to use may be an important part of its justification: after all, no-one buys a bicycle merely to lock it up. The High Court of Australia in *Glencore*, whilst clearly correct to dismiss B's argument that the presence of an immunity *necessarily* means that A is under a duty to B, may have come close to adopting the equally erroneous position that the presence of an immunity (against A's altering B's legal position in some way) necessarily means that A is *not* under a duty to B (not to act in a particular way).

For present purposes, however, the key point from *Glencore* is its attention to the different forms of legal relations which make up private rights. Such attention is also crucial, it can be argued, in understanding the operation of equitable estoppel as a cause of action and its relationship to the law of contract. Where, for example, proprietary estoppel operates as a means for B to acquire a right as a result of B's reliance on A's promise that B will acquire a right in A's land, it has been said that, like contract law, B's claim depends on a promise but, unlike contract law, the court has a discretion to give effect to B's claim without necessarily protecting B's expectation interest.[45] Such a model plays into the idea – also seen, for example, in relation to equitable interests in property[46] – that equitable doctrines operate as discretionary shadows of their common law equivalents. A different analysis emphasises instead the formal differences between the equitable estoppel claim and a contractual right and, it is submitted, better explains the nature and operation of that claim.

The point can be seen in the influential[47] judgment of Hoffmann LJ, as he then was, in *Walton v Walton*.[48] It was accepted that A's oral promise that B, her son, would inherit her farm was likely to have been subject to 'unspoken and ill-defined qualifications' and that B could not reasonably have understood A to be intending to enter into an immediately binding legal relationship. This barred any contractual claim as a contract 'subject to the narrow doctrine of frustration, must be performed come what may'.[49] Reversing the first instance judge, however,

[45] See, eg: *James v James* [2018] EWHC 43 (Ch), [51]-[52] (HHJ Paul Matthews).

[46] See, eg: *R v Tower Hamlets LBC, ex p von Goetz* [1999] QB 1019, 1023 (Mummery LJ).

[47] It is relied on for example by Lord Walker and Lord Neuberger in *Thorner v Major* [2009] UKHL 18, [2009] 1 WLR 776, at [52]–[57] and at [101] and in *Cowper-Smith v Morgan* [2017] SCC 61, [2017] 2 SCR 754 at [26] and [28] (McLachlin CJ, Abella, Moldaver, Karakatsanis, Wagner, Gascon, and Rowe JJ).

[48] *Walton v Walton* (Unrep, 14 April 1994).

[49] ibid [20], per Hoffmann LJ. Of course, the lack of formalities, as well as the absence of consideration, also prevented a contractual claim.

Hoffmann LJ held that this uncertainty did not prevent a claim based on equitable estoppel as, in contrast to contract law, the principle:

> does not look forward into the future and guess what might happen. It looks backwards from the moment when the promise falls due to be performed and asks whether, in the circumstances which have actually happened, it would be unconscionable for the promise not to be kept.[50]

Contrary to the view of, for example, Atiyah,[51] an equitable estoppel, therefore, is not simply a contract which is made enforceable because detrimental reliance operates as an alternative to consideration. As shown by *Walton v Walton*, the claim can arise even where other requirements of a valid contract, such as the intention to create legal relations, or a sufficiently certain agreement, or formalities, are also absent. Unlike a contract, the equitable estoppel does not give B an immediate claim-right against A. The traditional formulation is that, instead, an 'equity' arises,[52] which gives B the opportunity to go to court to seek a remedy against A: such a remedy will be granted where it would 'shock the conscience of the court'[53] were A free to leave B to suffer a detriment as a result of B's reasonable reliance on A's promise. In deciding if an equity has arisen, and in deciding how best to give effect to it, a court can take into account circumstances as they stand at the date of the trial, even where those circumstances affect only one of the parties and are not part of any bilateral dealings.[54] The discretion given to a court when applying the doctrine can thus be seen not as simply part of its equitable origins, but rather as a response to the particular legal relations involved in B's claim.

These features of an equitable estoppel claim are consistent with its giving effect to a primary liability of A, arising as a result of the prospect of B's suffering detriment as a result of B's reasonable reliance on A, rather than as responding to any actual or threatened breach of duty by A.[55] This means in turn that equitable

[50] ibid [21]. This is not to say that the certainty of a promise is irrelevant to a proprietary estoppel claim. On the contrary, as seems to have been the case in eg *Cobbe v Yeoman's Row Management Ltd* [2008] UKHL 55; [2008] 1 WLR 1752, it may prevent B's showing that B reasonably understood A's promise as seriously intended by A.

[51] Atiyah (n 3). See too analyses of §90 of the Restatement (Second) of Contracts which regard it as solely extending the circumstances in which promises may be binding: see eg Edward Yorio and Steve Thel, 'The Promissory Basis of Section 90' (1991) 101 *Yale Law Journal* 111.

[52] See, eg: Scarman LJ in *Crabb v Arun DC* [1976] Ch 179, 192–93.

[53] Lord Walker in *Cobbe v Yeoman's Row Management Ltd* (n 50) at [92].

[54] See, eg: *Moore v Moore* (n 35); *Habberfield v Habberfield* (n 35) [41] [72]. Note too that Dixon J's seminal discussion of the role of detriment in equitable estoppel in *Grundt v Great Boulder Pty Gold Mines Ltd* (1938) 59 CLR 641, 674–75 makes clear that the doctrine does not respond to a loss already suffered by B, but rather seeks to remove the prospect of detriment: 'the real detriment or harm from which the law seeks to give protection is that which would flow from the change of position if the assumption were deserted that led to it'.

[55] See, eg: McFarlane, *The Law of Proprietary Estoppel* (n 10) and McFarlane, 'Equitable Estoppel as a Cause of Action' (n 10); Andrew Robertson, 'Justifying the Law of Obligations' ch 10 in this volume. For analyses which instead see equitable estoppel as depending on an actual or threatened breach of duty by A, see, eg Michael Spence, *Protecting Reliance: The Emergent Doctrine of Equitable Estoppel* (Oxford, Hart Publishing, 1999); Ying Khai Liew, *Rationalizing Constructive Trusts* (Oxford, Hart Publishing, 2017) ch 7.

estoppel cases provide a very useful example of how such primary liabilities may operate in practice. One important question, where the claim relates to property held by A, concerns the position of third parties: what, for example, if A promises to give B a right in relation to A's property, and B reasonably relies on that promise in such a way that B would suffer a detriment were A wholly free to renege on the promise, but A then transfers the property to C? In such a case, a court must consider what rights B had in relation to the property at the time of the transfer from A to C.[56] This means a court should evaluate what order would have been made had it given effect to A's liability at that earlier point in time. This shows that, even if A's primary liability can be turned into a duty owed by A to B only by a court order, this does not mean that B has no right at all before such an order is made. Indeed, the standard formulation, that B, before a court order, has an 'equity by estoppel' nicely aligns B's position with other cases – such as where B has a power to set aside a transfer of a property right to A – where A is similarly under a liability.[57]

B. False Friends

The analysis of equitable claims is often impeded by an identification of those claims with common law 'equivalents'. It has already been suggested, for example, that regarding an equitable estoppel claim as simply providing an alternative to contractual consideration is an error: it obscures the fact that such a claim does not depend on A's coming under an immediate duty to B to honour a promise. Similarly, it would be a mistake to regard an equitable assignment as involving any transfer of A's right to B. As Tham has clearly shown,[58] the effect of A's equitable assignment of a legal chose in action to B is not that B steps into A's shoes as holder of the right; rather, it is much closer to that of A's keeping the right and holding it on trust for B.[59] The same point can be made when considering the

[56] See McFarlane, *The Law of Proprietary Estoppel* (n 10) ch 8.

[57] The equity by estoppel should not, however, be capable of binding a third party in all cases, as in some cases A's liability would be concretised simply by an order that A pay a sum of money to B, or allow B a licence: where, at the relevant time, the court would thus have imposed a duty giving B only a personal right against A, there is no reason why, prior to that court order, B should instead have a right capable of binding a third party. This view casts doubt on the interpretation of s 116(a) of the Land Registration Act 2002 preferred by the Law Commission in the Report which led to the Act: Law Com No 271, 5.29–5.31. See further B McFarlane, 'Proprietary Estoppel and Third Parties After the Land Registration Act 2002' [2003] *Cambridge Law Journal* 661 and McFarlane, *The Law of Proprietary Estoppel* (n 10) ch 8.

[58] Tham (n 2).

[59] ibid, chs 4–6. This explains why, for example, an equitable assignee of a legal chose in action must join the assignor in an action seeking to enforce the right: see eg: the discussion in *Roberts v Gill* [2011] 1 AC 240 (HL) [62]–[71]. Tham's view is that an equitable assignment involves both: (i) A's holding the chose in action on trust for B; and (ii) an irrevocable agency relationship's existing between A and B, so that B can give a good discharge to the debtor.

legal relations involved where B has an equitable interest in property: those relations are clearly distinct from those arising where B instead has a legal property right. As Maitland once observed, it is not uncommon to think of B's interest under a trust, for example, as 'just ownership pure and simple, though it is subject to a peculiar, technical and not very intelligible rule in favour bona fide purchasers'.[60] Such a view, however, obscures the particular way in which equity, by recognising the trust and other equitable interests, adds to the options available to a holder of a right.

A key characteristic of a legal property right is that the rest of the world is under an immediate, prima facie duty to the holder of the right: if, for example, O owns a bicycle then the rest of the world has a prima facie duty to O not deliberately or carelessly to damage or otherwise physically interfere with the bicycle. That is not, however, the case where A holds a right on trust for B. In *Shell UK v Total UK Ltd*,[61] for example, the Court of Appeal was keen to regard B, a beneficiary of the trust on which A held A's title to land, as the '"real" owner' of the land, given that A was 'little more than a bare trustee'.[62] Yet when the land was carelessly damaged by X, the Court of Appeal characterised the consequential loss suffered by B as purely economic loss. This view, it is submitted, is correct[63] as it recognises that strangers come under a duty to B in relation to property only in the relatively limited circumstances where B holds a legal property right.[64] So, whilst X may breach a duty owed to A (the trustee) when carelessly damaging the property, X does not automatically also breach a duty owed to B (a beneficiary). Rather than simply being a jurisdictional accident, this position can be justified in principle: even if X is already under a duty to A (and so would in any case come under a liability to pay damages to A for carelessly damaging the property), the imposition of an additional duty (and consequent liability) to B would be significant in practice and so the circumstances in which such a duty arises should be limited.[65]

[60] FW Maitland, 'Trust and Corporation' in D Runciman and M Ryan (eds), *State, Trust and Corporation* (Cambridge, Cambridge University Press, 2003) 94. Maitland there cites J Salmond, *Jurisprudence* (London, Stevens and Haynes, 1893) 278, where B is referred to as the 'real owner', with the trustee's ownership described as 'nominal' and 'fictitious'.

[61] *Shell UK v Total UK Ltd* [2011] QB 86 (CA).

[62] ibid [126].

[63] The correctness of this finding was then undermined by the Court of Appeal's very surprising finding (ibid at [132]–[144]) that a 'special relationship' existed between B and X, simply because B was the beneficiary of a trust. The existence of the trust, whilst evidencing a relationship between A and B, does not by itself create a special relationship between B and X, and such a relationship is required, on the Court of Appeal's own analysis, to allow for an exception to the 'exclusionary rule' preventing liability for carelessly caused pure economic loss. For criticism of the reasoning and result in the *Shell* case, see too, eg, KFK Low, 'Equitable Title and Economic Loss' (2010) 126 *Law Quarterly Review* 507; PG Turner, 'Consequential Economic Loss and the Trust Beneficiary' [2010] *Cambridge Law Review* 445; Edelman (n 14); McFarlane, n 14, 203–06.

[64] A possessory right is an example of such a legal property right, as in such a case B's possession gives B a relative title to the property: see, eg: *Healey v Healey* [1915] 1 KB 938; *Leigh & Sillivan Ltd v Aliakmon Shipping Co Ltd* [1986] AC 785, 812.

[65] See, eg: *Hill v Tupper* (1863) 2 H&C 122; *Cattle v Stockton Waterworks Co* (1875) LR 10 QB 453.

The relative width of the situations in which B may acquire an equitable (as opposed to legal) interest in property are inconsistent with a position in which such equitable interests necessarily impose such an additional duty on X. It is accepted, for example, that X owes no duty to the holder of a mere contractual right in relation to property, yet there is nothing in the rules as to the content or acquisition of an equitable interest that would make it any easier for X to discover an equitable interest, or reduce the burden on X of owing a duty to all holders of such an interest.

The third party effect of an equitable interest thus differs from that of a legal interest, and was summarised by Lord Sumption in *Akers v Samba Financial Group*.[66] He stated that 'an equitable interest possesses the essential hallmark of any right *in rem*', yet identified that hallmark as being 'that it is good against third parties into whose hands the property or its traceable proceeds may have come, subject to the rules of equity for the protection of bona fide purchasers for value without notice'.[67] That formulation appears to resemble the common misconception identified by Maitland,[68] but it contains some important differences.

Significantly, Lord Sumption went on to state that when an asset subject to an equitable interest is transferred to a third party, 'the question becomes whether the conscience of the transferee is affected'.[69] So, rather than recognising that B's equitable interest imposes a strict immediate duty of non-interference on third parties, his Lordship's own analysis of B's right is that only a particular group of third parties (recipients of the trust property or its traceable proceeds) come under a duty to B, and then only when their conscience is affected by having sufficient knowledge of the trust. B's interest is thus much closer to the concept of quasi-property, as explicated by Balganesh,[70] rather than to a classic right *in rem*. Rather than equating B's position to that of a holder of a legal property right, it is more helpful to note that the existence of a trust has a more limited effect on third parties.[71]

[66] *Akers v Samba Financial Group* (n 13).

[67] ibid [82].

[68] See n 60 above.

[69] ibid [89]. For similar remarks, see *Investec Trust (Guernsey) Ltd v Glenalla Properties Ltd* [2018] UKPC 7, [2018] 2 WLR 1465, [228] (Lord Mance).

[70] S Balganesh, 'Quasi-Property: Like, But Not Quite Property' (2012) 160 *University of Pennsylvania Law Review* 1889: see too, B McFarlane and S Douglas, 'Property, Analogy, and Variety' *Oxford Journal of Legal Studies* (forthcoming).

[71] Although the existence of a trust imposes a duty on the rest of the world not to dishonestly assist the trustee in a breach of trust (*Royal Brunei Airlines v Tan* [1995] 2 AC 378 (PC)), the duty is not strict and thus it offers less protection than a legal property right. Furthermore, its existence does not distinguish the trust from other *in personam* rights, as similar duties exist, eg, not to assist in a breach of fiduciary duty and not to procure a breach of contract (*OBG Ltd v Allan* [2007] UKHL 21, [2008] 1 AC 1). See, further, B McFarlane, 'Equity, Obligations, and Third Parties' [2008] *Singapore Journal of Legal Studies* 308. The decision in *Shell UK v Total UK Ltd* (n 61) whilst still requiring joinder of A where B brings a claim against X, does however seem to recognise at least a liability of X to B in relation to consequential loss caused to B by X's careless interference with the trust property but, as noted at n 63 above, the finding in that case is undermined by the confused reasoning of the court, and seems to be inconsistent with the decision of the House of Lords in *Leigh & Sillivan Ltd v Aliakmon Shipping Co Ltd* [1986] AC 785.

If they acquire a particular right from the trustee, and if they hold that right or its traceable proceeds with sufficient knowledge of the trust, only then will they come under a duty to B:[72] a duty not to use that right for their own benefit or otherwise inconsistently with the trust.

If then C is a donee of trust property transferred by the trustee without authority, equity fulfils its characteristic role of preventing C's assertion of a right in a way that is unconscionable as regards B.[73] It does so not because C has breached a pre-existing duty to B, but because it would now be unconscionable for C to act in a particular way. Equity does not undermine or usurp the common law by setting up a parallel, competing system of rights *in rem*. The fact that the proprietary effect of B's rights under a trust depends on the existence of a particular relationship between B and C confirms that B's interest under a trust is 'a kind of personal claim that has proprietary effects because it can be enforced against any trustee, including transferees of the trust property who become trustees by operation of law'.[74]

C. Meta-Rights

Much equitable intervention, it can be argued, takes the form of regulating, in favour of B, the acquisition or enforcement of a right by A.[75] A classic example is provided by *Hughes v Metropolitan Rwy Co*.[76] The decision provides a clear example of equity's second-order role in acknowledging the existence of a right, but then controlling the exercise of that right. A was prevented from exercising a contractual right to forfeit B's lease, as such a forfeiture would have allowed A to benefit from B's failure to complete repairs within a particular time, even though A had encouraged B to believe that B's inaction during a period when the parties where negotiating as to B's possible surrender of the lease would *not* lead to forfeiture of the lease. A did not thereby lose the contractual right; rather, A was prevented from asserting that right before the expiry of an additional period, so that the period in which negotiations had taken place did not count against B in assessing whether

[72] See too *ITS Ltd v GP Noble Trustees Ltd* [2013] Ch 91 (CA) [76], [81], [84]. At [76], for example, Lloyd LJ states that B's claim 'only extends to money (or its traceable proceeds) which was in [the third party's] hands at the time she was given notice of [B's] claim'. Adopting the analysis of Millett J in *Agip (Africa) Ltd v Jackson* [1990] Ch 265 (Ch), 290–91, Lloyd LJ also confirmed that: 'to the extent that, before [the third party recipient] had notice of the claim to the funds, she had disposed of any of the money without receiving traceable proceeds, she would not be liable [to B]'. See further S Agnew and B McFarlane, 'The Paradox of the Equitable Proprietary Claim' in B McFarlane and S Agnew (eds), *Modern Studies in Property Law*, vol 10 (Oxford, Hart Publishing, 2019).

[73] See, eg: McFarlane and Stevens (n 14). For further analysis of the position of C in Hohfeldian terms, see B McFarlane, 'The Essential Nature of Trusts and Other Equitable Interests: Two and a Half Cheers for Hohfeld' in S Balganesh et al (eds), *The Legacy of Wesley Hohfeld: Edited Major Works, Select Personal Papers, and Original Commentaries* (Cambridge, CUP, forthcoming).

[74] L Smith, 'Trust and Patrimony' (2008) *Revue Générale de Droit* 379, [10].

[75] See McFarlane and Stevens (n 21).

[76] *Hughes v Metropolitan Rwy Co* (n 6).

the repairs had been completed in time.[77] As B was not claiming that A had lost the initial contractual right, there was no need for B to show that the parties' contract had been varied; B was instead protected through equity's control of A's assertion of the contractual right. Indeed, the relevant principle can be seen as responding to a possible defect in the general contractual rules controlling A's acquisition of the power to forfeit the lease: whilst the condition for A's acquisition of the right (B's failure to complete repairs in the contractually agreed six-month period) had arisen, that condition consisted of particular action or inaction by B, and it would be unjust for A to be free to enforce the right where B's decision to adopt that course of conduct was based on A's encouragement to B that A would *not* acquire or enforce the right. A's action would seem to consist of precisely the sort of opportunistic behaviour which equity, on one view,[78] characteristically aims to prevent; it may be significant, however, that the opportunism consists specifically in trying to take advantage of the primary legal rules regulating the parties' rights.

This formal aspect of equitable intervention is perhaps clearest where A holds a particular claim-right or power, and is under a duty to B, the content of which relates specifically to that claim-right or power. It can be argued that the correlative claim-right of B, in such a case, operates differently from a purely personal right and instead has the hallmark of an equitable interest:[79] it can give B some protection too against C, a third party later acquiring A's right, or a right that depends on A's right. This result flows from the content of A's duty: it relates to something (A's right) which exists independently of A.[80] Such an analysis accords with the view that equity is a form of second-order, or meta law, but gives that view a specific formal consequence.

Two of the examples discussed thus far – equitable assignment and the trust – are cases in which, because A's duty to B relates to a specific right held by A, B can be said to have a claim-right which has the particular third party effect associated with equitable interests. Given that third party effect, it is understandable that, in particular contexts, B's right can be described as 'property'. In *Akers v Samba*,[81] for example, the Supreme Court confirmed that a right under a trust counts as property for the purpose of the very wide definition of that term used in the Insolvency Act 1986.[82] At the same time, the court confirmed that it is possible

[77] The ability of equity to regulate the enforcement of A's admitted right against B thus explains the 'suspensive' effect of this form of promissory estoppel, see eg: B McFarlane, 'Understanding Equitable Estoppel: From Metaphors to Better Laws' (2013) 66 *Current Legal Problems* 267, 282–86.

[78] See, eg: H Smith, 'Property, Equity and the Rule of Law' in L Austin and D Klimchuk (eds), *Private Law and the Rule of Law* (Oxford, Oxford University Press, 2014) 232–33; H Smith, 'Equity as Meta-Law' *Yale Law Journal* (forthcoming).

[79] See McFarlane and Stevens (n 12).

[80] The same model can also apply where A is under a liability to B, but the liability relates to a specific right held by A (as occurs, for example, when B transfers a right to A under a contract entered into after an innocent misrepresentation made by A to B).

[81] *Akers v Samba Financial Group* (n 13).

[82] Insolvency Act 1986 (UK), s 436. See, eg: *Akers v Samba Financial Group* (n 13) [42] (Lord Mance): 'The definition of "property" in section 436 is wide enough to embrace both equitable proprietary and purely personal interests'.

for an English court to recognise a trust in relation to property (in this case, shares), even if that property is situated in a jurisdiction which does not recognise the trust.[83] This reveals another difference between the practical treatment of an equitable interest and a legal interest,[84] one which is also seen when considering the question of jurisdiction: whilst the well-established traditional rule, for example, is that an English court does not have jurisdiction over claims to title to foreign land, claims to an equitable interest in such land (even one arising under a bare trust) can be heard by an English court.[85] The different approach in relation to equitable interests can be defended on the basis that, in such a case, B is not asserting a right directly in the foreign property, nor denying A's title to that property, but is rather looking to control A's exercise, as regards B, of that admitted right.

As for the choice of law question, it is worth noting the analysis, drawn on by Lord Mance in *Akers*,[86] of Cozens-Hardy MR in *British South Africa Co v De Beers Consolidated Mines Ltd*.[87] In applying the equitable rule against clogging the equity of redemption in relation to foreign land, the Master of the Rolls stated that:

> if A by an English contract agreed to give a mortgage to secure an English debt upon land in a foreign country, the law of which country does not recognize the existence of what we call an equity of redemption, *which was the case of our common law*, and if a mortgage was given and duly perfected according to the lex situs, I feel no doubt that our courts would restrain the mortgagee from exercising the rights given by the foreign law and would treat the transaction as a mortgage in the sense in which that word is used by us. In doing this our courts would not in any way interfere with the lex situs, but would by injunction, and if necessary, by process of contempt, restrain the mortgagee from asserting those rights. Similar observations would apply to a trustee, if the lex situs does not recognize trusts.[88]

The passing reference, emphasised above, to the common law indicates that the analysis of the relationship between English law and foreign law may also apply

[83] The shares in *Akers* were shares in a Saudi Arabian company, and it had been found as a matter of fact that the 'law of Saudi Arabia does not recognise trusts or any other distinction between the legal and beneficial interests in property': see *Akers v Samba Financial Group* (n 13) [80] (Lord Sumption).

[84] A further difference is demonstrated by the Supreme Court's holding that, where A transfers trust property to C, who is not affected by the trust, A does not thereby dispose of B's property: for discussion see McFarlane and Stevens (n 14).

[85] The rule in relation to claims to title to land is synonymous with *British South Africa Co v Companhia de Moçambique* [1893] AC 602; the different position in equity can be seen in eg *Penn v Lord Baltimore* (1750) 1 Ves Sen 444, 27 ER 1132. Similarly, Art 24(1) of the Recast Brussels Regulation (Regulation (EU) 1215/2012, [2012] OJ L351/1, amending Regulation (EC) 44/2001, [2001] OJ L12/1) gives exclusive jurisdiction to the courts of the Member State in which the property is situated, if proceedings have 'as their object rights *in rem* in immovable property or tenancies of immovable property', whereas in *Webb v Webb* [1994] QB 696; [1991] 1 WLR 1410 (Ch), it was confirmed that Art 24(1) did not apply to a claim that A held his title to land in France on trust for B.

[86] *Akers v Samba Financial Group* (n 13) [25].

[87] *British South Africa Co v De Beers Consolidated Mines Ltd* [1910] 2 Ch 502 (CA).

[88] ibid 514 (emphasis added).

to the relationship of common law and equity. Just as an English court taking jurisdiction, or enforcing a trust, in respect of foreign property, is not challenging the position that A holds the relevant property, so equity, in affording B an equitable interest, does not seek to undermine the common law position that A holds the property;[89] it rather regulates, in favour of B, A's use and enforcement of that right.

In the case where A holds, for example, a freehold of land on trust for B, the right of A to which A's duty to B relates is of course not simply A's claim-right against strangers not deliberately or carelessly to damage or otherwise physically interfere with the land: as Penner has noted,[90] A's duty also relates to the various liberties, powers and immunities that A holds as a result of A's freehold ownership. This may help to explain the somewhat automatic[91] nature of B's power to impose a duty on A, a trustee, in relation to traceable proceeds of the initial trust property – where, for example, A has sold the trust property without authority, then the money received by A derives from A's exercise of A's power to transfer the trust property and that power was impressed with a duty owed to B. As a result, it is no surprise that B then has the ability to impress the same duty on a right acquired by A through exercising that power. In contrast, the same logic does not apply in relation to legal interests: where O has title to property, the fact that third parties owe O a prima facie duty of non-interference in relation to a specific physical thing does not in itself mean that third parties must owe O the same duty in relation to something acquired by X when making an unauthorised use of O's property.

III. The Functions of Equity

A. Negative: Mitigating Risks

It was argued in Section II.A above that, where equitable estoppel operates as a cause of action, it does not respond to an actual or threatened wrong of A, but rather imposes a liability on A. Whilst such an analysis may assist in showing its

[89] See S Agnew and B McFarlane, 'The Nature of Trusts and the Conflict of Laws', *Law Quarterly Review* (forthcoming). The analysis here thus accords with Maitland's view as to the peaceful co-existence of common law and equity (see, eg: FW Maitland, *Lectures in Equity* (Cambridge, Cambridge University Press, 1929)) rather than with Hohfeld's criticisms of Maitland in WN Hohfeld, 'The Relations Between Equity and Law' (1913) 11 *Michigan Law Review* 537: see further B McFarlane, 'Avoiding Anarchy? Common Law v Equity and Maitland v Hohfeld' in PG Turner et al (eds), *Equity and Law: Fusion and Fission* (n 6) 331.

[90] JE Penner, 'The (True) Nature of a Beneficiary's Equitable Proprietary Interest under a Trust' (2014) 27 *Canadian Journal of Law and Jurisprudence* 473.

[91] See *Foskett v McKeown* [2001] 1 AC 102 (HL), confirming that the power does not depend on showing an unjust enrichment of A at B's expense. The analysis in this paragraph follows that of McFarlane and Stevens (n 14) 203–204.

compatibility with contract law and so perhaps overcome the concern in English law about extending the promise-based strand of equitable estoppel to promises unrelated to land,[92] the analysis does not mean that there are no limits on the types of promise that may give rise to liability. In *Waltons Stores v Maher*,[93] for example, Brennan J argued for a principle not confined to cases where A promises to give B a right in relation to land, on the basis that it is well-established that equitable estoppel can apply to a promise to extinguish or suspend a right,[94] and there is no relevant distinction between a 'change in legal relationships effected by a promise which extinguishes a right and a change in legal relationships effected by a promise which creates one'.[95]

Again, however, a careful focus on legal relations is necessary, as it challenges the logic of Brennan J's assertion. There *is* a difference between a principle that controls the acquisition or assertion of an existing right and one that instead imposes a new duty or liability. That difference is recognised at common law: for example, the rules applying to waiver of contractual rights differ from those applying to variation of a contract.[96] The basis of equitable estoppel in a case such as *Hughes v Metropolitan Rwy Co* may therefore be quite different from its basis in a case such as *Waltons Stores*.[97] This formal point does not mean that it is illegitimate to allow equitable estoppel to operate as a cause of action, but it does have consequences for the justification of the principle in such cases. It may nonetheless be possible, however, to justify Brennan J's focus on promises that relate to rights.[98] It can be argued, for example, that the existence of certain legal powers, provided by private law (such as the power to transfer a right, or to enter a contract), whilst advantageous overall, carries certain risks: a party may abuse such a power by, for example, causing another to suffer a detriment through reasonable reliance on a promise that such a power will be exercised.[99] A second-order rule can then

[92] For discussion, see, eg: B McFarlane and P Sales, 'Promises, Detriment, and Liability: Lessons from Proprietary Estoppel' (2015) 131 *Law Quarterly Review* 610.

[93] *Waltons Stores v Maher* (1988) 164 CLR 387.

[94] See, eg: the formulation of promissory estoppel provided by Robert Goff J in *BP Petroleum Co (Libya) Ltd v Hunt (No 2)* [1979] 1 WLR 783, 810.

[95] *Waltons Stores v Maher* (n 93) 425.

[96] Most notably, consideration is not required: see eg *Hickman v Haynes* (1875) LR 10 CP 598.

[97] See, eg: McFarlane (n 77) 282–86 where it is argued that the principle applied in *Hughes* does not in fact require A to have made a promise (see e.g *Birmingham & Land District Co v London and North Western Rwy Co* (1888) 40 Ch D 268 (CA)), nor that B would suffer a detriment as a result of reasonable reliance on A.

[98] The limitation in Brennan J's analysis, that equitable estoppel can operate as a cause of action only where A's promise relates to an actual or promised legal relationship between A and B, has however been challenged as too restrictive both in case-law (see eg *W v G* (1996) 20 Fam LR 49) and academic commentary (see eg A Robertson, 'Three Models of Promissory Estoppel' (2013) 7 *Journal of Equity* 226).

[99] Or, equally, by standing by and failing to disabuse B when A knows that B has a mistaken belief as to B's legal rights: such acquiescence cases are described by Lord Neuberger in *Fisher v Brooker* [2009] 1 WLR 1764 [62] as 'the classic example of proprietary estoppel'. B's mistake need not be specifically that A has exercised a power to give B a right, but must be a mistake as to B's rights: see eg *Ramsden v Dyson* (1866) LR 1 HL 129, 140–41 (Lord Cranworth) and 168 (Lord Wensleydale).

control the risk inherent in the powers established by the primary legal rules, by offering some protection to the relying party. It can then be argued that the 'shock' to the conscience of the court, justifying intervention,[100] does not come merely from the fact that B has been left to suffer a detriment. After all, as the law does not usually protect B from purely economic loss, even where A has acted carelessly, it is difficult to sustain the argument that we all owe each other a duty not to cause one another loss through any form of induced reliance. Rather, the 'shock' is more specific and comes from the risk of A's taking advantage of, or otherwise abusing, the existence of certain primary legal rules.[101] The conclusion that intervention is necessary to prevent such abuse, however, cannot come from simply applying a set of tests to A's past conduct; a court rather has to consider the parties' current positions and ask if it would *now* be unconscionable for A to leave B to suffer a detriment as a result of B's reasonable reliance.[102] The court's intervention is not about protecting B's pre-existing entitlement or enforcing A's pre-existing duty; it is rather concerned with mitigating a risk that comes from the existence of the power-conferring primary rules that form a key part of private law.

A functional link can be drawn here to the law of unjust enrichment. The action for money had and received, available for example where B has made a mistaken payment to A, has been famously described as 'equitable in origin and function'.[103] This chapter does not consider the origin of the action, but will support that view of its function, arguing that it is equitable not in a generalised sense of enforcing norms of fairness, but rather in a specific sense of operating so as to mitigate the impact of primary legal rules that govern the acquisition of private law rights. It thus shares a function with equitable estoppel and, if Stephen Smith's argument as to the nature of an unjust enrichment claim is accepted,[104] it also shares a form with that doctrine, as it too operates to impose a primary liability, rather than an immediate duty, on A. Indeed, it is significant that, in relatively recent cases, each of the Supreme Court and the High Court of Australia[105] has drawn links

[100] To adopt the language of Lord Walker in *Cobbe v Yeoman's Row Management Ltd* (n 50) at [92]. Note of course that, equally, the prospect of B's suffering detriment as a result of reliance on a promise by A is required. The mere fact that A has expressed an intention as to A's exercise of a legal power does not lead to liability, as noted by Robert Walker LJ (as he then was) in *Gillett v Holt* [2001] Ch 210, 228: 'It is notorious that some elderly persons of means derive enjoyment from the possession of testamentary power, and from dropping hints as to their intentions, without any question of an estoppel arising'.

[101] Note there is a link here to the analysis of M Harding, 'Equity and the Rule of Law' (2016) 132 *Law Quarterly Review* 278: equity can promote respect for the law by limiting the situations in which the application of the law itself leads to injustices.

[102] See Section II.A above for discussion of the 'backwards-looking' nature of liability in equitable estoppel.

[103] Cardozo J in *Atlantic Coast Line Railroad Co v Florida* 295 US 301, 309 (1935).

[104] See SA Smith, 'A Duty to Make Restitution' (2013) 26 *Canadian Journal of Law and Jurisprudence* 157; and Smith, 'The Restatement of Liabilities in Restitution' (n 8).

[105] See *Pitt v Holt* [2013] 2 AC 108 [124] where, in considering the circumstances in which a court can exercise, at B's request, the equitable jurisdiction to set aside a voluntary settlement, Lord Walker expressly referred to proprietary estoppel cases in stating that: 'the fundamental principle that equity is concerned to prevent unconscionable conduct permeates all the elements of the doctrine. In the end

to equitable estoppel in order to justify taking a wider set of factors into account when deciding if a restitutionary claim should be permitted.[106]

Consider a case where B initially holds a right. In such a case, primary legal rules give B a power to alter the legal relations of A and B, by for example transferring B's right to A. One of the obvious benefits of B's power is that it allows parties the freedom to structure their relations and to make plans on the basis of those relations. As the exercise of such a power also has consequences for third parties, there are good reasons for allowing the exercise of the power to be effective despite a subjective flaw in B's consent to the transfer. In justifying the effect of such primary rules on mistaken parties, however, the possibility of a restitutionary claim against the recipient may play a vital role.[107] In other words, as the location of the transferred right determines legal relations with third parties, it may be justifiable to find that a transfer has occurred notwithstanding B's mistake;[108] but that does not mean that the effect of such rules on B's position *as regards A* is necessarily justified. In a case where A remains factually better off, at least by the time A is aware of the mistake, there is a prima facie case for A paying the value of that benefit to B. The case is only a prima facie one and events occurring after the defendant's receipt, even if not resulting in a clearly measurable reduction of A's enrichment, can change the position so as to make it no longer unconscionable for A, even with knowledge of B's mistake, to retain the enrichment.[109]

the court must look at the matter in the round.' See too *Australian Financial Services v Hills Industries Ltd* (2014) 253 CLR 560 where, in considering the scope of the change of position defence to a personal restitutionary claim, French CJ (building on the earlier analysis of Gummow J in *Roxborough v Rothmans of Pall Mall Australia Ltd* (2001) 208 CLR 516) emphasised the 'general application of equitable considerations to restitutionary actions' ([13]) and regarded the change of position defence as not depending simply on whether or not A has been disenriched but as rather raising the wider question of the extent to which it would be unconscionable for A to retain any benefit acquired at the expense of B; see too the judgment of Hayne, Crennan, Kiefel, Bell and Keane JJ at [65]–[76].

[106] See too McFarlane (n 27). In *Prudential Assurance Co Ltd v Revenue and Customs Commissioners* [2019] AC 929 [69], Lord Reed, Lord Hodge and Lord Mance stated that, where a mistaken payment is received, 'an obligation arises immediately under the law of unjust enrichment to reverse the enrichment by repaying the money (or an equivalent amount). The cause of action accrues when the money is mistakenly paid'. The language of 'obligation', if intended in its strict meaning, is inconsistent with the liability model, but the limitation position is not, as it is reasonable for a limitation period to run from the point when B has the power to bring a claim.

[107] See B McFarlane, 'Unjust Enrichment, Rights, and Value' in D Nolan and A Robertson (eds), *Rights in Private Law* (Oxford, Hart Publishing, 2012) 579, 591, 606 and (n 89) 347–49; see too J Mee, 'Justifying Restitutionary Liability for Mistaken Payments' (paper presented at the Obligations IX conference, 2018).

[108] See, eg: *Cressman v Coys of Kensington (Sales) Ltd* [2004] 1 WLR 2775: the transfer of a registration number to A was valid, simply because A was registered as its holder; but the effectiveness of the transfer did not prevent a personal restitutionary claim. Indeed, as noted by Mance LJ at [24], it was a precondition of such a claim.

[109] See *Australian Financial Services v Hills* (n 105) [65]–[76]. Note also that, on the view in this chapter, it is not necessary for the change of position to have come from voluntary action of A: a different change of circumstances may also suffice. That appears to be the position in England (see eg *Scottish Equitable plc v Derby* [2001] EWCA Civ 369 [32] and [46]) and that view of the law in Australia is supported by eg J Edelman and E Bant, *Unjust Enrichment*, 2nd edn (Oxford, Hart Publishing, 2016) 340–41.

The intuitive appeal of this more limited generalisation of the money had and received claim, as related to an exercise of a power by B rather than by any transfer of value from B to A, is evident in what can be called 'proprietary' analyses: B's claim is said to be justified by the general need to ensure that an owner of property is not deprived of it, or at least its value, otherwise than as a result of a transfer to which B has freely and unqualifiedly consented.[110] On this view, the claim has the same aim as, for example, the tort of conversion, as it is focussed on the protection of B's pre-existing assets.[111] Such a view, however, makes it difficult to explain the well-established distinction between cases where the absence of, or flaw in, B's consent prevents the transfer of B's right at all (and so, in the case of chattels, allows B to maintain an actual conversion claim) and those where the transfer does occur and B has instead a personal restitutionary claim. The 'proprietary' emphasis may also be unhelpful: for example, even when a purely contractual right is not protected by the tort of conversion,[112] B can still have a personal restitutionary claim where B mistakenly gives A the benefit of such a right. A better way of building on the intuitive appeal of the proprietary analysis is to see the core case of the personal restitutionary claim as involving the valid, but mistaken, exercise of a legal power, where that exercise causes both B's loss of a right (or the imposition of a duty on B) and A's gain of a right (or loss of a duty).[113] This formulation can be both broader and narrower than a 'property' principle: broader as it includes any rights that B has the power to lose or waive; narrower, because it requires an exercise of a power by B.[114] On a power-focussed analysis, for example, B's mistaken entry into a contract with A can always be said to fall under the same principle as the mistaken payment case, as B has mistakenly exercised a primary legal power which has caused B to come under a duty and A to gain a right.[115] As in the case of

[110] See, eg: P Watts, 'Restitution – A Property Principle and a Services Principle' [1995] *Restitution Law Review* 49; and P Watts, 'Unjust Enrichment – The Potion that Induces Well-Meaning Sloppiness of Thought' [2016] *Current Legal Problems* 289; C Webb, *Reason and Restitution* (Oxford, Oxford University Press, 2016).

[111] Watts makes the link to conversion explicit, regarded the restitutionary claim and the property torts as 'cognate conservators': P Watts, 'Property and Unjust Enrichment: Cognate Conservators' [1998] *New Zealand Law Review* 151.

[112] See, eg: *OBG Ltd v Allan* (n 71).

[113] B McFarlane, 'Unjust Enrichment, Rights and Value' in D Nolan and A Roberston (eds), *Rights and Private Law* (Oxford, Hart Publishing, 2012). Note that this formulation extends the operation of the principle beyond cases where a right is directly transferred, so as to include, for example, transfers through bank accounts. For consideration of how such transactions can be incorporated within a model based on transfer, see eg, T Cutts, 'Modern Money Had and Received' (2018) 38 *Oxford Journal of Legal Studies* 1.

[114] Watts (n 110) for example, suggests that the 'property principle' should apply in a case involving A's gain through the loss of B's property right, even where no power has been exercised by B. This means, as Watts notes, that a claim should arise where material used by B in mistakenly building on A's land accedes to A's land. In English law, at least, no claim arises in such a case.

[115] In such a case, the rules permitting such a claim fall within the characterisation of Smith (n 104) 178, as rules which 'provide a means to fix a problem that is largely the law's own creation' (compare n 101 above). There is a debate as to whether the power to rescind an executory contract can be seen as part of the law of unjust enrichment. For example, L Smith, 'Unjust Enrichment: Big or Small?'

equitable estoppel, a focus on the function of mitigating the effects of other legal rules can thus assist in providing a limit to the scope of the claim. If, for example, B simply mistakenly performs a service for A then, on the analysis here, the strict liability principle applying to the mistaken payment case does not apply as B has not exercised any power to change the legal relations of A and B. This is consistent with the fact that the law does not generally recognise any strict personal liability of A in cases of mistaken services.[116]

B. Positive: Increasing Autonomy

Equity's second-order, or supplementary, nature allows it to play an important role in mitigating some of the risks that arise from having a system of private law rights. That same second-order nature has also allowed equity to play a more positive role, by increasing the means by which a holder of a right, A, can benefit from that right. It can be argued, as Hanoch Dagan has done,[117] that a principal aim of private law is to enhance parties' opportunities for self-determination by providing different means by which they can structure their legal relations; if so, equity makes a central contribution to that aim. As noted in Section I, for example, the possibility of making an equitable assignment of a chose in action provides A with a practically valuable means of dealing with that right.

It is also notable how, even if a particular equitable doctrine may initially have arisen to achieve a negative function, of mitigating the risks involved in a system of private rights, it may come to serve a positive, autonomy-enhancing function. For example, the classic form of use (and ultimately the trust), arising where S transfers a right to A to hold for B, can be seen as arising to prevent A's abusing A's power to receive such a transfer from S, by inducing the transfer through a promise to hold for B, and then attempting to breach that promise.[118] Once that

in S Degeling and J Edelman (eds), *Unjust Enrichment in Commercial Law* (Sydney, Lawbook, 2008) 35, 40-43 argues that B's power instead depends on an inherent defect in A's contractual right against B. On the analysis in this chapter, however, that feature, on the contrary, justifies seeing B's power as within the same liability principle as applying to the case of a mistaken payment.

[116] See, eg: *Blue Haven Enterprises Ltd v Tully* [2006] UKPC 17. For discussion see F Wilmot-Smith, 'Reasons? For Restitution?' (2016) 79 *The Modern Law Review* 1116, 1132–1133. Note that §10 of the Restatement (Third) of Restitution and Unjust Enrichment takes a different approach in relation to the mistaken improvement of land, allowing a prima facie liability, subject to the limits in eg §§49-52, but that approach seems to be influenced by betterment statutes and even the civil law (via the judgment of Justice Story in *Bright v Boyd* (1841) 4 Fed Cas 127 (No 1,875) (Cir Decisions, Maine)). For discussion of the position in Australia, see S Degeling and B Edgeworth, 'Improvements to Land Belonging to Another' in LB Moses et al (eds), *Property and Security: Selected Essays* (Sydney, Lawbook Co, 2010) 277.

[117] See n 31 above.

[118] Note that this basis for intervention can still be seen in cases where, owing to a failure to comply with a formality rule, it is impossible for B to show that S successfully exercised a power to set up a trust in B's favour: see, eg, *Rochefoucauld v Boustead* [1897] 1 Ch 196 (CA) as discussed by eg B McFarlane, 'Constructive Trusts Arising on a Receipt of Property *Sub Conditione*' (2004) 120 *Law Quarterly Review* 667; Ying Khai Liew, '*Rochefoucauld v Boustead* (1897)' in C Mitchell and P Mitchell (eds), *Landmark Cases in Equity* (Oxford, Hart Publishing, 2012).

structure of intervention is accepted, however, it can very quickly be used as a means to allow S to deal with S's right in different ways, increasing the options available to a holder of such a right. Perhaps the ultimate expression of this development is the (relatively late)[119] recognition of the self-declaration of trust: A has the power to set up a trust simply by having a right, and then declaring that A holds that right on trust for B. The fact that an oral, gratuitous declaration can have this momentous effect is, as Hackney noted, remarkable,[120] and it certainly causes difficulties for some conceptions of the nature of the trust.[121] Moreover, at least in the absence of any reliance by B, it is hard to say why it would be unconscionable, as regards B, for A, having thus declared the trust, to change his or her mind and use the right for A's own benefit. As suggested by Agnew and Douglas,[122] however, the power thus to declare a trust is now seen as an 'inherent prerogative of ownership, which the law should facilitate': in other words, given that the trust structure has been recognised, it is consistent with the autonomy-enhancing aims of private law to allow A to set up such a structure without the possible inconvenience of having to transfer A's right to another to hold on trust for B.[123] Rather than simply controlling, in B's favour, A's exercise of powers to alter legal relations, equity can also endow A with such powers.

IV. Conclusion

This chapter has attempted to knit together two distinct but significant strands of legal scholarship. The first pays careful attention to the nature of the legal relations involved in private law claims, and, based in particular on Stephen Smith's work, emphasises the particular role a court may have to play in giving effect, in B's favour, to a liability of A. The second strand aims to identify distinctive concerns of equity and thus to justify its continued existence as a distinct body of rules and principles.[124] Underpinning both strands is a sensitivity to the diversity of private

[119] *Ex p Pye* (1811) 18 Ves Jr 140, albeit preceded by an earlier decision of Lord Eldon in *Ellison v Ellison* (1802) 6 Ves Jun 656, is regarded as the crucial case-law development.

[120] 'I can informally transfer to you my economic advantages in chattels of huge value by a few significantly chosen words, and once simply done that act cannot be revoked. No other device in the legal system approaches the massive power of these spoken words in Equity: "I declare myself trustee of this for you."': J Hackney, *Understanding Equity and Trusts* (London, Fontana, 1987) 109.

[121] Such as the contractarian view: see JH Langbein, 'The Contractarian Basis of the Law of Trusts' (1995) 105 *Yale Law Journal* 625.

[122] S Agnew and S Douglas, 'Self-Declarations of Trust' (2019) 135 *Law Quarterly Review* 67, 85. They note the possible influence of Pothier's *Traité des Obligations*, published in English in 1806, in supporting this conception.

[123] The possibility of a self-declaration is particularly significant where A holds a non-assignable chose in action: see, eg, *Don King Productions Inc v Warren* [2000] Ch 291 (CA); *Barbados Trust Co Ltd v Bank of Zambia* [2007] EWCA Civ 148.

[124] As noted by McFarlane (n 27), different concerns have been emphasised: eg, I Samet, *Equity: Conscience Goes to Market* (Oxford, Oxford University Press, 2018) argues that equity makes a distinct substantive contribution, increasing the correspondence of law to morality; H Smith argues (in 'Fusing

law, both in the forms of legal relations that it employs and the different values it may adopt. An important theme of this chapter is that, by recognising different forms of legal relations, equity is not seeking to compete with or undermine the common law, but rather to supplement and support it by a limited, second order form of intervention.

To return to the complications set out at the start of this chapter, it cannot be denied that the existence of equity increases the rules relating to private rights, and thus increases the entities in need of justification. This should not, however, be feared: a system of private rights, like an analysis of it, needs to have the 'right kind of simplicity',[125] and attempts to simplify matters by eliminating distinct equitable doctrines may be misguided.[126] It is true that equity brings complications, but the complications are far from needless. Indeed, equity performs two necessary functions and, by doing so, both mitigates the risks inherent in any system of private law and increases the ability of such a system to serve the key aim of enhancing parties' opportunities for self-determination. To have a full picture of the operation of private law, and of the justification of private rights, the distinctive role performed by many equitable doctrines must be given adequate recognition.

the Equitable Function in Private Law' (n 21)) that equity characteristically performs specific functions which are well-suited to a secondary system. The analysis in this chapter (see too McFarlane (n 14 and n 27)) instead focuses on the distinct formal nature of much equitable intervention.

[125] Hohfeld (n 7) 20.

[126] See too Smith (n 21), noting the dangers of 'flattening-through-fusion'. That is not to say of course that there is always space for equitable doctrines: the decision in *Great Peace Shipping Ltd v Tsavliris (International) Ltd* [2003] QB 679 (CA) is that there is no conceptual room for a distinct equitable doctrine of common mistake as if the mistake is not of a type serious enough to make the contract void, it cannot then still be serious enough to justify giving B an equitable power to set the contract aside. The fact that the equitable doctrine would have a distinct form is not in itself enough to justify the existence of the doctrine.

12

Property, Therefore: Is an Equitable Doctrine of Relief against the Forfeiture of Contractual Rights Justifiable?

NICHOLAS A TIVERIOS*

I. Introduction

The doctrine to relieve against forfeiture is one of many legal rules in respect of which Australian courts are developing a distinct body of equitable jurisprudence in circumstances where there is no equivalent English development. The growing list of divergences includes the antipodean remedial constructive trust, the scope of estoppel, the scope of the penalties doctrine, the role of unconscionability in unjust enrichment, the vitiating factor of unconscionable dealing, the nature of knowing/dishonest assistance for breach of fiduciary duty, the calculation of substitutive equitable compensation for the misapplication of trust assets, and implied duties of good faith.[1] The general direction of travel is that, in each of these areas, Australian courts embrace a more expansive view of equity in circumstances where there is no equivalent English approach. The most recent addition to this growing list involves a disagreement regarding the elements that must be satisfied in order to engage the equitable doctrine of relief against forfeiture. This doctrine is commonly (but, it is submitted, misleadingly) described as concerning the long-established rule under which equity will prevent B from losing (or forfeiting) a proprietary or possessory right[2] on an event of default, even

* I am grateful for comments received from my fellow editors, and at the Justifying Private Rights workshop at UNSW, and also at the Obligations Group Contracts Conference hosted by University of Melbourne Law School in December 2019.

[1] See generally: P Finn, 'Common Law Divergences' (2012) 37 *Melbourne University Law Review* 509; NA Tiverios and C McKay, 'Orthodoxy Lost: The (Ir)relevance of Causation in Quantifying Breach of Trust Claims' (2016) 90 *Australian Law Journal* 231.

[2] It ought to be noted that many property scholars (it is submitted correctly) do not recognise the existence of a 'possessory right'. Possession is simply a way of acquiring a property right. See B McFarlane, *The Structure of Property Law* (Oxford, Hart Publishing, 2008) 155; S Douglas, *Liability for Wrongful Interference with Chattels* (Oxford, Hart Publishing, 2011) 31; MJR Crawford, *An Expressive Theory of Possession* (Oxford, Hart Publishing, 2020) 57–58.

where the strict legal effect of a transaction between A and B is to produce such a result. The requirement that B loses a proprietary or possessory right in order to enliven the doctrine has been reaffirmed in modern English jurisprudence. Australian courts have adopted an approach that clearly differs from their English counterparts. This is because, in Australia, the equitable doctrine to grant relief against forfeiture can seemingly apply in the context of the forfeiture of non-proprietary rights (eg, where B loses a contractual right on an event of default).[3] The central argument presented in this chapter is that the Australian approach is to be preferred: there is no clear moral, analytical or historical justification for the strict insistence on limiting relief against forfeiture only to those cases where B loses a proprietary or possessory right. Put simply, it is hard to provide a positive justification for the property requirement. Three arguments are given in support of this position. The *first* argument is that the property requirement is not essential as a matter of legal history (*the conservative argument*). The *second* argument is that the property requirement is not essential analytically or as a matter of moral philosophy (*the corrective justice and curtailing opportunism arguments*). The *third* argument is that the property requirement risks strained reasoning as to what constitutes a proprietary or possessory right (*the coherence argument*).

II. Restating the Basic Requirements for Relief against Forfeiture

Relief against forfeiture is said to concern a long-established[4] rule under which equity will restrain B from losing (or forfeiting) a proprietary or possessory right to A on an event of default, even where the strict legal effect of a transaction between A and B is to produce such a result.[5] Pursuant to Anglo-Australian

[3] *Mineralogy Pty Ltd v Sino Iron Pty Ltd (No 6)* [2015] FCA 825; (2015) 329 ALR 1, [981] (Edelman J). See too *Mineralogy Pty Ltd v Sino Iron Pty Ltd* [2017] FCAFC 55, [421]; *Auburn Shopping Village Pty Ltd v Nelmeer Hoteliers Pty Ltd* [2018] NSWCA 114; 19 BPR 38569, [25] (Bathurst CJ); *Ayers Rock SkyShip Pty Ltd v Voyages Indigenous Tourism Australia Pty Ltd* [2019] NSWSC 828; 19 BPR 39541, [106]–[107] (Drake J); *JPA Finance Pty Ltd v Gordon Nominees Pty Ltd* [2019] VSCA 159; 58 VR 393, [82]. However, Brereton JA in *Kay v Playup Australia Pty Ltd* [2020] NSWCA 33, [100]–[123], favoured the English approach and took a more restrictive reading of Australian law to conclude in *obiter* that 'the doctrine [of relief against forfeiture] is confined to proprietary or possessory rights, and does not extend to mere contractual rights' (Macfarlan JA and Simpson AJA not deciding this point).

[4] Sharing its origins with the penalties doctrine: *Jobson v Johnson* [1985] 1 WLR 1026 (CA); R Francis, *Maxims of Equity* (London, E & R Nutt and R Golsing, 1728) 42–52; DEC Yale (ed), *Lord Nottingham's Chancery Cases*, Vol 2 (London, B Quaritch, 1957–61) 15–30; H Potter, *An Introduction to the History of Equity* (London, Sweet & Maxwell 1931) 57; RW Turner, *The Equity of Redemption* (Cambridge, Cambridge University Press, 1931) 17–42; CJ Rossiter, *Penalties and Forfeiture* (Sydney, Law Book Co, 1992) 20; RP Meagher, WMC Gummow and JR Lehane, *Equity: Doctrines and Remedies* (Sydney, Butterworths, 1975) 372; NA Tiverios, *Contractual Penalties in Australia and the United Kingdom: History, Theory and Practice* (Sydney, Federation Press, 2019) 9–44.

[5] JD Heydon, MJ Leeming and PG Turner, *Meagher, Gummow & Lehane's Equity: Doctrines & Remedies*, 5th edn (Sydney, LexisNexis, 2015) [18-210], note that relief against forfeiture can apply absent a breach of obligation [18-315]. See also NA Tiverios and B McFarlane, 'Controlling Private

law, there are two conceptually distinct grounds on which equity may provide B with relief against the forfeiture of her property right.[6] The first ground can be termed the 'security rights' basis for relief.[7] That is, where A's right to the forfeiture of B's property is inserted into the contract as a matter of substance[8] to secure either B's payment of money or B's performance of some other transactional event, equity will relieve B from the forfeiture of her property on the condition that she compensates (including interest and costs) A for the failure of the secured event.[9] This ground of relief against forfeiture was recently described by Lord Neuberger in *Cukurova Finance International Ltd v Alfa Telecom Turkey Ltd*[10] as being the 'paradigm case for relief' applicable where:

> the primary object of the bargain is to secure a stated result which can be effectively attained when the matter comes before the court, and where the forfeiture provision is added by way of security for the production of that result.[11]

The second ground of relief against forfeiture applies beyond the context of security rights and involves circumstances where A has engaged in an unconscientious exercise of a legal right or a legal power (termed here the 'unconscionability basis').[12] That is, B may be entitled to retain her property right in circumstances where A's exercise of a legal right or power in order to acquire B's property right is affected by fraud, accident, mistake or surprise,[13] provided that A has sufficient

Punishment in Three Dimensions: Penalties and Forfeiture in England and Australia' in E Bant et al (eds) *Punishment and Private Law* (London, Hart Publishing, 2021) (*forthcoming*).

[6] *Shiloh Spinners Ltd v Harding* [1973] AC 691 (HL), 722 (Lord Wilberforce); *Legione v Hateley* (1983) 152 CLR 406 (HCA), 424–25 (Gibbs CJ and Murphy J); *Australia Capital Financial Management Pty Ltd v Linfield Developments Pty Ltd; Guan v Linfield Developments Pty Ltd* [2017] NSWCA 99; (2017) 18 BPR 36683 (NSWCA), [357] (Ward JA); Heydon, Leeming and Turner (n 5) [18-250].

[7] ibid. See also B McFarlane, 'Penalties and Forfeiture' in J McGhee (ed), *Snell's Equity*, 33rd edn (3rd supp) (London, Sweet & Maxwell, 2015) [13-022]; N Chin, 'Relieving Against Forfeiture: Windfalls and Conscience' (1995) 25 *UWA Law Review* 110, 122–23; L Smith, 'Relief Against Forfeiture: A Restatement' (2001) 60 *Cambridge Law Journal* 178, 191; S Worthington, 'What is Left of Equity's Relief Against Forfeiture' in E Bant and M Harding (eds), *Exploring Private Law* (Cambridge, Cambridge University Press, 2010) 249, 258.

[8] Worthington (n 7) 267; Smith (n 7) 191–2.

[9] McFarlane (n 7) [13-025]. *Waddington in Kreglinger (G&C) v New Patagonia and Cold Storage Co Ltd* [1914] AC 25 (HL), 49–50 (Lord Parker); *Shiloh Spinners Ltd v Harding* (n 6) 722–3 (Lord Wilberforce); Worthington (n 7) 254; Smith (n 7) 195–7.

[10] *Cukurova Finance International Ltd v Alfa Telecom Turkey Ltd* [2013] UKPC 25; [2016] AC 923 (PC).

[11] ibid [90]. See also *Peachy v Duke of Somerset* (1721) 1 Str 447; 93 ER 626, 630 (Lord Macclesfield).

[12] *Mineralogy Pty Ltd v Sino Iron Pty Ltd (No 6)* (n 3) [987] (Edelman J); *Shiloh Spinners Ltd v Harding* (n 6); *Legione v Hateley* (n 6) 447 (Mason and Deane JJ); *Stern v Mcarthur* (1988) 165 CLR 489 (HCA); *Tanwar Enterprises Pty Ltd v Cauchi* [2003] HCA 57; (2003) 217 CLR 315 (HCA), [58] (Gleeson CJ, McHugh, Gummow, Hayne and Heydon JJ); Heydon, Leeming and Turner *Meagher, Gummow & Lehane's Equity* (n 5) [18-340].

[13] *Shiloh Spinners Ltd v Harding* (n 6) 722–23 (Lord Wilberforce); *Australian Competition and Consumer Commission v CG Berbatis Holdings Pty Ltd* [2003] HCA 18; (2003) 214 CLR 51 (HCA), [42] (Gummow and Hayne JJ).

notice of the impugned circumstances such that A's retention of B's property right is unconscionable.[14]

Given this starting point – that there are two separate bases of relief against forfeiture in Anglo-Australian law – what is the relationship between those bases and the purported additional requirement at English law that B forfeits a proprietary or possessory right to A? The answer provided by this chapter is clear: as a matter of legal history, coherence and morality, there should be no proprietary or possessory right requirement to engage either the security rights basis or unconscionability basis for relief against forfeiture.

III. The Conservative Argument: Proprietary or Possessory Right Requirement Not Essential as a Matter of Legal History

The first argument presented here is that the proprietary or possessory right requirement for the engagement of the equitable doctrine to relieve against forfeiture is not an historically entrenched feature of the general law. This is true for both the unconscionability basis for relief and the security rights basis for relief. In making this claim, I am not suggesting that the common law and equity ought to be governed solely by a series of lessons derived exclusively from a close study of English legal history. The principled conservative acknowledges that a system without the means of change will fail ultimately to conserve itself.[15] It is thus an inherent feature of the common law and equity that judge-made legal principles need room to develop incrementally. The claim being made here is more modest: in a system of law governed by precedent, legal history forms an important body of knowledge from which lawyers can draw pre-existing answers to difficult legal questions.[16] Put simply, in a body of law which dates back a millennium, there is little new under the sun. Accordingly, lawyers have access to the relevant 'collected reason of ages',[17] being a treasure trove of decided cases and related justifications (both judicial and extra-judicial) against which to test arguments and properly to understand legal rules in the course of the continuous process of refining and restating the law. For present purposes, it suffices to note that the arguments deployed in this chapter are not entirely novel. This is for the simple reason that

[14] Relief on the unconscionability basis is often refused on the basis that A has done nothing that affects her conscience (particularly in the context of relief on the basis of surprise and fraud): *Tanwar Enterprises Pty Ltd v Cauchi* (n 12) [58] [63] (Gleeson CJ, McHugh, Gummow, Hayne and Heydon JJ); *Auburn Shopping Village Pty Ltd v Nelmeer Hoteliers Pty Ltd* (n 3), [60]–[65] (Bathurst CJ).

[15] Edmund Burke, *Reflections on the Revolution in France* (first published 1790, Oxford, Oxford University Press, 2009) 21.

[16] L Smith, 'Fusion and Tradition' in S Degeling and J Edelman (eds), *Equity in Commercial Law* (Sydney, Lawbook Co, 2005) 38.

[17] Burke (n 15) 95.

lawyers appearing before the Court of Chancery situated at either Westminster Hall or the Old Hall at Lincoln's Inn would not have insisted upon a proprietary or possessory right requirement when seeking relief against forfeiture.

Starting with the unconscionability basis for relief. The unconscionability basis for relief emerged as an identifiable legal principle from, at the very latest, the end of the reign of Elizabeth I (1558–1603).[18] During this period, Chancery continued to expand and refine the circumstances in which a defendant could be afforded relief from the strict legal enforcement of a conditional bond (being a form of written personal obligation evidenced under seal)[19] to those where the defendant had suffered an accident or extremity, made a mistake, was the subject of equitable fraud or had only made a trifling default, provided that the defendant compensated the plaintiff for any loss suffered.[20] The relevant principles on which equity would grant relief were captured in the opening pages of *Sir George Cary's Chancery Cases (1558–1602)*:

> [i]f a man be bound in a penalty to pay money at a day and place, by obligation, and intending to pay the same, is robbed by the way; or hath intreated by word some other respite at the hands of the obligee, or cometh short of the place by any misfortune; and so failing of the payment, doth nevertheless provide and tender the money in short time after; in these, and many such like cases, the Chancery will compel the obligee to take his principal, with some reasonable consideration of his damages (*quantum expediat*), for if this was not, men would do that by covenant which they do now by bond.[21]

These principles are continued on the second page of *Cary's Cases* and include circumstances of trivial default (albeit this time using one example concerning the forfeiture of a proprietary right):

> [t]he like favour is extendable against them that will take advantage upon any strict condition, for undoing the estate of another in lands, upon a small or trifling default.
>
> ...
>
> If the obligee have received the most part of the money, payable upon the obligation at the peremptory time and place, and will nevertheless extend the whole forfeiture

[18] AWB Simpson, 'The Penal Bond with Conditional Defeasance' (1966) 82 *Law Quarterly Review* 392, 395. Although it would be wrong to suggest that the development of these principles was linear. Lord Keeper Egerton (1596–1603) (latter known as Lord Ellesmere, the Lord Chancellor between 1603–16) is said to have been restrictive about granting relief from a bond: WJ Jones, *The Elizabethan Court of Chancery* (Oxford, Oxford University Press, 1967) 447; Yale (n 4) 15.

[19] On the nature of conditional bonds generally see: AWB Simpson, *A History of the Common Law of Contract* (Oxford, Clarendon Press, 1987) 90–92; David Ibbetson, *A Historical Introduction to the Law of Obligations* (Oxford, Oxford University Press, 1999) 28–30; NA Tiverios, 'A Restatement of Relief Against Contractual Penalties (I)' (2017) 11 *Journal of Equity* 1, 6; Tiverios (n 4) 9–44.

[20] See the case examples listed in Francis (n 4) 27–29.

[21] *Anon* (1558–1602) Cary 1–2; 21 ER 1. Sir George Cary (or Carew) was a master in chancery who recorded the principles on which the Court operated in the early seventeenth century based primarily on the notes of William Lambarde. See also Jones (n 18) 111–16, 436; Turner (n 4) 25; Simpson (n 18) 416; R Halson, *Liquidated Damages and Penalty Clauses* (Oxford, Oxford University Press, 2018) [1.16]; Tiverios (n 4) 9–44.

> immediately, refusing soon after the default to accept of the residue rendered unto him, the obligor may find aid in Chancery.[22]

The principles enunciated in *Cary's Cases* can be more succinctly covered by the classical formulation that equity is, at least in part, concerned with circumstances in which A takes advantage of B by virtue of the presence of 'fraud, accident [or] mistake'[23] or, put another way, that in equity '[t]hree things are to be helpt in Conscience; Fraud, Accident, and things of Confidence'.[24] What is most significant about this development concerning the unconscionability basis of relief is the interplay between different substantive legal principles operating at common law and in equity.[25] There was no strict requirement during this period that B forfeit a proprietary or possessory right to A.[26] Rather, equity was working (as it still does) as a body of second order legal rules owing to the strictness and generality of the common law. The unconscionability basis for relief commenced as a body of second order principles under which a particular outcome at law was assumed, but then equity disabled A's strict exercise of legal rights and powers in certain recognised circumstances which affected A's conscience as against B.[27]

In a similar vein, there was no inherent historical property requirement involved in the security rights basis for relief. This is most clearly illustrated by the shared history of relief against penalties and forfeitures in this context. Most notably, the fact that by (at least) the time of the Restoration (1660), equity would grant relief from a punitive security right *irrespective* of whether A's security right against B was personal or proprietary in character. The personal obligations evidenced by a penal bond with a conditional defeasance provided the archetypal (but not exclusive) historical example of a transaction that generally satisfied the criteria for relief (alongside the parallel development of a mortgagor's equity of redemption).[28] The two central criteria for relief in the post-Restoration authorities were: (i) the characterisation[29] of a purported penalty in favour of A enforceable against B as being in the nature of a security or collateral to ensure B's performance of a legal duty or the fulfilment of some other condition; and (ii) A (being the innocent party) being required to be compensated by B for B's failure

[22] *Anon* (1558–1602) Cary 2; 21 ER 1.

[23] Potter (n 4) 57. See too William Blackstone, *Commentaries on the Laws of England: Book III* (first published 1768, Oxford, Oxford University Press, 2016) 432; *Earl of Bath v Sherwin* (1710) 10 Modern 1; 88 ER 596. Although at times the expression 'fraud, trust and accident' was used.

[24] 1 Roll Abr 374.

[25] Jones (n 18) 422.

[26] However, it is not necessarily the case that the right will be forfeited *to* A, but that simply the impugned right will be forfeited. For example, in the case of lessor-lessee, if the latter forfeits the right, the former does not acquire it, *his* right is instead transformed from a freehold in reversion to a freehold in possession.

[27] Jones (n 18) 447. On a strand of equitable jurisprudence being thought of as curtailing opportunistic behaviour, see HE Smith, 'Equity and Administrative Behaviour' in PG Turner (ed), *Equity and Administration* (Cambridge, Cambridge University Press, 2016) 326, 330–35.

[28] Potter (n 4) 57, 99.

[29] Yale (n 4) 24–25; Several Gentlemen of the Respective Branches of Law (Anon), *A Supplement to Viner's Abridgement*, Vol V (London, A Strahan, 1805) 375; *Howard v Harris* (1681) 1 Vern 33; 23 ER 288;

to perform or fulfil the underlying secured duty or stipulation.[30] These criteria are set out in DEC Yale's analysis of Lord Nottingham's methodology in relief against penalty and forfeiture cases:

> [t]he principle that Lord Nottingham took was to test whether the impeached transaction was in the nature of a security. If it were, it was a proper occasion for compensation and would not be allowed generally to work a forfeiture or inflict a penalty.[31]

In this connection Richard Francis distilled the following general principle in his 1728 treatise *Maxims of Equity*: 'equity suffers not advantage to be taken of a penalty or forfeiture, where compensation can be made'.[32]

The penal bond with a conditional defeasance was a typical example of a transaction (and form of personal obligation) that generally satisfied these two criteria. That is, a transaction where a penalty was evidenced on the face of a bond to secure the performance of an underlying condition of defeasance: equity would restrain A's strict legal enforcement of the bond provided B could compensate A for the failure (or non-performance) of the condition of defeasance. For example, where A and B agreed that B would deliver a cargo of rice to A (on date X) for the sum of £10 recorded as a condition of defeasance on the back of a bond, which otherwise stated on its face that B would pay A the sum of £30 (the penalty) on date X+1, equity would look at the underlying substance of the transaction and treat (or mould) A's personal right to £30 as existing for the accessorial or collateral purpose of ensuring that A would have his cargo of rice on date X. If B failed to deliver the rice by date X, then, in equity, A would only be able to enforce the agreed remedy contained on the face of the bond (ie, the personal obligation that B pay to A £30) to the extent that it was compensatory in light of the condition that the sum secured. That is, A would be put in the same financial position as if the condition of defeasance had been fulfilled (ie, as if B had delivered the cargo of rice on time).[33] But A would not necessarily be able fully to enforce his strict legal right to the sum of £30.

Marks v Marks (1718) Prec Ch 486; 24 ER 218, 219 (Sir Thomas Powis and Sir Robert Raymond); *Peachy v Duke of Somerset* (n 11) 630 (Lord Macclesfield); *Roy v Duke of Beaufort* (1741) 2 Atk 191; 26 ER 519, 520 (Lord Hardwicke); *Lowe v Peers* (1768) 4 Burr 2225; 98 ER 160, 162 (Lord Mansfield); *Sloman v Walter* (1783) 1 Bro CC 418; 28 ER 1213, 1214 (Lord Thurlow); *Clark v Watkins* (1863) 1 New Rep 227, 228 (Stuart VC); *Thompson v Hudson* (1869–70) (1869–70) LR 4 (HL) 1, 15 (Lord Hatherley); *Protector Endowment Loan and Annuity Co v Grice* (1880) 5 QBD 592 (CA), 595 (Baggallay LJ).

[30] Where it was not possible to assess the damages which A had suffered relief from the strict enforcement of the penalty would not be granted: *Tall v Ryland* (1670) 1 Chan Cas 183; 22 ER 753.

[31] Yale (n 4) 24–25.

[32] Francis (n 4) 44 (there are plenty of non-property-based examples listed). See also JL Barton, 'Penalties and Damages' (1976) 92 *Law Quarterly Review* 20, 23: '[i]n the year 1700, the statement that a penalty is intended merely as security for the performance of an agreement expressed a well-understood fact of commercial life'.

[33] B had to pay to A the loss caused to A by the failure of the condition of defeasance, interest and any relevant legal costs.

The same analysis can be deployed with respect to the common mortgage. Under such a transaction, the mortgagor (ie, B) was subject to a penalty in favour of the mortgagee (ie, A) for the non-performance of a loan. Take the standard mortgage example from *Coke on Littleton* whereby B (the original owner) would transfer Whiteacre to A (a creditor) on the condition that: (i) if B repays a loan of £40 to A on a set date in six months' time then B shall have the land retransferred back to him; otherwise (ii) if B fails to make the required repayment then Whiteacre remains A's property.[34] Like our conditional bond example, in Chancery B was relieved (as a matter of course) from the strict legal consequences in the case of non-performance of the condition to repay the principal within six months. Importantly, equity did so by disabling A's strict insistence on his legal rights so as not to exact a punishment on B (ie, to mould A's right to Whiteacre into a security right and provide relief against a penalty) and not by reason of any special rule about mortgages or B losing a property right.[35] As Viscount Haldane correctly observed in *Kreglinger v New Patagonia Meat and Cold Storage Co Ltd*,[36] equitable relief in the case of a mortgage was: 'merely a special application of a more general power to relieve against penalties and to mould them into mere securities'.[37]

The idea that equity could grant relief from a personal security right that exacted a punishment on B does not rest solely on the influential post-Restoration Chancellorship of Lord Nottingham. Rather, it maps how the penalties doctrine and relief against forfeiture were commonly understood until a change of direction in the early twentieth century.[38] In penalties and forfeiture cases, equity was ensuring that such punitive security rights contained in a written obligation were only enforced insofar as they were required to secure the enjoyment of the related primary object of the transaction. It is for this reason that in *Thompson v Hudson*,[39] Lord Hatherley summarised a unified general underlying principle with respect to penalties and forfeitures:

[34] Edward Coke, *The First Part of the Institutes of the Laws of England: or, A Commentary upon Littleton*, 11th edn (London, Eliz Nutt and R Gosling, 1717) 322.

[35] On the common moral justification between penalties and forfeitures see too, WE Grigsby, *Story's Commentaries on Equity Jurisprudence*, 1st English edn, (London, Stevens & Haynes, 1884) 906.

[36] *Kreglinger v New Patagonia Meat and Cold Storage Co Ltd* [1914] AC 25 (HL).

[37] ibid 35. See also: *Boucaut Bay Co Ltd v Commonwealth* (1927) 40 CLR 98 (HCA), 103 (Starke J); *Campbell Discount Company Ltd v Bridge* [1962] AC 600 (HL), 630 (Lord Denning); *Forestry Commission of NSW v Stefanetto* (1976) 133 CLR 507 (HCA), 519 (Mason J); *Jobson v Johnson* (n 4) 1038 (Nicholls LJ); A Mason, 'Themes and Prospects' in PD Finn (ed) *Essays in Equity* (Sydney, Law Book Co, 1985) 248; M Evans, *Outline of Equity and Trusts* (Sydney, Butterworths, 1988) 121. But see: M Tilbury and CJ Rossiter, 'Relief Against Forfeiture' in P Parkinson (ed) *The Principles of Equity*, 2nd edn (Sydney, Thomson, 2003) 322.

[38] See generally: Tiverios (n 4) 9–44. WD Evans, *Pothier on the Law of Obligations: Volume II* (London, A Strahan, 1806) 85–94; F White and O Tudor, *A Selection of the Leading Cases in Equity Volume II*, 8th edn (London, Sweet & Maxwell, 1912) 255–95; Anon, *A Supplement to Viner's Abridgement* (n 29) 375; *Wheeler v Whithall* (1676) 2 Freeman 9; 22 ER 1023; *Howard v Harris* (n 29); *Peachy v Duke of Somerset* (n 11); 93 ER 626, 630 (Lord Macclesfield); *Roy v Duke of Beaufort* (n 29) 520 (Lord Hardwicke); *Lowe v Peers* (n 29) 162 (Lord Mansfield); *Sloman v Walter* (n 29) 1214 (Lord Thurlow); *Clark v Watkins* (n 29) 228 (Stuart VC); *Protector Endowment Loan and Annuity Co v Grice* (n 29) 595 (Baggallay LJ).

[39] *Thompson v Hudson* (n 29) 15 (Lord Hatherley).

> I take the law to be perfectly clear … namely, that where there is a debt actually due, and in respect of that debt a security is given, be it by way of mortgage or be it by way of stipulation that in case of its not being paid at the time appointed a larger sum shall become payable, and be paid, in either of those cases equity regards the security that has been given as a mere pledge for the debt, and it will not allow either a forfeiture of the property pledged, or any augmentation of the debt as a penal provision, on the ground that equity regards the contemplated forfeiture which might take place at law with reference to the estate as in the nature of a penal provision, against which equity will relieve when the object in view, namely, the securing of the debt, is attained, and regarding also the stipulation for the payment of a larger sum of money, if the sum be not paid at the time it is due, as a penalty and a forfeiture against which equity will relieve.[40]

It is for this reason that one can pick up a leading legal text from the eighteenth or nineteenth century and see little formal distinction between penalties and forfeitures (although the first English edition of *Story's Commentaries* published in 1884 notes, albeit critically, the emerging distinction[41] between penalties in the nature of a security and punitive forfeitures in the nature of security).[42] The analysis above should suffice to prove that, as a matter of legal history, no proprietary or possessory right requirement was necessary to support either the unconscionability or the security rights basis for relief against forfeiture. Both rules were more than capable of applying to personal obligations between A and B, the most obvious examples being cases concerning conditional bonds. The principal reason for this conclusion in the context of the security rights basis for relief is that the central mischief with which equity was concerned was the prevention of consent-based punishments. Such a mandatory rule ought to apply irrespective of whether B forfeited an asset or had to pay a fixed monetary sum to A. Properly understood in its historical context, the security rights basis for relief against forfeiture becomes no more than a context specific application of a wider equitable rule against the strict legal enforcement of penalties (ie, on this approach there is a unified and broad based equitable jurisdiction to relieve against security rights). Likewise, the operation of the unconscionability basis for relief looked more closely at A's opportunistic exercise of a legal right or power that was either procured or enlivened as a result of some factor which ought to put restraints on how A could exercise her

[40] ibid.

[41] That distinction being that relief against forfeiture was then being applied more narrowly only to circumstances whereby the secured default was the failure to pay a sum certain and not where 'the forfeiture arises from the breach of any other covenants of a collateral nature; as for example, of a covenant to repair'. The author of *Story* notes that this was a mere distinction rather than a positive justification for differing treatment. Noting that: 'in the case of a penalty, such a distinction is wholly repudiated; because the penalty is treated as a security. The forfeiture is also treated as a security, in the cases of non-payment of rent. And in other cases of covenant, if the damages are capable of being ascertained, and will, in a legal and equitable sense, be an adequate compensation, the reason is not very clear why, under such circumstances, the forfeiture may not be equally treated as a security for such damages': Grigsby (n 35) 912.

[42] See, eg: Francis (n 4) 44–52; Grigsby (n 35) 904–14.

right. Such factors, be it a mistake, accident, surprise etc., transcend whether A's behaviour concerns a legal right or power relating to B's proprietary or possessory right. As a matter of legal history and analytical structure, equity can restrain the exercise of legal rights and powers irrespective of whether those rights and powers relate to the acquisition or forfeiture of a right that would be exigible against third parties (ie, a proprietary or possessory right).[43]

IV. The Corrective Justice and Curtailing Opportunism Arguments: Property Requirement Not Analytically Essential as a Matter of Moral Philosophy

A. Security Rights Basis for Relief

The position taken in this chapter is that the security rights basis for relief against forfeiture is best explained as a rule of corrective justice. By this, it is meant that the security rights basis for relief ought to be best understood as no more than a specific application of equity's jurisdiction to relieve against penalties whereby the penalty in question concerns an asset and not simply the payment or forfeiture of an agreed monetary sum. This position is subject to one important caveat: many cases will be explained wholly by the objective intentions of the parties. For example, the typical consumer mortgage transaction is entered today on the express understanding that the mortgagee has no more than a security right over the mortgagor's property. In such circumstances, it is the parties who are exercising their legal powers to create consent-based obligations in a particular way pursuant to which A's right is objectively understood as being acquired for the limited purpose of security (ie, A's 'security' right against B was intended to be no more than a purposive right from the get-go).[44] Putting to one side such intention-based cases, it is worth unpacking the normative reasons why equity grants relief from forfeiture.

The argument presented here is that once A's legal right (or power) against B (whether contractual or proprietary in nature) is characterised[45] as being a

[43] See also JS Getzler, 'Forfeiture for Breach of a Time Condition' (2004) 120 *Law Quarterly Review* 203, 205: 'equity did not act in order to protect an estate contract from being unconscionably cancelled by [A], but rather scrutinized [A's] resort to a contractual power (rescission) in itself for possible taint'; *Hampton v BHP Billiton Minerals Pty Ltd (No 2)* [2012] WASC 285, [239]–[240] (Edelman J); *Mineralogy Pty Ltd v Sino Iron Pty Ltd (No 6)* (n 3) [988] (Edelman J).

[44] See, eg: R Calnan, *Taking Security*, 3rd edn (London, Jordans, 2013) [3.118].

[45] Meaning here not simply applying the linguistic or semantic meaning of the text but the ultimate legal effect a court is willing to give a text (ie, giving effect to the substance of the agreement and not merely its linguistic form): *Dunlop Pneumatic Tyre Co Limited v New Garage and Motor Company Limited* [1915] AC 79 (HL), 86 (Lord Dunedin); *Re Universal Management* [1983] NZLR 462, 470 (Cooke J); *Street v Mountford* [1985] AC 809; *Welsh Development Agency v Export Finance Co Ltd* [1992] BCC 270 (CA), 278 (Dillon LJ); 300 (Staughton LJ); *Re Spectrum Plus* [2005] 2 AC 680 (HL), [116]–[117] (Lord Scott).

security, equity has a set of default rules that restrain how such a right can be enforced. This approach of disabling A's strict exercise of an otherwise valid legal right accurately reflects the equitable origins of relief against penalties and forfeitures and the 'second order' analytical structure of equity in controlling the exercise of legal rights.[46] It is important to appreciate that the security rights basis for relief does not operate in the abstract. Rather, the doctrine evaluates the relationship between two consent-based rights and how those rights are exercised.[47] That is to say, the security rights basis for relief against forfeiture serves the purpose of ensuring that where the function of one right, going beyond its bare linguistic meaning, is to provide security for the performance of a primary or principal right (which would historically have been fully enforceable at common law)[48] then it would be punitive for A's security right to be enforced *beyond* that function.[49] If A is able to enforce her collateral or security significantly beyond the monetised value of the underlying secured primary right (or condition), the result would be that the impugned security right would have a punitive operation, thereby imposing an unjustifiable burden on B given the primary purpose of the transaction. Viewed in this way, for the security rights basis for relief to be applicable there must first be a collateral or security right that operates to ensure the performance or occurrence of a related underlying primary condition or obligation. In such circumstances, equity will restrain the exercise of A's security right in order to ensure that it is only enforced to the extent necessary to secure performance of the related primary condition (or the condition's monetised equivalent).

From this starting point it is axiomatic that most security rights taken over an asset will be inherently punitive in nature as: (i) the asset is unlikely accurately to reflect the monetary value of the underlying secured primary condition (even more so where the same asset is forfeit on the breach or failure of multiple stipulations);[50] and (ii) in any case where the asset secures the performance

[46] FW Maitland, *Equity: A Course of Lectures* (Cambridge, Cambridge University Press, 1936) 17–19. See also: WJV Windeyer, *Lectures on Legal History*, 2nd edn, (Sydney, Lawbook Co, 1957) 259; B McFarlane and R Stevens, 'What's Special about Equity? Rights about Rights' in D Klimchuk, I Samet and HE Smith (eds), *Philosophical Foundations of the Law of Equity* (Oxford, Oxford University Press, 2020) ch 9; B McFarlane, 'Avoiding Anarchy? Common Law v Equity and Maitland v Hohfeld' in J Goldberg, HE Smith and PG Turner (eds), *Equity and Law: Fusion and Fission* (Cambridge, Cambridge University Press, 2019) 331; HE Smith, 'Equitable Defences as Meta-Law' in PS Davies, S Douglas and J Goudkamp (eds), *Defences in Equity* (London, Hart Publishing, 2018) 17.

[47] *Hughes v Metropolitan Rly Co* (1876–77) LR 2 App Cas 439 (HL), 448 (Lord Cairns).

[48] See generally: n 19 above.

[49] See also: *Campbell Discount Company Ltd v Bridge* (n 37) 629 (Lord Denning): '[t]he whole system of equity jurisprudence proceeds upon the ground that a party, having a legal right, shall not be permitted to avail himself of it for the purpose of an injustice, or fraud, or oppression, or hard or vindictive injury'.

[50] See, eg: Calnan (n 44) [1.29], [5.13–[5.15], [8.09]. In order to mitigate risk most lenders seek security which is worth more in monetary terms than the underlying secured condition.

of a loan (or a series of ongoing contractual obligations) then the unrestrained full forfeiture of the asset will tend in the direction of becoming more punitive the closer the debtor or obligor gets to full performance (ie, the forfeiture of the asset scales towards being more punitive the longer A cannot quibble with B's performance).[51]

What conclusions can be drawn from this analytical overview of the security rights basis for relief against forfeiture? If we are to assess the security rights basis for relief in its most favourable light, there are two potential overlapping normative reasons why the law might want to prohibit A from fully enforcing her security right against B. Both reasons are derived from a theory of corrective justice which is commingled with Kantian deontology.[52] Importantly for present purposes, neither of these moral justifications hinge on A's right against B being proprietary in nature.

The first reason to limit the full enforcement of a security right is that it ensures that any consent-based remedy which A receives (or sanction B is subject to) serves as an accurate response to the transactional disadvantage that A suffers as a result of the failure of the underlying secured condition.[53] Where equity provides relief against forfeiture on the security rights basis A is disabled from receiving a windfall (and B from being subject to the corresponding detriment) in light of how the law attributes value to the fulfilment of the underlying secured primary condition. That is, A is being disabled from the strict enforcement of her legal rights beyond

[51] See, eg: *Kilmer v British Columbia Orchard Lands Limited* [1913] AC 319 (HL): a clause was held to be punitive where it allowed a vendor of real property to retain: (i) the land; and (ii) any purchase payments, where a purchaser in possession (B) defaulted in making an obliged purchase payment. As Lord Moulton observed at 325: '[t]he circumstances of this case seem to bring it entirely within the ruling of the *Dagenham Dock Case*. It seems to be even a stronger case, for the penalty, if enforced according to the letter of the agreement, becomes more and more severe as the agreement approaches completion, and the money liable to confiscation becomes larger'. See also: *Public Works Commissioner v Hills* [1906] AC 368 (PC), 375–76 (Lord Dunedin); *Donegal International Limited v Republic of Zambia* [2007] EWHC 197 (Comm); [2007] 1 Lloyd's Rep 397 (QB), [511] (Andrew Smith J); *Vivienne Westwood Ltd v Conduit Street Development Ltd* [2017] EWHC 350 (Ch); [2017] L&TR 23 (Ch), [54]–[65] (Fancourt QC); Tiverios (n 4) 147.

[52] See, eg: Aristotle, *Nicomachean Ethics* (Cambridge, Cambridge University Press, 2014) [1131a1]–[1131b26]; EJ Weinrib, *Corrective Justice* (Oxford, Oxford University Press, 2012) 96–98; 169–84; Smith (n 7) 188–89. On consent-based promises being binding as a matter of deontology see generally: Immanuel Kant, *Groundwork of the Metaphysics of Morals* (first published 1785, Cambridge, Cambridge University Press, 2012) [4:403], it can be deduced from strict logic that all promises must be taken seriously as a failure to make this a universal rule would make it 'futile to pretend my will to others with regard to my future actions, who would not believe this pretense'.

[53] Weinrib (n 52) 96–98, 172–75; EJ Weinrib, 'Corrective Justice in a Nutshell' (2002) 52 *University of Toronto Law Journal* 349, 349; Smith (n 7) 188–89; PS Davies and PG Turner, 'Relief Against Penalties Without a Breach of Contract' (2013) 72 *Cambridge Law Journal* 20, 23; Rossiter (n 4) 13; Tiverios (n 4) 61–67; J Gardner, *Torts and Other Wrongs* (Oxford, Oxford University Press, 2019) 336–41, who observes that the standard remedial response to a breach of contract is 'primarily reparative' and seeks to achieve 'primarily corrective justice' between the parties.

what is needed to correct the financial disadvantage or 'injury'[54] A has suffered due to the failure of the underlying secured condition. As a matter of mandatory policy, A's interests are primarily quantified by the underlying secured condition or obligation which, in turn, dictates what A would have received had the impugned transaction been performed or fulfilled. If B can fully compensate A for the failure of the underlying secured condition or obligation then it is justifiable for the court to interfere with A's enforcement of the accessorial security right (ie, 'it is the availability of compensation which generates the "equity" upon which the court intervenes; without it, the parties are left to their legal rights and obligations').[55] The extent to which A is entitled to enforce a security right in equity is determined by the value the law attributes to the underlying secured condition (ie, corrective justice considerations still enable the parties to a voluntary transaction to determine the price of the *substantive* transaction but equity is willing to intervene in order to limit the enforcement of collateral or accessional punitive consent-based sanctions or remedies).[56] The corollary of this point is that were A allowed fully to retain the forfeited asset, the full enforcement of the forfeiture clause would be in the nature of a penalty or punishment imposed upon B (given the value of the underlying secured condition or obligation).

It is common for any mandatory policy that interferes with consent-based transactions (such as the security rights basis for relief against forfeiture) to be critiqued on the basis that it detracts impermissibly from the parties' powers to form consent based transactions.[57] While there is much force in such critiques,[58] it is important to ensure that they are not erected in a manner that attacks a straw man. Accordingly, it is important to appreciate that, in one salient respect, the security rights basis for relief does *not* detract from the content of the parties' bargain: equity's power to disable the strict exercise of a security right ensures that A nonetheless receives the monetised value of the underlying secured primary condition or obligation. That is, A is always placed in the financial position in which she would have been had the underlying primary rights or conditions been properly performed or fulfilled. The court is giving effect to the parties' intentions insofar as the *fundamentals* of the contract are concerned but equity is treating the accessory security right as akin to an ineffective punitive deterrent

[54] Grigsby (n 35) 911.

[55] *Andrews v Australia and New Zealand Banking Group* [2012] HCA 30; (2012) 247 CLR 205 (HCA), [11] (French CJ, Gummow, Crennan, Kiefel and Bell JJ) citing with approval *Peachy v Duke of Somerset* (n 11) 630 (Lord Macclesfield). See also Chin (n 7) 123.

[56] The rejoinder to this point being that an agreed remedy clause (including a forfeiture clause) can nonetheless have a significant impact on: (i) the price of the bargain; or (ii) the creation of the bargain; and that (iii) any injustice that is imposed on B has been, at one point, been voluntarily assumed by B. See Tiverios (n 4) 88–89. See also *Re Newman; Ex Parte Caper* (1876) 4 Ch D 724, 729 (Bacon CJ).

[57] *Ringrow Pty Ltd v BP Australia Pty Ltd* [2005] HCA 71; (2005) 224 CLR 65 (HCA), [32] (Gleeson CJ, Gummow, Kirby, Hayne, Callinan and Heydon JJ).

[58] See generally: Tiverios (n 4) chs 2 and 3.

(ie, the court is not giving effect to the parties' intentions on the accessorial or 'side issue').[59] Likewise, B's primary expectations under the impugned transaction are also protected in that provided B compensates A, equity will restrain the full enforcement of the security right.[60] On the other hand, there is one key sense in which the security rights basis for relief is not respectful of the linguistic meaning of the parties' bargain. This is the potential for the doctrine to impose external principles onto the transactional text in order to mould the ultimate legal effect of A's right against B into serving the limited function of security for performance.

The second normative reason why A is restrained from fully exercising a security right against B is that the full enforcement of punitive consent-based sanctions should not be a function of civil courts, particularly when prompted to take action by private litigants. That is, the security rights basis for relief prevents private individuals from using courts and the common law to punish a transactional counterparty for their own benefit. This is because punishment is a function that typically attaches to breaches of public duties and is not a remedial response designed to redress a disadvantage caused to A by the failure of a consent-based transaction, perhaps save for particular exceptional circumstances governed by general law principles.[61] On this institutional approach to preventing the full enforcement of a security right, A is prevented from acting as a private prosecutor by inhibiting A from receiving a financial incentive (ultimately funded by B) as a result of enforcing fully an impugned security right.[62] The corollary of A's position being that the penalties doctrine and the security rights basis for relief against forfeiture shield B from being subject to private punishment without the protections commonly afforded under the criminal law. That is to say, while the security rights basis for relief prevents the imposition of a punishment (ie, B is not going to lose the full value of the family house when defaulting on a loan secured by a mortgage) it still allows A to receive fair recompense for the value of the breach of, or failure of, the underlying secured condition.[63]

[59] See also: PS Atiyah, *Essays on Contract* (Oxford, Oxford University Press, 1988) 369–74, suggests that the parties do not intend to be bound at all by such clause as they are not the 'primary purpose' of the contract but merely operate as an ineffective deterrent.

[60] Smith (n 7) 188–89.

[61] First, the remedy of an account of profits for breach of a fiduciary duty, although an unexceptional remedy in equity, stems from the nature of the accounting relationship between the fiduciary and her principal and is thus different in kind to the typical contractual relationship or typical contractual duty. Second, and perhaps more relevantly, the imposition of disgorgement or restitutionary damages for breach of contract in England (which is not the law in Australia) is limited to 'exceptional circumstances' governed by general law principles.

[62] Weinrib (n 52) 96–98, 170–71.

[63] See also: Simpson (n 18) 421; Yale (n 4) 16.

B. Unconscionability Basis for Relief

There is, similarly, nothing in the nature of the unconscionability basis for relief that necessitates that what B must forfeit to A is a proprietary or possessory right. This is because, at a high level of generality, the mischief at which equity appears to be directed is limiting A's opportunistic exercise of a legal right or power given the circumstances under which that right was acquired or the power exercised.[64] Put another way, equity is concerned with ensuring legal rights and powers are exercised with a baseline modicum of good conscience (ie, equity is acting as a body of second order principles which disables A's strict insistence on primary legal rights in order to prevent unconscionable conduct).[65] It stands to reason that such opportunistic conduct ought to be prevented *irrespective* of whether B's forfeited right is proprietary, possessory, personal or derived from statute (ie, the third party effects of such a right are by the by as between A and B). This general justification captures the more specific heads of relief pertaining to the special heads[66] of fraud,[67] accident,[68]

[64] See, eg: HE Smith (n 27) 330–35.

[65] In this connection see too JE Penner, 'We All Make Mistakes: A "Duty of Virtue" Theory of Restitutionary Liability for Mistaken Payments' (2018) 81 *Modern Law Review* 222, especially at 234–46.

[66] See, eg: n 12 above.

[67] Relief for fraud involves circumstances whereby B's forfeiture was caused by A's sharp practice (ie A's impugned conduct has caused or contributed to a significant degree to B's non-performance of a covenant, or non-fulfilment of a condition). One clear example of such conduct would involve circumstances where A's wrongdoing has resulted in B's default. As William Noy said in his seventeenth century treatise on the laws of England, to allow A to recover an agreed sanction or remedy in circumstances whereby A has relevantly stultified B's performance would enable A to use the courts as a mechanism by which A could take advantage of his own wrongdoing: W Noy, *A treatise of the principal grounds and maxims of the laws of this nation*, 4th edn (London, Sawbridge & Rawlins, 1667) 12. However, it is often observed that the concept of equitable fraud is wider than its common law equivalent such that this head of relief can apply in novel circumstances whereby A has not committed a legal wrong: Yale (n 4) 7; Turner (n 4) 24; Potter (n 4) 58; Heydon, Leeming and Turner (n 5) [18-255]. A wider understanding of equitable fraud could be used as a way of potentially understanding the decision in *Hughes v Metropolitan Rly Co* (n 47) 448 (Lord Cairns).

[68] Relief for accident involves circumstances whereby B's right has been fortified to A as a result of an unforeseen and unexpected event. That event must have occurred: 'external to [B, being] the party affected by it, and which [B's] own agency is not the proximate cause, whereby, contrary to his own intention and wish, [B] loses some legal right or becomes subject to some legal liability, and [A] acquires the corresponding legal right, which would be a violation of good conscience for [A], under the circumstances, to retain': JN Pomeroy, *A Treatise in Equity Jurisprudence Vol III*, 5th edn (San Francisco, Bancroft-Whitney, 1941) [823]; Heydon, Leeming and Turner (n 5) [18-255]. Such relief is somewhat akin to the doctrine of frustration whereby equity is providing B with relief from a forfeiture where an external and unforeseen event has caused B's default (ie the equity is reallocating the risk of B's default in a limited set of circumstances not comprehended by the parties). However, there are two substantial differences between the doctrine of frustration and relief on the basis of accident. First, relief against accident does not require performance of the contract to be rendered 'radically different' from the agreed terms. Indeed, A is seeking to enforce strictly the agreed legal terms. Rather, relief on the basis accident requires B's forfeiture to be triggered by an unforeseen and unexpected event. Second, the court will not provide B with relief where he ought to have guarded himself from the impugned event by virtue of the contract: *Tanwar Enterprises Pty Ltd v Cauchi Tanwar Enterprises Pty Ltd v Cauchi* (n 12) [66].

mistake[69] or surprise.[70] However, on this understanding of the unconscionability basis, each species or category within the broader genus of relief against the strict enforcement of a legal right or power needs to be (more specifically) justified on its own terms. Put simply, why should A be prevented from being a stickler for his legal rights? What constitutes opportunism such that equity will limit A's exercise of an otherwise lawful legal right or power? The specific answers to these more particular questions do not need to be addressed at present.

An alternative (and ultimately similar) view of a high level theoretical link between the various heads of equitable relief on the unconscionability basis would be as follows: equity acknowledges that A has a legal right but insists that he exercise that right in a *virtuous* manner, or in a manner which cleanses A's conscience,[71] given the totality of the facts of the case. Indeed, equitable relief from the strict application of legal rights on the basis of factors such as fraud, accident, hardship, surprise, mistake and trivial default was established in a period when ecclesiastical Lord Chancellors were heavily influenced by virtue ethics as provided by Aristotle's *Nicomachean Ethics* (including as mediated through theologians such as Thomas Aquinas and Jean Gerson).[72] Importantly, Aristotle's wider project in *Nicomachean Ethics* argued that to achieve *eudemonia* or happiness,[73] an individual ought to live their life in a manner that cultivates a set of virtues of character and intellect

[69] Relief for mistake concerns circumstances whereby B was under a misapprehension about the operation of her legal rights and that misapprehension was causative in B's forfeiture (and thus A acquiring a benefit): *Pitt v Holt* [2013] 2 AC 108 (albeit a case involving the creation of a trust). Importantly, so far as mistake is concerned, although it may not be necessary to demonstrate that the impugned mistake was caused (or perhaps contributed to or encouraged) by A's conduct: *Tanwar Enterprises Pty Ltd v Cauchi* (n 12) [58]. It will, however, still be necessary for B to point to some additional circumstances which make it 'unconscientious' for A to rely on her strict legal rights: *Auburn Shopping Village Pty Ltd v Nelmeer Hoteliers Pty Ltd* (n 3), [63]–[65].

[70] Relief for surprise involves circumstances whereby A exercises legal rights or powers in circumstances where A has created an impression that she would not be a stickler for her legal rights such that she contributed to B's default (from B's perspective, the relevant 'surprise' being B becoming wrong-footed by A's newfound insistence on her strict legal position). Such relief is akin to an estoppel whereby A is prevented from benefiting (or resiling) from B's detriment to which A has contributed (the initial legal contractual rights and powers are based on the initial promises between A and B, but equity disables the strict application of these legal rights by virtue of A and B's subsequent reliance based conduct): *Auburn Shopping Village Pty Ltd v Nelmeer Hoteliers Pty Ltd* (n 3) [61]–[62]; *Tanwar Enterprises Pty Ltd v Cauchi* (n 12) [58] (Gleeson CJ, McHugh, Gummow, Hayne and Heydon JJ). On the moral basis for reliance-based liability see generally: SA Smith, *Contract Theory* (Oxford, Oxford University Press, 2004) 78–96.

[71] Jones (n 18) 424. Penner has made this observation in the context of restitution for mistake: (n 65 above).

[72] It is possible that later (ie, post-Restoration) officers of the Court of Equity directly used Aristotle to the same ends: D Ibbetson, 'A House Built on Sand: Equity in Early Modern English Law' in E Koops and WJ Zwalve (eds), *Law & Equity: Approaches in Roman Law and Common Law* (Leiden, Martinus Nijhoff, 2014) 58, 70; I Williams, 'Christopher St German: Religion, Conscience and Law in Reformation England' in M Hill and RH Helmholz (eds), *Great Christian Jurists in English History* (Cambridge, Cambridge University Press, 2017) 69, 81–85; J Salmond, *Jurisprudence*, 6th edn, (London, Sweet & Maxwell, 1920) 36. For more on the influence of Aristotle on British intellectual life from the early modern period to twentieth century see W Durant, *The Story of Philosophy*, 2nd edn (London, Simon & Shuster, 1933) 103, where the author (originally writing in 1926) observes that Aristotle's *Nicomachean Ethics* moulded the British ruling mind for over three hundred years.

[73] This conception essentially means be 'favoured by the gods' albeit in a secular sense.

(including the character of 'justice').[74] Thus the ethically right course of action in a given set of circumstances becomes the course of action that fosters virtuous characteristics and therefore self-development.

Unlike a rights-based theory, applying Aristotle, A should not be a stickler for his legal rights in circumstances where A's conscience is affected by fraud, mistake, accident or surprise, because to do so would make A less virtuous and therefore stultify A's chances of personal development towards happiness. If A is coerced in equity into acting in a virtuous manner, future litigants will be encouraged to act virtuously and will not attempt to avail themselves of their legal rights, but instead will accept their 'fair share' in the circumstances of the case.[75]

The difficulty with considerations of virtue disabling the strict insistence on legal rights are well understood and can be briefly stated:[76] virtue ethics provides for a form of justice that, as Aristotle conceded,[77] can give a different answer on the same set of facts. What does one do when virtue is conflicted? For example, assume for present purposes that the virtuous person (i) tells the truth; and (ii) is kind to his friends and family without being a flatterer.[78] Now further assume that my wife has had a difficult week at work and has just returned home from the hairdresser with a haircut that I think looks terrible. She then asks me the inevitable question: 'how does my hair look?' What does the virtuous person in my position do? What does conscience compel me to do? There is no correct answer.

Given my wife's difficult week I would be justified in being kind and not telling the truth on this one occasion. Alternatively, I could be justified in telling the truth on the basis that if I lie about the little things, then I would be more inclined to lie in the future (perhaps about more important matters). Further, my wife might be unimpressed if she finds out that I was not honest with her in the first place. It is also important to emphasise that this problem cannot be resolved by saying that

[74] These virtues include: (i) courage (fear and confidence); (ii) temperance (bodily pleasure and pain); (iii) generosity (giving and retaining money); (iv) magnificence (giving and retaining money on a large scale); (v) greatness of soul (honour on a large and small scale); (vi) even temper (anger); (vii) friendliness (general social relations); (viii) truthfulness (honesty about oneself); (ix) wit (conversation); (x) justice (including equitable, corrective and distributive justice); (xi) friendship (personal relations).

[75] If the Lord Chancellor is concerned with individuals acting with good conscience then ideally the individual will not need to be compelled but will organically act for the right reason: Aristotle (n 52) [1100a]–[1104a]. This is because it could be argued that state mandated altruism is not true altruism. See Williams (n 72) 86–88, for a discussion of sixteenth century equity's concern for the soul, noting that the guidance of the conscience of individuals was a prominent purpose of St German's *Doctor and Student*. See too St Thomas Aquinas, *Aquinas's Shorter Summa* (Manchester, Sophia Institute Press, 1993) 197–98: 'To say that a man discharges his proper office is equivalent to saying that he acts virtuously; for virtue of any being is that which makes its possessor good and also make his work good, as is stated in the second book of Aristotle's *Ethics*. Accordingly, since the ultimate end of man is eternal life, of which we spoke previously, not all attain it, but only those who act as virtue requires'.

[76] Of course, if individuals choose to operate this way as a matter of personal morality then this is an entirely different matter. Thus, I do not wish to be taken as saying that individuals ought not choose to act virtuously, seek meaning or self-improvement on a day-to-day basis.

[77] Aristotle (n 52) [1106b]–[1109b]; [1128a]–[1129a]: what is virtuous can change given the circumstances.

[78] For a similar example see Aristotle (n 52) [1126b]–[1127a].

conscience in this case can be objectively determined by a curial process, by asking what a reasonable person in my position would do.[79] This is because there is no syllogism (ie, there could be no agreement on the major premise of the syllogism) that will produce a consistent and transparent answer: reasonable minds can and will differ and, accordingly, the objective person would be justified in going either way.[80] Thus if A's exercise of his legal rights are going to be restrained on the basis of vague and protean-based concepts of 'unconscionability' or 'virtue', then equity is beginning to slip back into the realm of discretionary justice based on the Lord Chancellor's assessment of the totality of the facts.

By modern standards, too much of a discretionary approach would be seen as antithetical to the principled and transparent application of the general law (as a judge's reasoning could be no more than a thing covering for what is a matter of individual judicial taste).[81] With respect to the importance of legal certainty, it is a truism that the general law and associated coercive power of the state should ultimately 'be used only in cases defined in advance by the law and in such a way that it can be foreseen how it will be used'.[82] Thus it is unsurprising that the noticeable trend in modern cases involving the unconscionability basis for relief bends towards the tightening of the circumstances under which a court is willing to disable A's legal rights (ie, relief against forfeiture on the unconscionability basis appears to be an exceptional remedy).[83] It could be that an area of law based with its origins in a more protean concept of virtue ethics and good conscience

[79] As a rejoinder to my argument, insofar as cases are commonly reasoned by analogy, decided cases will, over time, form a body of knowledge that would be relevant in deciding any future case. Thus, as more cases are decided, principles concerning how to balance concepts such as 'virtue' or 'conscience' may become more precise. See also: AH, *Equity and Trusts*, 8th edn (Abingdon, Routledge, 2015) 1310, where conscience is described as 'being an embodiment of an objective ethics to which the individual is intended to aspire and by reference to which her deeds and misdeeds will be judged by the civil courts'.

[80] Put simply, to strip the haircut example down to its basics, a reasonable person would be justified in considering facts A, B and C and then concluding therefore D (tell the truth). However, the same person would also be justified in considering facts A, B and C and then concluding therefore E (be kind to your spouse). Kant (n 52) [4:418]: 'one cannot therefore act on determinate principles, but only according to empirical counsels, eg, of diet, of thrift, of politeness, of restraint, and so on, which experience teaches on average [to] advance the well-being most. From this it follows that the imperatives of prudence cannot, to be precise, command at all'.

[81] *Stewart v Atco Controls Pty Ltd* [2014] HCA 31; (2014) 252 CLR 307 (HCA), [31]; P Birks, 'Equity in Modern Law: An Exercise in Taxonomy' (1996) 26 *UWA Law Review* 1, 97; *Australian Competition and Consumer Commission v CG Berbatis Holdings Pty Ltd* (n 13) [43]; and NA Tiverios, 'Raiders of the secured asset: The doctrinal rationalisation for the liquidator's lien or charge over a secured asset post-Stewart v Atco' (2015) 23 *Insolvency Law Journal* 101, 106.

[82] FA Hayek, *The Road to Serfdom* (London, Routledge & Kegan Paul Ltd, 1944) 62. See also: J Twining (ed), *Selected Writings of John Dinwiddy* (Stanford, Stanford, 2004) 54.

[83] Indeed, relief on the unconscionability basis is often refused on the basis that A has done nothing that affects her conscience (particularly in the context of relief on the basis of surprise and fraud): *Tanwar Enterprises Pty Ltd v Cauchi* (n 12) [58]–[63] (Gleeson CJ, McHugh, Gummow, Hayne and Heydon JJ); *Auburn Shopping Village Pty Ltd v Nelmeer Hoteliers Pty Ltd* (n 3) [60]–[65] (Bathurst CJ). *Australian Competition and Consumer Commission v CG Berbatis Holdings Pty Ltd* (n 13), [42] (Gummow and Hayne JJ); *Ayers Rock SkyShip Pty Ltd v Voyages Indigenous Tourism Australia Pty Ltd* (n 3) [119] (Drake J); *JPA Finance Pty Ltd v Gordon Nominees Pty Ltd* (n 3) [112] (McLeish JA).

has, over time, crystallised into a more precise and restrictive '*duty* of virtue'.[84] Important for present purposes, none of the analysis above turns on B forfeiting to A a proprietary or possessory right.

V. The Coherence Argument: Property Requirement Risks Strained Reasoning as to What Constitutes the Forfeiture of a Proprietary or Possessory Right

Having established that the property requirement ought not be necessary to engage the equitable doctrine to relieve against a forfeiture, it is worth considering the additional consequences of failing to be transparent over this issue. There are (at least) two potential problems. The first is that a disproportionate amount of time and effort (in both litigation and the provision of legal advice) will be directed to the question of whether the impugned forfeiture involves the requisite proprietary or possessory character.[85] Indeed, attention should be directed towards the more salient issues of: (i) whether the impugned right functions as a security; or (ii) whether A's conduct falls under one of the more specific and exceptional categories that constitute the unconscionability basis for relief such that A ought to be disabled from the strict exercise of her legal rights. Second, given that there are sound moral, historical and analytical reasons for granting relief against a forfeiture absent a proprietary or possessory right, there is a risk that judges may become tempted to strain what constitutes a 'proprietary' or 'possessory' right in order to do practical justice between A and B. This potential problem of strained reasoning creates two further issues which threaten coherence in the law: (i) if the concepts of property and possession are given a strained meaning in the context of relief against forfeiture, there is a risk that such meanings can cross pollinate back into other areas of the law where such concepts are settled;[86] and (ii) covert legal tools and legal fictions are generally unreliable in the long term[87] and are thus apt to produce an incoherent (or fractured) body of case law. Put simply, the focus on whether the forfeiture is proprietary or possessory in character may serve to mask the true basis for relief.

[84] See too Penner (n 65).

[85] See too *Mineralogy Pty Ltd v Sino Iron Pty Ltd (No 6)* (n 3) [985] (Edelman J).

[86] For scholarly works raising this issue in different contexts see, eg: W Swadling, 'Opening the Numerus Clausus' (2000) 116 *Law Quarterly Review* 354; McFarlane (n 2) 506; J Edelman, 'Two Fundamental Questions for the Law of Trusts' (2013) 129 *Law Quarterly Review* 66.

[87] Albeit in a different context see: KN Llewellyn, 'Review of the Standardization of Commercial Contracts in English and Continental Law' (1939) 52 *Harvard Law Review* 700, 702–03.

A good example of a case that puts in focus the coherence issues raised above is the recent decision of the Supreme Court of the United Kingdom in *Manchester Ship Canal Company Ltd v Vauxhall Motors Ltd (formerly General Motors UK Ltd)*.[88] The facts of the case can be stated briefly: in the 1960s a body corporate in control of the Manchester Canal (A) granted a motor vehicle company (B) a contractual licence (stated to be in perpetuity) in exchange for B paying to A a fee of £50 *per annum* which was to be paid in whole on a specified annual date. The licence conferred on B the right to discharge water (comprising of both surface water caused by rainfall and trade effluent created by B's manufacturing plant) into A's canal. The water would pass over A's land through a drainage system which was to be constructed and maintained by B. The terms of the licence specified that only B could use the drainage system and that B would be obliged to maintain and repair the system even though part of the drainage system was situated on A's land. The licence agreement contained a clause (clause 5) which stipulated the consequences of B's failure to pay the annual fee within 21 days of the due date; A could terminate the licence provided it complied with the relevant 28 day notice period and B did not cure the default during that notice period.[89]

Several decades after entering into the agreement, and in what appeared to be an expensive administrative oversight, B failed to pay to A an annual £50 licence fee. In response, A exercised its legal powers under clause 5 and terminated the licence after issuing a default notice with which B failed to comply. After A terminated the licence, B immediately made an offer to pay the arrears (ie, £50) to A. After over a year of negotiations concerning a new licence agreement B sought relief against the forfeiture of the original licence. The then market value of a right to discharge both surface water and trade effluent from B's land into A's canal was estimated to be in a range between £300,000 to £440,000 *per annum*.[90] The Supreme Court (affirming the decision of the Court of Appeal)[91] held that B was entitled to relief against the forfeiture of its contractual licence. The Court granted the relief in question for two key reasons. The position taken in this chapter is that only the second reason has weight.

First, the majority (Lord Briggs, with whom Lord Carnwath, Lady Black and Lord Kitchin agreed) held that relief from forfeiture was only available to B in circumstances where B 'forfeits' a proprietary or possessory right (although in a concurring judgment that is consistent with the position taken in this chapter, Lady Arden was less sanguine about applying a limit on relief based on the type of right B holds).[92] In so holding, the majority were reticent to interfere with what they described as the: 'careful development of the principled limitation of the

[88] *Manchester Ship Canal Company Ltd v Vauxhall Motors Ltd (formerly General Motors UK Ltd)* [2019] UKSC 46; [2019] 3 WLR 852 (UKSC).

[89] ibid [15].

[90] ibid [1].

[91] Per Lewison LJ with whom Floyd and David Richards LJJ agreed: *Vauxhall Motors Ltd (formerly General Motors UK Ltd) v Manchester Ship Canal Co Ltd* [2018] EWCA Civ 1100; [2019] Ch 331 (CA).

[92] *Manchester Ship Canal Company Ltd v Vauxhall Motors Ltd* (n 88) [83]–[89].

jurisdiction to the forfeiture of proprietary or possessory rights, worked out over many years in a succession of broadly coherent authorities'.[93] It is telling given the thesis put forward in this chapter that the 'broadly coherent authorities' to which the majority referred were all modern.[94] They stem from a literal reading of a speech of Lord Wilberforce in *Shiloh Spinners Ltd v Harding*,[95] and can be traced from that starting point to the speech of Lord Diplock in *The Scaptrade*,[96] the speech of Lord Templeman in *Sport Internationaal Bussum BV v Inter-Footwear Ltd*,[97] and then to the judgments of Dillon LJ in *BICC plc v Burndy Corpn*[98] and Robert Walker LJ in *On Demand Information plc v Michael Gerson (Finance) plc*.[99] Although the key authorities here, such as *Shiloh Spinners* and *The Scaptrade*, can be readily explained[100] without recourse to a proprietary or possessory right requirement.

As to why the property threshold was 'principled', the majority in *Manchester Ship Canal* adopted what can be termed a 'Goldilocks approach'.[101] The majority was ultimately required to respond to, on the one hand, A's submissions that

[93] ibid [50].

[94] PG Turner, 'What Delimits Equitable Relief From Forfeiture?' (2019) 28 *Cambridge Law Journal* 276.

[95] *Shiloh Spinners Ltd v Harding* (n 6) 722 (Lord Wilberforce): '[t]here cannot be any doubt that from the earliest times courts of equity have asserted the right to relieve against the forfeiture of property'.

[96] *The Scaptrade* [1983] 2 AC 694 (HL), 702 (Lord Diplock): where it is observed that the statement of Lord Wilberforce in *Shiloh Spinners Ltd v Harding* (n 6), 722 as to the security rights and unconscionability bases for relief was 'mainly [a] historical statement was never meant to apply generally to contracts not involving any transfer of proprietary or possessory rights, but providing for a right to determine the contract in default of punctual payment of a sum of money payable under it'.

[97] *Sport Internationaal Bussum BV v Inter-Footwear Ltd* [1984] 1 WLR 776 (HL), 794 (Lord Templeman): 'My noble and learned friend, Lord Diplock, at p 702 [of *The Scaptrade*] confined that power to contracts concerning the transfer of proprietary or possessory rights. Mr Wilson submitted that, in the present case, the licences to use the trademarks and names created proprietary and possessory rights in intellectual property. He admits, however, that so to hold would be to extend the boundaries of the authorities dealing with relief against forfeiture. I do not believe that the present is a suitable case in which to define the boundaries of the equitable doctrine of relief against forfeiture. It is sufficient that the appellants cannot bring themselves within the recognised boundaries and cannot establish an arguable case for the intervention of equity. The recognised boundaries do not include mere contractual licences and I can see no reason for the intervention of equity'.

[98] *BICC plc v Burndy Corpn* [1985] Ch 232 (CA).

[99] *On Demand Information plc v Michael Gerson (Finance)* plc [2001] 1 WLR 155 (CA), 170 (Walker LJ).

[100] First, it is true that in *Shiloh Spinners* Lord Wilberforce described the doctrine as concerning the ability of a court to 'relieve against the forfeiture of property'. However, not only did his Lordship's reasoning overlook the historical cases outlined in this chapter (including earlier decisions of the House of Lords) but the case involves an otherwise orthodox application of the security rights basis for relief in circumstances where B would lose its assigned rights under a lease on an event of default (thus statements concerning the 'property' requirement would appear to be, at best, *obiter dicta*). Second, relief was refused in *The Scaptrade* for three reasons: (i) any grant of relief from the forfeiture of B's contractual rights on the facts before the House would be akin to the court granting specific performance of an employment or personal services contract; (ii) A's power to withdraw the vessel was not considered to be a punitive security right (ie the contractual power to determine that charter had a legitimate non-security function); (iii) the time charterparty (as opposed to a charter by demise) vested in B no proprietary rights. Important for present purposes is that the thesis put forward in this chapter does no harm to the first two arguments deployed by Lord Diplock in *The Scaptrade*.

[101] See the note on the case: NA Tiverios, 'The Forfeiture of Contractual Rights' (2020) 79 *Cambridge Law Journal* 17.

no relief ought to be given from the forfeiture of a contractual licence which granted possession over land (as to do so would make the law too uncertain given the commercial importance of real property); and, on the other hand, B's submissions that relief ought to be available from any right to *use* property (ie whether or not that right to use property is ultimately characterised as personal, proprietary or possessory in nature). In response to these positions, the majority adopted the intermediate approach of affirming a proprietary or possessory right requirement.[102] This intermediate approach made the law 'just right' by achieving an adequate balance between considerations of commercial certainty and an equitable rule that interferes with the parties' powers to enforce consent based transactions to their letter. This approach effectively mirrors the earlier appeals to commercial certainty by Robert Goff LJ in the Court of Appeal decision in *The Scaptrade*.[103]

In response to the majority's reasoning in *Manchester Ship Canal*, the position taken in this chapter is that legal certainty is an important value in and of itself. If, for example, you and I are playing a game of chess it is important that the rules are settled ahead of time. There are, nonetheless, difficulties with certainty *simpliciter* as a positive justification for a particular legal rule. This is because 'it is to the interest of legal certainty that, *other things being equal*, the rules of law should be as clear of application as possible'.[104] The important point for present purposes is that, before one can appeal to legal certainty, the fundamental question arises as to whether the 'other things' are indeed equal. Those who would, on balance, prefer to remove the 'proprietary or possessory' right threshold (and Lady Arden in her concurring judgment can, it seems, be counted in their ranks)[105] can point to both the conservative and normative arguments set out in this chapter. Further, as should become clear from the analysis below, the outcome in *Manchester Ship Canal* can also be critiqued on the basis that it detracts from legal certainty and coherence.

Returning to the substantive reasoning in *Manchester Ship Canal*, having reaffirmed the proprietary or possessory right threshold, the majority went on to hold that the contractual licence in that case granted to B such rights and thus the first bar to B seeking relief against forfeiture was cleared.[106] According to the majority, the principal reasons why the rights granted by the contractual licence were characterised as possessory in nature were (i) they conferred on B factual possession (ie, B had a contractual liberty to create, and ongoing obligations to maintain, drainage infrastructure and B had, as a matter of fact, availed itself

[102] *Manchester Ship Canal Company Ltd v Vauxhall Motors Ltd* (n 88) [35]–[47].

[103] *The Scaptrade* (n 96) 540 (Robert Goff LJ).

[104] G Williams, 'Language and the Law (II)' (1945) 61 *Law Quarterly Review* 179, 185 (emphasis added).

[105] *Manchester Ship Canal Company Ltd v Vauxhall Motors Ltd* (n 88) [76].

[106] Essentially mirroring the approach adopted by the Court of Appeal: *Vauxhall Motors Ltd (formerly General Motors UK Ltd) v Manchester Ship Canal Co Ltd* (n 91) [68].

of such rights and obligations) and (ii) these factors pointing to factual possession were coupled with B's exclusive right to use the infrastructure under the terms of the licence. These further facts illustrated that B had also manifested an intention to control the relevant infrastructure.[107] In reaching this conclusion the majority (as had the Court of Appeal) superimposed a test derived from the law of adverse possession[108] to the contractual licence. In doing so the majority observed that the analysis of Lewison LJ in the Court of Appeal correctly dealt with this issue with 'conspicuous care and detail'.[109] In the Court of Appeal, Lewison LJ observed that:

> the licence cast upon [B] the responsibility for the physical construction of the infrastructure and the sole primary responsibility for its maintenance and repair. It did not reserve to [A] any rights to use the infrastructure or (except in case of default by [B]) to carry out works to it. Those rights over the physical property, coupled with its physical characteristics and the clear intention that [B] would be the only entity able to use and maintain it, amount, in my judgment, to a sufficient degree of physical custody and control of the infrastructure (although not of the soil in which it was placed), having regard to the nature of the property and the manner in which property of that character is commonly enjoyed. [B] plainly intended to exercise those rights (and fulfil those responsibilities) on its own behalf and for its own benefit. The combination of those elements means that the rights granted by the licence were possessory in nature and thus opened the way to the exercise of the equitable jurisdiction to grant relief against forfeiture.[110]

It is submitted here that a key oversight in the reasoning of the Supreme Court and Court of Appeal appears to be the *non-sequitur* that 'the rights granted by the licence were possessory in nature'.[111] This is because the statement is inconsistent with two basal principles of common law. First, it is inconsistent with the doctrine of privity of contract, which provides that only parties to a contract can be bound by the mutual promises which were created by the parties' powers to create consent-based obligations.[112] Second, the statement is inconsistent with the principle that there are a closed number (*numerus clausus*) of recognised legal rights that the law will consider to be proprietary in nature (ie, there are a limited set of legal rights which place third parties under obligations not to interfere with a particular asset).[113] The principal reason why both these principles are inconsistent

[107] *Manchester Ship Canal Company Ltd v Vauxhall Motors Ltd* (n 88) [52]–[57]; see too at [89] (Lady Arden).

[108] The test being derived from: *JA Pye (Oxford) Ltd v Graham* [2003] 1 AC 419.

[109] *Manchester Ship Canal Company Ltd v Vauxhall Motors Ltd* (n 88) [54]-[59].

[110] *Vauxhall Motors Ltd (formerly General Motors UK Ltd) v Manchester Ship Canal Co Ltd* (n 91) [68].

[111] ibid.

[112] NC Seddon and RA Bigwood, *Cheshire & Fifoot Law of* Contract, 11th edn (Sydney, LexisNexis, 2018) [7.1]; E Peel, *Treitel's Law of Contract*, 14th edn, (London, Sweet & Maxwell, 2015) [14-004]; A Burrows, *A Restatement of the English Law of Contract* (Oxford, Oxford University Press, 2016) 240; *Tweddle v Atkinson* (1861) 1 B & S 393; 121 ER 762; *Dunlop Pneumatic Tyre Co Ltd v Selfridge & Co Ltd* [1915] AC 847 (HL); *Trident v McNiece* (1988) 165 CLR 107 (HCA), 114.

[113] *Keppell v Bailey* (1834) 2 My & K 517, 535; 39 ER 1042, 1049 (Lord Brougham); McFarlane (n 2) 137; Swadling (n 86).

with the reasons given in *Manchester Ship Canal* is that the Supreme Court did not delineate properly between the fact that where there is a licensee in possession of an asset (or land) there are two independent sources of legal rights in play. First, there are the *in personam* contractual rights and obligations between A and B (which is what the decision in *Manchester Ship Canal* concerned).[114] Second, there are the *in rem* possessory rights that a licensee in possession has against the rest of the world (save for those with better title such as the true owner of an asset) which derive from the fact of possession, thereby both arising and persisting by operation of law *independently* of any contractual licence that B has with A (indeed, a thief, adverse possessor or a finder of lost property each have similar rights derived from the mere fact of possession).[115]

Once these two sources of rights are identified, it becomes difficult to see how the contractual licence enforceable only between A and B conferred on B a possessory right (ie, a right enforceable against the world at large not to interfere with the relevant drainage infrastructure). In this connection it is telling that the majority resorted to applying a test derived from the law of adverse possession in order to reach the conclusion that B had acquired a 'possessory' right in a dispute between A and B. Understood this way, key aspects of the Supreme Court's reasoning pertaining to the identification of B's possessory rights fall away as being mere background noise that detract from the true signal of the judgment: the Court was nonetheless substantively granting B relief against the forfeiture of its contract rights with A (ie the court ultimately preserved B's contractual liberty against A and not merely B's separate possessory rights enforceable against the rest of the world). Indeed, any possessory rights which B had acquired against the rest of the world would have persisted notwithstanding the position between A and B being altered by the termination of the contractual licence between A and B. That is to say, those rights which B had by virtue of the fact of possession would continue to bind all those without a superior property right over the drainage infrastructure (C, D, E, F *ad infinitum*) *irrespective* of the forfeiture of the contractual licence. It follows that all that results from the forfeiture of the contractual licence is that B would now become a trespasser against the owner of the freehold of the land[116] (ie, A) by virtue of the revocation of B's *in*

[114] On the nature of a licence being no more than a personal liberty of the licensee against the licensor: WN Hohfeld, 'Fundamental Legal Conceptions as Applied to Judicial Reasoning' (1913) 23 *Yale Law Journal* 16, 32–44; McFarlane (n 2) 502–07; Swadling (n 86).

[115] ibid. See too *Armory v Delamirie* (1722) 1 Str 505; 93 ER 664; *Gollan v Nugent* (1988) 166 CLR 18 (HCA), 28 (Brennan J): 'there is clear authority that a right of recovery founded on possession is not affected by illegality in the manner in which the plaintiff acquired possession'; *Costello v Chief Constable of Derbyshire* [2001] EWCA Civ 381; [2001] 1 WLR 1437 (CA), 1446 [22] (Lightman J); *Government of the Islamic Republic of Iran v The Barakat Galleries Ltd* [2007] EWCA Civ 1374; [2009] QB 22 (CA), 32 [15]; *McMillan Properties Pty Ltd v W C Penfold Ltd* [2001] NSWSC 1173; (2001) 40 ACSR 319, 325 [44] (Young CJ in Eq); *Bride v Shire of Katanning* [2013] WASCA 154, [72] (Edelman J). Note too, the authorities listed in n 2 above.

[116] Although note that such a person need not be a freeholder. A could be a leaseholder or (in Australia) a life tenant.

personam contractual liberty against A to use the impugned land. So understood, the decision in *Manchester Ship Canal* becomes a case about the forfeiture of B's contractual rights with A despite the statements to the contrary. The acquisition of the 'property right' in the *Manchester Ship Canal* case was original, and not derivative from the contract. The 'property right' in play was acquired *because* of an act of possession.

The second essential reason in *Manchester Ship Canal* as to why B was entitled to relief against forfeiture was that A's power to terminate the contract on B's default was construed as being a security right to ensure that B complied with its underlying contractual obligations (eg, making timely payment of the licence fee and keeping the infrastructure in good repair). Indeed, before the Supreme Court it had become 'common ground' between the parties that A's power to terminate the contract on B's default was in the nature of a security right with the primary purpose of ensuring that B complied with its underlying contractual obligations (but this point had been contentious before the High Court and Court of Appeal).[117] Accordingly, A's legal power to terminate the licence was disabled and the court affirmed the orthodox approach of a court of equity in granting relief from the strict enforcement of a security right. Relief was therefore granted from A's strict exercise of a contractual power on the terms that B pay what was due plus A's costs. Thus, the trial judge's order stands:

> I would grant relief from forfeiture substantially on the terms suggested by Mr Edwards [counsel for B]. I would reserve to the Master the assessment of the losses suffered by [A] by the [failed] negotiations. Further argument is needed on the extent of the costs payable by [B].[118]

Given the position taken in this chapter it is submitted that the security rights issue ought to constitute the real crux of the decision in *Manchester Ship Canal*. Focusing on whether A's right functions as security for B's performance of an underlying condition is seemingly how the case would have been decided in Australia. Although, since this chapter was originally drafted, Brereton JA in the Court of Appeal of the Supreme Court of New South Wales has, in *obiter dicta*, expressed a preference for the English proprietary or possessory right requirement.[119]

[117] *Vauxhall Motors Ltd (formerly General Motors UK Ltd) v Manchester Ship Canal Co Ltd* (n 91) [70].

[118] *General Motors UK Ltd v Manchester Ship Canal Co Ltd* [2016] EWHC 2960 (Ch) [160].

[119] See the authorities in n 3 above. See too, Rossiter (n 4) 201; Tiverios (n 4) 222–26, and see further, the line of final level appellate authorities in Australia that are difficult to reconcile with the view that property is central to the concept of a security right. These are the cases in which B (a purchaser) has been granted relief against termination of the contract by A (the vendor) for B's purchase of A's land despite B not yet having a proprietary interest in the land in question (although B has possession). See further, *Legione v Hateley* (n 6); *Ciavarella v Balmer* (1983) 153 CLR 438 (HCA); 48 ALR 407. A similar approach is adopted in some parts of the United States of America whereby relief against forfeiture on the security right basis is granted where a purchaser of property defaults on instalments payments (in circumstances whereby the vendor retains ownership of the property until all instalments are paid): G Nelson and D Whitman, *Real Estate Finance Law*, 4th edn (Saint Paul, West Group, 2001) [3.29].

VI. Some Additional Considerations

As a matter of completeness there are two further arguments that can be deployed to support the removal of the proprietary or possessory requirement in order to engage the equitable rule against forfeiture. One additional issue needs to be considered as it provides a further piece of broader contextual background to the decision in *Manchester Ship Canal* which may explain the divergences between English and Australian law in this area. The first further argument is that, as noted above, there are English authorities that support the proposition that relief against forfeiture is only available to protect B from the loss of a proprietary or possessory right. A fundamental limitation, however, with relying on these cases is that such authorities have struggled to provide a positive legal analysis as to why the doctrine should be so confined. In this connection, Edelman J in *Mineralogy Pty Ltd v Sino Iron Pty Ltd (No 6)* raised the question for those who insist on the imposition of the proprietary or possessory right requirement:

> One difficulty with the insistence that relief against forfeiture operates only to relieve from forfeiture of proprietary rights is the issue of the principle. *Why* should the doctrine be confined to property rights? None of the cases addresses this point.[120]

Since Edelman J's observation, the closest that English law has got to providing such a justification is the bare appeal to legal certainty by the Supreme Court in *Manchester Ship Canal*. Naturally, the approach advocated in this chapter does not overlook the importance of certainty. It is submitted here that in the context of the security rights relief against forfeiture cases, asking whether A's right against B is 'proprietary' or 'possessory' is to ask the wrong question. The salient question ought to be whether A's right to an agreed remedy (whether proprietary or personal) is a security right.[121] Certainty can then be achieved by a detailed consideration of whether or not the impugned right has some other legitimate non-security function[122] such that relief will only be afforded 'where the security purpose stands ahead of any other'.[123] Further, given that the moral justification for the security rights basis for relief appears to be best explained by considerations of corrective justice, relief ought only be granted where the impugned forfeiture would have a punitive effect on B (eg, in *Manchester Ship Canal* the loss of the entire perpetual licence on the failure to pay £50 would have been punitive). Likewise, relief against forfeiture in the context of the 'unconscionability basis' can be refined by restricting tightly the circumstances when A is prevented from exercising her legal rights or by having such cases governed by the principles pertaining to the various species of equitable estoppel.

[120] *Mineralogy Pty Ltd v Sino Iron Pty Ltd (No 6)* (n 3) [983] (Edelman J).
[121] Worthington (n 7) 261; McFarlane (n 7) [13-023].
[122] See further, Tiverios and McFarlane (n 5).
[123] Turner (n 94) 279, cited with approval by Lady Arden in *Manchester Ship Canal Company Ltd v Vauxhall Motors Ltd* (n 88) [70].

The second further argument that relief against forfeiture ought not be limited to proprietary or possessory rights is that, on present authority, personal rights are often at the core of a security right and the associated equitable jurisdiction to relieve against forfeiture. For example, hallmarks of modern commerce such as charges over book debts or bank accounts involve no actual property but merely impose an equitable encumbrance over wholly personal rights.[124] Nonetheless, equity's jurisdiction to relieve against forfeiture on the basis of security rights clearly applies in such contexts.[125] The fact that the somewhat misleading label of equitable property[126] is deployed in such contexts does not detract from the reality of the situation: there is no tangible property to speak of (ie, no rights of non-interference enforceable directly against third parties concerning an asset) but merely underlying personal rights in play.[127]

As a final observation, it is worth noting the wider relationship between penalties and forfeitures in England. Although unstated and unexplored in *Manchester Ship Canal*, this relationship points to a further reason as to why it may ultimately prove difficult to remove the proprietary or possessory right threshold under English law. That is, removing this threshold effectively breaks down the formal distinction between the penalties doctrine and relief against forfeiture. This is for the simple reason that once this step is taken, relief against forfeiture becomes available to regulate all manner of agreed contractual remedies or sanctions. For example, in *Andrews v Australia and New Zealand Banking Group*,[128] the High Court of Australia adopted an approach to the penalties doctrine which reaffirmed the equitable origins of the rule and realigned the penalties doctrine in a manner that is conceptually similar to the security rights basis of relief against forfeiture. Under this Australian approach relief against penalties and forfeitures both involve equity disabling A's strict enforcement of an agreed remedy or sanction in order to prevent consent-based punishments. However, in *Cavendish Square Holding BV v Makdessi*[129] the Supreme Court held that the English rule against penalties is properly characterised as a rule of common law and not, as in Australia, a rule of equity. In doing so, the Supreme Court criticised the reasoning in *Andrews* and adopted a restrictive approach in holding that the English penalties doctrine

[124] On the nature of equitable property: McFarlane (n 2) 23–32; B McFarlane and R Stevens, 'The Nature of Equitable Property' (2010) 4 *Journal of Equity* 1, 1–3; Edelman (n 86).

[125] See eg: *Re Kent & Sussex Sawmills* [1947] Ch 177, 181 in which an equity of redemption over an assignment of personal rights by way of security was recognised. See too decisions listed in n 118 above.

[126] For favourable obiter dicta on the availability of relief against the forfeiture of personal rights see too, *Chaka Holdings Pty Ltd v Sunsim Pty Ltd* (1987) 10 BPR 18,171 (NSWSC), 18,182 (Young J); *Milton v Proctor* (1988) 4 BPR 9654 (NSWCA), 9659–60 (McHugh JA), where McHugh JA notes that the English approach 'may not, represent the law as it is understood in Australia' although his Honour did not expressly decide the point Further, it ought to be noted that *Milton* involved the forfeiture of an additional equitable interest which, importantly for present purposes, is not proprietary or possessory in character.

[127] McFarlane (n 7) [13-023].

[128] *Andrews v Australia and New Zealand Banking Group* (n 55) [10].

[129] *Cavendish Square Holding BV v Makdessi* [2015] UKSC 67; [2016] AC 1172 (UKSC), [42].

involves ascertaining whether or not A has acquired a valid legal right against B to an agreed remedy and does not involve equity controlling the enforcement of an otherwise valid agreed remedy. On the other hand, the English law concerning relief against forfeiture involves circumstances under which it is accepted that A has a valid legal right against B but equity controls, in B's favour, the assertion of A's otherwise valid legal right. The fundamental analytical difference between penalties and forfeitures under English law lies in the fact that the equitable forfeiture rule limits the assertion of a legal right whereas the common law penalties rule concerns the valid creation of such a right in the first place. Put simply, any removal of the 'proprietary' or 'possessory' right threshold in the context of forfeitures will have the result of blurring the distinction between penalties and forfeitures.[130] The High Court of Australia has taken this first step in *Andrews*, but the Australian approach to the penalties doctrine was expressly rejected in *Cavendish Square Holding*. Once this piece of the broader contextual puzzle falls into place it is perhaps unremarkable that the majority in *Manchester Ship Canal Co Ltd* maintained the proprietary or possessory right requirement.

VII. Conclusion

A hybrid of arguments has been presented in this chapter to illustrate that a satisfactory positive justification in support of the proprietary or possessory right requirement necessary to engage the equitable doctrine of relief against forfeiture in England and Wales remains wanting. While in an ideal world the normative arguments concerning corrective justice and curtailing opportunistic behaviour presented in this chapter would suffice to suggest that such a justification is likely to prove elusive, it cannot be expected that all lawyers will respond in the same way to each species of argument. Therefore, some of the arguments deployed are inherently conservative (or Burkean): as a matter of legal history there is nothing anomalous about the position taken in this chapter (ie, that there are periods in history where equitable relief was granted from the strict exercise of non-proprietary legal rights and powers on either the security rights or unconscionability bases for relief). Other arguments deployed here are normative: considering whether there is any rational connection between: (i) on the one hand the strict requirement (still persisting at English law) that B forfeits a proprietary or possessory

[130] Differences nonetheless remain as to the timing of when a court will assess whether to grant relief against penalties and forfeitures. For example, a penalty clause to be judged according to the circumstances at the time of its making, and, in contrast to relief against forfeiture, not at the point when A seeks to enforce it: see, eg: *Else (1982) Ltd v Parkland Holdings Ltd* [1994] 1 BCLC 130 (CA); *Australia Capital Financial Management Pty Ltd v Linfield Developments Pty Ltd* (n 6); 18 BPR 36683, [326] (Ward JA); *Kay v Playup Australia Pty Ltd* (n 3) [100]–[123] (Brereton JA). On these differences and the potential for these principles to be reconciled, see further, Tiverios (n 4) 219–26; Tiverios and McFarlane (n 5); Smith (n 7) 198.

right (ie, a requirement which looks to the third party effect of B's right on C, D, E *ad infinitum* etc …); and (ii) on the other hand, legal rules that seek to impose norms based on corrective justice or curtailing opportunistic behaviour (ie, normative justifications relevant only between A and B). Further still some of the arguments deployed in this chapter are based on coherence: the requirement that B forfeits a proprietary or possessory right to engage either the security rights or unconscionability bases for relief is creating a muddled body of case law in England which is increasingly difficult to reconcile. Not only does such a fractured body of case law serve to mask the true basis for equitable relief but strained curial definitions as to what constitutes a 'proprietary' or 'possessory' right risks a cross contamination of such ideas into other areas of law where such concepts are settled.

INDEX

www.ingramcontent.com/pod-product-compliance
Lightning Source LLC
Chambersburg PA
CBHW071301180926
51613CB00001B/96